This book is given
in honor of
Ben A. Stacke
by
Dr. Robert, Mary
& Sarah K. Stacke
May 1999

Dilemmas of Reform in China

"Joe Fewsmith has given us the definitive study of economic reform policy debates of the 1980s that set the agenda for the politics of the 1990s. He has also given us much more. Through wide-ranging interviews with many of the key economic advisors, and comprehensive and painstaking analysis of the documents of the time, he has opened a window into the basic nature of prevailing Chinese elite politics. His introduction and conclusion highlight both the irreversible shift to economic performance as the basis of regime legitimacy, and also explain why and how personalistic power struggle at the top still inhibits the politics of compromise essential to steady and sure modernization in China."

—Carol Lee Hamrin,
The Johns Hopkins University

"Professor Fewsmith's fine-grained analysis of the politics of the reform era cogently interweaves economic policy disagreements with struggles over political power. The book both provides fresh insights into the substantive debates over economic reform and also shows how the workings of the political system itself—the structure of power, roles of bureaucracies, and evolving state/society relations— have affected the major outcomes. Professor Fewsmith on balance focuses attention heavily on the apex of the system where, he argues, the spotlight should focus in a book that seeks to understand China's zigzag path to reform since 1978. This book is wide ranging and compelling. It considerably enhances our understanding of economic reform debates and politics in China."

—Kenneth Lieberthal,
University of Michigan

★ SOCIALISM AND ★ SOCIAL MOVEMENTS

Series Editor: Mark Selden

★ *Socialism and Social Movements*

Dilemmas of Reform in China

Political Conflict and Economic Debate

JOSEPH FEWSMITH

An East Gate Book

M.E. Sharpe
Armonk, New York
London, England

An East Gate Book

Copyright © 1994 by M. E. Sharpe, Inc.

Library of Congress Cataloging-in-Publication Data

Fewsmith, Joseph, 1949–
Dilemmas of reform in China: political conflict and
economic debate / Joseph Fewsmith
p. cm.—(Socialism and social movements)
"An East Gate book."
ISBN 1–56324–327–X.—ISBN 1–56324–328–8
1. China—Economic policy—1976– 2. China—Economic
conditions—1976– 3. China—Politics and government—1976–
I. Title. II. Series.
HC427.92.F49 1944
338.951—dc20
93[34487
CIP

Printed in the United States of America

The paper used in this publication meets the minimum requirements of American National Standard for Information Sciences— Permanence of Paper for Printed Library Materials, ANSI Z 39.48-1984.

BM (c)   10   9   8   7   6   5   4   3   2   1
BM (p)   10   9   8   7   6   5   4   3   2   1

For Irene

Contents

Acknowledgments

Writing a book of this sort is inevitably a collaborative effort, and one of the pleasures of finishing such a work is the opportunity to acknowledge in some small way those who have provided so much help. Those who read this volume will recognize the very great intellectual debt that I continue to owe Tang Tsou, my mentor some years ago at the University of Chicago. It is perhaps with some chagrin that I note that his influence on my thinking has grown over the years since I have left his tutelage, though those who know Professor Tsou's work will understand why I and others return to it periodically for inspiration.

Over the years I have honed my understanding of Chinese politics, and discovered the limits of my knowledge, in countless conversations with Cliff Edmunds, Carol Hamrin, H. Lyman Miller, and Terry Weidner. I have also benefited greatly from discussions with Gary Zou, with whom I have collaborated on *Chinese Economic Studies*.

The writing of this book began with a two-month stay in the fall of 1990 as a Visiting Scholar at the University of Michigan's Center for Chinese Studies, where Michel Oksenberg, Kenneth Lieberthal, Robert Dernberger, and others provided a warm and intellectually stimulating atmosphere that was conducive to research and writing.

I have also benefited greatly by participation in two conferences, that on "The State Council and Economic Development," sponsored by The Johns Hopkins School of Advanced International Studies and the U.S. Department of State, in Washington, DC, October 24–25, 1991; and that on "Leaders, Institutions and Politics in the People's Republic of China," sponsored by The Center for Modern China, in La Jolla, California, August 28–30, 1992.

Over the years, this book has benefited tremendously from the insights provided by numerous Chinese scholars. For reasons that readers will understand, these contributions are recognized in the footnotes simply as "author's interviews." Though they deserve much more, here I will simply say "thanks." In addition, Nancy Hearst of the Fairbank Center at Harvard University has been extraordinarily helpful in locating important sources.

As this project neared completion, I have received particularly extensive comments from Jean Oi and Mark Selden. In addition, Corrina-Barbara Francis,

ix

Edward Friedman, Nina Halpern, Gwendolyn Stewart, Edwin Winkler, Brantly Womack, and Zhao Suisheng have provided valuable comments on parts of the manuscript. If I have not always responded adequately to their comments, the book is nevertheless a better product for their raising of important issues.

Doug Merwin and Angela Piliouras at M.E. Sharpe have been a pleasure to work with, gently hammering the manuscript into a more readable book.

It is also a pleasure to thank my wife, Irene Kiedrowski, for all her support and good humor over the years. And perhaps now Stephanie and Andrew will see a bit more of "Daddy."

Dilemmas of
Reform in China

Introduction:
Some Perspectives on the
Chinese Political System

The economic reforms that have been implemented in China since the watershed Third Plenary Session of the Eleventh Central Committee in December 1978 are of unquestioned magnitude and importance, affecting the lives of over a billion people and contributing to the peace and stability of East Asia. In terms of economic growth and restructuring, the accomplishments of the decade from 1978 to 1989 (and since) are impressive. In 1978, the average per capita income of urban residents was 316 yuan and that of peasants was only 134 yuan. A decade later, in 1988, those figures were 1,119 yuan and 545 yuan, respectively. In 1978, national income stood at 301 billion yuan; by 1988 it had risen to 1,153 billion yuan. In the same period, foreign trade expanded from U.S. $20.6 billion to U.S. $80.5 billion.[1]

In political terms, this process has been more problematic. The failure of the Chinese political system was all too visible to the world in the tragic events of June 3–4, 1989, but the tensions within the leadership that formed the backdrop against which the popular protest emerged, and which led ultimately to its violent suppression, differed only in degree from the tensions that had long existed among the leadership. One would have hoped that the economic successes of the reform would have provided a basis for an easing of leadership tensions and the establishment of institutional mechanisms that could have provided for long-term political stability. Unfortunately, that was not the case. As China's reforms deepened and new problems emerged, cleavages among China's leaders deepened. Eventually, divisions within the leadership and the societal frustrations that emerged as a by-product of the reforms led to the tragedy of Tiananmen and the collapse, albeit only temporarily, of the reform process.[2]

In using the term "reform process," I mean to indicate a decision-making process in which conflicts, however severe, can be contained within certain bounds. Those bounds were clearly broken by the events surrounding Tiananmen and the purge of Zhao Ziyang, then general secretary of the Chinese Communist Party (CCP). Although it is true that the economic reforms were not as a whole rolled back following Tiananmen, it is nevertheless evident that party conservatives sharply challenged the reform agenda that had been followed at least since 1984. In contrast to any previous time since the inauguration of reform, there was an effort to change fundamentally what was meant by reform. As the immediate political crisis passed, the reform process has been reconstituted in the early 1990s, although sharp cleavages within the CCP leadership remain apparent. This reconstitution of the reform process may in time lead to a new form of politics in China and to peace and prosperity in the post–Deng Xiaoping era, but this trend remains nascent and uncertain. Whatever the future may hold, it is apparent that the reform process in the pre-Tiananmen period was not sufficiently institutionalized to contain the tensions that the reforms engendered.

The major task of this book is to trace the emergence of China's economic reforms, the conflicts that accompanied them, and the sharpening of leadership disputes that led to the collapse of the reform process in 1988–89. It approaches this task first and foremost from the perspective of the most influential policy advocates who argued publicly and privately over the course of economic reform. This approach permits viewing as comprehensively as possible the ideas and issues that guided and frequently obstructed the reform process. Close reading of the debates over economic reform can provide the outsider with an understanding of the conceptual frameworks of the participants and how those frameworks changed with the passage of time. One can also gain a finer-grained understanding of the issues that informed and inhibited decision making as well as an understanding of how and when issues rose and fell, sometimes to rise again.

This volume traces the main lines of economic debate in the decade between the inauguration of reform in around 1978 and the Tiananmen crackdown in 1989, trying to clarify the sources of ideas and issues that were central to the debate at any specific point in time. Only by considering various economic concepts in some detail can one gain a sense of the economic and political rationales behind various approaches to economic reform and how and why different approaches to reform changed with time. Moreover, this approach allows one to attach names to arguments, permitting one to go beyond sweeping generalizations about "reformers" and "conservatives" by being more specific about which individuals advocated which concepts.

Focusing on the writings of economists makes one aware that such writings constitute a complex tapestry in which each written piece is part of an ongoing dialogue that does not simply involve the views of individual economists, but rather involves debates among fairly clearly defined (if constantly evolving) schools of thought. Although there is a great diversity of thought about economics in China, and there are many different concerns and approaches, it nevertheless seems appropriate to speak of "schools of thought." In general, economists seek to build support for their ideas by cultivating a following of like-minded economists who conduct research that supports these ideas and who participate in the polemics on economic policy in various papers, journals, and meetings. To speak of "schools of thought" is not meant to suggest that such schools are fixed and unchanging, but rather that writers of a given school share common concerns and approaches to problems over a given period.

It is also important to keep in mind that the writings of Chinese economists occurred within the context of historical debates over Marxian political economics and involved the entire socialist world. Thus, economic debate within China reflects the influence of these historical understandings and debates, as well as the history of economic debate in the People's Republic of China (PRC).

These schools of thought do not exist independently of the political process but are part and parcel of a continuing debate over public policy and power. That political process sets the parameters of the debate, including the vocabulary that is used, even as the debate attempts to affect the policy-making process and thus push the parameters of the debate in different directions.

It is precisely because writings by economists are part of an ongoing debate over public policy and are intertwined with the political aspirations of various leaders that this study follows a chronological approach. Without sensitivity to the political situation at any given time and to the positions articulated by other economists, it is easy to misunderstand why economists are writing what they are; their articles are always intended as a contribution to an ongoing debate about public policy. Moreover, a chronological approach allows one to better understand the evolution of economic thought over the course of time. New ideas are inevitably a response to ideas that have preceded them and especially to the economic problems that emerge in the course of reform.

It is also because the debates of Chinese economists and economic bureaucrats are integrally related to China's political process that this volume focuses attention on leadership politics. As just suggested, it is the leadership that sets the framework in which economic issues are debated, even if those debates seek to alter the parameters of that framework. Much of China's decision-making process remains elusive, but careful reading of public sources and interviews with participants allows some judgments to be made about this process. This volume attempts to provide as comprehensive an overview as possible of the interaction between Chinese economists and decision makers, in the hope that this will provide some insight into the Chinese political process as well as stimulate responses and new research that will further our understanding.

The concerns of this volume inevitably focus on elite participants within the Chinese political system. Some readers may feel that too little consideration has been given to the implementation (as opposed to the making) of decisions and the changing relations between state and society.[3] In looking at the decision-making process, however, I am intensely aware that this process is not occurring in a vacuum. On the contrary, as I try to remind the reader throughout this volume, the changing economic and social conditions in society are constantly impinging on the deliberations of economists and decision makers, sometimes giving greater credence to one side in the debate and sometimes to another side. Moreover, as noted in Chapters 5 and 6 in particular, the different estimates of economists about the capacities of the state to effect reform, and their different judgments about a desirable relationship between state and society, are an integral part of their approaches to and proposals for reform. In short, though this volume does not focus primarily on what is happening "on the ground," that reality is always present, shaping debates and creating pressures to which decision makers must respond.

Although economic and social reality has been vital in shaping the broad contours of the development of reform, this book argues that China's reform process has been driven first and foremost by the top leadership. Time and again, policy makers have intervened to make critical decisions to speed up, slow down, or change the direction of reform. Without the support of central leaders, China's rural reforms could not have developed. Similarly, however favorable may have been the economic conditions at the time, the decisions of central policy makers were what inaugurated the second phase of reform that began in 1984.

It might be said that economists and economic bureaucrats mediate between the economy and the policy makers, interpreting economic trends for the leadership and offering broad cognitive maps in the hope of influencing both specific decisions and the conceptual understanding of the leadership. It must also be said, however, that economists respond to the political agendas of individual leaders. Frequently what is demanded of economists is that they find economic solutions to the political dilemmas facing the party's leadership. Thus, what apparently drives the process all too often is the political needs of particular leaders; economists then find themselves in the role of shaping economic policies that support the political position of individual leaders.

As these comments suggest, the process of economic policy making in the reform period has been considerably less incremental than the results of reform would seem to indicate. Although it is true that marketization of the Chinese economy has progressed steadily over the past decade and more, the policy-making process that has guided, or attempted to guide, economic reform has been deeply contentious. Both the *goals* and *methods* of reform have been the subjects of sharp debate at all points in the process of reform. As a result, economic policy has had a lurching, discontinuous quality that contrasts with the generally more incremental process of marketization.

This is not to suggest that the policy-making process and economic trends exist on separate levels, the one having little to do with the other. On the contrary, leadership decisions frequently have an important impact on the economy, though not always what was expected or desired by the leadership, and economic trends inevitably fuel leadership conflict. Economic developments engender political conflict because individual leaders have different visions of both reform and economic trends, and problems are always considered to support or refute one or another vision of reform. It should also be said that the Chinese leadership faced no easy choices in the course of reform.[4] Whichever course they chose, they were bound to encounter serious problems. Such problems then led to recriminations that in turn exacerbated political conflict and hobbled the formulation of new policies. This conflictual process ultimately contributed to breakdown of the reform process in 1989.

Over the course of the decade, much progress was made both in the sophistication of economic analysis and in the breadth of discussion of economic issues; there was a very real learning curve. Specialists learned much about economic forecasting, conducting feasibility studies, and economic theory.[5] There is no question that by 1988 China had a much more sophisticated economics community than it had had ten years earlier. There were also new think tanks established and new ways for economists to communicate with the leadership. Not only was the economy more marketized, but the planners were better. Nevertheless, despite this evident progress, economic policy, particularly the critical decisions about the direction of reform and macroeconomic policy, were inextricably intertwined with the struggle for power.

The struggle for power has long been a central feature of the Chinese Communist political system. As Tang Tsou pointed out many years ago, "the basic assumption of CCP politics has been that a group or a coalition of groups can and does decisively defeat a major rival group or coalition, and eliminate it."[6] Although Tsou wrote this in the mid-1970s and was undoubtedly influenced by the experience of the Cultural Revolution, he did not build his case on the Cultural Revolution. On the contrary, Tsou argued that of all periods in CCP politics, that of the Cultural Revolution most closely approximated the factional model proposed by Nathan.[7] Even in the period of the Cultural Revolution, however, Tsou maintained that CCP politics were "based on the assumption that the major rival opponents and groups could defeat and eliminate one another."[8]

If it can be accepted that Tsou's contention about Chinese political actors having a fundamental assumption of being able to decisively defeat their opponents describes accurately a central feature of CCP politics before the inauguration of reform, to what extent can we extend his observation into the 1980s? In the early 1980s Tsou himself seemed to be optimistic that this tradition of "merciless struggle" within the CCP could be brought to an end. With the Third Plenary Session of the Eleventh Central Committee in December 1978, as Tsou observed, the party abandoned the idea of "struggle *between two lines*" and adopted the concept of a "struggle *on two fronts*," that is, against "leftism" on the one hand and "bourgeois liberalization" on the other.[9] By carving out a "middle course," the Chinese leadership seemed to be trying to bring an end to the era of struggle, both between the state and society and within the party.

A decade later, in the wake of the Tiananmen tragedy, Tsou was considerably less sanguine about the prospects for jettisoning this tradition of struggle for total victory. For him, the party's long-standing "pattern of disagreement, conflict, struggle, confrontation, and outcome" was critical in the evolution of events that culminated in the brutal crackdown.[10]

To what extent can we say that the struggle for total victory remains a central feature of Chinese politics in the era of reform? Many observers of China believe that the struggle for total victory is no longer, if it ever was, a central feature of Chinese politics and most discussions have looked at the political system in terms of bureaucratic or factional politics. There is some reason to believe that the tradition of striving for total victory in CCP politics is less central to Chinese politics than it was in the era before reform. After all, the veteran cadres who returned to power in the late 1970s were so scarred by the near destruction of the party in the Cultural Revolution that they developed a very strong norm against the sort of mass purge that Mao had conducted. Moreover, no leader in the present era is able to dominate the political scene as Mao could. Deng Xiaoping both made a virtue of necessity and rallied the veteran party leaders to his cause by turning away from the personality cult and asserting that no one leader should occupy a position above the party as Mao had done. In part because of these reasons (others will be considered in the Conclusion), the chief political rivalry in the reform period—that between Deng Xiaoping and Chen Yun—has not resulted in a decisive struggle; a decade and a half after their return to power, despite the evident deep disagreements between them, both remain as powerful actors on the political scene.

Nevertheless, it seems evident that the party's long history of struggle for total victory continues to haunt the conduct of politics in various ways. The party veterans who returned to power in the late 1970s were repelled by Mao's leadership style and the ruthless inner-party struggles that he had visited upon them, and this revulsion appears to have been one reason that they considered, for a while, reform of the political structure. However, that reform failed, and it failed at least in part because those same veteran party leaders could not agree on institutions and procedures that would limit their own conflict. The traditions of "one-man rule" and "party line" were too deeply embedded to yield to legal-rational decision making.

The party's tradition of a struggle for total victory also finds expression in a structure of power that continues to revolve around a one-man core.[11] Deng Xiaoping has been particularly blunt about this feature of Chinese politics, telling the newly formed Politburo Standing Committee in June 1989 that "a leadership without a core is unreliable." Deng said that just as Mao had been the core of the first generation of leadership, he (Deng) is the core of the second. (He also claimed, perhaps wishfully, that Jiang Zemin would be the core of the third.)[12]

The notion of a one-man core is closely related to the articulation, however ambiguously, of a "line" that defines the policy direction preferred by the core leader. Political "lines" in contemporary China are less clear and more overlapping with potentially competing lines than they were in Maoist China, but the idea of a political line remains important. Line links policy to leadership; line is one of the things that distinguishes the practice of Chinese politics from the exercise of purely personal power. The notion of political line does not mean either that all policy preferences are clearly defined or that policies are not changed or even reversed in response to changing circumstances or political opposition. Instead, line defines a policy direction or orientation rather than a set of specific policies. In the case of Deng Xiaoping, the political line includes marketization and diversification of the economy, the depoliticization (not liberalization) of society, opening to the outside world, and, as argued below, higher rates of economic growth.

These complementary notions of core leadership and line are important for two reasons. First, the existence of a core leader suggests the degree to which Chinese politics is personalized rather than institutionalized. The core leader is neither elected nor exerts power on the basis of institutionalized position (as Deng Xiaoping's current status of being an ordinary party member amply demonstrates!). Second, political line is what connects policy to power. As Domes once wrote, "One cannot separate the issues of policy disputes from the individual persons who hold divergent views, for the rivals engage in conflicts for positions of power which will enable them to enact the policies and strategies they advocate."[13]

There are two consequences that follow from this structure of power. First, the core leader will always attempt to maximize his or her (mostly his) power while rival leaders, whether or not they intend to challenge for power, try to undermine the ability of the leader to set the political and economic agendas for the country. That is to say, the structure of Chinese politics inevitably gives rise to a struggle for dominance. Second, because policy and power are linked, criticisms of policy preferences and initiatives associated with the core leader are inevitably political assaults on the power of the leader—and are intended as such. If left unanswered, the ability of the leader to function as the core would be undermined, perhaps even leading to his removal. Thus, efforts to define and redefine the political and economic line are always part of the struggle for power.

Because of these features of Chinese politics, leaders, particularly those of the older generation, appear to act on the belief that total victory is possible. This belief is reflected in the recent decision of the Fourteenth Party Congress to write Deng Xiaoping's theory of "building socialism with Chinese characteristics" into the party constitution. At least on paper, Deng's line has emerged triumphant over all rivals, both past and present. Moreover, to the extent that political actors have internalized the pattern of "disagreement, conflict, struggle, confrontation, and outcome" from their past experience, it shapes their present actions.

Arguing that the tradition of struggle for total victory continues to influence the pattern of politics in China does not mean that there is no bargaining or compromise within the system. As the work of Lieberthal, Oksenberg, Lampton, and others has shown, there is extensive bargaining throughout the economic system.[14] However, the model of China's policy-making process as a "bargaining treadmill" or a type of "fragmented authoritarianism," as Lieberthal has recently noted, was constructed around studies of investment projects; its utility for analyzing elite politics and the determination of policy lines appears to be less significant.[15] Because of the structure of politics, such issues are inherently more conflictual than the sort of investment projects that have been most frequently studied. It should be noted, however, that the fragmentation of power and the bargaining processes conveyed in these works is very relevant to the implementation of policy and thus forms a real constraint on policy makers. This in turn affects elite politics.

Chinese leaders can and do strike political bargains, but such bargains reflect temporizing rather than the politics of compromise. Under the assumption that there will be struggle and confrontation at some point in the future, the deals struck among the elite are undertaken as efforts to better position oneself for these conflicts. As Tsou wrote in his analysis of the Tiananmen tragedy:[16]

> It is true that at times there were compromises, concessions, admissions of defeat, negotiations, and even cooperation with such opposing forces, but those were tactical measures that did not lead to permanent institutions and fundamental processes according to which all political forces would have to conduct their contestations, promote their interests, and accept the results.

This complex game of maneuver and counter-maneuver infused the entire decade under consideration. The absence of institutionalized procedures or a consensus-building mechanism meant that policy, rather than evolving incrementally, tended to lurch, sometimes rather dramatically, from one extreme to another. For instance, the campaign against "spiritual pollution" in 1983 was followed in 1984 by the most extensive reforms to date, despite the absence of significant leadership changes. In the years between 1978 and 1989, such swings in policy, as well as the momentum of the ongoing reforms, tended to exacerbate leadership conflict. Whatever chance there might have been in the early years of the decade to forge a genuine politics of compromise was lost.

Since the inauguration of reform in 1977–78, the central political relationship has been that between Deng Xiaoping and Chen Yun. Although the two were closely allied at the beginning of the reform period—Chen's strong support for Deng's leadership at the Central Work Conference in November 1978 was critical in Deng's rise to preeminence—their relationship steadily deteriorated over the course of the decade. In the 1980–82 period Chen increasingly asserted his influence over economic policy at Deng's expense; with the adoption of the 1984 "Decision on Economic Structural Reform," Deng signaled his rejection of Chen's approach. In the late 1980s, the differences between the conservative and reform wings of the CCP increased dramatically. The victory of party conservatives at the Third Plenum of the Thirteenth Central Committee in October 1988 fueled the political tensions that became so evident the following spring.

The tension between Deng and Chen is rooted both in the traditional assumption, referred to above, that one policy line must predominate and in the different temperaments and resources of the two men. Deng returned to power in the late 1970s as a leader purged twice by Mao Zedong. Despite his previous career as one of Mao's closest allies, Deng could not secure legitimacy through allegiance to Mao Zedong Thought. Moreover, the stance of ideological loyalist was already taken by Party Chairman Hua Guofeng, who raised the slogan of the "two whatevers" ("whatever decisions Chairman Mao made, we resolutely support; whatever instructions Chairman Mao made, we will steadfastly abide by") to prevent Deng and other veteran leaders from returning to power. Deng launched his comeback by using one of the most powerful themes in the Maoist canon, the criterion of practice, to undermine Hua Guofeng and Mao Zedong Thought as it had developed since the inauguration of the Great Leap Forward in 1958. At the same time, Deng attacked two important Maoist symbols, the Dazhai model in agriculture and, less frontally, the Daqing model in industry. His claim to legitimacy thus rested squarely on his ability to "deliver the goods." His position in the political order virtually demanded breaking precedent and producing high growth rates.

In contrast, Chen Yun has always been concerned with, and had responsibility for, the details of economic affairs, particularly the management of the planned economy. As an economic specialist rather than a political generalist, he is much more conscious of the economic imbalances that occur when economic growth is pursued too quickly. Whereas Deng was willing to challenge fundamental elements of the Maoist order in order to produce higher growth rates and to pursue China's perennial search for "wealth and power," Chen's approach to reform was to work within the basic framework of the planned economy.[17] Strictly speaking, Chen was more of a reformer than Deng. Chen believed that it was possible to reform the socialist economic system that had been established to make it more scientific and more efficient. He desired a more streamlined and efficient planning system, not the development of a market-based system.

If economic growth exceeds certain levels, or if wages rise too quickly, or if decentralization and extrabudgetary investment proceed too quickly, tensions are inevitably introduced into the economic system, affecting the balance so prized by Chen and other planners. They then find it necessary to tighten central control, reduce investment, and control wages to cool off the economy. Such measures slow reform, and thus Chen is inevitably in the position of "correcting" Deng's mistakes and undermining his reform efforts.

The relationship between Deng and Chen is undoubtedly also exacerbated by their very different personalities. Hot tempered and bold, Deng takes chances, both politically and economically. Although highly intelligent (Mao once called him a "living encyclopedia"), Deng has no patience with abstract theory and has a reputation for not reading.[18] Chen, on the other hand, is known for meticulous attention to detail; as he summarized his approach, it was necessary to spend 90 percent of one's time on study and investigation and only 10 percent on making decisions.

There has thus always been an economic line associated with Deng that has emphasized a higher rate of growth, bolder experimentation with various forms of reform, allowing nonsocialist economic forms to grow, rapid and full integration of the Chinese economy into the world economy, and extensive marketization of the economy. In contrast, Chen's economic line has always been associated with "steady and proportional growth of the economy," maintaining the leading position of the state-run (and planned) sector, and with concerns that integrating the Chinese economy into the world economy would lead to economic and political dependence on the outside world.

It should also be said that political ideology has played a very different role in the thinking of Deng and Chen. Deng has consistently shown himself willing to jettison ideological orthodoxy and stake his (and the party's) claim to legitimacy on the ability to improve the livelihood of the people. Chen, on the other hand, has seen Deng's attitude toward ideology as being rather cavalier and undermining control over both the cadre force (those charged with carrying out the decisions of the party and state) and the population at large; without an emphasis on ideology, Chen seems to fear, reform will weaken discipline within the party, breed corruption, and ultimately undermine the basis of party rule.[19]

Although there are certainly areas of agreement between Deng and Chen— including the need for reform of some sort, the importance of political and social stability, the need to avoid large-scale political campaigns that mobilize the masses, and the ruling position of the CCP—there are also obvious differences. In a different sort of polity, such differences could lead to compromise; indeed, to outsiders it often seems as though the strengths of Deng compensate for the weaknesses of Chen and vice versa. The tradition of struggle for power within the party, however, makes this relationship much less benign. When reform is progressing rapidly Deng's power waxes visibly, while during periods of economic retrenchment Chen's influence grows at Deng's expense. There is no political mechanism by which the approaches and powers of the two men can be either integrated or institutionalized in a form of checks and balances.

The relationship between Deng Xiaoping and Chen Yun on the one hand, and the long-standing assumption of CCP politics that only one line can prevail on the other hand, cast a long and harmful shadow over the policy-making process throughout the decade. The exercise of power in China has always been highly personal. At the top of the regime there is an absence of institutionalization. At a recent conference, Kenneth Jowitt characterized the Chinese leadership as a "war band," each member of which possessed "plenipotentiary powers."[20] If one does not take this as implying an equality of status, there is much truth in this. The leader who fails to demonstrate power through the exercise of authority loses the ability to do so. It was no accident that approximately one-third of state-allocated construction expenditures in the Sixth Five-Year Plan, according to Song Ping, then head of the State Planning Commission, were approved by the notes of individual leaders.[21]

It should be said, however, that the "plenipotentiary powers" possessed by second-echelon leaders such as Hu Yaobang and Zhao Ziyang were of a different order than those held by party elders, particularly Deng and Chen. It seems apparent that neither Hu nor Zhao, despite their positions in the Politburo Standing Committee and as heads, respectively, of the party organization and government bureaucracy throughout much of the 1980s, had the status in the party to discuss issues with party elders on anything approaching an equal basis. Depending on their standing in the party and their relations with Deng, some party elders could talk more or less freely with him. Associates of Hu and Zhao maintain that those leaders could not.[22] The relationship between Deng and the other party elders on the one hand and Hu and Zhao on the other was one between superiors and subordinates. As inferiors, Hu and Zhao could report on their work and ask for instructions (*huibao, qingshi*); they could not sit down and discuss problems and possible solutions with party elders.

The very real differences between Chen and Deng, the gap in authority between party elders such as Deng and Chen and second-echelon leaders such as Hu and Zhao, and the absence of institutions or procedures to delimit the "plenipotentiary powers" of the leaders had a major impact on the functioning of the system and the course of reforms. For instance, as head of the party organization and with ultimate responsibility for ideological matters, Hu Yaobang maintained close contact with a network of intellectual supporters with whom he discussed ideas for ideological and other reform.[23] It was inevitable that Hu and his intellectual supporters would come into conflict with Deng Liqun, the head of the CCP Propaganda Department for much of the 1980s, who relied on a very different group of people (and also regarded himself as a more appropriate choice for general secretary). Such conflict was inevitable because the responsibilities of the two leaders overlapped and because Hu, despite his superior institutional position in the party, had no authority to remove his antagonists. Such personnel questions were decided at a level higher than Hu's. Ultimately, Hu's antagonists were successful in undermining his authority and bringing about his downfall.

Similarly, the overlapping responsibilities of Hu Yaobang and Zhao Ziyang brought them increasingly into conflict. For the general secretary to have forsaken dealing with the economy, particularly in an era in which the focus of the party's work was officially declared to be economic construction, would have amounted to self-emasculation. For Zhao, however, the economy was his focus of responsibility and he clearly resented Hu Yaobang's intervention.

This structure of power had a very real impact on the course of reform. With respect to the economy, it meant that there were at least four different foci of lobbying efforts: Deng Xiaoping, Chen Yun, Zhao Ziyang, and Hu Yaobang.[24] Provincial leaders could and did appeal to Hu Yaobang for exceptions to policies laid down by Zhao. Reformers could address their proposals to Zhao Ziyang, either personally or via think tanks, or they could try to find bureaucratic allies to pressure Zhao from a different direction. Conservative bureaucrats, unhappy with the effects of reform, would collect data and send it to Yao Yilin, the head of the State Planning Commission during much of the decade, and Chen Yun. In short, where it was possible to make appeals that bypassed the responsible leader and institutional means of making an authoritative decision were lacking, there was no reason to compromise (although there might have been reason to temporize).

This structure of power had very real implications for the policy-making process and the strategies of leaders. For instance, Hu Yaobang's power as general secretary was limited, as just noted, by his inability to control his own Propaganda Department or the state bureaucracy. Given his limited authority over the party organization, it is no wonder that he relied on intellectuals, who were more respected than feared, and on his network of supporters from the Communist Youth League, which he had long headed.

Similarly, Zhao Ziyang's power, first as premier and then as general secretary, was circumscribed, like Hu's, by the party elders. Zhao had to present and modify his policies in various ways out of deference to the views of the elders, especially when he was pursuing goals at variance with theirs. Zhao has sometimes been called a weak leader. One might say that one of the reasons he was chosen for the job of premier was that his natural inclination was to find a way to move forward without directly confronting his opponents. He was, for instance, much more willing to advocate halfway measures in early stages of rural reform than the more confrontational Anhui party secretary, Wan Li.

Zhao also had to deal with the central bureaucracy, particularly the State Planning Commission and the Ministry of Finance, which were powerful, comprehensive organs with overall command over the planned economy. This is not to say that they wholly opposed change, but they were guardians of the state's interests, and especially the well-being of the approximately 8,000 large and medium-sized state-owned enterprises that make up the core of China's planned economy and provide the bulk of Beijing's financial revenues.

Zhao was not a product of this structure and never came to dominate it. His pre-1980 career was entirely in the provinces and he lacked the necessary ties throughout the central bureaucracy to control them. Moreover, Zhao apparently never pressed for control over the State Planning Commission and the Ministry of Finance. Yao Yilin, the vice premier in charge of the State Planning Commission, was a long-time protégé of Chen Yun; Wang Bingqian, the minister of finance, had long-standing ties to Chen Yun and Li Xiannian. Given the dominance of the party elders in the system, Zhao had little choice but to acquiesce in the continuation of conservative control over these bureaucracies.

Conservative control of the State Planning Commission and Ministry of Finance virtually dictated a strategy of enterprise reform that circumvented the bureaucracy rather than being promoted through the bureaucracy. An analogy might be made to the rural reforms. In the rural sector, reformers offered "policies" more than funds or programs; that is to say, reformers loosened restrictions on localities and peasants so that they could carry out reform. Similarly, in the course of urban reform, Zhao did more to loosen restraints on localities and enterprises than to reform the bureaucracy. Such a strategy soon encountered difficulties because it failed to confront many of the intractable issues in reform; however, it was dictated in large measure by the structure of power in Beijing.

In circumventing the central bureaucracy, Zhao turned for advice to the various think tanks that were established and maintained through his patronage. Although the growth of think tanks brought to light new data and stimulated debates about important policy issues, thus improving the quality of information available to decision makers and enhancing the quality of decisions made, the relationship between the think tanks and the professional bureaucracies was more antagonistic than complementary.[25] In general, the think tanks brought a different type of information into the system, rather than more information of the same type. What the think tanks could do was to conceptualize reform and suggest strategies for attaining reform goals. The bureaucracies, on the other hand, were better at providing detailed information on specific problems (e.g., the effect on ex-factory prices of raising the price of coal). Thus, the role of the think tanks was much more prominent in periods of rapid reform, whereas the central bureaucracies came to the fore in periods of retrenchment and strengthened state controls.

The structure of power that I have tried to sketch in the preceding paragraphs had a great impact on the development of reforms, including their timing and pace, as well as on the course of economic debate. To anticipate the discussion in Chapters 1 and 2, both the rural reforms and the early enterprise reforms emerged as part of the struggle for power against Hua Guofeng and the wing of the party that he represented. This is not to say that this was their only source, but it is doubtful that in the absence of such inner-party struggle the reforms would have emerged as quickly or as fully as they did. The reform program was indeed a part of a campaign that undermined the economic policies of Hua Guofeng and justified the return to power of Deng Xiaoping and his supporters. It does not seem accidental that the push for reform slowed after Hua Guofeng and his associates were removed from power (although this was not the only reason for its slowing).

Similarly, whereas Deng Xiaoping and Chen Yun were able to make common cause in the late 1970s and early 1980s, their relationship was clearly strained by 1983 and 1984. Deng increasingly felt that Chen's policies were too conservative, and the "Decision on Economic Structural Reform" adopted at the Third Plenary Session of the Twelfth Central Committee in 1984 clearly marked a parting of ways. The inauguration of the "second wave" of reform, as Hamrin has called it, thus marked more than a restoking of the dimmed embers of the first wave.[26] It marked the ascendance of a different vision of reform, one that went well beyond the limits considered in the earlier period. It is no wonder that conservative economists, in the aftermath of Tiananmen, began to speak in terms of two periods of reform, the first of which went well and the second of which, beginning in 1984, went increasingly awry.

These two phases of reform defined the political contours in which economic debates unfolded. In the beginning of the first phase, reform-minded economists directed their criticism primarily against the economic policies, both urban and rural, associated with Hua Guofeng. Reformers were not all of one mind, however, and as the economic planners associated with Hua were ousted and as Chen Yun became dominant in the economic policy arena, more liberal ideas were subjected to harsh criticism. The momentum for reform slowed visibly.

In the second phase of reform, more liberal-minded reformers were ascendant, but the continued presence of conservatives, who looked to Chen Yun for leadership, sharply constrained the formulation and implementation of any reform plan. Faced with such constraints and confronted by real problems in the economy, it is no wonder that reform-minded economists soon began criticizing each other more than they criticized the conservatives. The contentious debates among reform-minded economists reflected the uncertainty and political difficulties Zhao faced as he tried on the one hand to defend himself against conservative criticism and on the other hand to forge ahead with reforms that were likely to create more problems before bearing results. Finally, with the ill-advised intervention of Deng Xiaoping on the issue of price reform, the problems became overwhelming and Zhao's position collapsed. With Tiananmen and Zhao's ouster, conservatives again gained control over economy policy, at least for a while.

Notes

1. Foreign trade figures are from Nicholas R. Lardy, *Foreign Trade and Economic Reform in China, 1978–1990*, p. 12.
2. This is not to say that elite conflict was the only cause of the Tiananmen tragedy. Obviously the tremendous changes in society and in the relationship between state and society wrought by the reforms were fundamental to the emergence of popular protest. Nevertheless, elite conflict contributed greatly to the political atmosphere in which the protests occurred, as well as to the way in which the regime responded.
3. Three recent works that focus on the changing state-society relationship are Arthur Lewis Rosenbaum, ed., *State and Society in China: The Consequences of Reform*; Mark Selden, *The Political Economy of Chinese Development*; and Gordon White, *Riding the Tiger: The Politics of Economic Reform in Post-Mao China*.

4. The phrase "no easy choice" is borrowed from Samuel P. Huntington and Joan M. Nelson's book *No Easy Choice*, which analyzes the dilemmas leaders of developing countries face in the course of economic development.

5. See, in particular, Carol Lee Hamrin, *China and the Challenge of the Future*, especially pp. 123–128.

6. Tang Tsou, "Prolegomenon to the Study of Informal Groups in CCP Politics," p. 99.

7. Andrew J. Nathan, "A Factionalism Model for CCP Politics."

8. Tsou, "Prolegomenon to the Study of Informal Groups in CCP Politics," p. 100.

9. Tang Tsou, "Political Change and Reform: The Middle Course," p. 222.

10. Tang Tsou, "The Tiananmen Tragedy," p. 293.

11. Tsou, "The Tiananmen Tragedy," p. 293.

12. Deng Xiaoping, " 'Full Text of Gists' of Deng Xiaoping's Speech to Members of the New Politburo Standing Committee," *Tung fang jih pao*, July 15, 1993, p. 6, trans. FBIS, July 18, 1993, pp. 13–15.

13. Jurgen Domes, "The Pattern of Politics," *Problems of Communism*, vol. 23, no. 5 (September–October 1974), pp. 21–22, quoted in Harry Harding, "Competing Models of the Chinese Communist Policy Process: Toward a Sorting and Evaluation."

14. See Kenneth G. Lieberthal and Michel Oksenberg, *Policy Making in China: Leaders, Structures, and Processes*; and David Lampton, "Chinese Politics: The Bargaining Treadmill," pp. 11–41.

15. Kenneth G. Lieberthal, "The 'Fragmented Authoritarianism' Model and Its Limitations," p. 14.

16. Tsou, "The Tiananmen Tragedy," p. 319.

17. The term "wealth and power" is borrowed from Benjamin Schwartz's classic study *In Search of Wealth and Power*.

18. During his highly publicized trip to Shenzhen in the spring of 1992, Deng made a point of saying that he had never read *Das Kapital*.

19. On the relationship among economic, political, and ideological thought in Chen Yun, see Qu Anzhen and Zhu Yushan, "Chen Yun on Party Style," in *Jiefang ribao*, May 15, 1991, p. 6, trans. FBIS, May 23, 1991, pp. 40–42.

20. Conference on "The Chinese Political Process in Comparative Context," held in Washington, DC, October 7–8, 1991. Although, as noted above, the primary political relationship in China since the late 1970s has been that between Deng and Chen, there are certainly other leaders who possess "plenipotentiary powers," albeit to a lesser degree than Deng and Chen. I take the term "plenipotentiary powers" to indicate both that power is personal (though different persons exercise different degrees of power) and that the scope in which power is exercised is not circumscribed by institutions or procedures (though the scope varies with the individual's position in the system). This means, as discussed below, that leaders' spheres of power inevitably overlap, that there are no institutional means for resolving such conflicts, and that such conflicts are readily personalized.

21. Chen Yizi, *Zhongguo: Shinian gaige yu bajiu minyun* (China: Ten Years of Reform and the Democratic Movement of 1989), p. 51. Author's interviews.

22. Author's interviews.

23. See Merle Goldman, "Hu Yaobang's Intellectual Network."

24. There were other foci of lobbying on a variety of issues both big and small, but these four leaders had the ultimate responsibility within their (overlapping) spheres of authority.

25. Nina Halpern has suggested that the formation of the think tanks forced the bureaucracies to respond by arguing their cases with better information, thus bringing about a pattern of "competitive persuasion" and improving the overall decisionmak-

ing process. The relationship between bureaucrats and those in the think tanks, however, was generally antagonistic; those in the bureaucracy looked down on those in the think tanks as fuzzy-headed idealists who did not really understand how the economy worked while the latter were often contemptuous of the bureaucrats' inability to think conceptually about the economy. Moreover, because the bureaucracy and the think tanks looked to different elements of the leadership for support, they had little incentive to cooperate. See Nina Halpern, "Information Flows and Policy Coordination in the Chinese Bureaucracy."

26. Hamrin, *China and the Challenge of the Future*, Chapter 4.

1

The Emergence of
Rural Reform

No reform in the Dengist period has had a more profound effect on the political economy of China or affected the lives of as many people as the rural reforms that were implemented gradually from 1978 onward. Not only did these reforms stimulate a sharp increase in grain production and permit the rapid development of nonagricultural sideline production (such as native crafts) and rural industry that greatly raised the income of peasants, but they also greatly affected the urban economy by providing a model of reform, creating new markets for goods produced in the cities, and by releasing underemployed peasants to participate in the growth of rural industry as well as in urban industry and trade, among other effects. The rural reforms have not been without problems, as new difficulties have arisen in the wake of old ones, but they have radically changed the face of China, altering the relationship between central and local authorities and perhaps providing China's best single hope of making the transition to a post-Communist world with a minimum of trauma.[1]

How did a reform of such magnitude come about? Looking at the history of the late 1970s, it becomes apparent that the reform emerged neither from a groundswell of peasant demand for reform, as some romanticized renditions of this period maintain, nor as a coherent program adopted by the top leadership.[2] Rather, it emerged from a highly complex process in which local leaders provided peasants with the opportunity to experiment with reform and then argued, both directly and indirectly, with the central leadership to allow the experiments to continue and eventually to be expanded. Perhaps most important, the launching of rural reform was part of a struggle for leadership as veteran cadres, purged during the Cultural Revolution, returned to power and began challenging the existing leadership of China, headed by Hua Guofeng, over both positions and policy.

In the wake of the death of Mao and the arrest of the "Gang of Four," Hua Guofeng had attempted to bolster his legitimacy by stressing that he was Mao's chosen successor (Mao had written a note to Hua, "With you in charge, I am at ease") and by sanctioning his policies in Maoist terms. As pressure mounted to allow veteran cadres to return to their posts, Hua had explicitly raised the slogan of the "two whatevers" ("whatever decisions Chairman Mao made, we resolutely support; whatever instructions Chairman Mao made, we will steadfastly abide by") to impede their advance and prevent them from challenging his policies.[3]

In this period, agricultural policy was under the purview of Ji Dengkui and Chen Yonggui, the latter being the former party secretary of the Dazhai Production Brigade, who had been promoted on the basis of his apparent success in making Dazhai, a poor and barren area in the hills of Shanxi Province, prosper. Generally speaking, the Dazhai model referred to taking the production brigade (rather than the lower-level production team) as the basic unit of account (that calculated and divided income), abolishing the cultivation of private plots, and emphasizing ideological rather than material incentives. Following the arrest of the Gang of Four, Chen Yonggui made common cause with Hua Guofeng, and Hua rewarded this support by touting the Dazhai model.[4]

The economic planners associated with Hua Guofeng, Ji Dengkui, and Chen Yonggui, however, miscalculated the seriousness of the situation in the countryside and overestimated the ability of the state to redress the problems of the rural economy. Instead of relaxing policies toward the countryside, Hua Guofeng's government called for accelerating rural modernization, setting a goal of rural mechanization within ten years.[5] Rural communes were too impoverished to purchase agricultural machinery on a large scale, and such policies were doomed from the start. The lack of understanding of the rural situation and the unrealistic policies adopted after the death of Mao left Hua politically vulnerable on the critical issue of rural policy.

The challenge to the Dazhai model was posed earliest and most forcefully by Anhui Province, where Wan Li had been appointed CCP secretary in June 1977. In Sichuan, Zhao Ziyang also supported rural reform, but Zhao's approach emphasized the relaxation of agricultural policies and the search for compromise solutions.[6] It was Wan Li who confronted head-on the issue of rural collectivization and staunchly supported the "household responsibility system" in which production decisions were devolved to the family. Wan was a determined opponent of "leftist" policies. In 1975, when Deng Xiaoping was struggling against the Gang of Four, he called on Wan Li, then the minister of railways, to root out leftists in the railway system and restore efficiency to the system.[7] As a provincial leader, Wan had no more tolerance for the Dazhai model than he had for the "leftists" in the railway system; he condemned the communes as "labor camps."[8] Wan combined his genuine empathy for the peasants with unusual moral courage and absolute loyalty to Deng Xiaoping. In 1976, when the Gang of Four used the outpouring of popular grief for Zhou Enlai in Tiananmen Square to persuade Mao Zedong to purge Deng again, a nationwide campaign to criticize Deng was launched. Few officials could stand up to the pressure to criticize Deng. Even

Zhao Ziyang issued a statement condemning Deng, albeit in the mildest language possible. Wan Li did not. This display of moral courage in the face of intense pressure gave Wan enormous prestige within the party when the Gang of Four was arrested the following October, not to mention the gratitude of Deng Xiaoping.

Even before Wan Li arrived in Anhui, local leaders were making efforts to reevaluate rural policy. In the spring of 1977, Chuxian Prefecture organized 394 cadres to inspect 401 communes and brigades.[9] Chuxian Prefecture was headed by Wang Yuzhao, who would soon become one of Wan Li's chief allies in the forging of a new rural order and who would subsequently be rewarded by being promoted to the State Council's Research Center for Rural Development, and it encompassed such counties as Feixi and Fengyang, which would soon become famous for their efforts in pioneering rural reform.

By October 1977 at the very latest, Wan Li had taken charge of an effort to evaluate the rural situation and draw up a new set of provincial regulations to guide agriculture in Anhui. Wan's efforts drew heavily on the rural investigations conducted under Wang Yuzhao and, after three months of investigation and discussion, the province drew up "Regulations on Several Questions of Current Rural Economic Policy" (which became known as the "Six Articles"). These regulations stressed respecting the autonomy of the production team, encouraging sideline production, and restoring private plots. Anhui's policies were clearly an effort to criticize the Dazhai model and were therefore part of the broader effort to undermine the Hua Guofeng wing of the CCP.

In national-level meetings that took place in November and December 1977, some areas criticized the Dazhai model by stressing the autonomy of the production team, protecting private plots, and promoting household sideline production—precisely the points emphasized in Anhui's regulations. *People's Daily* even went so far as to prepare an editorial to support the new emphasis in agricultural policy, but this initiative was quashed by those in charge of agricultural policy before it could be published.[10]

Despite this apparent victory for proponents of the Dazhai model, it soon became apparent that their opponents had the strength and willingness to publicly contest the Dazhai model. In February 1978 *People's Daily* published a front-page article describing in detail the formulation of Anhui's agricultural regulations. The article was accompanied by an "editor's note" indicating that the article had high-level backing, which is likely to have come from Deng Xiaoping.[11] The publication of this article in the wake of the December meeting made clear that the reform wing of the party was challenging the leadership of Hua Guofeng by putting forth a contrary agricultural policy. Three months later, Hua's authority would be challenged publicly with the inauguration of the discussion on practice as the sole criterion of truth.

Poverty was the critical issue as reformers began challenging Hua Guofeng. According to statistics compiled in 1976 and 1977, the production of some 200 counties—about 10 percent of China's total—remained at the same level as at the time of the establishment of the PRC, with some counties' production even below this. Statistics from the summer of 1980 would reveal that over one-quarter of China's rural population had an annual per capita income of less than 50 yuan.[12] Chen Yun, the senior economic specialist in the party, bluntly warned the critical central work conference that preceded the Third Plenum that if the livelihood of the peasants did not improve, party secretaries would lead peasants into the cities to demand food.[13] At the same time, Deng argued that egalitarianism should be opposed and that some peasants should be allowed to get rich first.[14] Nevertheless, there were limits on how far Deng and his allies were willing, or able, to go.

The watershed Third Plenary Session of the Eleventh Central Committee, which was held in December 1978, marked Deng Xiaoping's rise to leadership (though not undisputed) within the party, affirmed the discussion on practice as the sole criterion of truth, and called for shifting the focus of the party's work from class struggle to economic construction. It also approved two documents on rural policy: the "Decisions on Some Questions Concerning the Acceleration of Agricultural Development (Draft)" and "Regulations on the Work in Rural People's Communes (Draft for Trial Use)." These documents were necessarily compromise documents, but they nevertheless marked an important step away from the Dazhai model. Despite reaffirming the mass movement to learn from Dazhai, they implicitly undermined the Dazhai model by emphasizing the authority of the production team and permitting the practice of awarding work points according to fixed work quotas.[15]

The seriousness with which the CCP leadership viewed the rural situation was reflected in its decision to stimulate grain production through a major increase in the procurement price of grain. The price for grain procured within the state quota would be raised 20 percent and an additional bonus of 50 percent would be paid for grain sold to the state beyond the quota. This policy measure, combined with the rural reforms that were yet to appear, would have a major impact on grain production (and the central government's financial burden) in the years that followed.

Although the emphasis on the authority of the production team and material incentives moved significantly away from the Dazhai model, the central authorities did not at this time contemplate the decollectivization of agriculture. On the contrary, the affirmation of the production team as the basic unit of account was in accord with the Sixty Articles approved by Mao Zedong in 1962, and the use of price policy to stimulate grain production reflected an administrative effort to stimulate production. At this point, the reformers at the center were neither strong enough nor certain enough to push for more radical measures of reform; the decision on accelerating agriculture specifically forbade the adoption of the household responsibility system ("*bu xu baochan daohu*").[16]

Even as the Third Plenum was feeling its way toward a compromise, Anhui Province was pushing ahead with a liberalization of rural policy that would soon sweep China. In 1978 a severe drought hit Anhui, the sort of drought said to happen but once in a century. Rainfall was two thirds below normal, and the famous fog surrounding Mount Huang, the scene of so many landscape paintings, disappeared. Dysentery, type B encephalitis, infectious hepatitis, and other diseases began to spread. Hundreds of thousands of people fled the devastation; militia men in Shanghai tried to stanch the flow of refugees into that city. A movie made for internal reference is said to have made the elderly leaders of the Politburo "cry out, cover their faces with their hands, and weep."[17] The land was baked dry. Neither hand tractors nor animal-drawn plows could break through it. The only way to prepare the ground for planting was by backbreaking, intensive manual labor. This drought would provide Wan Li with an opportunity to push the radical agricultural policies that became China's rural reform.

The peasants were not willing to engage in the backbreaking labor needed for planting without assurances of a return on their efforts. When the party secretary of Shannan district (in Feixi County in Chuxian Prefecture) went to the Huanghua Production Brigade of Shannan Commune to investigate, the peasants demanded a return to "the old ways" (*lao banfa*).[18] What they meant by "the old ways" was the household responsibility system. Although never officially approved since the founding of the PRC, the household responsibility system had been implemented in at least some areas of the country on three occasions. That history cut two ways. On the one hand, previous efforts to implement some form of the household responsibility system provided the precedents on which the rural reforms would be built, and had previously gained the support of such leaders as Deng Xiaoping and Chen Yun. On the other hand, each such attempt had been ruthlessly criticized, leaving many cadres fearful of supporting another round of decollectivization while making other cadres determined to defend the agricultural policies on which they had built their careers.

Political Conflict and the Household Responsibility System

The household responsibility system was first implemented in the PRC in 1956 following the introduction of higher-level Agricultural Producer Collectives (APCs). Mao's July 31, 1955, speech, in which he had ridiculed his more moderate colleagues for "tottering along like a woman with bound feet," had ushered in a period of accelerated collectivization. By the end of 1955, 63 percent of the nation's rural households were enrolled in APCs, and by the end of March 1956 the number had risen to 88.9 percent. Over half of all peasant households were organized into higher-level APCs.[19]

It was soon clear that the pace of collectivization had outstripped peasant willingness and cadre capabilities. In May 1956, Deng Zihui, who was head of the CCP's Rural Work Department, admitted that there were many defects in the APCs, and the party began to back away from its harsh policy of the previous year. A policy directive adopted in September 1957 instructed cadres to dissolve large APCs and transferred production authority from APCs down to production teams and subsidiary occupation groups.[20] In this atmosphere, many areas began to experiment with varieties of the household responsibility system.

One such area was in Zhejiang, which had been hostile to collectivization even before Mao had demanded that its pace be stepped up. Yongjia County of Wenzhou Prefecture was particularly resistant to efforts to collectivize the countryside, and Li Yunhe, the county deputy party secretary in charge of agriculture, organized an experiment in the household responsibility system (which was called *baochan daohu shengchan guanli zeren zhi*). Li's experiment came under attack in the prefectural newspaper, but Zhejiang Provincial Party Secretary Lin Hujia (who would become mayor of Beijing in the early 1980s and was associated with the so-called Petroleum Faction), who was in charge of agriculture, supported Li's efforts. As a result, in January 1957, *Zhejiang Daily* published an article written by Li defending the results of the household responsibility system in Yongjia. This was the first article in China to openly advocate the household responsibility system (*baochan daohu*).[21]

Despite the more relaxed ideological atmosphere of early 1957—Mao gave his speech "On the Correct Handling of Contradictions Among the People" in February—there was strong opposition to the household responsibility system. In March the Zhejiang provincial party committee—despite Lin Hujia's previous support—ruled that the household responsibility system was "a mistake of orientation" and ordered Yongjia County to abolish it. Local cadres and peasants initially resisted this order, but the launching of the antirightist campaign in July made resistance futile. In July 1957, the Wenzhou prefectural newspaper published an editorial entitled "Strike Down the Household Responsibility System, Protect Socialism," and in August the same paper criticized Li Yunhe by name as having committed "rightist opportunist errors." These actions were subsequently supported by Beijing. In October, *People's Daily* published an article entitled "Wenzhou District's Correction of the 'Baochan Daohu' Mistake," and in February 1958 Li was named a "rightist element," expelled from the party, and sent down (*xia fang*) for labor.[22]

Two years later, as the excesses of the Great Leap Forward were causing obvious hardship in the countryside, the party leadership met at the second Zhengzhou Conference and began to take some measures to rein in the worst aspects of the Great Leap. These actions provided a somewhat more relaxed atmosphere, and peasants in various places once again began to engage in the household responsibility system. Not long after its reemergence, however, Peng Dehuai challenged Mao at the Lushan Plenum, resulting in Peng's fall from power and a renewed campaign against "rightist" policies. In November 1959, a Commentator article in the party theoretical journal *Red Flag* accused "rightist elements" of wanting to use the household responsibility system to "lead the rural areas back onto the capitalist road." A Commentator article in *People's Daily* shortly thereafter similarly accused the household responsibility system of ιeing an "extremely backward, retrogressive, reactionary method."[23] Accusaιions that the household responsibility system was leading to the restoration of ιapitalism went considerably beyond the criticisms of 1957, which stopped at ιondemning the system as a "rich peasant" policy.

The household responsibility system was revived once again in the wake of ιhe mass starvation and privation caused by the Great Leap Forward. This time ιhe system was implemented more widely and for a longer time than in previous ιeriods, but the shadow of past criticisms caused local officials to devise a ιariety of new names for the practice. In Henan, officials called it "lending land" ιjie di); in Anhui, officials called the land given to households to farm "responsiιility land" (zeren tian). Ever more direct, the peasants in Anhui, one of the ιrovinces worst hit by the disasters of the Great Leap Forward, called this land ιlife-saving land" (jiuming tian).

Reeling under the impact of Great Leap policies, Anhui Province, which had been among the most active of China's provinces in endorsing the Great Leap policies, quickly reversed course in an effort to stabilize production and halt the mass starvation occurring there. Zeng Xisheng, first secretary of the province, urged the adoption of the household responsibility system at a meeting of the East China Bureau in March 1961 and then reported on the plan to Mao Zedong. Mao allegedly said, "Try it out! If you make a go of it and can increase output by 100 million jin of grain that will be important!" But shortly thereafter, Mao modified his instructions, saying "Responsibility fields may be tried out on a small scale." Mao did not reply to a letter from Zeng that further elaborated on the advantages of the household responsibility system.[24] By the summer of 1961, three quarters of the production teams in Anhui had instituted the household responsibility system, and by October the figure had increased to 84.4 percent.[25] Across China, more than ten provinces and regions implemented some sort of responsibility system, accounting for some 20 percent of the cultivated land in China.[26]

In December 1961, Mao met with Zeng Xisheng in Wuxi in Jiangsu Province. Mao said, "Production has begun to revive, shouldn't this plan [i.e., responsibility fields] be changed?" Mao had become hostile toward the household responsibility system. At the 7,000 cadre conference in January 1962, Zeng Xisheng was criticized both for "leftism"—because he had enthusiastically supported the Great Leap Forward, thereby incurring disaster in Anhui—and for "rightism" because of the extreme remedies he had adopted in response to the disasters of the Great Leap. In March the Anhui party committee was reorganized.[27] The new party committee convened a cadre conference and declared that the system of "responsibility land" was an error in orientation.[28]

Zeng's purge did not end debate over the responsibility system. After all, Mao had been forced to make a self-criticism, albeit a mild one, at the 7,000 cadre conference, and Mao's article "Oppose Bookishness" was reprinted to drive home the point that rigid adherence to dogmatic theory was not the way to build socialism. There remained much debate over the household responsibility system, and many investigations of rural conditions were conducted, particularly by the teams sent by Deng Zihui, head of the party's Rural Work Department, who supported the household responsibility system. These investigations found that areas that implemented the household responsibility system fared better than those that did not.[29]

The most important of the investigations conducted in this period was by Chen Yun. Chen spent two weeks in Qingpu County outside of Shanghai, an area in which Chen had organized peasants in 1927 and with which he had maintained close contact following the founding of the PRC. Prior to going, Chen asked Xue Muqiao to lead a small team to the same area to do a preliminary investigation; then, from late June to early July 1961, Chen himself led an investigation team. After his investigation, Chen wrote a letter to Deng Xiaoping, then general secretary of the party, to which he appended three documents addressing the issues of allowing peasants to raise pigs privately and increasing the size of private plots.[30] In the spring of 1962, while resting in Hangzhou, Chen became aware of Anhui's experiments with "responsibility land," which were then being promoted by Deng Zihui. Chen said that it was an extraordinary measure for extraordinary times and that it did not matter whether the policy was called "dividing the land among households" or "household responsibility system" (*baochan daohu*). Chen returned to Beijing in early July 1962, and on July 6 wrote a letter to Mao Zedong requesting a meeting. On the evening of July 9, Chen talked with Mao for over an hour. Although Mao did not express his opinion that evening, he was very angry the following morning, sharply criticizing Chen's views as "dividing the land and individual farming" (*fentian dangan*), as destroying the collective economy, and as Chinese-style revisionism. It was, Mao said, a question of which road China should take.[31]

Chen was not the only senior leader who supported the household responsibility system in this period. On July 7, Deng Xiaoping, in receiving delegates to the Seventh Plenary Session of the Third Chinese Communist Youth League (CYL), said, "Whatever form the peasants are willing to adopt, they should adopt; those that are illegal should be legalized." He also said that it was possible to legalize the household responsibility system (*baochan daohu*). It was in this talk that Deng said:[32]

> Comrade Liu Bocheng frequently uses a Sichuan phrase: "yellow cat, black cat, whichever catches mice is a good cat." This was said in reference to fighting war. The reason we were able to defeat Chiang Kai-shek is that we did not follow old rules or fight according to old ways. Everything was determined by the circumstances; winning is what counted. Now if we want to restore agricultural production, it is necessary to look at the situation. We should use whatever form [of production] arouses the enthusiasm of the masses. Now it seems that whether in industry or in agriculture it is not possible to advance without first retreating.

Later that same day, Deng learned that Mao was not pleased with his remarks and he called Hu Yaobang's office (Hu Yaobang was then head of the CYL) to have them deleted from the transcript of his talk that would be circulated to the delegates to the CYL Plenum. The following morning he called Hu again to insert some other comments in the place of the offending passage.[33]

It was the personal and strong intervention of Mao Zedong that stopped the spread of the household responsibility system and decided the intraparty debate in favor of continuing collective agriculture. Two days after Chen's talk with Mao, a notice was issued convening a Central Work Conference in Beidaihe. On the first day of the Beidaihe meeting, Mao gave a talk on contradictions and class struggle. The conference then sharply criticized views that "opposed the people's communes" and favored the "household responsibility system" and "individual farming."[34] It was at this meeting that Mao raised the slogan "Never forget class struggle."

The household responsibility system continued to be implemented for a while in some areas, but by the fall of 1963 it had been effectively suppressed. Some observers believe that if it had not been for Mao's personal and strong opposition to the household responsibility system at this time, the rural reforms associated with the late 1970s and early 1980s would have been implemented and developed almost two decades earlier.

Local Initiative and the Emergence of Rural Reform

It was against this background of local initiatives and intraparty debate—and the judgment, enforced for more than fifteen years, that the household responsibility system was a mistake of line and a question of capitalism versus socialism—that the peasants of Huanghua Production Brigade in Anhui urged the adoption of the "old methods." When the party secretary of Shannan district was presented with this demand, he indicated neither approval nor disapproval. Taking this as tacit approval, cadres of the Huanghua Production Brigade began fixing responsibility for production to individual households.[35] Other production brigades in the same commune soon got wind of Huanghua's example and began to implement the household responsibility system themselves.

The drought that Anhui was facing facilitated reform. As early as the beginning of 1978, the Anhui provincial party committee proposed that "land that cannot be cultivated by the collectives can be lent to commune members to cultivate; whoever plants should harvest, the state will not collect grain or assign procurement responsibilities." Moreover, the committee specifically pointed out that each person could be "lent" a portion of the land that was being contracted out. This regulation broke the long-standing "taboo" on individual management of the land and gave localities the sense that they could push ahead on their own.[36] In March 1978, Mahu Commune in Fengyang County became the first area to specifically link production and reward.[37] The system used in Mahu

Commune, however, was not the household responsibility system (*baochan daohu*) but the small-group responsibility system (*baochan daozu* or *da bao gan*).[38] In May, Wang Yuzhao, party secretary for Chuxian Prefecture, explicitly approved of Mahu Commune's experiment and the small-group responsibility system.[39]

Despite the open-minded attitude of the prefectural and provincial authorities, the history of criticism of the household responsibility system was cause for caution. Even in Fengyang County, where the party leadership vigorously supported the small-group responsibility system, it was dangerous to go further and adopt the household responsibility system. When peasants and cadres in the extremely poor Xiaogang Production Brigade in Liyuan Commune in Fengyang County decided to put the household responsibility system into effect in the spring of 1978, they first convened and swore an oath of loyalty in which the eighteen households in the community vowed to take care of the dependents of any production team cadres who were arrested for allowing the household responsibility system to go into effect (since the cadres would have been held responsible). The oath read as follows:[40]

1. The contracting of production to individual households is to be kept strictly secret and not divulged to any outsider.
2. When the grain is harvested, the amount to be rendered to the state will be rendered to the state, and the amount to be rendered to the collective will be rendered to the collective. Should there be a large amount of grain, more should be contributed to the state, with no one shirking.
3. Should they [the cadres] come to grief because we are contracting production to individual households, we are willing to raise the children of village cadres until they are eighteen years of age.

Although Fengyang County soon gave special permission to Xiaogang Production Brigade to experiment with the household responsibility system, it later reversed itself as other areas started demanding the same right.[41]

The household responsibility system remained confined to Feixi County and a few other locations, such as Xiaogang Production Brigade, but the small-group responsibility system spread quickly. Within three months of its inauguration, over 15 percent of Anhui's production brigades had adopted the production responsibility system.[42]

However, the household responsibility system—as opposed to the small-group responsibility system—continued to face strong opposition. Shortly after the household responsibility system began to be adopted, in Feixi County, one county leader objected bluntly: "We have engaged in collective agriculture for twenty years. Now in one step we have retreated to pre-liberation times, engaging in individual farming. . . . How is this worthy of Chairman Mao?"[43] On several occasions the county leadership issued documents and sent people to Shannan district to "correct" their work. Moreover, as noted above, the very success of the household responsibility system in Xiaogang Production Brigade aroused the envy and opposition of nearby brigades and communes, leading the Fengyang County leadership to force Xiaogang to adopt the small-group responsibility system in late 1979. In addition, Anhui's policies came under attack from other provinces, apparently with the support of Chen Yonggui. As Wan Li said in a January 1979 provincial meeting, Anhui was criticized for "chopping down Dazhai's red flag" because its regulations stressed the production team, instead of the production brigade. As Wan put it, the "struggle was very sharp."[44]

The victory of Deng Xiaoping at the Third Plenary Session of the Eleventh Central Committee in December 1978 created an atmosphere that facilitated the implementation of reform in Anhui. In January 1979, after inspecting Fengyang and other rural counties, Wan spoke with unusual bluntness:[45]

> Now we must not be biased; we must see what sort of method increases production. The only type of biases we oppose are egalitarianism and individual farming (*dan gan*). Any method that can mobilize the enthusiasm of the masses is permissible. Anything that can increase production, make greater contributions to the state, consolidate (*zhuang da*) the collective economy, increase the masses' income, and improve their standard of living is a good method. You say the peasants can become prosperous by doing it [the small-group responsibility system, *da bao gan*] for three years, then let them do it. If there are other methods that can mobilize the peasants' enthusiasm, we can let them try. Now, what we fear is that enthusiasm cannot be aroused. Also, family sideline production should not be restricted, let them do it. Don't be afraid of their earning 10,000 yuan. *In fact, individual farming is nothing to get excited about.* There is individual farming in Yugoslavia, but it is still recognized as a socialist country. At present, landlords in our country have been eliminated and the means of production are under the public ownership system. Now the question is one of getting the masses to raise productivity. I only fear that production will not be raised. As long as production is increased, any method is fine.

In the wake of the Third Plenum, the production responsibility system developed rapidly. In February 1979 a work team from the Provincial Agricultural Committee Policy Research Office arrived in Shannan district of Feixi County to convey the contents of the two documents on rural work adopted by the Third Plenum. They soon learned that Shannan had gone beyond the system of contracting work to small teams by implementing the household responsibility system and that it was seeking higher-level approval. When researchers asked the peasants how to increase production, the peasants reportedly said, "If you want rapid [development], mass action will not work. If the household responsibility system is adopted, 80 percent will become wealthy."[46]

The Policy Research Office was sympathetic to the household responsibility system. The office was headed by Zhou Yueli, who had been Zeng Xisheng's secretary in 1961. When Wan Li arrived in Anhui in 1977, he had found the provincial party "Dazhai office" strongly opposed to reform and so had naturally turned to Zhou and his office. Thus, it was under Zhou's direction that Anhui had formulated the six articles.[47] When the work team from the Policy Research Office reported the situation to Wan Li, he declared that Feixi County should be allowed to continue the household responsibility system on an experimental basis.[48] With regard to the experiment, however, Wan instructed that "it should not be publicized, it should not be promoted, and it should not appear in newspapers. Let practice demonstrate whether or not it is correct."[49]

Wan Li's support for the production responsibility system in general and the household responsibility system in particular was being watched carefully, and not always with admiration, by other areas in China. In March 1979, just as spring planting was getting under way, this opposition received high-level support when *People's Daily* published a "letter to the editor," signed by one Zhang Hao, that sharply criticized the household responsibility system for destroying the three-level ownership system of the communes. Zhang Hao's letter had in fact been prepared in the office of Wang Renzhong, head of the State Agricultural Commission and a strong opponent of the household responsibility system. An "editor's note" introducing the front-page article and indicating that it had high-level support said that those areas that had already begun implementing the household responsibility system should restudy the decision on rural work adopted by the Third Plenum—which had explicitly forbidden the household responsibility system.[50]

This article had an immediate and unnerving effect on local cadres in Anhui, but it also provoked the staunch opposition of the provincial party leadership. The minutes of a party committee meeting in Fengyang County on March 17, that is, only two days after the article appeared, recorded party secretary Chen Tingyuan's words as follows:[51]

After *People's Daily* published the letter and editorial note regarding the production responsibility system, the reaction was not small. Should we continue to engage in the small-group responsibility system or not? There are several sorts of circumstances. Yesterday [Anhui Provincial CCP Deputy Secretary] Wang Guangyu came to Fengyang and said not to change anything. Last night, Wan Li was in Chuxian and asked old Zhang to give a call. Wan Li said practice should be the test. If production is increased, we should continue [the production responsibility system] next year.

Two weeks after Zhang Hao's letter to the editor was published, *People's Daily* published a rebuttal in the form of another letter to the editor and another "editor's note." The letter to the editor was signed by two people from Anhui's provincial agricultural commission, strongly suggesting that Wan Li had demanded that *People's Daily* issue a correction. They complained that Zhang Hao's letter and the accompanying editor's note had caused "confusion" (*hunluan*) in Anhui; cadres in places that had divided work into groups (i.e., the small-group responsibility system) and had linked production to rewards were afraid that they would again be criticized. Reminding the center that spring had already arrived, the letter suggested that areas that had already implemented such systems be allowed to continue them and that their experience be summed up in the future. The accompanying editor's note admitted that the previous editor's note, which had accompanied Zhang Hao's letter, had been imprecise. Party policy, it said, was that the system of contracting responsibility to small groups (the *baochan daozu* system) was permissible but that contracting responsibility to households (*baochan daohu*) and individual farming were not.[52]

Although this letter and the accompanying editor's note had the effect of "correcting" the previous one and protecting the embryonic agricultural reforms taking place in Anhui and elsewhere, the argument over the course of agricultural policy was far from over. In the fall of 1979, for instance, Wang Renzhong had an angry exchange of words with Wan Li over the phone. Wang accused Wan of allowing the socialist ownership system to be changed, while Wan replied that it did not matter how good a policy seemed to be if the peasants could not eat their fill.[53]

Despite this opposition to the household responsibility system, when the Fourth Plenum of the Eleventh Central Committee met in September 1979, it made a significant revision in the draft agricultural document that had been adopted by the Third Plenum the preceding December. In place of the blanket prohibition on the household responsibility system contained in the draft, the Fourth Plenum added the following passage:[54]

> It is not permitted to divide up the farmland for individual farming. Except for those with special requirements to develop sideline production and the few individual households in remote hilly areas with poor communications, the fixing of output quotas based on the household *should not* be practiced.

This passage marked a departure from the draft passed by the Third Plenum in two ways. First, while not endorsing the household responsibility system, it permitted "remote hilly areas" to practice it. Thus, areas like Fengyang County in Anhui, which were contracting production to small groups, were allowed to continue to do so. Second, it changed the blanket condemnation of the household responsibility system contained in the draft to "should not"—a considerably less stringent prohibition. Nevertheless, the document as adopted by the Fourth Plenum hardly constituted an endorsement of the household responsibility system. Without more positive support from the center, the system could not expand rapidly and the status of cadres implementing it would continue to be uncertain.

Over the following two years, this first tentative endorsement of the household responsibility system would be gradually extended until it was adopted throughout China. The process through which these early reforms were initiated and later extended throughout the country suggests the critical importance of local leadership, particularly that of Wan Li and Wang Yuzhao. Wan Li, however, was only able to defend the early reforms because he had the support of

Deng Xiaoping. In the policy debates that followed and during the gradual extension of the household responsibility system, agricultural reform received support from the Economic Research Office of the State Planning Commission (then headed by Xue Muqiao); from Deng Liqun, then vice president of the Chinese Academy of Social Sciences; from central leaders including Deng and Chen Yun; and from a group of young intellectuals who collected vast amounts of data and lobbied ceaselessly on behalf of reform. As compared to the course taken by the development of enterprise reform, the process of rural reform was remarkably decentralized and open. Although the support of central party leaders was essential to it, the process was not dominated by China's establishment intellectuals and bureaucratic apparatus. This was partly because of the unique political and social circumstances prevailing in China in the late 1970s and early 1980s and partly because rural policy had always been under the purview of the party rather than the state bureaucracy.

Lobbying Beijing

The process of lobbying Beijing for approval not only of the principle of linking reward to production but also of allowing production to be fixed at the household level began in the summer of 1979 when Guo Chongyi, a member of the Anhui provincial Chinese People's Political Consultative Conference, came to Beijing with a report on the success of the household responsibility (*baochan daohu*) system in Anhui's Feixi County. This report, which was circulated immediately among at least some of the CCP's top leadership, appears to have been the first such report to support the household responsibility system in the Dengist period. Guo reported that because of the implementation of the household responsibility system in Feixi County, the summer grain harvest in 1979 had increased one and a half times over that of the previous year, despite the drought. Arguing that the household responsibility system was socialist, Guo refuted the charge that it would lead to "individualism" and "polarization."[55]

However, because the household responsibility system violated central policy, several officials, including those of the State Agricultural Commission, declined to meet with Guo when he tried to present his findings in Beijing. When he arrived at the Agricultural Institute of the Chinese Academy of Social Sciences (CASS), the open-minded but cautious head of the institute, Zhan Wu, also declined to meet with Guo, although Zhan nevertheless introduced him to people in the institute, including Lu Xueyi and Chen Yizi.[56]

Lu had originally been a philosophy student at Beijing University in the late 1950s and early 1960s and had joined the Philosophy Institute at the Chinese Academy of Sciences (CAS) in 1962. He became interested in agricultural problems shortly thereafter when he was sent to the countryside during the Four Cleanups Movement. At that time, Lu had become aware of the problems of the commune system and was therefore a sympathetic listener when Guo met with him.

Chen Yizi, who was thirty-eight years old in 1978, came from a family of intellectuals. His grandfather had been a reform-minded official under the Qing dynasty, and his father was a hydroelectric engineer who believed that science was the way to save China. This family background gave Chen Yizi a sense of intellectual superiority and historic mission. As a student first of physics and then of literature at Beijing University, Chen was a leader in the Communist Youth League. In 1957, Hu Yaobang, then head of the CYL, carried out investigations ("squatted") at Beijing University and became acquainted with the young activist. During the antirightist campaign of 1959, Chen, from a sense of idealism, wrote a letter to the Central Committee complaining that people who had offered sincere criticisms of the party were being unjustly punished. As a result, Chen himself was sent down to the countryside. He did not, however, lose his belief in Communist ideology or his sense of nationalism.[57]

Chen spent most of the Cultural Revolution in Henan Province, where he rose to be party secretary of a commune. There he met Deng Yingtao, the son of Deng Liqun, who was working as a production team leader. The younger Deng would emerge as one of the most important young intellectuals involved in promoting rural reform. Through this connection, Chen got to know Deng Liqun, formerly Liu Shaoqi's political secretary, with whom he became quite close. Chen also kept up ties with Hu Yaobang, visiting him when he returned to Beijing during the Spring Festival time.

Such ties proved vital for Chen. In early 1979, it was Hu Yaobang who recommended that Chen be allowed to move back to Beijing. He took a position in the Agricultural Institute of the Chinese Academy of Social Sciences, where Deng Liqun was vice president.[58]

Chen was so excited by Guo's report on the success of the household responsibility system in Feixi County that he sent it to Deng Liqun and Hu Yaobang on the same day that he received it. That evening, Hu granted permission for Feixi County to continue the household responsibility system on an experimental basis. This was the first direct expression of party support for the household responsibility system.[59]

Lu Xueyi was also excited by Guo's report. He soon went to Anhui with two other CASS researchers, Jia Dexin and Li Lanting, to investigate the situation. When they returned in the summer of 1979, they wrote a report entitled "The Household Responsibility (*baochan daohu*) System Should Be Restudied." The report said that peasants in Feixi County were demanding to know the answers to such questions as: "Why isn't a method that has been proven to greatly increase production allowed?" and "Is 'practice is the sole criterion of truth' permissible in the rural areas?"

Like Guo, Lu and his colleagues rebutted accusations against the household responsibility system. Moreover, they asked that the case against Zeng Xisheng, the Anhui secretary whom Mao had purged in 1962, be reevaluated. Unless Zeng's case were redressed, they argued, cadres would be afraid to allow the household responsibility system to continue.[60] Their report was published in October 1979 in *Weiding gao* (literally, "unfinalized drafts"), CASS's internal (*neibu*) journal. Deng Liqun frequently used *Weiding gao* to float ideas and proposals that undermined Hua Guofeng's policies, which is one reason why Deng supported the publication of the article by Lu and his colleagues.

The Origin of the Chinese Rural Development Research Group

The Chinese Rural Development Research Group (*Zhongguo nongcun fazhan wenti yanjiu zu*, hereafter, Rural Development Group), which would lobby intensively for rural reform and become China's first real think tank, reflected the unique political and social atmosphere prevailing in the late 1970s and early 1980s. Its formation and role in the policy-making process reflected the Cultural Revolution on the one hand and the demand for reform on the other.

The formation of the Rural Development Group reflected the experience of the Cultural Revolution in at least three ways. First and foremost, it was because of the Cultural Revolution that the urban-educated youths who came to form the group spent so much time in the countryside and became intimately familiar with its conditions and the attitudes of the peasants. They saw firsthand the extensive poverty of the rural areas, the dysfunctionality of the rural communes, and the discontent of the peasants. Second, it was because of their participation in Red Guard organizations and their travel throughout China in the "great linking up" (*da chuan lian*), by which they were to share their revolutionary experiences, that these young intellectuals—members of the so-called third generation—developed extensive personal networks with each other and a profound sense of their generational identity.[61] Many of the key members of the Chinese Rural Development Group got to know each other during the Cultural Revolution.

Perhaps the most unexpected result of the Cultural Revolution was the bridge that it created between this third generation and that of their parent's generation—the high-level cadres who made up the "first generation." The two generations were able, at least for a while, to bridge the years that separated them. The understanding forged during this time provided the basis for veteran cadres, when they returned to office, to turn to young intellectuals for information and advice. It was during the Cultural Revolution that Chen Yizi got to know first Deng Yingtao and then his father, Deng Liqun. Without the Cultural Revolution, people like Deng Liqun would never have had time to reminisce with their children and others of the third generation, passing on their knowledge of the past and their uncertainty over the future. Similarly, Chen Yizi got to know Hu Yaobang better during the Cultural Revolution, visiting Hu at his Beijing home when Chen returned annually to the capital. After the death of Lin Biao, the political atmosphere relaxed significantly, and Hu's home became a gathering place to which young people and intellectuals could come and chat. Unlike most officials, Hu was without pretense, talking frankly with all visitors. He made no bones about his disdain for the Gang of Four and leftist policies.[62]

Shortly after returning to Beijing in 1979, Chen Yizi began looking up old friends. One of the most important was He Weiling, a former classmate from Beijing University. Many of He's ancestors were distinguished scholars, including Xu Fang, a well-known tutor to China's last emperor. His grandfather had received first place in the military examinations in the Qing Dynasty and had gone on to tutor the warlord Feng Yuxiang in the military arts—not the best credentials for a descendant working in revolutionary China. His parents were graduates of Yanjing and Peiping Universities, and his father had been general secretary of the Yong An Company in Shanghai. He Weiling overcame his poor political background through hard work and great intellect. He developed a reputation as one of the brightest students in Beijing University's physics department, earning the respect of classmates and professors alike. His roommate was Deng Pufang, Deng Xiaoping's son, who was also a student in the physics department, and he also came to know Hu Deping, Hu Yaobang's son.[63]

The discussions that Chen had with He Weiling and other young intellectuals such as Deng Yingtao formed the basis for a group that would become known as the Chinese Rural Development Research Group in 1980. Some of the early members of the group were Yang Xun, then a lecturer in the economics department at Beijing University; Bai Ruobing, the son of former Beijing deputy mayor Bai Jiefu; Jiang Baichen; Zhang Musheng; and Bai Nanfeng. They would receive advice, guidance, and strong support from Wang Gengjin, deputy head of CASS's Agricultural Institute. The connections that this group had, and would develop, provided it with access to some of the highest leaders in China.

These young people, most of whom were in their late twenties and early thirties, many of whom were not party members, and almost all of whom were without formal position in the party or government, came to play a role in the formation and development of rural policy in the early 1980s that was unprecedented in the history of the PRC.[64] That they were able to play such a role was due to their personal characteristics, their ties to policy makers, and the needs of the policy makers.

Although many of these people who would go on to form the Rural Development Group were just enrolling in college in 1977 (the first year in which higher education was restored to normal function after the Cultural Revolution), they had indeed been "tempered" by the experience of the Cultural Revolution. Most of them had visited many parts of China during the early period of the Cultural Revolution and had then become familiar with rural conditions by living in the countryside for extended periods. Most members of the group had spent from two to five years in the countryside, although some, like Deng Yingtao, had spent as many as ten years in rural areas.

Having "gone up the mountains and down to the countryside" (*shangshan xiaxiang*), these young people constituted a group of politically and socially experienced youth who had spent many years pondering the problems of the Chinese economic and political order. As bright, extremely energetic people, they were able to combine their personal experience with the new knowledge they were gaining as they returned to Beijing, enabling them to think clearly about and research systematically the problems in the countryside.

During the early years of the Rural Development Group, it was Deng Liqun who provided its members with their primary patronage. The close connection between the embryonic group and Deng Liqun in particular and the "conservative" wing of the CCP in general bespeaks a very different political atmosphere in the late 1970s and early 1980s than emerged later and indicates personal relationships that crossed strict ideological bounds. Deng Liqun, like Chen Yizi, had come from an intellectual family and had joined the party out of intellectual commitment. A widely read and highly intelligent person, Deng filled his house not only with scores of old books but also with the writings of Marxist dissidents from the Soviet Union and Eastern Europe (the presence of Marxist dissident writings in Deng Liqun's house was at least in part due to his participation in the campaign to oppose revisionism in the early 1960s). The Cultural Revolution afforded people like Chen Yizi, Deng Liqun, and Deng Yingtao the leisure to read widely and debate vigorously a wide variety of ideas.[65]

Deng Liqun was keenly aware of China's lack of economic progress, a frustration that could only have been deepened by his November 1978 trip to Japan. His astonishment at what he saw is palpable in his report of his trip. Deng reported that the Chinese interpreter who accompanied his delegation had grown up in Japan but had visited Tianjin in the early 1950s. At that time she had felt that Tianjin was more comfortable than Yokohama. Twenty-some years later the situation was "vastly different." Deng reported such facts as that one out of every two Japanese households owned automobiles and that over 95 percent of Japanese households had television sets, refrigerators, washing machines, and other amenities. He also noted the variety—and cleanliness—of clothes worn by the people, observing that: "One Sunday we went out to a busy street. Of all the women we saw, no two wore the same style of clothes. The female workers accompanying us also changed clothes every day."[66] Deng Liqun saw in people like Chen Yizi a like-minded idealism and nationalism that was determined to reform socialism and make it attain its ideals.

Deng's support of the Rural Development Group was also based on personal and political considerations. On a personal level, his son Deng Yingtao was a core member of the group, which would have made it very difficult for the elder Deng not to have supported the group. On a political level, the ideas and proposals of the group not only could bolster the position of the returned veteran cadres vis-à-vis Hua Guofeng's wing of the CCP but could also provide support for Deng Liqun himself. Deng was still expanding his influence in the party, and he sought to use his positions as deputy head of CASS and head of the party's Policy Research Office to build his influence. The ideas presented by the Rural Development Group were useful in this regard.

The young intellectuals around Chen Yizi were not the only ones to seek out the patronage of the conservative wing of the party. At the same time that the Rural Development Group was taking shape, another informal group of young intellectuals, known as the "four gentlemen"—Huang Jiangnan, Wang Qishan, Weng Yongxi, Zhu Jiaming—was also forming ties with senior leaders. In the early reform period, the four gentlemen were more influential than the Rural Development Group, and like the latter group they relied on personal relations both to rise quickly and to pass reform proposals to senior leaders through personal connections. Weng Yongxi's rise was the most spectacular of the four; he was promoted to become deputy head of the party's Rural Policy Research Office under Du Runsheng in 1980. Subsequently Weng was criticized by those envious of his success for having criticized Deng Xiaoping during the Cultural Revolution, and Deng ordered him removed.[67] Although the success of the four gentlemen paralleled that of and in many ways prepared the ground for the Rural Development Group, they never developed the structure or membership that characterized the latter group. Hence, their success and influence was more individual. They never constituted a think tank and hence lacked the continuous involvement in policy making that characterized the Rural Development Group.

The fact is that in the late 1970s, the ideas of the conservative wing of the party differed little from those of Deng Xiaoping, particularly with respect to economic policy. Headed by Chen Yun, this conservative group of economic policy makers had throughout the 1950s and 1960s provided the most consistent and systematic alternative to Maoist policies.[68] Chen Yun played a critical role in the 1978 Third Plenum, fully supporting Deng Xiaoping's efforts to change the focus of party policy to economic work and modernization. Strongly committed to socialism, including central planning, such people found their vision of socialism mocked by the poverty of China in general and of the countryside in particular. They wanted a strong, economically advanced socialist nation; they were willing to reform the economic system if it would bring about an increase in economic development, maintain stability in the countryside, and provide a basis for strengthening the party's rule.

The Formation of the Rural Development Group

By the fall of 1980, the young intellectuals around Chen Yizi felt they needed a more permanent organizational structure both to carry out systematic research and to present their research results to the leadership of the CCP. It was in September of that year that about thirty young intellectuals founded the Chinese Rural Development Research Group. The members of the new group came from a variety of organizations scattered around Beijing, including CASS, CAS, the Chinese Agricultural University, Chinese People's University, Beijing University, Beijing Economics Academy, Beijing Agricultural University, Beijing Normal University, Central Nationalities University, and *People's Daily*.[69]

The name for the new group was chosen with care. It conveyed a self-conscious effort to distinguish the approach of the new group from the way in which rural problems had been studied and discussed in the past. Previously, rural problems had invariably been described with the term *nongye* ("agricultural undertaking"), which connoted production in a quantitative sense. The founders of the new group sought to emphasize their break with the Stalinist past by using the term *nongcun* ("rural"), a more comprehensive term that suggested that the problems of the countryside extended beyond increasing production to the need to reorganize rural society as a whole. Similarly, the term "development" was chosen to convey a Western sense of social development in contrast to the traditional emphasis on quantitative growth.[70]

The group was headed by Chen Yizi; He Weiling and Wang Xiaoqiang served as deputy heads. Chen wanted He in the group because of his excellent connections, particularly with Deng Pufang and Hu Deping. At first, He was wary of Chen's passionate personality, but he was soon convinced that the new group could do something for China's future. Nationalism was the driving force. Wang Xiaoqiang was chosen because of his celebrity status among young intellectuals. He had published in *Weiding gao* an article entitled "Critique of Agrarian Socialism" that had been picked up and touted by Japanese scholars, giving Wang a unique status among young intellectuals at that time.[71]

This new group was well organized, possessed of both a sense of mission and an elaborate division of labor. The group had a General Section (*zonghe zu*), Secretarial Section (*mishu zu*), Current Situation Section (*xianzhuang zu*), Methodology Section (*fangfa zu*), and Theory and History Section (*lilun lishi zu*). Research projects were overseen and coordinated by a seven-member Executive Small Group (*zhixing xiaozu*) headed by Wang Gengjin, Yang Xun, and Chen Yizi. Like any organization trying to get off the ground, the Rural Development Group had problems; a report of the General Section complained that some members were extremely busy while others were idle; moreover, because members were drawn from units all over Beijing there was a lack of coordination and information sharing.[72]

The Current Situation Section was headed by Chen Yizi. This section tried to publicize the work of the new group and to generate publicity on behalf of the household responsibility system. It was this section that edited a book entitled *Selected Materials on the Household Responsibility System*, which brought together important articles on the history of the household responsibility system with contemporary research reports on its progress and achievements. The material in this book remained so controversial that it had to be taken to Chuxian County in Anhui, where the rural reforms were under way, to be published.[73] People who had a background in the natural sciences, like He Weiling and Luo Xiaopeng, gravitated toward the Methodology Section. They drew on theories of cybernetics, information theory, and Pregojian theory to try to articulate a rationale and method for change in social systems. This group produced an important essay entitled "On Strategic Research," which helped introduce the whole concept of strategic thinking to China and drew the attention of such eminent intellectuals as Yu Guangyuan and Ma Hong.[74]

Drawing on concepts of strategic studies that had developed in the West since the Second World War, the essay argued that there was a need for an intermediate level of study between basic research and applied research. As an interdisciplinary study, strategic research could draw on the results of basic research in many fields to determine long-term social and economic goals and thereby better guide the development of applied research. This intermediate level of research was self-consciously intended to provide systematic information and strategic options to China's policy makers. To this end, the authors argued that strategic research must be conducted by a relatively independent research organization that would not be overly influenced either by the day-to-day work of government or by the biases of various ministries.

The young intellectuals in the Rural Development Group were both self-conscious about the role they were carving out for themselves and extremely ambitious in terms of their intellectual agenda. They set as their goal nothing less than the determination of strategic goals for China's development, including the shape of the new structure that was to evolve from reform. This not only required accurately analyzing the current circumstances of China but also absorbing the results of basic research in such fields as psychology and culture as well as "grasping the history, present, and future, of an entire people's cultural background."

The authors also saw themselves as practitioners of the "art of the possible," working within the constraints—economic, social, as well as political—of the existing system to provide accurate and unbiased information to China's decision makers so as to enable them to make accurate and scientific decisions about policy. In the past, the authors said, research specialists had been frustrated by the failure of the leadership to pay sufficient attention to their results while the leadership had been frustrated by the lack of systematic plans on which they could base intelligent decisions. Decision making in the reform period, the authors argued, should be based on practical incrementalism—"crossing the river by feeling the stones" (a phrase they picked up from Chen Yun's speech to the December 1980 Central Work Conference)—as well as on systematic thinking about alternative courses of development. Strategic research could bring theory and practice together to provide policy makers with systematic programs based on the collection and analysis of empirical evidence and theoretical research. Such information could only be provided by a relatively independent research organization that would be free both from the pressures of day-to-day governing and from the institutional biases of China's ministries. In short, there was a need to establish "think tanks."[75]

The newly established Rural Development Group found itself under considerable pressure from opposite ends of the political spectrum, suggesting both the novelty and precariousness of what they were trying to do. As might be expected, many older party members and party organizations looked upon this new group as subversive, both ideationally and organizationally. At the same time, the emergent democratic movement in China looked askance on the group for its willingness to collaborate with the power holders. In a new twist on the old issue of problems and "isms," those involved in the democratic movement accused the Rural Development Group of working too closely with the Communist party; the problem in their view was indeed one of "isms"—they viewed the ideal of communism as out of date. In contrast, the members of the Rural Development Group viewed the participants in the democratic movement as idealists; their ideas were noble but their methods impractical. Those in the Rural Development Group preferred to seek the solution to real problems within the framework of the existing power structure.

The Rural Development Group was unprecedented in that it was an organized group providing information and advice to the central leadership but not part of the vast bureaucratic party and state apparatuses. It was nevertheless a quasi-official group. Five months after its inauguration, the group held a second and more formal founding meeting. Both Deng Liqun and Du Runsheng addressed the meeting, thereby giving it official dispensation if not recognition. The group was finally given official status in November 1981, when it was approved by the CCP Secretariat and domiciled in CASS's Agricultural Institute, albeit as a separate entity with its own budget. Nevertheless, the group continued to think of itself and to operate as a separate think tank rather than as part of China's bureaucratic system.

This existence outside of China's bureaucratic structure proved both a strength and a weakness of the Rural Development Group. On the one hand, it gave the group a degree of flexibility and freedom that it could not otherwise have enjoyed. Group members reported directly to Du Runsheng and Deng Liqun. Access to such high-level leaders—which soon extended to include Wan Li, Hu Yaobang, and Zhao Ziyang—meant that the group's ideas and research findings had an impact far greater than its position in the bureaucratic structure would suggest. In particular, the group had a great impact on the concepts embodied in the CCP's annual rural policy documents—referred to as "Documents No. 1" because they were the first party document (*zhongfa*) of each year—which began to be issued in 1982.

On the other hand, the group's lack of bureaucratic status meant that it worked with comparatively few resources and had no power to secure compliance from other bureaucracies. Ultimately, it could propose policies but could not command resources. When, in the early Dengist period, rural reform depended more on policies than resources, the Rural Development Group had great success. Later, as issues became more complex, greater bureaucratic clout was needed to defend policies, and more resources were needed to deal with issues, the influence of the group diminished.

Most important, the group's lack of bureaucratic status meant that its influence depended on personal relationships. This made its work particularly difficult in 1983, during the campaign against "spiritual pollution." The close association of the group with Deng Liqun and the presence of Deng Yingtao in the group made Zhao Ziyang and Hu Yaobang wary of dealing with the group.[76] Nevertheless, as the campaign passed, the group was able to switch its primary relationship from Deng Liqun to Zhao Ziyang (not without strain in the group since Deng Yingtao remained a core member). However, it was still dependent on political patronage for its influence. This not only weakened the group's ability to defend its policy agenda against bureaucratic rivals, but it also meant that it could not survive Zhao's fall from power.[77]

Continued Conflict Over The Household Responsibility System

The sharp conflict over agricultural policy between Wang Renzhong, head of the State Agricultural Commission, and Wan Li throughout 1979 suggested both the degree of opposition to decollectivization at very high levels of the Chinese government and the critical role played by Wan Li as a provincial leader in protecting the first efforts to reform the agricultural system. However, official policy, as restated by the March 30, 1979, editor's note in *People's Daily*, restricted itself to permitting only limited experimentation with contracting to small groups (the *baochan daozu* system); the household responsibility system was still equated with individual farming (*fentian dangan*). Over the next two years, policy evolved from permitting the household responsibility system to recognizing and then popularizing it. This evolution in policy was due to Deng Xiaoping's political success, Deng Liqun's support for the household responsibility system, the investigations and reports of the Rural Development Group, and the economic success of the household responsibility system, which made it ultimately impossible to stop. Nevertheless, at each step of the way agricultural reform encountered opposition.

Rural reform would not have been possible without the political success of Deng Xiaoping, particularly in routing those within the party who had been the primary supporters of Hua Guofeng's "two whatevers" policy. Deng's success was apparent at the party's Fifth Plenum, held in February 1980. The so-called "little gang of four"—Wang Dongxing, Ji Dengkui, Wu De, and Chen Xilian—were removed from the Politburo. At the same time, Hu Yaobang and Zhao Ziyang were added to the Standing Committee of the Politburo, and Hu was named general secretary of the Central Committee.[78] At a meeting of the National People's Congress Standing Committee in April 1980, Zhao Ziyang and Wan Li were named as vice premiers of the State Council. In a victory that marked a personal triumph, Wan replaced his nemesis, Wang Renzhong, as head of the State Agricultural Commission. The person who had pushed agricultural reform more resolutely than any other leader in China was thus put in charge of agricultural policy.

It was against this background that Deng Xiaoping made his first "public" statement on agricultural policy—a talk with Deng Liqun and Hu Qiaomu that was circulated internally among party leaders. Deng's statement came against the background of lobbying efforts by Chen Yizi and Deng Liqun. Even before conducting his first survey, Chen had been arguing strongly on behalf of the household responsibility system. Although supportive of the household responsibility system, Deng Xiaoping had two concerns: its economic viability and its political acceptability. The data—preliminary though they were—that people like Guo Chongyi and Lu Xueyi provided made the case for reform in economic terms; anecdote helped make the case politically. Through Deng Liqun, Chen Yizi passed on the enthusiastic reactions of the peasants, including such ego-pleasing sayings as, "Mao Zedong allowed us to renew our lives (spiritually); Deng Xiaoping has allowed us to fill our bellies" (*Mao Zedong rang women fanshen; Deng Xiaoping rang women chibao*). A meeting Wan Li had with Deng Xiaoping in March 1980, at which Wan was able to report on the situation in Anhui, appears to have been of decisive importance.[79] The following month, in Sichuan, Guanghan County's Xiangyang became the first commune in China to declare itself a township. In May, Deng endorsed the changes in Anhui, stating:[80]

> Since rural policies have been relaxed, some places that are suitable for house-hold contracting have implemented household contracting. In Feixi County in Anhui the great majority of production teams have contracted production to households; the results have been very good and the changes very fast. The vast majority of production teams in Fengyang County, where the "flower drums of Fengyang" are sung, have engaged in contracting to small groups (*da bao gan*); they have transformed (*fanshen*) themselves and changed their circumstances in a year.

Despite the much-improved political atmosphere, rural reform, and especially the household responsibility system, remained extremely controversial. Even in Anhui, the most radical of China's provinces, the household responsibility system was still not widely accepted. Although Feixi County had adopted the system from the beginning, most of Anhui had adopted the alternative system of contracting to small groups. In Fengyang County, which became famous for pioneering the system of contracting to small groups, Party Secretary Chen Tingyuan staunchly supported linking production to small groups but opposed the household responsibility system. As noted earlier, the Fengyang party committee had originally allowed the Xiaogang Production Brigade to adopt the household responsibility system, only to reverse itself when Xiaogang's example disrupted the implementation of contracting to small groups in nearby areas. Although Wang Yuzhao, party secretary of Chuxian Prefecture, supported the household responsibility system, local cadres, particularly at the county level, resisted.[81]

In 1980, as the household responsibility system spread at the local level and large increases in production were recorded, attitudes began to change, at both the local and national levels. One of the greatest contributions of the Rural Development Group was to collect and analyze data on the rural reforms, transmitting their findings not only to the CCP leadership but just as importantly to other agricultural specialists in Beijing. In short, they helped build a policy community in support of rural reform, including the household responsibility system.[82]

The Rural Development Group's efforts to collect information on rural reform began in the spring of 1980, when Chen Yizi spent three months—from April 15 to July 15—investigating several counties and prefectures in Anhui Province.[83] This was perhaps the most detailed survey up to that date. Rather than relying on the "typical example" so beloved by Chinese leaders, Chen investigated the area systematically, drawing data from a sample of wealthier areas as well as poor areas. He talked with peasants as well as local cadres, and he paid particular attention to cadres at the town level. If such cadres opposed the household responsibility system, they could put up formidable opposition to it. Much to his relief, Chen found that the town-level cadres also benefited from the reforms.

Chen was very excited when he returned to Beijing, calling the household responsibility system "a great creation of the Chinese peasants." Stimulated by the results of Chen's investigation, Lu Xueyi then collaborated with Wang Xiaoqiang on an investigation of the household responsibility system in Gansu, where Song Ping, the party secretary, was supportive of the system.[84]

During the summer of 1980, there was a meeting of the Chinese Agricultural Association (*Zhongguo nongye jingji xuehui*), at which arguments over the household responsibility system became heated. Most of those in the older generation continued to view the household responsibility system as too radical. Some, like Li Youjiu, an influential scholar and official in agricultural work, supported the cooperative system, rather than either the commune or household responsibility system, through a genuine belief that cooperativization would work in China. Others, like Wang Renzhong, continued to oppose the household responsibility system because their reputations were staked to the old system.[85]

The conflict over the household responsibility system in Beijing was mirrored in the provinces. With opinions in Beijing divided, the household responsibility system became the focal point of debate in the provinces. Some were in favor while others opposed it; still others were divided. In those provinces in which the provincial party committee was divided in its opinion about the household responsibility system, lower levels pursued different policies. Some prefectures favored the system while others opposed it; not infrequently, different counties within a given prefecture followed different policies.

Conflict was intense. When Zhang Jingfu replaced Wan Li as first party secretary of Anhui in 1980, he began to roll back the household responsibility system in the province. Some lower-level cadres supported him while others staunchly defended the household responsibility system. Similarly, in Jiangxi, where the provincial leadership was divided, Jian Prefecture promoted the household responsibility system while neighboring Yichun Prefecture developed a competing model known as the "specialized contract system" (*zhuanye chengbao*). This system divided production tasks within the production team so that there would be both a division of labor (as called for by the household responsibility system) and collectivization (as called for by traditional understandings of socialism). This system enjoyed a brief period of support from high-level leaders, including Zhao Ziyang and Du Runsheng, who were looking for a compromise solution.[86] Other leaders, such as Wan Li, uncompromisingly supported the household responsibility system.

The "Broad Road" Versus the "Single Plank Bridge"

Because of the divisions of opinion and policy described above, the atmosphere was tense and the arguments sharp when a special conference of provincial-level party secretaries was convened in Beijing in September 1980. Anhui, Gansu, and Sichuan took the lead in arguing for the household responsibility system, while the majority of other provinces, led by Jiangsu, Zhejiang, Heilongjiang, Jilin, and Guangdong, opposed it. The opposition of places like Jiangsu, Zhejiang, and Guangdong was based on their relatively more successful efforts to develop the collective economy. As wealthier provinces, they worried that the household responsibility system would undermine their collective enterprises and hurt their economies. Heilongjiang's opposition was based on its development of large-scale agricultural production, which it feared would be undermined by the household responsibility system, and perhaps the greater "leftist" ideological influence in the province.

The argument at the conference centered around the "broad road" of collective agriculture versus the "single-plank bridge" of the household responsibility system. The term "broad road" derived from a July 1980 meeting on commodity grain bases in the northeast that was convened by the State Agricultural Commission. The meeting held that Heilongjiang had good conditions for agricultural mechanization and should not "blindly" follow the experience of others, but should rather follow the path of "modernized, large-scale agriculture." This was what was known as the "broad road" (*yang guan dao*).[87]

In a speech in mid-November 1980, Heilongjiang party secretary Yang Yizhen described the household responsibility system as the product of the difficult circumstances in other provinces, a way to "advance one step by retreating two steps." At the September meeting, he said that "some comrades were envious of our good conditions; some said that we were taking the 'broad road' while they were only able to take the 'single-plank bridge.' . . . Why should we give up the broad road and follow those areas that are forced to go by way of a single-plank bridge?"[88]

This argument was the subject of a long and important article by Wu Xiang that was published in *People's Daily* on November 5, 1980. Wu was a former Xinhua reporter based in Anhui who had been an early proponent of the household responsibility system. Wan Li brought him to Beijing, where he worked with Du Runsheng in the party's Rural Policy Research Office and was very influential in the formulation of rural policy at the time of his article. In his article, Wu defended strongly the household responsibility system against the charge that it was nothing more than a "single-plank bridge." Pressing on the sore point of continuing rural poverty, Wu underscored the shame of the socialist system, in that after some two decades of collectivization, the production of some 200 counties (about 10 percent of the total) throughout the country was about the same as, or even below what it had been when the communists had come to power. In contrast, survey data showed that the household responsibility system had successfully aroused the enthusiasm of peasants in poor areas and had raised their incomes.

Suggesting the tense ideological atmosphere at the September meeting, Wu said that some people believed that the household responsibility system "turns collective management into individual management, runs counter to the socialist road, basically degenerates into individual farming, and thus is a *mistake in orientation*." Invoking Lenin, Wu argued that any system that had public ownership and implemented the principle of "to each according to his work" is a socialist system and should be upheld. By this interpretation, said Wu, the household responsibility system was not an abandonment of socialism but rather a way to break through the stagnation of the past and remain on the socialist road. If people insisted on speaking of the household responsibility system as a "single-plank bridge," Wu concluded, then they should realize that the only way in which they could reach the "broad road" was by first crossing this single-plank bridge.[89]

As Yang Yizhen's mid-November comments indicate, many people continued to oppose Wu's argument and the continued spread of the household responsibility system. In fact, about two-thirds of China's provinces opposed the household responsibility system at the September 1980 meeting. However, because Wan Li was the head of the State Agricultural Commission and a confidant of Deng's, the document that was adopted by the meeting—which came to be referred to by its number as "Document No. 75"—upheld the legitimacy of the household responsibility system despite the opposition to it of the majority of China's provinces. Although the document emphasized that the "collective economy is an unshakable foundation for the advance of our agriculture toward modernization," it went on to provide explicit permission for those areas that had embarked on the household responsibility system to continue to do so. In compromise language that was contributed by Hu Yaobang, the document said that communes "could" give work points according to the achievements of quotas, "could" give work points based on an evaluation of time spent in labor, and *"could also"* link compensation to production with rewards given for production exceeding a quota (a passage referred to among Chinese by its famous phrasing *keyi, . . . keyi, . . . ye keyi*).

This was the first central document in the history of the CCP to give explicit permission to implement the household responsibility system.[90]

The promulgation of a party document permitting the implementation of the household responsibility system did not, however, end debate over the subject. On the contrary, as more and more areas, encouraged by the document, began to adopt the system, defenders of collective agriculture resisted it all the more strongly. Thus, in the spring of 1981, a number of local leaders again raised the accusation that the household responsibility system really meant dividing the land and used various methods to oppose its implementation. A municipal leader in Sichuan openly published a talk in which he labeled the household responsibility system a mistake in orientation and called for its "correction." This talk was sharply criticized by the top leadership of the party, cooling the opposition to the household responsibility system and in the process further encouraging its development.[91]

It was perhaps in the summer of 1981 that the young intellectuals of the Rural Development Group made their greatest contribution to rural reform and in doing secured a place for their group as the first permanent think tank in China. As a group, they faced two challenges in the spring and summer of 1981. On the one hand, with controversy over the household responsibility system reaching a climax, there was a pressing need to carry out a new investigation to collect data on how the system had performed after two years of implementation. On the other hand, the members of the Rural Development Group were prompted to action by the threat posed by other young intellectuals. The four gentlemen—Huang Jiangnan, Wang Qishan, Weng Yongxi, and Zhu Jiaming—had achieved great success. Wang had been appointed deputy director of the liaison department in Du Runsheng's Agricultural Development Center, thus taking up an important bureaucratic position. Weng was already Du Runsheng's deputy, and Zhu had emerged as an influential advocate of reform in a group organized under the State Council (see Chapter 2). Threatened by this competition, the members of the Rural Development Group decided that they had to act in order not to be swept aside. But they had to wait for the time of their summer vacation. Most in the group were still in college, taking classes and writing examinations.[92]

The group's members reported on their proposal to undertake a new survey of Chuxian Prefecture in Anhui to Deng Liqun and Du Runsheng, both of whom strongly supported the idea. Thus, when the summer vacation arrived, Chen Yizi led some thirty young intellectuals on a forty-day investigation of rural Anhui.[93] Returning to Beijing, Chen Yizi enthusiastically reported on conditions in Chuxian to Deng Liqun, who in turn reported these findings to higher levels. Participating in this survey was no doubt a heady experience for the young researchers. Armed with a letter of introduction from both the Policy Research Office of the Central Secretariat and the State Agricultural Commission, they experienced a real taste of power. Local officials were solicitous and gave them every convenience.[94]

At the same time that the Rural Development Group was investigating Chu-xian, the State Agricultural Commission (now headed by Wan Li) was sending more than 140 investigators to fifteen provinces and regions. Many of these people were cadres in various state organs who doubted the feasibility of the household responsibility system. Participating in these investigations and seeing the results of the household responsibility system with their own eyes apparently convinced many of them that it was indeed a viable approach.[95]

The formal report of the Rural Development Group, which ran to some 200,000 characters, was not finished until October 1981, but it was completed in time to have an effect on the National Agricultural Work Conference that was held the same month. For the first time, members of the Rural Development Group were asked to participate in such a conference, and Zhang Musheng presented the views of the group to the conference. Owing in part to the investigations of the Rural Development Group, in part to the investigations of the State Agricultural Commission, and in part to the continuing proliferation of the household responsibility system throughout China, this conference adopted a resolution that for the first time in the history of the PRC declared the household responsibility system to be a form of production responsibility system within the socialist collective economy. On January 1, 1982, the "outline" of this meeting was circulated as Document No. 1 of the new year—the first of five Documents No. 1 that would be issued on the first of each year to outline rural policy.[96] It was a historic breakthrough.

A breakthrough of another sort was made the following month when the CCP Secretariat formally affirmed the work of the Rural Development Group, thus completing its transition from informal discussions among friends to the formation of an unofficial, extra-bureaucratic organization, to a part, albeit a very special part, of China's bureaucracy. This was China's first think tank and the first time that a group of young intellectuals was able to influence official policy in a sustained fashion.

Bureaucratically, the group was located within CASS's Agricultural Institute, although its funds and leadership came from Du Runsheng's office.[97] At this time, there were about twenty members in the group. It was headed by Chen Yizi, and its deputy chairmen were Wang Xiaoqiang, Zhou Qiren, and Chen Xiwen. Although China's agricultural policy was always subject to negotiation among the leadership and the provinces, the ideas of the Rural Development Group had an important impact, particularly on the historic Documents No. 1 of 1983 and 1984.

It was almost exactly at the time that the "outline" from the National Agricultural Work Conference was being finalized that Chen Yun made an important intervention in the policy-making process. Although originally supportive of China's rural reforms, Chen was by now concerned that the reforms were undermining the state's control of the countryside and its ability to extract resources from the rural areas. Thus, in a meeting with party secretaries from China's provinces, Chen reemphasized the importance of planning:[98]

> The agricultural economy also needs to take the planned economy as primary and market adjustment as supplementary.
> The reason for raising this question is because following the implementation of various sorts of production responsibility systems it seems as though agriculture can do without planning. In fact, this is not the case.

Chen's remarks, which went on to call for strengthened planning in industry and to oppose staunchly the creation of new Special Economic Zones in Jiangsu or any other province, had a major impact on the development of enterprise reform and on the reform movement as a whole (as discussed in Chapter 3), but they had very little impact on rural policy despite the fact that rural policy topped the list of his concerns.

Chen's comments had little impact on rural policy because, first and foremost, rural policy was under the purview of Wan Li, and because the household responsibility system retained the support of Deng Xiaoping, Hu Yaobang, and Zhao Ziyang. Document No. 1 of 1982 was issued despite whatever reservations Chen may have had about the policy. And with the promulgation of Document No. 1, rural reform became unstoppable. As of October 1981, 45 percent of China's production teams had already adopted some form of the household responsibility system (7.1 percent of production teams contracted output to households [baochan daohu] and another 38 percent of production teams contracted tasks to households [baogan daohu]). Six months after Document No. 1 was promulgated, in June 1982, the household responsibility system had spread to 72 percent of production teams (67 percent of contracting tasks to households and 5 percent of contracting production to households.[99]

The underlying reason for the weak effect of Chen's call for a renewed emphasis on planning was that there was no perceived crisis in agriculture to make central and local leaders willing to pay the necessary social and perhaps economic costs to reimpose control. Agricultural production was up, from 305 million tons in 1978 to 325 million tons in 1981, and the state did not encounter difficulties in procuring grain from the countryside. Without such a crisis, there was no galvanizing motive for reestablishing state control.[100]

At a deeper level, the inability of Chen to rein in the rural reforms reflected the unique circumstances of the agricultural sector that had allowed the reforms to develop in the first place. Because agricultural production was dispersed among thousands of communes in more than 2,000 widely varying counties throughout China, there was simply no way in which the central bureaucracy could be familiar with conditions throughout countryside—particularly after the Cultural Revolution had so disrupted China's bureaucratic structure. Hua Guofeng's efforts to promote rural mechanization reflected this bureaucratic ignorance. It was this opening that local party officials and young intellectuals, particularly the members of the Rural Development Group, were able to use to defend local experiments and gather the data needed to convince central decision makers of the viability of rural reform. After four years of reform, there was no reason to believe that China's bureaucracy was more capable of directing rural production than it had been at the start of the reform process.

Bureaucratic weakness vis-à-vis the rural sector was also due to the fact that rural policy had traditionally been under the purview of the party organization rather than the state bureaucracy. For the most part, China's rural reform developed in extra-bureaucratic channels. The support of the central leadership was of course necessary—the rural reforms that were implemented could never have proceeded without the support of central leaders like Deng Xiaoping and Chen Yun—but this support was secured via party and personal relations rather than state bureaucratic channels. If rural policy had been dominated by the state bureaucratic apparatus, it is unlikely that local leaders such as Wan Li or a quasi-official organization such as the Rural Development Group could have played the important roles they did in the reform process. Industry was under greater bureaucratic control, and the history of enterprise reform followed a very different trajectory.

Notes

1. In 1993 there was an upsurge of rural violence attributable to stagnating or declining agricultural incomes in some areas and to increasing exactions by local cadres, sometimes for public works but also apparently to feather their own nests. This outburst of rural disorder has provoked expressions of concern from the highest leadership in China as well as a series of new policy initiatives. Unless greater attention and resources can be devoted to the rural sector, particularly areas that do not have well-developed township and village enterprises, the hope that the rural areas will provide a basis of stability in the transition to the future may prove misplaced. See Joseph Fewsmith, "Reform, Resistance, and the Politics of Succession," *China Briefing, 1994*.

2. Recently, Daniel Kelliher has argued that the political and economic situation in China in the late 1970s did indeed allow the peasants to repeatedly exceed the limits of policy and "invent" the household responsibility system. Basing his account of the development of the household responsibility system in Anhui almost entirely on a single article, Kelliher ignores the voluminous written and oral evidence from the period that points to a much more complex process than he allows. There is no question that peasants welcomed the new policies and—once they were initiated—adopted them with a rapidity and enthusiasm that surprised much of the political leadership. But there is also no question that Wan Li was aware of the experiments from the beginning and could have stopped them had he desired to do so. His own personal inclinations and courage as well as the dynamic of political struggle at the time led him to adopt a very different attitude. See *Peasant Power in China: The Era of Rural Reform, 1979–1988*, especially pp. 55–64.

3. The "two whatevers" were raised in an editorial, entitled "Study Well the Documents and Grasp the Key Link," published jointly by *Renmin ribao, Hongqi*, and *Jiefangjun bao* on February 7, 1977, trans. FBIS, February 7, 1977, pp. E1–E3. On the Hua Guofeng period, see Richard Baum, *Chinese Politics in the Age of Deng Xiaoping*, Chapter 2.

4. Sun Qimeng and Xiong Zhiyong, *Dazhai hongqi de shengqi yu duoluo* (The Rise and Fall of the Red Flag of Dazhai), pp. 304–308.

5. Hua introduced the ten-year plan for economic development at the Fifth National People's Congress in February 1978. This plan called for large investment in heavy industry, the import of state-of-the-art turn-key plants from industrialized nations, and the mechanization of agriculture—something that far exceeded the capacity of rural finances and organization. See Hua Guofeng, "Unite and Strive to Build a Modern, Powerful Socialist Country," Xinhua, March 6, 1978, trans. FBIS, March 7, 1978, pp. D1–37.

6. As discussed below, it was Anhui that first countered the Dazhai model through the formulation of the "Regulations on Several Questions of Current Rural Economic Policy." According to Wang Lixin, Deng Xiaoping recommended this policy to Zhao during a trip to Sichuan. Later, Zhao supported the system of contracting to small groups (*baochan daozu*) that was a less radical reform than contracting to households. See Wang Lixin, "Life After Mao Zedong: A Report on Implementation of and Consequences of Major Chinese Agricultural Policies in Anhui Villages," *Kunlun*, no. 6 (December 1988), pp. 4–53, trans. JPRS-CAR–89–079 (July 28, 1989), p. 27.

7. Tan Zongji and Zheng Qian, eds., *Shinianhou de pingshuo* (An Evaluation Ten Years Later), pp. 108–110.

8. Author's interviews.

9. Wang Yuzhao, "Fengqi yunyong de biange langchao" (The Sweeping Tide of Change), p. 9.

10. An Gang et al., "Zhongguo nongye zhenxing youwang" (There Is Hope for the Vigorous Development of Chinese Agriculture), *Renmin ribao*, July 9, 1981, p. 2. Tang Tsou, "The Responsibility System in Agriculture," p. 191. The proposals raised at the party meetings apparently went beyond the Anhui regulations since the article by An Gang et al. refers to eight points in the proposal whereas the Anhui regulations only had six points.

11. "Yi fen shengwei wenjian de tansheng" (The Birth of a Provincial Committee Document). See also Wang Gengjin et al., eds., *Xiangcun sanshi nian: Fengyang nongcun shehui jingji fazhan shilu (1949–1983 nian)* (The Countryside Over Thirty Years: A Veritable Record of Fengyang's Social-Economic Development, 1949–1983), vol. 2, p. 385.

12. Wu Xiang, "Yang guan dao yu du mu qiao" (The Broad Road and the Single-Plank Bridge).

13. Chen Yun, "Jianchi an bili yuanze tiaozheng guomin jingji" (Readjust the National Economy in Accordance with the Principle of Proportionality), p. 226.

14. An Gang et al., "Zhongguo nongye zhenxing youwang."

15. Tsou, "The Responsibility System in Agriculture," p. 192.

16. "Decision of the CCP Central Committee on Some Problems in Accelerating Agricultural Development (Draft)," *Zhanwang*, no. 417 (June 16, 1979) and no. 418 (July 1, 1979), trans. FBIS, August 31, 1979, pp. L22–37. This policy was subsequently elaborated in the "Regulations on the Work in Rural People's Communes."

17. Wang Lixin, "Life After Mao Zedong," pp. 2–4.

18. Although there appear to have been many areas in Anhui and the rest of the country that began adopting various forms of the household responsibility system at about this time, both Chen Yizi and Lu Xueyi give credit to the Huanghua Production Brigade as being the first. See Chen Yizi, "Nongcun de shouguang, Zhongguo de xiwang" (Rural Radiance, China's Hope), p. 33; and Lu Xueyi, *Lianchan chengbao zerenzhi yanjiu* (Studies on the Production Responsibility System), p. 65.

19. Parris H. Chang, *Power and Policy in China*, p. 21.

20. Chang, *Power and Policy in China*, pp. 35–36.

21. Lu Xueyi, *Lianchan chengbao zerenzhi yanjiu*, pp. 35–38. Li Yunhe, " 'Zhuan guan zhi' he 'baochan daohu' shi jiejue shenei zhuyao maodun de hao banfa" (The "Specialized-Management System" and the "Household Responsibility System" Are Good Methods to Solve the Important Contradictions Within the Commune").

22. Lu Xueyi, *Lianchan chengbao zerenzhi yanjiu*, pp. 39–40. See also "Wenzhou zhuanqu jiuzheng 'baochan daohu' de cuowu zuofa" (Wenzhou District's Correction of the "Household Responsibility" Mistake).

23. Lu Xueyi, *Lianchan chengbao zerenzhi yanjiu*, p. 43; and "Jiechuan 'baochan daohu' de zhen mianmu" (Expose the Real Face of the Household Responsibility System).

24. Wang Lixin, "Life After Mao Zedong," p. 17.

25. Ibid., p. 19.

26. Lu Xueyi, *Lianchan chengbao zerenzhi yanjiu*, pp. 48–49. By early 1962, some 85 percent of production brigades in Anhui were implementing this method. See Lu, p. 53. The figure of 20 percent is given in Gong Yuzhi, *Sixiang jiefang di xin qidian* (A New Starting Point for the Emancipation of the Mind), p. 77.

27. Wang Lixin, "Life After Mao Zedong," p. 19.

28. Lu Xueyi, *Lianchan chengbao zerenzhi yanjiu*, p. 53.

29. Ibid., p. 56. Deng Liqun, "Zai Zhongguo, nongcun fazhan wenti yanjiu zu taolunhui shang de jianghua" (Talk at the Symposium of the Chinese Rural Development Research Group), p. 4.

30. Chen Yun, "Qingpu nongcun diaocha" (Rural Investigations in Qingpu), pp. 167–169.

31. Zhou Taihe, "Chen Yun tongzhi sici xia nongcun diaocha de qianhou" (Before and After Comrade Chen Yun's Four Rural Investigations), pp. 167–169.

32. Deng Xiaoping, "Zenyang huifu nongye shengchan" (How Can Agricultural Production Be Restored?), p. 305. According to Gong Yuzhi, Deng first employed his aphorism about the color of the cat in a meeting of the CCP Secretariat on July 2, and then repeated his comments five days later. Deng's remarks to the CCP Secretariat are not included in his selected works. Deng almost certainly had discussed the agricultural situation with Chen Yun before making his remarks on July 7 and perhaps even before speaking on July 2. See Gong Yuzhi, *Sixiang jiefang di xin qidian*, p. 76.

33. Author's interviews. Deng's original remarks are what are published in *Deng Xiaoping wenxuan (1938–1965)*. If Mao had already expressed his attitude on this issue on July 7, it raises the question of why Chen went to argue in favor of the household responsibility system on July 9.

34. Zhou Taihe, "Chen Yun tongzhi sici xia nongcun diaocha de qianhou," pp. 167–169.

35. Lu Xueyi, *Lianchan chengbao zerenzhi yanjiu*, p. 65.

36. Wang Gengjin et al., eds. *Xiangcun sanshi nian*, vol. 2, p. 386.

37. Ibid.

38. Under the *baochan daozu* system, production teams signed contracts not with individual households but with small groups. Normally there would be four or five groups (*zu*) to a production team. The *baochan daozu* system thus preserved the principle of collective agriculture. For a discussion of Mahu's adoption of the *baochan daozu* system, see Wang Gengjin et al., eds., *Xiangcun sanshi nian*, vol. 2, p. 391. It is important to note that at this time, the term *da bao gan* was used interchangeably with *bao chan dao zu* to refer to the practice of contracting to small groups. Later the meaning changed to "comprehensive contracting," under which all production was contracted to the household.

39. Wang Gengjin et al., eds., *Xiangcun sanshi nian*, vol. 2, p. 386.

40. Wang Lixin, "Life After Mao Zedong," p. 57. See also Pi Shuyi, "Without Reform, There Would Be No Way Out," *Renmin ribao*, April 25, 1992, pp. 1–2, trans. FBIS, May 11, 1992, p. 19.

41. Sun Qimeng and Xiong Zhiyong, *Dazhai hongqi de shengqi yu duoluo*, p. 305; Lu Xueyi, *Lianchan Chengbao zerenzhi yanjiu*, p. 69; and Wang Gengjin et al., eds., *Xiangcun sanshi nian*, vol. 2, pp. 399–402. In Fengyang, the Xiaogang Production Brigade of Liyuan Commune pioneered the household responsibility system. Liyuan Commune was known as a poor commune in one of Anhui's poorest counties, and Xiaogang was one of Liyuan's poorest production brigades. In 1956, the first year in which Xiaogang adopted agricultural cooperatives, it sold over 40,000 *jin* (1 *jin* = 1.1 pound) of grain to the state. That was the last time before 1979 that it sold grain. In 1957, Xiaogang was hit by the antirightist movement, followed by the Great Leap Forward the following year. In 1960, Xiaogang, which originally had 34 households, 175 people, and 30 head of livestock, was left with only ten households, 39 people, and one water buffalo. Over 60 people had starved to death, wiping out six households, while another 76 people had fled to other areas. Repeated political campaigns brought a constant turnover of local leadership and tense personal relations, making any form of cooperation impossible. In the spring of 1979, the Xiaogang Production Brigade was divided into four groups in accordance with the *baochan daozu* system. When this failed, it was divided into eight groups. Finally, it simply adopted the household responsibility system. The commune leadership decided to ignore Xiaogang's violation of party policy, believing that letting one production brigade adopt the household responsibility system would not matter. But in 1979, Xiaogang harvested 132,370 *jin* of grain—as much as it had harvested cumulatively in the five years from 1966 to 1970—and sold 24,995 *jin* to the state. Xiaogang's example deeply influenced other areas, angering local cadres. As a result, Xiaogang was forced to organize production by groups to accord with the *baochan daozu* system.

42. Sun Qimeng and Xiong Zhiyong, *Dazhai hongqi de shengqi yu duoluo*, p. 305.

43. Lu Xueyi, *Lianchan chengbao zerenzhi yanjiu*, p. 67. See also Chen Yizi, *Zhongguo: Shinian gaige yu bajiu minyun* (China: Ten Years of Reform and the Democratic Movement of 1989), p. 26.

44. Wan Li, "Zai shengwei gongzuo huiyi shang de jianghua" (Talk at a Work Meeting of the Provincial Party Committee), January 3, 1979, quoted in Wang Gengjin et al., eds., *Xiangcun sanshi nian*, vol. 2, p. 386.

45. Cited in Wang Gengjin et al., eds., *Xiangcun sanshi nian*, vol. 2, p. 390. Emphasis added.

46. Cited in Chen Yizi, "Nongcun de shouguang, Zhongguo de xiwang," p. 34.

47. On Zhou, see Wang Lixin, "Life After Mao Zedong," p. 25.

48. Wang Gengjin et al., eds., *Xiangcun sanshi nian*, vol. 2, p. 390; Lu Xueyi, *Lianchan chengbao zerenzhi yanjiu*, p. 66; Chen Yizi, *Zhongguo: Shinian gaige yu bajiu minyun*, p. 26.

49. Wang Lixin, "Life After Mao Zedong," p. 26.

50. " 'Sanji suoyou, dui wei jichu' tinggai wending" ("Three-Level Ownership with the Production Team as the Foundation" Should Be Stabilized), *Renmin ribao*, March 15, 1979, p. 1.

51. Wang Gengjin et al., *Xiangcun sanshi nian*, vol. 2, p. 392. See also Lu Xueyi, *Lianchan chengbao zerenzhi yanjiu*, p. 73; Chen Yizi, *Zhongguo: Shinian gaige yu bajiu minyun*, p. 34; and Lu Xueyi, Jia Xinde, and Li Lanting, "Baochan daohu wenti yingdang chongxin yanjiu" (The Question of the Household Responsibility Syatem Should Be Restudied), p. 26.

52. Xing Sheng and Lu Jiafeng, "Zhengque kandai lianxi chanliang de zerenzhi" (Correctly View the Responsibility System That Links Remuneration to Output), *Renmin ribao*, March 30, 1979, p. 1. See also "Tiaodong nongmin jijixing de yixiang youli cuoshi" (An Effective Measure for Arousing the Enthusiasm of Peasants), *Renmin ribao*, May 20, 1979, p. 2.

53. Chen Yizi, *Zhongguo: Shinian gaige yu bajiu minyun*, p. 33.

54. "Zhonggong zhongyang guanyu jiakuai nongye fazhan ruogan wenti de jueding" (Decision of the CCP Central Committee on Some Problems in Accelerating Agricultural Development), p. 65. Emphasis added.

55. Guo Chongyi, "Zeren daohu de xingzhi ji qi youguan wenti" (The Nature of Devolving Responsibility to the Household and Related Questions), pp. 15–25. Guo's report is dated August 1979.

56. Chen Yizi, *Zhongguo: Shinian gaige yu bajiu minyun*, pp. 27–28.

57. On Chen's background, see Judith Shapiro and Liang Heng, *After the Nightmare*, pp. 88–89.

58. Chen Yizi, *Zhongguo: Shinian gaige yu bajiu minyun*, p. 4.

59. Author's interviews.

60. Lu Xueyi, Jia Xinde, and Li Lanting, "Baochan daohu wenti yingdang chongxin yanjiu," pp. 26–33.

61. On the shared generational experiences and common sense of identity of this generation, see Yang Fan, *Zhonghua renmin gongheguo de di dan dai* (The Third Generation of the PRC). Distinguishing generations in China is sometimes difficult, particularly in light of Deng Xiaoping's statement that he is the core of the "second generation" of CCP leaders (as opposed to Mao, who was the core of the first generation of leadership). Most people who participated in the Cultural Revolution, however, lump Mao and Deng together in the first generation of leadership, refer to leaders like Jiang Zemin and Li Peng as belonging to the second generation, and think of themselves as constituting the third generation. I have followed this usage.

62. Author's interviews.

63. On He's background, see Shapiro and Liang, *After the Nightmare*, p. 79; and Zhu Jiaming, "Diaonian wo de pengyou He Weiling" (Mourning My Friend He Weiling), *Zhongguo zhi chun*, August 1991, p. 29.

64. Getting membership in the party for most of the members of the Rural Development Group was one of the challenges the group faced in its early development. Generally, the group was successful in gaining membership for its members, but there were some who had problems of one sort or another and were never admitted into the party.

65. Author's interviews.

66. Deng Liqun, "FangRi guilai de sisu" (Thoughts Upon Returning from Japan), in Deng Liqun, Ma Hong, Sun Shangqing, and Wu Jiajin, *FangRi guilai de sisu* (Thoughts Upon Returning from Japan), p. 2.

67. Apparently these accusations were not without foundation, but they nevertheless appear to have been based on personal jealousy. Author's interviews.

68. See Nicholas R. Lardy and Kenneth G. Lieberthal, eds., *Chen Yun's Strategy for Development: A Non-Maoist Alternative*.

69. Secretarial Section, "Zhongguo nongcun fazhan wenti yanjiu jihua tigang (cao'an)" (Outline of the Research Plan on Problems in China's Rural Development, Draft), p. 24.

70. Author's interviews.

71. Wang's article was subsequently published openly in *Nongye jingji wenti*, no. 2 (February 1980).

72. On the organization of the group, see General Section, "Guanyu 'Zhongguo nongcun fazhan wenti yanjiu' diyi jieduan de gongzuo yijian" (Views on the First Stage Work on "Studies on China's Rural Development Problems"), pp. 27–28; and Secretarial Section, "Zhongguo nongcun fazhan wenti yanjiu jihua tigang (cao'an)," pp. 23–24.

73. Chinese Rural Development Research Group, ed., *Baochan daohu ziliao xuan* (Selected Materials on the Household Responsibility System). Author's interviews.

74. In February 1981, Yu began hosting a bimonthly "forum on China's economic and social development strategy," a forum that continued on for years. The Chinese Rural Development Research Group's article on strategic development was written in June, suggesting that the notion of "strategic development" was very much on the minds of Chinese intellectuals in this period. On Yu's forum, see Yu Guangyuan, "A Well Received Forum," *Shijie jingji daobao*, March 25, 1985, p. 5, trans. FBIS, April 4, 1985, pp. K24–25.

75. Deng Yingtao et al., "Lun zhanlue yanjiu," pp. 267–268.

76. Shapiro and Liang, *After the Nightmare*, p. 95.

77. After the Tiananmen incident on June 4, 1989, the group was officially disbanded. Some members of the group remained in China and were able to join other research organs while other members went abroad to do research.

78. "Communiqué of the Fifth Plenary Session of the Eleventh Central Committee of the Communist Party of China," Xinhua, February 29, 1980.

79. Author's interviews.

80. Deng Xiaoping, "Guanyu nongcun zhengce wenti" (On Question of Rural Policy), p. 275.

81. Wang Gengjin et al., eds., *Xiangcun sanshi nian*, vol. 2, p. 403.

82. The Rural Development Group had close ties with the agricultural daily, *Zhongguo nongmin bao*, which became one of their chief allies in publicizing the new reforms.

83. Chen Yizi, "Nongcun de shouguang, Zhongguo de xiwang."

84. Lu Xueyi and Wang Xiaoqiang, "Baochan daohu de youlai he jinhou de fazhan" (The Origins of the Household Responsibility System and Its Future Development), pp. 54–68.

85. Author's interviews.

86. Author's interviews. The minutes of an August 1980 meeting in Fengyang County refers to a letter by Zhao Ziyang in which he calls for "stabilizing" the number of areas practicing the household responsibility system. See Wang Gengjin et al. eds., *Xiangcun sanshi nian*, vol. 2, p. 409. For Du Runsheng's support of the *zhuanye chengbao* system, see his speech at the September 1980 meeting of provincial party secretaries "Guanyu nongye shengchan zeren zhi" (On the Agricultural Responsibility System).

87. Editorial Committee on the History of Agricultural Cooperativization in Heilongjiang, *Heilongjiang nongye hezuo shi* (History of Agricultural Cooperativization in Heilongjiang), p. 483.

88. Ibid., p. 485.

89. Wu Xiang, "Yang guan dao yu du mu qiao."

90. Lu Xueyi, *Lianchan chengbao zerenzhi yanjiu*, pp. 77–78. "Guanyu jinyibu jiaqiang he wanshan nongye shengchan zerenzhi de jige wenti" (Several Issues Concerning Further Strengthening and Perfecting the Production Responsibility System in Agriculture), pp. 409–411. Author's interviews.

91. Lu Xueyi, *Lianchan chengbao zerenzhi yanjiu*, pp. 79–80.

92. Author's interviews.

93. Chen Yizi, *Zhongguo: Shinian gaige yu bajiu minyun*, p. 37.

94. Author's interviews.

95. Lu Xueyi, *Lianchan chengbao zerenzhi yanjiu*, p. 80.

96. "Quanguo nongcun gongzuo huiyi jiyao" (Outline of the National Rural Work Conference), *Renmin ribao*, April 6, 1982; and Lu Xueyi, *Lianchan chengbao zerenzhi yanjiu*, pp. 81–82.

97. Chen Yizi, *Zhongguo: Shinian gaige yu bajiu minyun*, p. 37.

98. Chen Yun, "Jingji jianshe de jige zhongyao fangzhen" (Several Important Directions in Economic Construction), p. 275.

99. Lu Xueyi, *Lianchan chengbao zerenzhi yanjiu*, p. 84.

100. This is not to say that there were not problems in rural reforms that would lead to difficulties later on. As Bernstein points out, rural reform progressed through ambiguities and half measures, including a lack of definition of property rights. Such ambiguities were useful in the early years, but they provided little incentive for peasant investment, thus bringing about difficulties in later years. See Thomas Bernstein, "From Anti-Leftism to Household Farming: A Limited Breakthrough," unpublished manuscript.

2

The Emergence of
Enterprise Reform

The process of early enterprise reform differed in important ways from that in the countryside, reflecting the very different relationship between the two sectors and China's central bureaucracy. The operation of agriculture was local, and revenues from agriculture were not important in the state budget; in contrast, China's industrial enterprises were mutually interdependent and their profits directly sustained the national government. Whereas an area such as Anhui could push ahead with agricultural reform without directly affecting conditions in other provinces,[1] any significant reform of enterprises—such as granting greater decision-making authority, reforming the price structure, or changing the tax structure—could have major and unforeseen consequences for other industries either in the same province or elsewhere. Most important, any significant misstep could quickly undermine the fiscal solvency of the central government and produce an economic disaster for the whole country. In short, the very nature of industrial organization in China biased the reform process toward tighter centralized control and marginal changes.

This is not to say that bottom-up demands from industries and localities played no role in the early enterprise reforms; on the contrary, enterprise demands for greater operational autonomy and experiments in enterprise reform undertaken in areas such as Sichuan provided an important force supporting reforms. However, in contrast to the case with rural reforms, the force of this bottom-up push was blunted by the hierarchical structure of Chinese industrial organization. The organization of major industrial enterprises into vertical "systems" (*xitong*) emanating from Beijing had led to the formation of strong vested interests that fought vigorously over the course of the decade against reforms that undermined their authority.

The centralization of such a large percentage of industrial production under the direct control of Beijing's ministries, as well as the potentially adverse consequences for industrial production, labor unrest, and the financial revenues of the central government if reform went awry, suggest why enterprise reform emerged as a much more centralized, top-down process than rural reform. Moreover, there was already a large cadre of officials, bureaucrats, and professional economists who were intimately familiar with the organization and operation of China's industrial enterprises. Against this phalanx of senior managers and intellectuals, there was little room (albeit some) for young intellectuals to play a role in enterprise reform analogous to that that they undertook in the countryside.

The impetus for enterprise reform derived from a combination of genuine problems in the economy, the open intellectual atmosphere that prevailed in the wake of the campaign for practice as the sole criterion of truth, and the competition for political power. As intellectuals returned to Beijing after the Cultural Revolution and after the establishment of CASS in 1977 (prior to the Cultural Revolution, social science research had been under the direction of the Chinese Academy of Sciences), an intellectual atmosphere of unprecedented openness developed quickly. As with thinking about rural policy, this trend was fostered by Deng Liqun, who used CASS as an almost personal policy organ. As noted in the previous chapter, Deng Liqun sponsored the establishment of CASS's internal journal *Weiding gao*, which published some very radical articles in the late 1970s. Biweekly seminars convened at CASS provided intellectuals with a forum for vigorous debate.[2]

The push for enterprise reform was also fostered by political competition. When industrial reform got under way in late 1978, economic policy was largely in the hands of a group of bureaucrats known as the "Petroleum Group." The Petroleum Group was composed of officials who had made their careers and risen to the top of the Chinese political system through their development of China's petroleum industry, particularly the Daqing oil field. The head of this group was the one-armed Long March veteran Yu Qiuli, who as Minister of Petroleum had moved to Daqing in the early 1960s to direct development of its oil field. His top assistants at that time, Kang Shien, Tang Ke, and Song Zhenming, followed Yu's assent up the political ladder.[3] In late 1964, Mao turned away from the economic policies envisioned in the early drafts of the Third Five-Year Plan—drawn up under the supervision of Chen Yun—and turned to Yu Qiuli and his associates to draw up a plan that would allow faster development and massive investment in the interior of China—the so-called Third Front.[4] Mao created a "Small Planning Commission" (*xiao jiwei*) that took over the task of planning from the State Planning Commission, which had been under the control of Li Fuchun. Joining Yu on the Small Planning Commission were Vice Chairman of the State Economic Commission Gu Mu and Zhejiang party official Lin Hujia—the same official who had supported Zhejiang's household responsibility system in 1956.[5]

Yu Qiuli came under sharp criticism in the early part of the Cultural Revolution but, with the help of Zhou Enlai, survived to guide what planning took place in that period. With Lin Biao's demise in 1971, and especially after Deng

Xiaoping's return to power in 1973, Yu Qiuli, with Deng's support, began draw-ing up plans for extensive imports of foreign technology and equipment. With Deng's fall in 1976, Yu's plan—derided as the "three poisonous weeds"—was sharply criticized for "selling out" the interests of China, but the Petroleum Group was not purged.[6] When the Gang of Four was arrested in October 1976, the Petroleum Group, under the patronage of Hua Guofeng and Vice Premier Li Xiannian, again dominated China's planning process.[7]

In 1977 and 1978, this group of planners stepped up their investment in heavy industry, relying in part on the infusion of foreign credit that became available as relations with the West improved. In July 1977, the State Planning Commission proposed an eight-year plan, covering the last three years of the Fifth Five-Year Plan (1975–79) and the Sixth Five-Year Plan (1980–85), that called for spending 8 to 9 billion yuan a year—about one-fifth of China's capital construction budget—on importing technology and complete plants. In November 1977, the National Planning Conference proposed that steel production double to 60 million tons by 1985 and that oil production should reach 250 million tons. This trend of rapid expansion of China's industrial base reached a climax in a State Council theoret-ical meeting (*wu xu hui*) that was held from July 6 to September 9, 1978. That meeting judged that the rapid recovery of the economy in the previous two years had shown that the economic damage caused by the Gang of Four could be rapidly overcome.[8] Shortly thereafter, with fiscal revenues increasing more rap-idly than expected, the State Council agreed to add an additional 4.8 billion yuan to the 1978 budget for capital construction, thus bringing the capital construction budget for that year from the 33.2 billion yuan originally proposed to 41.5 billion yuan—an increase of 34.5 percent. This raised the accumulation rate from 32.3 percent in 1977 to 36.6 percent in 1978.[9] In 1978 alone China had agreed to import 22 large-scale plants worth U.S. $13 billion. In 1981 and 1982, when the costs for these projects would reach their peak, capital outlays would rise to about 13 billion yuan per year.[10]

The Dengist coalition, whose political predominance was confirmed by the 1978 Third Plenum, opposed the Petroleum Group's approach to economic pol-icy. This critique was not led by Deng Xiaoping, who had worked harmoniously enough with Yu Qiuli in the mid-1970s, but rather by Chen Yun, whose views had been set aside in the mid-1960s in favor of those of the Petroleum Group. In the 1978–79 period, Chen Yun backed both an expansion of market forces in the economy, accompanied by greater autonomy for enterprises, and the restoration of "balance" to the economy through a policy of "readjustment." The two goals of marketization and readjustment differed from each other, and different groups of intellectuals and policy advisors would soon cluster around these two poles. Their intellectual assumptions differed in important ways, and these differences would come into sharp conflict beginning in 1980 (see Chapter 3).

Enterprise reform in the Dengist period can perhaps be dated to Hu Qiaomu's well-known report to the State Council in July 1978, entitled "Act in Accordance with Economic Laws, Step Up the Four Modernizations."[11] This report, which was subsequently published in *People's Daily* in October 1978,[12] can be seen as part of a three-pronged attack on the policy and authority of Hua Guofeng. The first prong was the attack on the Dazhai system discussed in Chapter 2. The second, and most public, prong was the launching of the discussion on "practice as the sole criterion of truth" in May 1978, in direct opposition to Hua's "two whatevers." The third prong, like the attack on the Dazhai model, undermined another powerful symbol of the Maoist era—the Daqing model with which the Petroleum Group was so closely associated. This attack on the Daqing model, however, was never as explicit or public as the attack on Dazhai because Ji Dengkui and Chen Yongkui, who backed the Dazhai model, were clear opponents of Deng's new coalition and were quickly removed from power; Deng and his allies would coexist with Yu Qiuli and the Petroleum Group until the fall of 1980, and even then Deng expressed support for Yu by naming him head of the PLA's powerful General Political Department and member of the Central Secretariat. Together, these initiatives amounted to a campaign platform that criticized Hua Guofeng on agricultural policy, ideology, and general management of the economy.

Hu Qiaomu's report had its origins in internal discussions on how to carry out criticism of the Gang of Four so as to undermine Hua Guofeng and lay a foundation for Dengist leadership. These internal discussions took up such issues as how to defend the principle of distribution according to labor against charges made during the period of the Cultural Revolution that this principle led to "economism" (i.e., emphasizing the economy to the neglect of politics) and how to defend attention to economic matters against charges of "productionism" (*wei shengchanli lun*) (again, paying attention to the economy and neglecting politics). Discussions also took up the issue of the aim of socialist production (*shehui zhuyi shengchan de mudi*), which criticized the mentality of production for production's sake that was said to have prevailed during the Cultural Revolution. These issues, whatever their economic ramifications, were fundamentally ideological issues, and the task of putting forth the Dengist program thus fell to those drawn from the ideological sphere.

In June 1975, when Deng was still first vice premier, he established a Political Research Office (*Zhengzhi yanjiu shi*) under the State Council in an effort to compete with the Gang of Four's influence in the ideological sphere. At the time, this office was staffed by Hu Qiaomu, Wu Lengxi, Hu Sheng, Xiong Fu, Yu Guangyuan, and Deng Liqun. The office participated in the editing of volume 5 of Mao Zedong's *Selected Works* and helped draft many important documents, including the "three poisonous weeds" ("Twenty Articles on Industry," "Outline Report on the Work of the Academy of Sciences," and "On the General Program of Work for the Whole Party and Country").[13] When Deng was purged in 1976, this office ceased work, but it was not officially disbanded.

Thus, when Deng began his comeback in 1977, this research office was able to resume its activities. At that time, Hu Qiaomu, Deng Liqun, and Yu Guangyuan were joined by Feng Lanrui and Lin Jianqing, the elder brother of the well-known economist Lin Zili. The research office not only played an important role as Deng's policy organ but also in the establishment and organization of CASS, which was established as a separate institution in 1977. Hu Qiaomu became the first president of CASS, and two of his vice presidents were Deng Liqun and Yu Guangyuan.[14]

It was the Political Research Office that drafted Hu Qiaomu's report to the State Council. What is striking is that Deng and his allies did not first defeat Hua politically and then sit down and think about economic reform but rather formulated an approach to the economy as part of the attack on Hua. It is ironic, but altogether in keeping with Chinese politics then and since, that the Dengist economic reforms, which have tried to decrease the role of ideology in the system, were nonetheless rooted in an ideological statement.

Although Hu's report marked a stark challenge to Hua Guofeng and his allies, it seems a surprisingly cautious document when compared to the bold actions Wan Li was undertaking in Anhui or the discussion on practice as the sole criterion of truth that had been launched only two months before it. The central thesis of Hu's report is that economic laws are objective. "Politics itself," Hu said, "cannot create a law beyond the objective economic laws and impose it on economics." Citing Engels, Hu argued that while state power can help the economy develop faster, if used incorrectly it can also cause "much waste in manpower and material resources." Moreover, because socialist economies are planned economies and economic and political power are concentrated, mistakes in economic work can easily become a "national crisis." The socialist economic system itself, Hu said, "cannot automatically guarantee that we will act according to objective economic laws." This was a startling statement given the political atmosphere of the time and the rhetoric of the previous three decades, but Hu pointed out that the experience of both the Soviet Union and China proved his thesis. The socialist economic system can only create the possibility that economic growth will be greater than in capitalist societies; it cannot guarantee it.

Hu's statement about the objectivity of economic laws was part of the ongoing redefinition of ideology in the early Dengist period so as to take into account the "relative autonomy" of specific fields of knowledge and the limits of state control. First enunciated in the field of economics, this "sociological postulate," as Tang Tsou has characterized it, was gradually—and with great controversy—extended to other fields. As Tsou put it, this sociological postulate held that "every sphere of social life and its activities has its special characteristics (*te-dian*) and is governed by special laws"; the corresponding injunction is that "the political leadership can and should create the general conditions favorable to the operation of these laws and even use these laws to promote development, but it cannot violate these laws without suffering serious consequences."[15]

Hu's emphasis on the objectivity of economic laws and the need to study such laws more systematically to "sum up both positive and negative experiences" in economic management played an important role in stimulating economic research and discussion. Hu's report admitted, first, that socialism was subject to economic crises and, second, that it was necessary for Chinese economists to study the economic management of capitalist societies, thus opening up new fields of inquiry. Citing Marx, Hu argued that capitalist management consisted of two parts, "the special function engendered by the nature of the course of social labor that belongs to this course" and "the function of exploitation in the course of social labor." In other words, there was a universal aspect that derived from the division of labor and modern management and an exploitative aspect that was a specific function of the capitalist system. The former, Hu said, "is indispensable to all kinds of social labor under various systems." Thus, Hu concluded, it is necessary to "combine the superiority of the socialist system with the advanced science and technology and advanced management experiences of the developed capitalist countries and combine all the useful experiences of foreign countries with our own concrete conditions and successful experiences."[16]

In the context of mid-1978, Hu's statement provided a major pillar of support for reform, justifying in systematic and authoritative fashion the study of economic laws, the reform of the economic system, and the opening of the PRC to the outside world. Nevertheless, it is apparent that traditional concepts of the importance of planning continued to influence the thinking of Hu and the rest of the CCP leadership.

One of the "laws" that Hu demanded be followed in economic work was that of "proportionate development in a planned way"—one of the central tenets of Chen Yun's economic thought. Describing this as a "basic characteristic" of the socialist system, Hu argued that only in this way could China avoid the "anarchist or semianarchist" conditions of capitalist societies. At the time, this demand to develop the economy proportionately and in a planned way meant the strengthening of planning. After the Cultural Revolution, Hu said, economic management work had been reduced to a "semi-planned" status and it was necessary to raise this to a "fully planned" status.[17] Doing so meant that construction undertaken outside state plans should be included in local plans at various levels, and that localities "must yield to the state's overall interests."[18]

Another "law" that Hu said had to be obeyed was the "law of value," which he called a "universal law in commodity economics." Reflecting the influence of China's most famous economist, Sun Yefang (who was excoriated during the Cultural Revolution as "China's Liebermann" and ended up spending seven years in jail), Hu stated that the law of value determined that the "value" of commodities is determined by the working time needed by society to produce it, and that the price of a commodity is based on its value.[19] This definition of the law of value implied nothing about supply and demand. Hu's assumption remained that the value of a commodity was something that could be objectively determined, and that a fair price could therefore be set for it if those doing economic work adhered to objective economic laws. Thus, as important a step forward as Hu's speech was in the context of the times, it did not pose a challenge to the basic assumptions of the Stalinist economic system: that prices are "objectively" determined through the amount of labor embodied in the product, that these prices can be determined by planners without the use of markets, that planning can be made rational by adhering to "objective" economic laws, and, further, that plans are determined by the needs of the society (the state) as a whole and are not a reflection of supply and demand relations in society.

The Wuxi Conference

The publication of Hu Qiaomu's report to the State Council stimulated public discussion of issues related to reform, particularly the "law of value," which was the focus of "several tens" of meetings of various sizes held in Sichuan, Fujian, Jilin, and elsewhere.[20] These meetings culminated in the Wuxi Conference, held in April 1979. Although more by coincidence than by plan, the date of April 1979 was of historical significance. Twenty years earlier, in April 1959, economists had gathered in Shanghai to discuss the relationship between market and plan. That meeting, called in response to the failures of the Great Leap Forward the year before, was the first time Chinese economists had held public discussions on the relationship of plan and market. Further discussions of the topic were cut short by the Lushan Plenum in the summer of 1959, when Mao, responding drastically to Peng Dehuai's challenge, moved to reaffirm the disastrous course he had set the year before.

Twenty years later, in the wake of the Cultural Revolution, Chinese economists gathered once again to discuss the law of value, the role of enterprises, and the relation of plan and market. More than three hundred scholars attended. Xue Muqiao, in his opening address, referred to the gathering as a "meeting of elites" (qun ying hui), a phrase that perhaps carries much irony in the wake of Tiananmen when "elites" (accused of having masterminded the Tiananmen demonstrations) have come in for so much criticism. The Wuxi Conference was not an academic symposium in the Western sense of that term; neither did it reflect the sort of local experimentation and informal lobbying (and sharp policy conflict) that had characterized the early rural reforms. On the contrary, the Wuxi Conference was a semi-official meeting of officials and establishment intellectuals that was preceded by elaborate preparations involving many offices in China's state bureaucracy.[21]

Prior to the convening of the Wuxi Conference, the Economic Research Office of the State Planning Commission (then headed by Xue Muqiao) and the Planning and Statistics Department of Chinese People's University convened four preparatory meetings between December 1978 and February 1979, which focused on the relationship between plan and market.[22] In addition, several ministries of the State Council participated in three other discussion meetings that were held in January and February 1979 on the question of the relationship between the law of value and the independence of enterprises.[23] The State Price Bureau also presided over four discussion meetings on the question of price formation.[24]

The elaborate process of bureaucratic consultation that preceded the Wuxi Conference contrasted sharply with the more informal convening of the well-known conference on ideology that took place in the same period—from mid-January to early April—and appears to have prevented the sharp challenges to official thinking that appeared in the theory conference.[25] Nevertheless, participants in the Wuxi Conference were apparently worried about the implications for their own deliberations of Deng Xiaoping's March 30 speech on upholding the four cardinal principles; Xue Muqiao, in his opening remarks, took pains to reassure them that upholding the four cardinal principles in no way contradicted the principle of "letting a hundred schools of thought contend."[26]

Not only did preparations for the Wuxi Conference involve a broad cross-section of China's industrial bureaucracy and establishment intellectuals, but Chen Yun clearly endorsed the tenor of the discussions if not all of the conclusions reached. It was at the time of the discussions preceding the Wuxi Conference that Chen Yun wrote a letter to the Central Committee of the CCP on the relationship of plan and market, suggesting that he was responding to the economic issues raised in the course of planning for the Wuxi conference. In his letter, Chen stated clearly that the planned economy is "primary" and that market regulation is "secondary," but he also said that the problem then facing China was the near absence of market regulation. As he put it, "Now, the plan is too rigid and it encompasses too much. The inevitable result is the absence of an element of spontaneous market regulation."[27]

These comments indicate that in the spring of 1979, Chen supported the main thrust of the critique of planning that unfolded in Wuxi. As will become evident, that critique was largely based on an interpretation of the economic history of the PRC that was at odds with Chen Yun's interpretation, and it pointed to remedies for the Chinese economy that differed from those favored by Chen Yun. These differences would soon become evident, particularly in 1980, as Chen and his supporters moved to emphasize "readjustment" over "reform." Although there was already tension between these two trends of thought in 1979, the conflict was not yet serious. Most of those who advocated readjustment also believed that reform was necessary. Reform was mostly a matter of theoretical discussion and some pilot projects; it did not yet affect readjustment and the "balance" of the national economy. Moreover, discussions of reform were inevitably critiques of the economic management system as it had developed under the Petroleum Group and so played a role in undermining the power of Chen's bureaucratic rivals.

At the Wuxi Conference, a group of officials, including Xue Muqiao, then head of the Economic Research Office at the State Planning Commission; He Jianzhang, then Xue's subordinate as deputy head of the Economic Research

Center; and Li Chengrui, deputy director of the State Statistical Bureau, joined with a group of CASS economists including Liu Guoguang, Sun Shangqing, Zhao Renwei, Chen Jiyuan, and Zhang Zhuoyuan to stress the need to "integrate" plan and market and to give greater decision-making authority to enterprises.

The importance of the Wuxi Conference derives from its systematic, though not explicit, criticism of orthodox Marxist economics as enshrined in Stalin's 1952 book *Economic Problems of Socialism in the U.S.S.R.*, a work that had tremendous impact in China.[28] At the time of its publication, Stalin's work marked an innovation in Soviet Marxist thinking (at least as it had existed since the early 1930s), justifying the continued existence of commodity relations in the socialist period (causing some Chinese at that time as well as later to consider it "revisionist"). But Stalin's reasoning was narrowly based. He argued that commodity-monetary relations had been abolished within the sphere of enterprises owned by the whole people, and hence that the law of value was no longer operative in that arena. However, Stalin argued that commodity relations and the law of value continued to exist within the collective ownership system, which was based on a lower level of socialization. Because these two systems of ownership exchanged goods, there was a need for commodity-monetary relations to continue. Stalin's expectation was that as the socialist system matured, the ownership of the whole people would gradually expand to the whole economy, eliminating both the collective economy and the need for commodity-monetary relations.[29] This view, among other things, helped to justify efforts in China that began in the mid-1950s to continually increase the size and raise the level of ownership of enterprises, thus eliminating commodity-monetary relations.

Stalin's view had originally been criticized in China in 1956 by Sun Yefang. Sun had held that because different economic interests continued to exist in the socialist period, and would continue to exist in the communist period, it was impossible—and undesirable—to eliminate the law of value. On the contrary, in Sun's view, it was necessary to base all economic work—in both collective enterprises and those owned by the whole people—on the law of value. The law of value derives from Marx's theory that the "value" of a good is due to the amount of labor in that good, which is distinguishable from the "exchange value" of the good, or what society will pay for it. Sun's contribution to Marxist discussions of the law of value was to emphasize that the value of a good derived from the "socially necessary labor"; thus, a good was not more valuable because slow labor and poor technology went into it. But Sun always held that the law of value did not depend on markets. In his view, it was possible to make the appropriate calculations to determine "socially necessary labor" and thus apply the law of value in setting prices.[30]

At the Wuxi Conference, theorists from the State Planning Commission's Economic Research Office, the State Statistical Bureau, and CASS attacked the planning system as it had existed in China over the prior three decades.[31] The brunt of their critique was that the planning system overconcentrated authority and managed excessively, stifling the initiative of enterprises. The result was that enterprises produced for the plan, not for market needs, so that unneeded products piled up in warehouses while needed goods were not produced. Moreover, a one-sided emphasis on "output value" caused enterprises to ignore costs and efficiency, contributing to horrendous waste. In addition, the plan concentrated resources on heavy industry, ignoring the need for consumer goods.

Those attending the Wuxi Conference argued that the fundamental reason that the planning system had not functioned well in the past was that the law of value had not been brought to bear. In order to bring out the importance—and the legitimacy—of the law of value, participants believed that it was necessary to criticize fundamentally Stalin's view that the law of value did not operate within the sphere of ownership by the whole people. Stalin's artificial separation of the economy into two distinct spheres (ownership by the whole people and collective ownership), theorists argued, led to the conception of plan and market being related to each other as two separate pieces—"planks and boards"—(bankuai jiehe) that have no integral relation to each other.

In contrast to understandings of Marxism based on Stalin's work, Liu Guoguang, Zhao Renwei, and others argued that individuals and enterprises continued to have their own distinct material interests in the socialist period. Because both individuals and enterprises make different contributions to society, it was necessary to recognize this by exchanging goods at equal value. And the only way of exchanging goods at equal value was by recognizing the law of value. This was as true of enterprises owned by the whole people as it was of those collectively or even individually owned; it followed that the law of value operated equally throughout the economy. Hence, in opposition to the board-and-plank notion of integration, Liu, Zhao, and their colleagues put forward the view that plan and market should be "organically integrated" (youji jiehe). Moreover, they argued, this "organic integration" of plan and market expressed the "essence of socialism."[32]

This criticism of board-and-plank integration, it would become evident, was directed at Chen Yun's idea that the plan should concentrate on the most important aspects of the economy, while the market should regulate commodities of lesser importance that could not be effectively included in the plan. The idea that an organic integration of plan and market represented the "essence" of socialism directly challenged the orthodox view that the planned economy expressed the "essence" of socialism. Two years later, in a more conservative climate, Liu's views would be criticized and refuted (see Chapter 3).

Sun Shangqing, Chen Jiyuan, and Zhang Zhuoyuan of CASS's Industrial Economics Institute argued along similar lines. They asserted that plan and market should be "mutually interpenetrating" (xianghu cantuo). This concept appears to be no different from the notion of "organic integration" as articulated by Liu Guoguang and Zhao Renwei. It was used to emphasize the point that market forces should help regulate production and exchange within the planned part of the economy, just as the plan should help arrange production in those parts of the economy not subject to the state plan. Such integration could, in Sun, Chen, and Zhang's view, be based only on the law of value, and the law of value could not—contrary to both Sun Yefang and Hu Qiaomu—be separated from the market.[33]

Closely related to this call for integrating plan and market was a strong appeal to expand the decision-making authority of enterprises. This appeal to expand the authority of enterprises was based on an analysis of the PRC's history of repeated cycles in which authority had been centralized, then delegated, only to be recentralized once again. As the common saying had it: "Enterprises die as soon as they are controlled, there is chaos as soon as they are released, as soon as there is chaos they are controlled again, and as soon as they are controlled they die again" (yi tong jiu si, yi fang jiu luan, yi luan you tong, yi tong you si). Experience, it was argued, showed that centralized control, which was based on vertical (tiao tiao) ministerial relations, cut off horizontal relations, limiting economic relations between enterprises. Delegation, however, gave control over enterprises to localities (kuai kuai), which helped coordinate relations within a given area but made it difficult to coordinate the transfer of materials from other areas or the circulation of goods among areas. This traditional inability to resolve the problem of vertical and horizontal (tiao tiao kuai kuai) relations had led to the tendency for enterprises to become self-sufficient ("large and complete," da er chuan, or "small and complete," xiao er chuan), thus reducing specialization and economic efficiency as well as creating demands for redundant construction.[34]

The solution to this problem, argued a number of theorists—including Xue Muqiao, Liu Guoguang, Zhao Renwei, Sun Shangqing, Chen Jiyuan, Zhang Zhuoyuan, He Jianzhang, Liu Chengrui, Hu Naiwu, and Yu Guanghua—lay in expanding the authority given to enterprises. Enterprises needed to have greater authority over their own finances and wages, the prices of their goods, and especially over investment in order to force them to cut costs, reduce waste, and produce more for the market. Such theorists also argued that there should also be competition among enterprises with the less efficient being eliminated (taotai). These theorists, while building on the work of Sun Yefang, went way beyond him in recognizing that the law of value could not, in fact, be separated from the market.[35]

The articles that came out of the Wuxi Conference reflected an unprecedented openness in Chinese economic thinking and a willingness to challenge long-held understandings of Marxism, including the views of more open-minded economic policy makers and intellectuals such as Chen Yun and Sun Yefang. Their ideas, however, were far from radical. In arguing for an "organic integration" or "mutual interpenetration" of plan and market, such theorists were consciously arguing that the principles of plan and market could be harmonized (as in "market socialism") and were thus rejecting the radical view that market relations must predominate—a view that was put forth by some economists attending the Wuxi Conference.[36] For instance, Liu Guoguang and Zhao Renwei argued that it was necessary to "avoid one-sidedly expanding the market economy." We "cannot allow Adam Smith's 'invisible hand' to control our economic development," they argued, because "if individual consumers on the market make their decisions and individual enterprises make decisions based on their own economic interests, this will not necessarily accord with the general interest of society. . . . Without planning it would be extremely difficult to realize the rational distribution of the forces of production and especially the development of backward areas." Sun, Chen, and Zhang similarly argued that one could not simply abandon the plan in favor of the market. The successes of the early 1960s proved that the law of value could be implemented under the plan and had moreover attained results that would not have been possible by relying on market forces alone.[37]

In order to harmonize plan and market, such theorists called for reforming the planning system in various ways. For instance, He Jianzhang called for gradually changing mandatory plans into guidance plans.[38] Liu Guoguang and Zhao Renwei, like Sun Shangqing, Chen Jiyuan, and Zhang Zhuoyuan, called for a system of contracts between higher and lower administrative levels. The plan should start from the bottom level, they argued, and be harmonized with state needs and capabilities through a system of negotiation and contracts that would be executed at each successive level of the hierarchy. Such a process, it was hoped, would make the plan more responsive to societal needs while preventing the "blindness" and "anarchy" of capitalism.[39]

It is important to point out that in arguing for an "integration" between plan and market and for granting greater economic authority to enterprises, such theorists were consciously rejecting a reform of the ownership system. It was not felt at the time that either expanding the authority of enterprises or giving greater weight to market forces necessarily entailed a need for ownership reform. One theorist who disagreed with this was Dong Fureng, a researcher in CASS's Economics Institute. In January 1979, Dong published a seminal article, which anticipated by several years Chinese discussions on ownership reform, in *Jingji yanjiu* (Economic Studies), the journal of CASS's Economics Institute. In Dong's views, the cycle of centralization and decentralization that had been repeated throughout the history of the PRC was a direct result of state ownership and the consequent mingling of administrative and economic systems. In Dong's view, disentangling the administrative and economic systems necessarily entailed a change in state ownership, moving toward a new form of "ownership by the whole people" that would more closely resemble collective ownership.[40] This was not a call for a capitalist system; Dong remained firmly within a Marxist framework. But it did raise one of the central and most sensitive issues of socialist reform. Dong's views were discussed actively by his colleagues at CASS and elsewhere. Eventually they had a major impact on reform thinking, but at the time most of his colleagues rejected his ideas. The critique of the planning system that was presented at the Wuxi Conference accepted the need to separate the administrative and economic systems, but it rejected the notion that such a separation would affect the ownership system. Liu Guoguang is said to have held Dong's views in "contempt" at the time, although Liu himself later came to espouse the need for ownership reform.[41]

Not surprisingly, given the extensive discussions held prior to the Wuxi Conference, the approach advocated by so many theorists at the conference was supported by the Party's Central Work Conference in April 1979, which endorsed the slogan "readjustment, reform, rectification, and improvement" (*tiaozheng, gaige, zhengdun, tigao*). That conference called for implementing "the principle of integrating planned adjustment and market adjustment, with planned adjustment as primary but at the same time giving full importance to the role of market regulation."[42] This official formulation of the relationship between plan and market gave surprising weight to the role of the market; two years later it would be revised to reemphasize the role of the plan. Its adoption in 1979, however, did reflect the economic difficulties of the time, the desire to challenge the Petroleum Group and Hua Guofeng, and the relative openness of economic thinking in the wake of the campaign for practice as the sole criterion of truth.

Xue Muqiao's Theory of Socialist Reform

During this early period of discussion of the reform of the economy, the most systematic and authoritative effort to articulate a theory of socialist economics to underpin the emerging Dengist reforms was Xue Muqiao's *Studies on China's Socialist Economy*. Xue, who had been vice minister of the State Planning Commission and head of the State Statistical Bureau in the 1950s, was appointed an advisor to the Economic Research Office (*jingji yanjiu suo*) of the State Planning Commission following the arrest of the Gang of Four. In December 1978, in apparent concert with the Third Plenum, Xue and several colleagues left Beijing to hammer out *Studies on China's Socialist Economy*. An initial draft was completed in only three months, and revisions were made in April and May 1979. The draft was finalized in August and the book was published in December 1979.[43] As this process suggests, the book was not the product of one person. Indeed, a veritable who's who of China's economic establishment participated in the drafting and discussions that led to the book, suggesting its authoritativeness as a programmatic statement of the Dengist reform program.[44]

At least three aspects of the book are significant. First, although it supported an expansion of market forces, it by no means looked forward to the full marketization of the Chinese economy. In Xue's view, the Cultural Revolution had undermined the plan, and the economy had "descended into a semi-anarchic situation."[45] It was, according to Xue, necessary and possible to increase *both* planned management and the decision-making authority of localities and enterprises.[46] Far from looking toward a time when the planned economy would be a thing of the past, Xue argued that "Even in the future, administrative organs will still be necessary. . . . [P]lanning commissions will still be responsible for maintaining comprehensive balance—and plans will still have to be implemented."[47] Xue's book, then, was clearly a statement of economic reform, not of economic transformation.

Second, mirroring its caution on the issue of plans and markets, Xue's book is surprisingly cautious in theoretical terms. For instance, in discussing the sensitive issue of commodity-monetary relations, Xue was not as bold as many of the theorists at the Wuxi Conference. Whereas Liu Guoguang and others had elaborated a theoretical explanation of why the products of enterprises owned by the whole people were commodities and should be exchanged at equal value, Xue and his colleagues were not willing to go that far. In the chapter on commodities and money, Xue consistently uses the terms "commodity production" and "commodity exchange" but avoids the theoretically more sensitive term "commodity economy." In fact, his discussion of exchange in socialist societies rises barely above that contained in Stalin's *Economic Problems of Socialism*. Following Stalin's explanation, Xue argues that the primary reason for commodity exchange in a socialist society is that two different forms of public ownership coexist: ownership by the whole people and collective ownership. When it came to the critical and sensitive theoretical issue of whether exchange between state-managed enterprises constituted commodity exchange, Xue avoided a direct response. Acknowledging debate over the issue, he fell back on the weak explanation that such exchange is "like" the exchange of equal value between enterprises of different ownership.[48]

Third, in contrast to this general theoretical caution, Xue's book accepts the view that China was only in the "low stage of socialism" (*shehui zhuyi de diji jieduan*) or the "initial stage of socialism" (*shehui zhuyi chuji jieduan*).[49] The notion that China's socialism was less than pure was widely discussed and accepted among theoretical circles in 1978, when the unfolding discussion on practice as the sole criterion of truth created a more open intellectual atmosphere. At the theory conference held in early 1979, Marxist theoretician Su Shaozhi and economist Feng Lanrui had presented a paper on this concept that was subsequently published in *Jingji yanjiu* in May 1979.[50] Su and Feng suggested that the period between the socialist transformation of the means of production and the arrival of full socialism be subdivided into two subperiods: the first extending from the victory of the proletarian revolution to the socialist transformation of the ownership of the means of production, and the second extending from that point until full socialism is reached. Drawing on Lenin and Mao, they suggested that the second subperiod be called "undeveloped socialism" (*bu fada de shehui zhuyi*) to distinguish it from the "developed socialism" that Marx and Lenin envisioned. This suggestion sounded to some like an argument that China was not yet a socialist country, and Deng Liqun organized a meeting to criticize Su and Feng's article. This resulted in a sharp rebuttal that was published in *Jingji yanjiu* in August.[51]

The notion of undeveloped socialism was controversial in ideological terms because it could be used to justify a return to the more open policies of the new democratic phase of China's revolution. In economic terms, however, the concept of undeveloped socialism (or the initial stage of socialism—there was no set formulation in this period) was useful because it could be used to justify expanding the individual economy, which was necessary to relieve pressures from unemployment, and to criticize the overemphasis on socializing production that had typified much of Chinese economic theory from 1958 to 1978. The criticism of the term "undeveloped socialism" as an ideological concept thus contrasted with its acceptance in a generally cautious statement of economic principles. It was as if the party were willing to accept the economic consequences of this concept but resisted the ideological implications. The 1981 history resolution reflected this ambivalence, affirming that China was in the initial stage of socialism but emphasizing that China was definitely socialist.[52] This compromise ultimately proved untenable, and the party revisited the issue in 1987 when Zhao Ziyang tried to underpin his efforts at economic reform by making the concept of the initial stage of socialism the centerpiece of his report to the Thirteenth Party Congress.

Drawing Up Reform Plans

The Wuxi Conference and Xue Muqiao's book marked important efforts at a systematic conceptualization of what was wrong with China's economic management system and the direction in which reforms should lead. In this sense they can be taken as the intellectual baseline from which economic reform proceeded. They were, however, efforts to conceptualize and legitimize reform, not concrete policies to effect change. In March 1979, the CCP approved the establishment of a Finance and Economic Commission under the State Council. Some of the top leadership, including Hu Yaobang, Hu Qiaomu, Deng Liqun, and Yao Yilin, discussed a proposal to convene an economic theory conference, but they decided that not enough was known about the state of the economy to justify such a meeting.[53] Not long afterward, in accordance with Yao Yilin's views, the Research Office of the Central Committee's General Office, the five economic research institutes of CASS, and the research organs of economic organs under the State Council jointly undertook studies on the state of China's economy and how to effect reform.[54] These research efforts were coordinated by the Small Group for the Study of Economic Structural Reform (*Jingji tizhi gaige yanjiu xiaozu*), which was established in June 1979 and headed by Zhang Jingfu. Initially, three research groups were established as follows:[55]

1. China Economic Reform Group, headed by Xue Muqiao, director of the Economic Research Office of the State Planning Commission, and Liao Jili.
2. China Economic Structure Research Group, headed by Ma Hong, concurrently a vice president of CASS and director of its Industrial Economics Institute, and Sun Shangqing.
3. Technological Transfer Research Group, headed by Wang Daohan, vice minister of economic relations with foreign countries.

After these groups were established, Yu Guangyuan, a vice president of CASS and concurrently a vice minister of the State Science and Technology Commission, proposed the organization of a fourth group on theory and method. This was approved (apparently by the Finance and Economics Commission), and Yu took charge of it. Yu was assisted by Dong Fureng, deputy director of CASS's Economics Institute.[56]

The establishment of these groups marked a further effort to organize thinking about reform, both theoretical and practical, in high-level policy research groups. As Hamrin has pointed out, many of these people had previously worked closely with Chen Yun and with each other, which enabled them to come together quickly after the arrest of the Gang of Four and formulate a common approach to economic reform. These groups were tied very closely to the highest levels of the government—Ma Hong, for instance, left his position as head of CASS's Industrial Economics Institute to move into Zhongnanhai, the compound in which China's leaders work, where he directed studies on China's economy.

These policy research groups, it should be pointed out, stood in marked contrast to the sort of semi-independent policy research group that Chen Yizi's Rural Development Research Group would become. Although some of these groups, particularly under Yu Guangyuan's leadership, thought about reform over the medium and long term, the agenda of the economic reform groups (those headed by Ma Hong and Xue Muqiao) appears to have been driven by the pressing problems of the economy and the State Council's immediate concerns.

Shortly before these groups were established, the Central Work Conference of April 1979 had endorsed Chen Yun's call for a "readjustment" of the economy. The policy of readjustment was directed against the high-growth economic policies associated with Hua Guofeng (see Chapter 3), and its approach was no doubt shared by many top economic bureaucrats, such as Xue Muqiao, Ma Hong, and Liao Jili. Working under the recently adopted guidelines, the groups headed by such people soon produced work that emphasized the need for readjustment.

The primary example of this orientation was the important two-volume study of the Chinese economic structure produced under the general editorship of Ma Hong and Sun Shangqing.[57] This study recommended correcting the proportions between heavy industry and light industry by accelerating the development of the latter until each sector accounted for about half of industrial production (in

1978, heavy industry accounted for 57 percent of China's industrial production). At the same time, the study called for correcting imbalances within the heavy industrial sector so as to reduce the rate of growth of the steel and machine-building industries and increase the development of such basic industries as transportation and the energy sector. In addition, it called for implementing the responsibility system in agriculture and accelerating agricultural development through greater investment, greater diversification of crops, and increased cooperation among regions. Finally, it emphasized the need to raise the living standard of the people by reducing the accumulation rate, allowing more for consumption.[58]

There was nothing new in this approach. It was vintage Chen Yun. But the survey data generated under the auspices of Ma Hong and Sun Shangqing were a sharp indictment of the economic mismanagement that had occurred during the Cultural Revolution and was continuing with the support of Hua Guofeng.

One of the most interesting products of Ma Hong's group was China's first economic reform plan, "Preliminary Ideas on the Overall Reform of the Economic Management System," which was approved by the Economic Structural Reform Small Group Office of the State Council's Finance and Economic Commission.[59] This plan reflected, at least in part, the influence of the so-called four gentlemen: Huang Jiangnan, Wang Qishan, Weng Yongxi, and Zhu Jiaming. These four got to know each other through meetings of young intellectuals held in early 1979 at both the *Chinese Peasant Daily* (*Zhongguo nongminbao*) and the then newly established Marxism-Leninism Institute under CASS. Huang and Zhu were graduate students of Ma Hong and worked with him on the Economic Structural Reform Group. Weng became an editor of the *Chinese Peasant Daily*, where he came into contact with Du Runsheng, who brought him to the Policy Research Office of the State Agricultural Commission. He was later promoted very rapidly to the position of a deputy head of Du Runsheng's Rural Policy Office under the Central Secretariat and then, as noted in Chapter 1, was purged by Deng Xiaoping, who was angered at reports that Weng had criticized him during the Cultural Revolution. Wang Qishan was then working in CASS's Modern History Institute. The group had good connections. Both Huang and Weng were children of high-level cadres, and Wang Qishan, as the son-in-law of Vice Premier Yao Yilin, was the best connected of all.

Working within the framework of the reform proposals then being aired in Beijing, these four drafted a report that was intended to provide an overall conceptual framework for reform. As the first effort to define a direction for economic reform, the plan attracted considerable attention at high levels in Beijing. It was published in *Neibu wengao* (*Internal Reports*), the internal publication of the party theoretical journal *Hongqi* (*Red Flag*), in January 1980, as well as in *Neibu qingyang* (*Internal Situation*), a highly restricted publication intended for the use of China's top leadership. The report was subsequently praised by Chen Yun, making the "four gentlemen" famous among young intellectuals.

It also brought these four to the attention of some of China's top leaders, including Zhao Ziyang, who spent several hours discussing reform ideas with some of them.[60]

One by-product of the fame achieved by these four young intellectuals was to arouse the ambitions of many other young intellectuals. Having shown that it was possible for young people to participate meaningfully in China's reform, many others began to use their connections to become policy advisors. This was one impetus behind Chen Yizi's formation of the Chinese Rural Development Research Group. The good side of this youth movement was that it brought many bright, energetic young people into the reform movement, creating a countercurrent to the "crisis of faith" then (and later) being suffered by so many youth. The negative side was that in the resulting competition many young intellectuals or groups sought to advance their own careers at the expense of others'. Not infrequently, the political divisions at higher levels were replicated by those who sought to climb this very unbureaucratic ladder of success.

The analytic thrust of "Preliminary Ideas on the Overall Reform of the Economic Management System," like much of the discussion at the Wuxi Conference and Xue Muqiao's book, was that the core of reform must be to change the relationship between the political authorities and the enterprises. It juxtaposed this approach to two others that were being discussed in political circles at the time. The first approach, like previous efforts to change the economic system, centered around adjusting the relationship between the central government and the localities. There were those who wanted to adjust this relationship in favor of Beijing by strengthening the central government's control over the localities, and others who wanted to adjust it in the opposite direction by strengthening the role of the provinces. Indeed, much of the management of the economy in the period after the ouster of the Gang of Four revolved around this issue, mostly to the benefit of Beijing. For instance, Xue Muqiao noted in his book that in the previous couple of years, most documents issued by the center had "emphasized unified management."[61]

The other approach rejected by the reform plan was to discard the idea of adjusting relations between the center and the localities in favor of making the provinces the unit of planning. All enterprises would be given over to the localities, and the national government would be responsible only for such things as railroads, civil aeronautics, communication trunk lines, customs, and national defense. This approach was based on the expanded authority that had been granted on an experimental basis to Guangdong and Fujian provinces.

It is apparent from the text of this plan that those who favored readjusting the relationship between the government and the enterprises faced substantial challenges from both centralizers, who wanted to tighten up the planning system, and radical decentralizers, who favored greatly increasing the authority of the provinces. This situation would not change throughout the decade.[62]

While outlining an approach that, if implemented, would substantially reform the Chinese economic system, the proposal was notably cautious when it came to recommending implementation. No doubt reflecting both bureaucratic opposition to this sort of reform and Chen Yun's guideline that gave priority to readjustment over reform, the proposal emphasized the wide-ranging effects that reforming the relationship between the state and enterprises would have and China's inexperience in carrying out reform. It therefore concluded that if reform were put ahead of readjustment, then "not only would it be impossible to implement reform smoothly but it is also possible that the arrangements made for readjustment would be destroyed and the national economy would suffer unnecessary losses."[63] The thrust of the report thus differed significantly from the tenor of the Wuxi Conference.

Implementation of Reform Experiments

As the Wuxi Conference, Xue Muqiao's work, and the work of the study groups under the State Council demonstrated, the chief thrust of reform thinking in 1979 was to reform the economic system by redressing the relationship between the state and enterprises. Enterprises should be given greater decision-making authority as well as material incentives to stimulate their development. As this work also showed, there was already a sense that the twin tasks of readjustment and reform conflicted to a greater or lesser extent, a feeling that would become much more acute over the following year. Although, as noted above, this approach to reform was developed primarily by economic bureaucrats and establishment intellectuals, it was also true that those thinking about reform were responding to some extent to pressures from below, particularly from enterprises and local authorities who demanded greater authority to stimulate greater production.

At the central government level, such pressures received the most favorable hearing from the State Economic Commission (SEC), the organ most responsible for the day-to-day implementation of state plans. Unlike the State Planning Commission and the Ministry of Finance, whose planning and taxation tasks naturally led them to try to increase their control over enterprises, the SEC worked directly with enterprises on plan implementation and frequently shared the enterprises' own sense of frustration with the restrictions on enterprise behavior that undermined economic rationality and hurt production. The SEC thus became a bureaucratic force for increasing the decision-making authority of enterprises.[64]

As early as May 1979, the SEC and five other ministries issued a joint circular approving the selection of eight enterprises in three cities (Beijing, Tianjin, and Shanghai) to be given greater decision-making authority on a trial basis. Four months later, in July, the State Council approved five documents granting greater decision-making authority to a small number of enterprises.[65]

At the same time that the central government was beginning to approve pilot projects in enterprise reform, provinces such as Sichuan, Anhui, and Zhejiang took the lead in promoting enterprise reform at the local level. Of these, the most important was Sichuan, where Zhao Ziyang was party secretary (even after moving to Beijing, Zhao retained close ties with Sichuan). A brief look at both the theory and practice of enterprise reform in Sichuan Province shows that there were important differences between the way in which reform developed there and the incremental, top-down process of reform taking place in Beijing.

Two of the most important of Zhao's brain trusts on economic reform were Jiang Yiwei and Lin Ling, the former working in Beijing and the latter in Sichuan. Jiang had begun to study economic issues in 1953, when he became deputy director of the Policy Research Office under the First Ministry of Machine Building. He was very much influenced by the head of the ministry, Huang Jing, who was an early advocate of expanding enterprise authority. In 1959, Jiang was named a rightist and sent to a factory in Zhengzhou, Henan. He worked his way up from the workshop level, learning in a firsthand manner how enterprises worked. Jiang then taught economics in Hubei for two years before the Cultural Revolution broke out and he was named a black element. In 1978, Jiang finally returned to Beijing, becoming deputy director of CASS's Institute of Industrial Economics.[66]

In a highly controversial 1979 article, Jiang followed the same approach as He Jianzhang and others at the Wuxi Conference, but gave the argument for expanding enterprise authority a sharper twist by calling for an "enterprise-based economy."[67] In Jiang's views, enterprises should be independent (not relatively independent) entities, whose activities should be based on and motivated by their own material interests. In order to do this, Jiang argued, they must have the ability to purchase (or not to purchase) raw materials on the market, establish economic relations with other enterprises, establish wage rates, and even dismiss unproductive or superfluous workers. Contributing a new metaphor to Chinese economic discourse, Jiang argued that enterprises must be like the "living cells" (*xibao*) of an organism, not like the lifeless bricks of a huge building. Building a robust economy meant recognizing that enterprises have a life of their own and that the vitality of the total organism depended on the vitality of its cells. This is what Jiang meant when he called for an "enterprise-based economy."[68]

Although Jiang stated the case for independent enterprises as boldly and persuasively as anyone at that time, he nevertheless implicitly accepted certain limitations on that independence. "Under the socialist system," he wrote, "the interests of the part should be subordinated to those of the whole."[69] Although Jiang envisioned the state using indirect (i.e., legal and economic) means to control this conflict of interest, he clearly assumed that the free interplay of partial and "private" interests was ultimately incompatible with, or at the very least in tension with, the overall and "public" interests, and that it was the state's responsibility to harmonize these conflicting interests. This is a belief that has deep roots both in Chinese intellectual history and in Marxism, and it is not surprising to see that even as reform-minded a person as Jiang shared such ideas along with his more conservative counterparts—even though they disagreed on how serious a problem this was and how to respond to it. Nevertheless, such beliefs are suggestive of the failure of most reformers, particularly in the late 1970s and early 1980s but in many cases extending throughout the decade, to break with certain fundamental assumptions about the nature of state-society relations.[70]

The concepts of expanding enterprise authority and an enterprise-based economy were not simply theoretical explorations of possible approaches to reform; rather, they were being developed alongside efforts being undertaken in Sichuan, under Zhao Ziyang's personal guidance, to delegate greater authority. After being appointed first party secretary in Sichuan in 1975, Zhao took a personal interest in the research activities of the Sichuan Academy of Social Sciences. Perhaps foreshadowing the reliance he would put on think tanks after his move to Beijing, Zhao personally ordered the establishment of the Economics Institute under the academy, paying great attention to the people appointed there.[71]

In 1977, Zhao accompanied Hua Guofeng on the latter's trip to Eastern Europe and was particularly impressed by Yugoslavia's experiments with enterprise self-management. This was an important influence on Zhao's thinking about enterprise reform in Sichuan.[72] These experiments got under way in the fourth quarter of 1978, when the Sichuan provincial government granted expanded authority to six enterprises. At the time, the experiments were quite limited. Profit targets were fixed, and the factories were allowed to keep a limited amount of their profits above these quotas.[73] The Third Plenum decision in December 1978, which signaled an important victory for Deng Xiaoping, created a more favorable atmosphere for reform, and Sichuan extended its experiment to 100 industrial enterprises and 40 commercial enterprises. By 1981, expanded authority had been given to 417 industrial enterprises and 250 commercial enterprises.[74]

One of the people who worked closely with Zhao on this reform was Lin Ling, a close collaborator of Jiang Yiwei. During the 1940s, Lin had studied physics at Beijing Normal University, where he was involved in the communist underground. After graduating in 1948, he worked for a while as deputy chairman of the labor union at the Shijingshan Iron and Steel Factory (later the Capitol Iron and Steel Factory) before going to the Southwest, where he worked first in the Southwest Office of the General Labor Union and then, beginning in 1954, at the Chongqing Iron and Steel Company, where he rose to be party secretary. From 1958 to 1962 he worked at the Sichuan party committee's party journal, *Shangyou* (*Upriver*). After being forced to step down from this post in the early phase of the Cultural Revolution, he returned in 1972 to head the policy research office of the Sichuan party committee. In 1978, he was named vice president of the Sichuan Academy of Social Sciences, where he was in charge of organizing economic research. It was precisely at that time that Zhao was turning his attention to economic reform and the two gradually became well acquainted. Lin would continue to be one of Zhao's brain trusters until Zhao's ouster in 1989.[75]

Lin's concept of enterprise reform differed from that of many economists in Beijing in that he viewed expanding the decision-making authority of enterprises as the critical "breakthrough point" (*tupo kou*) in the reform of the economic structure. The essence of expanding enterprise authority, in Lin's view, was in a sense negative: it approached reform by removing the restraints on enterprises. With administrative restraints removed, enterprises would be capable of better production, both quantitatively and qualitatively. Perhaps more important, Lin viewed expanding enterprise authority as an important "bottom-up" impetus that would force administrative organs to respond as enterprises began operating more in accordance with economic laws. Thus, it was not necessary to negotiate or try to design a top-down reform, a project that Lin envisioned as leading to delay and unlikely to yield the same economic benefits as expanding enterprise authority. Moreover, Lin viewed expanding enterprise authority as minimizing the risk of major disruptions in the economic system (which could be brought about by a misguided attempt to reform the system from the top down). By starting with basic-level enterprises, reform could proceed both experimentally and in a step-by-step manner, reducing risks of disruption and allowing for corrections as reform proceeded.

Lin's advocacy of expanding enterprise authority was in conscious opposition to proposals then being considered that took a very different approach to reform (as discussed in Chapter 3). At the time, some people argued that what China needed was not further decentralization, which had been greatly extended throughout the course of the Cultural Revolution, but rather centralization. Some such proposals argued for the formation of specialized administrative companies that would bring related enterprises under unified administrative control, thus enhancing coordination among enterprises and rationalizing relations within a given economic sector. Lin refuted such proposals, arguing that they were not based on economic laws, since they would force enterprises into such hierarchies without regard to their individual economic interests. Moreover, such proposals did not address what Lin viewed as the fundamental problem of reform: providing enterprises with an *internal* motivation to expand production, improve efficiency, and cut costs.

Another intended effect of expanding enterprise authority was to pave the way for price reform. Lin, like most economists of the day, was keenly aware that the prevailing price structure in China was irrational. As Lin put it, "market regulation is in the final analysis a problem of price."[76] The prices of processed goods were too high while those of basic industrial goods and energy were too low. The result was that the profits of an enterprise did not reflect the quality of its management. Lin proposed to address this situation through a combination of price reform and tax reform. Looking at the early results of Sichuan reforms, Lin said that the old, rigid price structure was already being "pounded" by the expanded authority given to enterprises. As a result, four different kinds of prices had emerged: fixed price, floating price, negotiated price, and free price.[77] This opening up of the price system was gradually bringing about a more rational price system that better reflected the relative scarcity of goods. Because of the extreme sensitivity of price reform as an issue, Lin recommended proceeding with it gradually, using provisional methods such as adjusting the amount of profits that different factories should be allowed to retain and using adjustment taxes increasingly to better equalize the external conditions facing industry.[78]

By Lin's own testimony, the process of expanding enterprise authority in Sichuan encountered a number of problems as it was implemented—problems that were later mirrored in other areas. Reflecting on the first two years of reform in Sichuan, Lin pointed out that various problems had emerged in the initial reforms. In particular, the profit-retention system led to "whipping the fast ox," that is, punishing those who were more efficient. Under the profit-retention system, state quotas for profit delivery would increase as profits increased. If, for an example, an enterprise's initial target were set at profits of 1 million yuan but it earned profits of 1.5 million yuan, then its profit quota would be set at 1.5 million yuan the following year. Fearing that unforeseen difficulties might make it impossible to attain the ever-increasing profit targets, thus affecting their ability to retain profits, enterprises had an incentive not to exceed their profit quotas by very much. Thus, there was a tendency for enterprises to slow their production in the third and fourth quarters of the year. Moreover, although the profit-retention system did give enterprises an incentive to increase their profits, it could not deal with the problem of deficit enterprises. Enterprises would retain profits if they were profitable but the state would still have to cover deficits if they were not. In short, the profit-retention system did not deal effectively with "the big pot" system.[79]

In order to deal with such problems, Sichuan in 1980 began to experiment with enterprises that bore responsibility for their own profits and losses (ziying fukui). First undertaken in only five enterprises, the experiment was expanded to include ten industrial enterprises and ninety commercial enterprises in the second half of 1980. Under this system, instead of delivering profits to the state, the enterprises would pay taxes—an income tax (suode shui), an industrial and commercial tax (gongshang shui), and a fee for the use of fixed capital (guding zichan zhanyong fei)—at predetermined rates, which were fixed for a period of three years. After it had paid taxes, the profit that an enterprise retained would be divided into four funds: a production development fund, a collective welfare fund, an incentive fund, and a reserve fund. The linkage of profits to wages provided a strong incentive to increase production. The initial results of the experiment were satisfying. Among the five industrial enterprises that had implemented the system for all of 1980, production rose by 50 percent, profits rose by

30 percent, and tax payments rose by 50 percent. According to Lin, the economic results of this experiment were much better than they were under the profit retention system.[80]

The approach of Jiang Yiwei and Lin Ling had an impact not only on the enterprise experiments being conducted in Sichuan but also on enterprise reform in other parts of China. The Capitol Iron and Steel Factory was one of the first eight factories granted expanded decision-making authority by the State Economic Council in 1979. Its importance as a reform model derived from its size; it was one of the ten largest iron and steel factories in China and by far the largest of the eight experimental enterprises. In 1981, the Capitol Iron and Steel Factory, with the strong backing of Vice Premier Wan Li, negotiated a fifteen-year contract with the State Economic Commission that set a base figure against which its annual financial obligations to the state would be calculated (originally, it was to increase its profit payments to the state by 5 percent per year; a year later this figure was raised to 7.2 percent). In 1982, on the basis of a research report by Jiang and Lin, the Capital Iron and Steel Factory's experience was codified as a model of the "contract responsibility system" (or contracted management responsibility system, *chengbao jingying zirenzhi*).[81] In 1982, Hu Yaobang promoted the contract responsibility system, only to encounter serious problems. Zhao subsequently promoted a change of the profit-delivery system into a system in which taxes, instead of profits, would be paid, but in 1987 he supported the adoption of the contract responsibility system throughout the nation (see Chapters 4 and 7). Ironically, by that time, Jiang and Lin had abandoned their support of the contract responsibility system to become firm advocates of ownership reform.

Although the local experiments with enterprise reform begun in Sichuan and elsewhere were important laboratories of reform—and significant harbingers of future trends—what is striking about this early period is the degree to which the reform process was launched from and controlled by the center. In contrast to Wan Li's semi-covert subversion of the Dazhai model in Anhui, enterprise reform was launched by Hu Qiaomu's thoroughly vetted policy speech to the State Council and then followed by important theoretical efforts to define the approach and content of industrial reform. Moreover, the coordination of wide-ranging research efforts by the research groups under the Small Group for the Study of Economic Structural Reform stood in marked contrast to the far less coordinated, more informal lobbying process that characterized the course of rural reform. Though young intellectuals such as the four gentlemen could play some role in this process, there was no room for the sort of unofficial and later quasi-official role played by the Rural Development Group.

It also seems apparent that the process of rural reform was less ideological than that of early enterprise reform. The expression "crossing the river by feeling the stones," which was adopted by members of the Rural Development

Group, does convey the sense of the process of experimentation and incremental implementation that prevailed in the rural reforms. This was a strategy that appears to have been self-consciously adopted to defuse ideological questions that, had they been raised all at once at the beginning of the process, would have generated intense opposition and probably ended the process of rural reform. It was also a strategy that both recognized the obvious differences in rural conditions throughout the country and utilized them to implement reform in backward and mountainous areas, and then gradually extended them to other areas of the country.

In contrast, Hu Qiaomu's report to the State Council was drafted by Marxist-Leninist theoreticians, not economists or enterprise managers, and defended the reform program on theoretical grounds. Precisely because reform of the enterprise system was so closely related to the Dengist leadership's claim to power, defining and defending the task of enterprise reform in ideological terms was very important from the very beginning. There was no gathering comparable to the Wuxi Conference or book comparable to Xue Muqiao's *Studies on China's Socialist Economy* in the early stages of rural reform.

Specifically because enterprise reform raised theoretical questions about the nature of socialism, because the process of enterprise reform was controlled more tightly from the center than that of rural reform, and because the performance of the industrial sector was directly related to the revenues of the state and affected the state's ability to attain its goals, the center could halt or at least slow the process of enterprise reform in a way that was not possible in the countryside. Moreover, debate over the process of enterprise reform was directly related to the party's line and thus had a direct bearing on power relations at the center. In the period from 1980 to 1982, the center moved to emphasize economic readjustment over reform, and in the process, Chen Yun began to assert much greater influence over economic policy.

Notes

1. Reforms in Anhui and elsewhere had a substantial political impact on other locations and therefore generated considerable hostility, but they did not have a direct economic impact.

2. There had been similar seminars held at CASS in the 1950s and 1960s, but participants in those held in the late 1970s say that in scope and openness the late 1970s seminars were unprecedented. As noted in Chapter 1, *Weiding gao* not only published the article on the household responsibility system by Lu Xueyi, Jia Dexin, and Li Lanting, it also published Wang Xiaoqiang's controversial article on agrarian socialism.

3. This account of the Petroleum Group is based on Lieberthal and Oksenberg, *Policy Making in China*, pp. 169–206.

4. Barry Naughton, "The Third Front: Defence Industrialization in the Chinese Interior," *The China Quarterly*, no. 115 (September 1988), pp. 351–386.

5. Lieberthal and Oksenberg, *Policy Making in China*, p. 169.

6. On the "three poisonous weeds," see Baum, *Chinese Politics in the Age of Deng Xiaoping*, Chapter 1.

7. Li Xiannian's role in this period was recently confirmed in an eulogistic article by Cheng Zhensheng, who was part of the editorial group that produced *The Selected Works of Li Xiannian*. According to Cheng, Li was responsible, among other projects, for the 1.7-meter rolling mill of the Wuhan Iron and Steel Plant and the construction of the Baoshan Iron and Steel Plant, both of which were criticized for exemplifying the attitude of "production for production's sake" that was said to characterize the Petroleum Group. See Cheng Zhensheng, "Not Claiming Credit for Oneself, Not Putting the Blame on Others—Learning From Li Xiannian's Lofty Moral Character," *Qiushi*, no. 15 (August 1, 1992): 24–25, trans. FBIS, September 24, 1992, pp. 31–33.

8. Fang Weizhong, ed., *Zhongguo renmin gongheguo jingji dashiji (1949–1980)* (Record of Major Economic Events in the People's Republic of China, 1949–1980), pp. 603–604.

9. Ibid., p. 607.

10. Ibid., p. 610.

11. Hu Qiaomu, "Act in Accordance with Economic Laws, Step Up the Four Modernizations," Xinhua, October 5, 1987, trans. FBIS, October 11, 1978, pp. E1–22.

12. According to Baum, publication of this report was delayed by the opposition of Wang Dongxing. See Baum, *Politics in the Age of Deng Xiaoping*, Chapter 2.

13. Tan Zongji and Zheng Qian, eds., *Shinianhou de pingshuo*, p. 123. After Deng Xiaoping was purged, members of the research office were pressured to provide incriminating evidence against him. Deng Liqun steadfastly refused; Hu Qiaomu cooperated. In May 1977 Deng Xiaoping made light of Hu's criticism, saying "Qiaomu is still our number one pen" and that he should still be used. See Wang Zhen's notes of Deng Xiaoping's remarks to Deng Liqun. A handwritten copy is available in Harvard University's Fairbank Center.

14. Author's interviews.

15. Tsou, "Political Change and Reform: The Middle Course," p. 220.

16. Hu Qiaomu, "Act in Accordance with Economic Laws," p. E4.

17. Ibid., p. E5.

18. Ibid., p. E6.

19. Ibid., p. E7.

20. Sun Shangqing, "Guanyu jiazhi guilu zuoyong wenti taolunhui de choubei qingquang he huiyi de kaifa" (The Preparations for and Opening of the Symposium on the Role of the Law of Value), vol. 2, pp. 770–771.

21. This is not to say that everyone held the same view at the meeting. On the contrary, the essays presented to the meeting reveal a considerable range of opinion. Nevertheless, it seems fair to say that these opinions revolved around a series of essays, to be discussed below, that represented the main thrust of the meeting.

22. Those presenting their views were the Economic Research Office of the State Planning Commission, the Economics Institute of CASS, the Planning and Statistics Department of Chinese People's University, the General Office of the State Planning Commission, the State Statistical Bureau, the General Planning Bureau of the State Material Department, and the Finance Research Institute of the Ministry of Finance. See *Jingji yanjiu* (March 1979), pp. 61–71.

23. These ministries included the First Ministry of Machine Building, the Ministry of Metallurgy, Ministry of Coal Industry, Ministry of Forestry, State Construction Commission as well as economic departments from Beijing Municipality. See *Jingji yanjiu* (March 1979), pp. 61–71.

24. *Jingji yanjiu* (March 1979), pp. 61–71.

25. On the theory conference, see Goldman, "Hu Yaobang's Intellectual Network."

26. Xue Muqiao, "Jianchi baijia zhengming, jianchi lilun lianxi shiji" (Uphold a Hundred Schools of Thought Contending, Uphold Linking Theory to Reality). The reference to Deng's speech is on p. 5. Deng gave his well-known speech on upholding the four cardinal principles primarily in response to the vociferous critics of the Chinese political system raised at the Theory Conference to which his speech was given. Another factor prompting Deng's conservative turn at this time may have been his vulnerability to the criticism from other socialist states. It is said that while the Theory Conference was in session, Kim Il-sung made a secret visit to China and grilled Deng Xiaoping on whether or not he was intending to become another Khrushchev, whether or not he intended to uphold socialism, whether or not he would maintain the leading role of the Communist party, and so forth. Deng, whose power was not yet secure, feared that he would indeed be labeled another Khrushchev. Author's interviews.

27. Chen Yun, "Jihua yu shichang wenti" (The Question of Planning and Markets), p. 221. There is no note identifying the person or group to whom this letter was addressed.

28. Joseph Stalin, *Economic Problems of Socialism in the U.S.S.R.*

29. Ibid.

30. Sun's classic essay in this regard is "Ba jihua he tongji fang zai jiazhi guilu de jichu shang" (Place Planning and Statistics on the Foundation of the Law of Value). See also Barry Naughton, "Sun Yefang: Toward a Reconstruction of Socialist Economics."

31. See especially Xue Muqiao, "Shehui zhuyi jingji de jihua guanli" (The Planned Management of a Socialist Economy); Liu Guoguang and Zhao Renwei, "Lun shehui zhuyi jingji zhong jihua yu shichang de guanxi" (The Relationship Between Plan and Market in the Socialist Economy); He Jianzhang, "Woguo quanmin suoyouzhi jingji jihua guanli tizhi cunzai de wenti he gaige fangxiang" (The Problems of the Structure of Planned Management in China's System of Ownership by the Whole People and the Direction of Reform); Sun Shangqing, Chen Jiyuan, and Zhang Zhuoyuan, "Shehui zhuyi jingji de jihuaxing yu shichangxing xiang jiehe de jige lilun wenti" (Several Theoretical Questions of Integrating the Planned and Market Natures of the Socialist Economy); and idem., "Zai lun shehui zhuyi jingji de jihuaxing yu shichangxing xiang jiehe" (Another Discussion of Integrating the Planned and Market Natures of the Socialist Economy).

32. Liu Guoguang and Zhao Renwei, "Shehui zhuyi jingji zhong jihua he shichang xiang jiehe de biranxing" (The Inevitability of Integrating Plan and Market in the Socialist Economy), p. 48.

33. Sun Shangqing, Chen Jiyuan, and Zhang Zhuoyuan, "Shehui zhuyi jingji de jihuaxing yu shichangxing xiang jiehe de jige lilun wenti," and idem., "Zai lun shehui zhuyi jingji de jihuaxing yu shichangxing xiang jiehe."

34. See in particular He Jianzhang, "Woguo quanmin suoyouzhi jingji jihua guanli tizhi cunzai de wenti he gaige fangxiang." In arguing that the expansion of enterprise authority was the necessary first step in reform, Sun, Chen, and Zhang put forth the practical argument that any attempt to implement reform from the top down would inevitably bog down in bureaucratic argument and indecision. They maintained that bureaucratic impediments to reform could best be broken down by expanding enterprise autonomy, forming markets, and letting the bureaucracy respond to the new needs of the economy.

35. See Xue Muqiao, "Shehui zhuyi jingji de jihua guanli"; He Jianzhang, "Woguo quanmin suoyouzhi jingji jihua guanli tizhi cunzai de wenti he gaige fangxiang"; Sun Shangqing, Chen Jiyuan, and Zhang Zhuoyuan, "Shehui zhuyi jingji de jihuaxing yu shichangxing xiang jiehe de jige lilun wenti"; and idem., "Zai lun shehui zhuyi jingji de

jihuaxing yu shichangxing xiang jiehe," respectively; and Liu Chengrui, Hu Naiwu, and Yu Guanghua, "Jihua he shichang xiang jiehe shi woguo jingji guanli gaige de jiben tujing" (Integration of Planning and Market Is the Fundamental Path of China's Economic Management Reform).

36. See especially Tang Zongkun, "Jiazhi guilu, shichang jizhi he shehui zhuyi jihua jingji" (The Law of Value, the Market Mechanism, and the Socialist Planned Economy). See also the rebuttals to both "conservative" and "liberal" criticisms in Sun Shangqing, Chen Jiyuan, and Zhang Zhuoyuan, "Zai lun shehui zhuyi jingji de jihuaxing yu shichangxing xiang jiehe."

37. Sun Shangqing, Chen Jiyuan, and Zhang Zhuoyuan, "Shehui zhuyi jingji de jihuaxing yu shichangxing xiang jiehe de jige lilun wenti," p. 102.

38. He Jianzhang, "Woguo quanmin suoyouzhi jingji jihua guanli tizhi cunzai de wenti he gaige fangxiang," pp. 74–95.

39. Liu Guoguang and Zhao Renwei, "Lun shehui zhuyi jingji zhong jihua yu shichang de guanxi"; He Jianzhang, "Woguo quanmin suoyouzhi jingji jihua guanli tizhi cunzai de wenti he gaige fangxiang"; and Sun Shangqing, Chen Jiyuan, and Zhang Zhuoyuan, "Shehui zhuyi jingji de jihuaxing yu shichangxing xiang jiehe de jige lilun wenti."

40. Dong Fureng, "Guanyu woguo shehui zhuyi suoyouzhi xingshi wenti" (The Form of Socialist Ownership in China), especially pp. 22, 25, and 26.

41. Author's interviews. Liu's views on ownership reform are discussed below.

42. Cited in Deng Liqun, "Zhengque chuli jihua jingji he shichang tiaojie zhi jian de guanxi" (Correctly Handle the Relation Between the Planned Economy and Market Regulation), p. 79. Deng goes on to note that in a talk he had given to a research group sponsored by the State Economic Commission in March 1979, he had said that there should be "strict planned regulation for that part of production and construction that is necessary for society and affects the national livelihood; apart from this, there should be market regulation." In other words, in the spring of 1979, Deng, like Chen Yun, accepted a much greater role for the market economy and the use of the terms "planned regulation" and "market regulation." Two years later, both would reject this terminology for implying that plan and market were equal. See below, Chapter 3.

43. Wu Kaitai, "Qiushi he yanjin de makesi zhuyi jingji xuejia—Xue Muqiao zhuanlue" (A Truth-Seeking and Serious Marxist Economist—A Brief Biography of Xue Muqiao), p. 254.

44. According to Xue Muqiao, senior economists Xu Qiao and Wu Shuqing helped in the writing of some parts of the original draft, while Su Xing, He Jianzhang, Xu Xueben, and Wu Kaitai joined in the discussions and revisions that produced the final draft. In addition, Xue thanks many other economists, including Ma Hong, Ji Chongwei, Liao Jili, Yang Peixin, Liao Suinian, Liu Guoguang, Zhou Shulian, Wang Haibo, and Wu Jinglian, who contributed ideas to the final version. See Xue Muqiao, *Zhongguo shehui zhuyi jingji wenti yanjiu* (Studies on China's Socialist Economy), pp. 12 and 271–272.

45. Ibid., p. 183.

46. Ibid., See also pp. 192–195.

47. Ibid., p. 198.

48. Ibid, p. 105. See also p. 261, where Xue writes that "it is necessary to recognize that exchange between state-managed enterprises fully has the nature of commodity exchange," thereby again stopping short of stating that such exchange is of a commodity nature.

49. Ibid., pp. 7–10. Apparently reflecting the fluidity of theoretical discussions at that time, Xue not only employed these two terms but also referred to Chinese socialism as "not completely mature and perfected socialism." See, for instance, p. 204.

50. Su Shaozhi and Feng Lanrui, "Wuchan jieji qude zhengquan hou de shehui fazhan jieduan wenti" (The Question of Developmental Stages Following the Proletariat's Attainment of Political Power).

51. Zhu Shuxian, "Ye tan wuchan jieji qude zhengquan hou de shehui fazhan jieduan wenti" (Also Discussing the Question of Developmental Stages Following the Proletariat's Attainment of Political Power).

52. "Resolution on Certain Questions in the History of Our Party Since the Founding of the PRC."

53. The need for such a meeting, given the just concluded Wuxi Conference, is not clear, although the proposed status as a theoretical work conference might have given it additional weight. See Yao Yilin, "Tongxin xieli zuohao jingji gaige de diaocha yanjiu" (Unify to Investigate Well Economic Reform), p. 1.

54. Deng Liqun, "Guanyu jingji wenti de diaocha yanjiu" (On Investigating Economic Problems), p. 8.

55. On the establishment of the three groups, see Yao Yilin, "Tongxin xieli zuohao jingji gaige de diaocha yanjiu," pp. 2–3. See also Zhongguo baike nianjian, 1980, p. 292; and Nina Halpern, "Making Economic Policy: The Influence of Economists," pp. 137–140. The listing of heads of the groups given here differs somewhat from that given in Hamrin, China and the Challenge of the Future, pp. 34–35.

56. On Yu Guangyuan suggesting the establishment of this group, see Yao Yilin, "Tongxin xieli zuohao jingji gaige de diaocha yanjiu," p. 5. Yao says that after Yu proposed this group, "we agreed," apparently referring to the Central Finance and Economic Commission, of which he was a leading member. On Dong's participation, see Hamrin, China and the Challenge of the Future, p. 35.

57. Ma Hong and Sun Shangqing, eds., Zhongguo jingji jiegou wenti yanjiu (Studies on the Chinese Economic Structure). The afterword to this study says that the economic structure group (headed by Ma Hong and Sun Shangqing) brought together over 700 people to study the economic structure of China and that a report based on their research was produced in May 1980. The two-volume study that was subsequently published was based on this research.

58. See especially the preface and first chapter (Zhou Shulian, "Sanshi nian lai woguo jingji jiegou de huigu" [Looking Back on China's Economic Structure Over the Past Thirty Years]) of Ma Hong and Sun Shangqing, eds., Zhongguo jingji jiegou wenti yanjiu. On adopting the policy of readjustment, see Dorothy J. Solinger, From Looms to Lathes: China's Industrial Policy in Comparative Perspective, pp. 96–103.

59. Office of the Economic Structural Reform Group of the State Council Finance and Economic Commission, "Guanyu jingji tizhi gaige de chubu yijian" (Preliminary Ideas on the Overall Reform of the Economic Management System).

60. Author's interviews.

61. Xue Muqiao, Zhongguo shehui zhuyi jingji wenti yanjiu, p. 200.

62. Office of the Economic Structural Reform Group of the State Council Finance and Economic Commission, "Guanyu jingji tizhi gaige de chubu yijian." Liu Guoguang and Wang Ruisun similarly outlines the policy fault lines at that time in "Restructuring the Economy," pp. 84–85. It is sobering to note how much of this debate remains hidden from the view of outside observers. What can be traced in academic publications and the general media are arguments about the role of enterprises that were supported by reformers. The arguments of those who advocated centralization or expanding the approach taken in Guangdong and Fujian do not appear in publicly available sources.

63. Office of the Economic Structural Reform Group of the State Council Finance and Economic Commission, "Guanyu jingji guanli tizhi gaige zongti shexiang de chubu yijian," p. 17.

64. The State Economic Commission was also responsible for the allocation of funds for technological transformation, which meant that enterprises could frequently bargain directly with the SEC, agreeing to comply with its demands if the SEC would grant them greater technological transformation funds in the future. The SEC and enterprises thus

developed a symbiotic relationship (though not one that was free of tension), and the SEC frequently expressed the position of enterprises at high-level government meetings.

65. The documents were "Some Regulations on Expanding the Economic Management Authority of State-Managed Industrial Enterprises," "Regulations on Implementing Profit Retention in State-Managed Enterprises," "Provisional Regulations on Collecting the Fixed-Assets Tax in State-Managed Industrial Enterprises," "Provisional Regulations on Increasing the Depreciation Rate on Fixed Assets in State-Managed Industrial Enterprises and Methods for Improving the Use of the Depreciation Fund," and "Provisional Regulations on Using Bank Loans for All Circulating Capital in State-Managed Industrial Enterprises." See Gao Shangquan, *Zhongguo de jingji tizhi gaige* (China's Economic Structural Reform), pp. 324–325.

66. See the biography of Jiang in his book *From Enterprise-Based Economy to Economic Democracy*, which is published in both Chinese and English.

67. "Qiye benwei lun" (On an Enterprise-Based Economy). Jiang's article first appeared in a shorter form in *Jingji guanli* in June 1979, and it was later expanded and published in *Zhongguo shehui kexue* in 1980. It has since been republished in several places. See Jiang Yiwei, *Jingji tizhi gaige he qiye guanli ruogan wenti de tansuo* (An Exploration of Several Problems in Economic Structural Reform and Enterprise Management), pp. 3–35.

68. Jiang Yiwei, "Qiye benwei lun." Xue Muqiao also refers to enterprises as cells in his book *Zhongguo shehui zhuyi jingji wenti yanjiu* (see p. 57). Whether he borrowed this usage from Jiang or whether it was in general currency in intellectual discussions is not clear, but Jiang appears to have utilized the concept more fully to support his notion of an enterprise-based economy.

69. Jiang Yiwei, "Qiye benwei lun," p. 34.

70. See Andrew J. Nathan, *Chinese Democracy*; and Joseph Fewsmith, "The Dengist Reforms in Historical Perspective."

71. Author's interviews.

72. Ibid.

73. Lin Ling, "Jingji tizhi gaige de lianghao kaiduan" (A Good Start in Economic Structural Reform) p. 12; and Lin Ling, ed., *Sichuan jingji tizhi gaige* (Economic Structural Reform in Sichuan), pp. 10–48.

74. Lin Ling, "Zhongguo jingji tizhi gaige zai Sichuan de shiyan" (The Experiments with Chinese Economic Structural Reform in Sichuan), p. 106; and Lin Ling, ed., *Sichuan jingji tizhi gaige*, pp. 10–48.

75. On Lin Ling's career, see *Chao liu*, no. 32, October 15, 1989, pp. 23–25.

76. Lin Ling, "Zhongguo jingji tizhi gaige zai Sichuan de shiyan," p. 208.

77. Ibid.

78. Lin Ling, "Guanyu jingji gaige zhong de jige wenti" (Several Problems in Economic Reform), p. 52.

79. Lin Ling, "Sichuan jingji tizhi gaige tichulai de xin keti" (New Problems Brought Out by Sichuan's Economic Structural Reform), p. 218.

80. Ibid., pp. 218–219.

81. See Jiang Yiwei and Lin Ling, "Cong Shoudu gangtie gongce kan tizhi gaige" (Looking at Structural Reform from the Perspective of the Capitol Iron and Steel Company), pp. 89–101. See also Jiang Yiwei, "Shougang zai gaige zhong kuabu qianjin" (Capitol Iron and Steel Company Taking Large Steps in Reform). There are several special features of the contract responsibility system adopted by Capitol Iron and Steel. In particular, the contract was (at least nominally) with the whole body of workers rather than the management alone (as was the case with many of the contracts in 1987). Under this approach, there is a contract system within the factory so that every workshop and individual worker is bound by the terms of the

contract. Moreover, the profit retained by the factory is to be spent in the following proportions: 60 percent on developing production, 20 percent on collective welfare, and 20 percent on wages and bonuses. Wages are linked to profits, so that wages increase 0.8 percent for every 1 percent increase in profits. For details on Capitol Iron and Steel's contract responsibility system, see *Shougang zhubian hua chengbao* (Major Changes in Capitol Iron and Steel Company Under the Contract Responsibility System) and the March 1991 issue of *Xuexi yu yanjiu* (Study and Research).

3

From Reform to Readjustment

The Wuxi Conference and the early experiments in enterprise reform were important in articulating an approach to reform and in testing that approach, however tentatively, against reality. The exigencies of economic management, however, forced those working in the research groups under Zhang Jingfu's supervision to direct their attention toward readjustment, redressing proportional imbalances in the Chinese economy by directing more resources to weak sectors such as agriculture and light industry. For some senior economic bureaucrats, such as Xue Muqiao, readjustment was seen as a way of preparing the conditions for reform rather than as a goal in itself. For others, however, readjustment represented a policy direction in and of itself, and starting in late 1979, such people began to gain in influence.

The growing influence of those who favored readjustment came in the context of the ongoing struggle for control over economic policy between Chen Yun and his followers on the one hand and the Petroleum Group on the other. Even though the April 1979 Central Work Conference endorsed the call for readjustment, the Petroleum Group continued to hold considerable influence. Yu Qiuli, for instance, continued to head the powerful State Planning Commission. Calls for readjustment, including sharp reductions in capital construction, grew louder as state revenues continued to lag seriously behind expenditures. In 1979, falling revenues and increased expenditures resulted in a budget deficit of 17 billion yuan (compared with a budget surplus of 1 billion yuan the previous year), and in 1980 a deficit of 12 billion yuan. Such deficits and mounting inflationary pressures (in 1980 the cost of living for urban residents increased by about 5.5 percent over the year before) would be used to bring about the ouster of Yu Qiuli and the Petroleum Group in the fall of 1980.[1]

As supporters of readjustment increased their influence in late 1979 and early 1980, however, they directed their attack not only against the Petroleum Group but also against reformers, particularly Jiang Yiwei, who became a favorite target of pro-readjustment policy advocates. As the influence of readjusters grew in the 1980–82 period, they levied a barrage of criticism against the approach to reform that had been articulated at the Wuxi Conference—despite the fact that Chen Yun had given his support for the general direction taken at that conference. Moderate reformers like CASS economist Liu Guoguang were forced to backtrack. By late 1982, the atmosphere for reform was much less open than it had been three years earlier; those in favor of readjustment had emerged as politically and ideologically ascendant.

This cycle of reform and retrenchment,[2] which occurred not only in the economic realm but also in the ideological sphere, contrasts sharply with the continued development of rural reform from 1979 to 1982. As pointed out at the end of Chapter 1, efforts to curtail rural reform had little effect, but similar efforts with regard to the industrial economy were much more successful. The contrast between the ongoing and highly successful process of rural reform and the continued assertion of central economic and ideological controls in the realm of the urban industrial economy generated sharp differences of opinion within the CCP leadership, leading to the campaign against "spiritual pollution" in the fall of 1983 and then to the critical decision on economic reform that was adopted in the fall of 1984.

Those who favored readjustment looked to Chen Yun for intellectual and political leadership. Chen Yun's views can properly be called "conservative" in the sense that he sought to "conserve" what he saw as the essential elements of the Marxist-Leninist party-state that had been created in China during the preceding three decades. With regard to economic policy, Chen's conservative approach needs to be clearly distinguished from "Stalinism." Chen's views took shape in the mid-1950s precisely as a critique of Stalinism. Chinese conservatives consider themselves to be realists who take the "national conditions" of China—especially its large population, limited financial resources, and geographic size and diversity—into account. What conservatives objected to in the Stalinist approach was, first, the overemphasis on heavy industry to the neglect of agriculture, light industry, and the people's standard of living, and, second, the neglect of the law of value. They believed that a more balanced approach to economic development would ultimately bring about faster growth than a one-sided emphasis on heavy industry (which they believed to be responsible for the sharp ups and downs in China's economic development) and provide a better basis for political stability. Although strong believers in planning, conservatives felt that there was room for market forces, particularly with regard to China's rural areas and consumer goods. This approach to planning recognized the limitations on planning in China. Its adherents believed that a plan that focused on essentials—the proper balance among economic sectors and the production and supply of essential products—would prove to be better than a plan that attempted to be all-inclusive.[3]

Chen's economic thought took shape in the mid-1950s, particularly in response to the economic problems associated with the "little leap" of 1956 and preparations for the formulation of the Second Five-Year Plan. In June of 1956, Chen Yun called for an economic slowdown, and in a series of speeches that fall, including his address to the Eighth Party Congress in September, he warned against "rashness" and excessive construction. The urge to do too much too quickly, Chen said, was leading to shortages of goods and inflationary pressures.[4]

These warnings against "reckless advance" (*ji cao chong jin*) were summed up in Chen's famous January 1957 speech to party secretaries of provinces, autonomous areas, and special municipalities. Called "The Scale of Construction Should Be Compatible with National Strength," Chen's speech warned: "The scale of construction must be suited to the national financial and material capacity. Whether it is suited or not determines whether there is economic stability or instability. . . . There will be rashness and economic chaos if the scale of construction exceeds the national and financial capacity." Chen argued that economic development must be "balanced." Specifically there should be a balance between financial revenue and expenditure, between bank loans and repayment of credit, and between the supply and demand of goods and materials.[5] Summarized as the "three great balances," this view emphasized the intimate links among different sectors of the economy; heavy industry could not forge ahead at the expense of agriculture and light industry, and accumulation could not squeeze out consumption. The key to maintaining these balances was proper planning and finance, said Chen, particularly by the Ministry of Finance.

Chen's thought was not opposed to reform. Chen clearly supported the early rural reforms and, at least in 1979, supported greater reliance on market mechanisms and the general thrust of the critique of the existing economic system that had been put forth at the Wuxi Conference. There were issues on which Chen clearly disagreed with Deng Xiaoping. He opposed the creation of Special Economic Zones, for instance, and he would later split with Deng on the issue of hiring labor. Whereas Deng was willing to countenance both a more concerted and far-reaching assault on the traditional system of economic management, the more cautious Chen favored strengthening and improving the economic management system even while allowing greater scope for market forces.

Those who looked to Chen for leadership accepted that there were problems in the planning system, that it was impossible to have a comprehensive plan covering all goods, that it was necessary to introduce market forces, and that enterprises should have greater decision-making authority. Their acceptance of these ideas, however, was conditioned by their fundamental belief that "comprehensive balance" (*zonghe pingheng*) was the key to all economic work, and that maintaining a comprehensive balance required a strong role for the central government in matters of pricing and taxation. Moreover, they believed that planning was absolutely necessary. As we shall see below, this approach was based on a fundamentally different view of the "law of value" than that espoused by the reform-minded economists who attended the Wuxi Conference—not to mention the far more radical economists who would emerge in the latter half of the decade.

Chen Yun's Call for Economic Readjustment

Almost immediately after Chen's return to power, he began to challenge the policy direction charted by the Petroleum Group. He called for economic readjustment in the October 1978 Central Work Conference, and he repeated that call in January 1979, criticizing the gaps that had been left in the plan for that year. As a result of a March 1979 meeting of the State Construction Commission, 222 large and medium-sized projects were stopped. Nevertheless, because those projects that were stopped were relatively small, and a number of large projects were started, in-budget investment in capital construction did not decline significantly, remaining above 15 billion yuan.[6]

On March 14, 1979, with the establishment of the Finance and Economics Commission of the State Council, chief responsibility for economic policy making was turned over to Chen. But Chen's control was far from complete. Politburo member Li Xiannian, the chief political supporter of the Petroleum Group, was named vice chairman of the commission.[7] In an apparent compromise document, Chen Yun and Li Xiannian, on behalf of the new commission, addressed a letter to the Central Committee. They declared that there was a "relatively serious" imbalance in the economy and that it was necessary to spend two to three years on readjustment in order to correct it.[8]

A week later, on March 21, Chen Yun forcefully reiterated his view that retrenchment and readjustment were the first priorities for China's economy. Addressing a Politburo meeting called to discuss the 1979 plan and the problem of readjustment, Chen criticized the July–September 1978 State Council theoretical meeting (*wu xu hui*) for not allowing an airing of divergent opinions and for not viewing realistically the weaknesses in the Chinese economy. Chen called for reducing the number of large and medium-sized capital construction projects, closing a number of inefficient small plants, and concentrating greater resources on improving people's livelihood. Chen also singled out the Ministry of Metallurgy—then headed by Yu Qiuli's associate Tang Ke—for special criticism. According to Chen, "The Ministry of Metallurgy, first of all, views problems too simply, and, second, views problems in an isolated fashion."[9]

The policy of readjustment was officially adopted at a Central Work Conference convened from April 5 to 28, 1979. Addressing the opening session of the conference, Li Xiannian laid out the official position that despite the rapid recovery of the economy in the previous two years, the fundamental imbalances in the economy had not yet been straightened out. Revealing that state finances were tight—revenue collections in the first quarter of 1979 were 5.3 percent below those for the same period of the year before—Li officially proposed the policy orientation of "readjustment, reform, consolidation, and improvement" (*tiaozheng, gaige, zhengdun, tigao*). In accordance with this orientation, Li called for the number of large and medium-sized capital construction projects to be reduced from over 1,700 to under 1,000 and proposed that target quotas for such heavy industrial products as steel be lowered. He also criticized excessive reliance on foreign loans for purchasing technology and complete plants, saying that "to place all of our hopes on foreign loans is unreliable and dangerous."[10]

The official adoption of the policy of readjustment was important. More resources were diverted to agriculture as procurement prices were increased and to light industry, which was encouraged to develop more rapidly. However, these policies, which did contribute to bringing about a more balanced economy, were not matched by cutbacks in capital construction, about which leadership opinion—despite Li Xiannian's apparent endorsement of Chen's views—remained divided. Although Chen Yun headed the Finance and Economics Commission, those favoring heavy industry—including Yu Qiuli, Gu Mu, and Kang Shien—were well represented on it. As a result, spending on capital construction did not decrease significantly, as noted above. Moreover, the decisions to raise the procurement price for grain by 20 percent and to raise the wages of workers—decisions which were consistent with the policy endorsed by Deng and Chen of trying to improve the livelihood of the people and to stimulate their productive "enthusiasm"—greatly increased expenditures. Together the failure to decrease expenditure on capital construction and the increase in expenditures for agricultural produce and wages led to a 17 billion yuan deficit in 1979.

Despite the gloomy budget picture that was emerging by the fall of 1979, the State Planning Commission proposed that in-budget capital construction for 1980 be set at 25 billion yuan and that the 4 billion yuan of funds needed for investment related to twelve complete plants that were being imported come from foreign loans that would be separated from China's domestic budget. This plan, which left a budget deficit of several billion yuan and a gap of U.S. $8.9 billion between expenditures and receipts of foreign exchange, drew a sharp rebuke from Chen Yun. Chen reiterated his belief that capital construction could not proceed on the basis of fiscal deficits, and he labeled the idea of foreign exchange being separated from the domestic budget as "impossible."[11]

Not surprisingly, the senior economic bureaucrats working under Zhang Jingfu's leadership supported Chen Yun's year-long crusade to implement economic retrenchment. Xue Muqiao's essays in this period increasingly emphasized readjustment, and top economic bureaucrats such as Ma Hong and Liao Jili also offered strong support for it.[12] But there were differences in approach toward readjustment between reformers and conservatives. These became apparent in debates in late 1979 and early 1980 that were kicked off by the "discussion of the aims of socialist production."

This discussion was initiated in October 1979 by a Contributing Commentator article in *People's Daily* that sharply but implicitly criticized the Petroleum Group. This article was written by Wu Zhenkun, then of the Central Party School, suggesting that Hu Yaobang played an important role in inaugurating this debate. The article criticized the traditional planning system, saying that it concentrated on the production of a few key goods to the neglect of the people's standard of living. The whole planning process, the article complained, had been centered around the needs of heavy industry, especially steel, with the result that "heavy industry has served itself a great deal but has served agriculture, light industry, and the people's livelihood very little." This orientation, the article continued, had brought about "production for the sake of production," ignoring the proper "aims of socialist production," namely, satisfying the "ever increasing material and cultural needs of the whole society." This tendency to "blindly seek high targets" and squeeze out the consumption needs of the people, the article said, was a manifestation of "leftist" ideology. Anticipating a theme that would become prominent in the latter half of the 1980s, the article criticized "some comrades" for "failing to see the role played by consumption in promoting production."[13]

The discussion on the aims of socialist production was closely associated with Yu Guangyuan, then the deputy director of the State Science and Technology Commission, a vice president of CASS, and a protégé of party secretary Hu Yaobang. Yu contributed a lengthy article on the subject to *People's Daily* on October 23 and then followed up with a lengthier version of the same article that was published in the leading economic journal, *Jingji yanjiu*. Yu clearly laid out an agenda for reform of the economic system by juxtaposing three different approaches to planning: the "resource approach," the "departmental approach," and the "end-products approach." The first approach—clearly intended to describe the type of planning favored by Chen Yun—proposed planning on the basis of the objectively available national resources, while the second approach—that which had in fact dominated policy making and was associated with the Petroleum Group—was based on drawing up targets for products in various sectors of the economy.

Rejecting these two approaches to planning, Yu then laid out an approach based on end products—a concept that obviously built on Western economic notions of final demand (although Yu denied that they were analogous concepts). The end products that were intended to drive the planning process included "most importantly" consumer goods for individuals but also goods for such other sectors as science, education, national defense, and export. In short, in attacking the Petroleum Group's approach to planning, Yu proposed an economic system that gave much greater weight to the market and consumer demand. The differences between Yu Guangyuan's conception of the economy and Chen Yun's approach to planning became apparent as conservative economists associated with Chen campaigned vigorously to implement a policy of readjustment.[14]

Xu Yi and the Campaign to Implement Readjustment

The person most publicly associated with the campaign to implement Chen Yun's vision of readjustment was Xu Yi, the influential head of the Ministry of Finance's Economic Research Institute. For Xu, the first three decades of the

PRC's history vividly demonstrated the correctness of Chen Yun's economic approach. The economy had done well in the first years of the PRC, especially during the early part of the First Five-Year Plan (1953–57). In 1956, however, with the completion of the socialist transformation, a mood of "reckless advance" had taken over and investment in basic construction and agriculture had become excessive at the same time that the numbers of workers and their wages had increased too quickly.[15] It was after this "little leap forward" that Chen Yun had articulated his view that the scale of capital construction must be kept within the bounds of the national strength and the corresponding thesis of the "three great balances." For Xu, the rapid and correct response of financial authorities in 1957 to the problems that had developed the year before proved the "responsiveness" of the socialist financial mechanism.[16]

In 1957, however, the antirightist movement had spilled over into criticism of financial work, and the "three great balances" were criticized as "negative balances." This leftist tide of thought led to the Great Leap Forward and disastrous financial and economic consequences, which ultimately had to be corrected through the retrenchment policies that were adopted in 1961 and codified in the eight-character principle of "readjustment, consolidation, supplementation, and improvement" (*tiaozheng, gonggu, chongshi, tigao*) that was officially adopted in the following year. The success of this period of readjustment was, in Xu's opinion, due to the success of financial organs "strictly guarding the pass" (*yange baguan*).[17] This period was also marked by a new level of thinking about and systematization of financial theory. In 1964 the First Theoretical Symposium on Finance was convened in Dalian, and the "three great balances" were a central point of discussion.[18] In 1965, the Second Theoretical Symposium on Finance was held in Beijing, and participants discussed creating a unified, level-by-level control system for managing China's economy.[19]

The positive effect of this period, in both theory and practice, was subsequently wiped out by the Cultural Revolution, when the Ministry of Finance was reduced to only "several tens" of people and unified fiscal control became out of the question. The Cultural Revolution destroyed not only the balance between accumulation and consumption but also the appropriate proportions among agriculture, light industry, and heavy industry. The one-sided emphasis on heavy industry had distorted China's economic growth, placing a heavy burden on finance, as well as preventing the people's living standard from increasing.[20] Moreover, the Cultural Revolution had destroyed the relationship between the "bones" (productive construction) and the "flesh" (nonproductive construction). It was important to maintain such things as the growth of housing as well as steel production "bones."[21]

There was a critical difference between this view of Chinese economic history and that held by moderate reformers such as Liu Guoguang, Chen Jiyuan, and He Jianzhang (much less more radical reformers such as Jiang Yiwei and Lin Ling).[22] At the Wuxi Conference, such reformers had argued that there were fundamental problems in the Chinese economic management system, problems that were not reducible to the interference of "leftists." The reason why Liu and others argued for increasing the "relative independence" of enterprises was that, in their view, the cycle of centralization and decentralization—the so-called *tiaotiao kuaikuai* problem (the problem of coordinating control between vertical administrative hierarchies and horizontal, geographic units)—could never be solved unless the relationship between enterprises and the state was addressed and changed. Similarly, Liu's and others' criticism of the board-and-plank model of integrating plan and market was based on a fundamentally different conception of the role of planning in society; market forces needed to be brought into the planned sector of the economy, and planning, in the sense of forecasting and industrial planning, had to be extended to the market-dominated sector of the economy. It was on this basis that they had called for the reduction of mandatory planning in favor of guidance planning.

In contrast, conservatives such as Xu Yi were arguing that there was nothing inherently wrong with the economic system itself; the success of the First Five-Year Plan and the three-year economic readjustment period proved that the economic system could function well. The problem was that "leftist" policies had frequently prevailed, with the result that incorrect macroeconomic policies had been adopted.[23] The lesson for Xu and like-minded people was that balanced and stable economic growth required firm, scientific, and planned central control. Financial work was the key to this, and maintaining "comprehensive balance" was the key task in financial work. The key to maintaining a comprehensive balance was to set an appropriate ratio between accumulation and consumption and then stick to it.[24]

A central issue on which reformers such as Liu Guoguang differed from conservatives such as Xu Yi was that of the law of value. Whereas reformers believed that utilizing the law of value to manage the economy necessarily meant adjusting prices so that they more closely reflected their relative scarcity, conservatives argued that "conscious" use of the law of value meant using the difference between "price" and "value" to direct production and consumption along paths desired by the party and state. In other words, conservatives such as Xu Yi believed that it was right and proper for prices not to reflect relative scarcity; if they did, prices would be set by the market "spontaneously," and economic development would be "blind." "Will it do if the law of value plays its role spontaneously?" Xu asked, and then answered his own question with a firm, "It will not." The whole point of a planned economy, in Xu's view, was to develop the economy in the direction that the state deemed to be in the long-term best interest of society, which necessarily meant overriding the short-term, partial interests of society. It was on this basis that Xu sharply criticized economists who, when discussing the law of value, emphasized only the exchange of goods at equal value and the general principle of price adhering to value.[25]

Xu tried to balance local initiative with centralized direction of the economy. Perhaps as a result of his decades of work in the Ministry of Finance, he was aware that the Chinese economy was too large and complex to be run effectively by means of a detailed plan. What Xu urged was drawing up a long-term plan (*gui hua*) that would specify the proper proportions among various economic sectors and set developmental tasks for each geographic area of the country. With such an overall plan, it would be unnecessary for the central government to approve each item of construction; it would suffice for the state to inspect and ensure that the projects being done by the various regions were in accord with the predetermined developmental plan. The state could focus its attention on the implementation of the long-term plan. This was Xu's solution to the old *tiaotiao kuaikuai* problem; there would be both concentration of authority and management and also a division of labor and responsibility. The old cycle of centralization and stagnation followed by decentralization and chaos could be avoided by appropriate long-term planning.[26]

There was, however, nothing *laissez-faire* about this vision of economic development. Xu was a firm believer in the necessity of centralized and authoritative power to maintain order in the economic system. In the absence of such authority, both economic and ideological chaos were sure to ensue. Thus, as Xu wrote in a passage worth quoting at length:[27]

> We say that reform is necessary and that it is permissible to discuss every type of conception, but reform must proceed in accordance with leadership, the steps must be stable, and it must proceed from reality and be adopted to local circumstances (*yindi zhiyi*). On questions that affect the overall situation, it is necessary to strengthen unified leadership. It is impermissible for everyone to have his own policy and do what he wants. Emancipating thought, science knows no taboos, let a hundred schools of thought contend—these are correct. But if we blindly pursue the blooming of a hundred flowers and everyone does as he pleases, then we will inevitably make the mistake of the Great Leap Forward and the ten years of calamity [i.e., the Cultural Revolution] and will not be adhering to the "four cardinal principles." Some people say that [enterprises] can hire and fire labor freely, give bonuses without restriction, have capital expenditures without restriction. Then how can the state handle the ratio between accumulation and consumption? How can our planned economy be manifested?

Xu was neither an armchair theorist nor a behind-the-scenes bureaucrat— suggesting that securing major changes in macroeconomic policy require both internal lobbying and public campaigning. Xu was an incessant activist for his ideas. In December 1979 he helped found the Chinese Finance Society (*Zhongguo caizheng xuehui*). Bo Yibo was named honorary president, and former Vice Minister of Finance Rong Zihe served as president. The first meeting of the new society, held in Foshan in late December 1979 and early January 1980, stressed its continuity with the readjustment policies of the early and mid-1960s by calling itself the Third Theoretical Symposium on Finance. As noted above, the first two such symposia, held in 1964 and 1965, had elaborated Chen Yun's economic thought, and the new society intended to do the same.[28]

In his address to the first meeting of the Chinese Finance Society, Xu made clear that his call for retrenchment, readjustment, and the reestablishment of comprehensive balance in the economy was directed not only at the Petroleum Group but also at the decentralization and expansion of enterprise authority. Putting the issue in unusually blunt terms, Xu said that there had been a difference of views since the adoption of the policy of "readjustment, reform, consolidation, and improvement" in April 1979 about whether readjustment or reform was the central concern. Xu made clear that his view—in marked contrast to that espoused by Liu Guoguang, Chen Jiyuan, and others at the Wuxi Conference—was that readjustment was the central focus.

Taking explicit aim at Jiang Yiwei's "enterprise-based economy" thesis (qiye benwei lun), Xu said:[29]

> If the 400,000 enterprises throughout the country are each taken as a basis (benwei), then how can a planned economy be implemented? Everybody now says that enterprises cannot eat their fill. Will they be able to eat their fill if authority is devolved to them? At present some enterprises have expanded their authority and are permitted to go everywhere to buy materials and exchange goods. The result is that some enterprises have prospered, but can the national economy as a whole prosper like this? . . . Can there be speed without comprehensive balance, without proportional development, without calculating economic benefits? I think there cannot be high speed.

Reform Versus Readjustment

It is thus apparent that by the beginning of 1980 there were three distinct approaches to macroeconomic policy. First, the State Planning Commission, under the direction of Yu Qiuli, continued to favor a large investment program in capital construction, relying on foreign loans and the hope that increased oil revenues would generate sufficient revenues to pay for the program. Second, the Ministry of Finance wanted to cut back sharply capital construction and limit the expansion of enterprise authority and local power in the hope that finances could be centralized and balanced. Finally, reformers like Yu Guangyuan shared the concern of conservatives about the economic distortions caused by the overdevelopment of heavy industry, but they believed that readjustment should be used not to increase centralization and administrative controls but rather to strengthen competitive pressures in the economy. In sharp contrast to conservatives like Xu Yi, Yu saw readjustment and retrenchment as forcing enterprises to rely more than ever on their own resources and ingenuity to secure supplies and market their products.

Thus, even as press commentary in favor of readjustment increased throughout 1980, political leaders and economists continued to debate which should be given priority, reform or readjustment. Writing in the party journal *Red Flag* (*Hongqi*), Zhao Ziyang—then still Sichuan party chief but soon to be tapped as vice premier and then premier—cast readjustment in terms similar to those of Yu Guangyuan, seeing in it an opportunity to expand enterprise autonomy and market forces. The readjustment of the economy would leave a large number of enterprises with no state-assigned tasks, argued Zhao, forcing them to gear their output to market needs. Thus, among the priority tasks for Sichuan in the coming year, said Zhao, were doing well in the expansion of enterprise authority, carrying out reforms, and introducing market regulation.[30]

Also defending reform were such economists as Lin Ling, Lin Zili, Sun Xiaoliang, and Jiang Yiwei. Lin Ling, Zhao's brain truster in Sichuan, strongly defended the results of expanding enterprise authority in Sichuan, saying that it had already changed enterprises in that province from being passive to being active; enterprises now paid attention to costs and to the market and had moreover been able to closely link the interests of the state, the enterprise, and the individual. Admitting that because it was a "profound reform," the expansion of enterprise authority had brought about some new problems, Lin argued that these could be solved through further reforms of the enterprises and the administrative organs. Implicitly opposing the calls for a greater concentration of authority, Lin argued that enterprise authority must be further expanded so that enterprises could become responsible for their profits and losses. At the same time, said Lin, administrative organs had to be reformed so that they "served" enterprises.[31]

Similarly, in a lengthy article, Lin Zili, an influential economist with the Policy Research Office of the CCP Secretariat, defended the results of the experiments in expanding enterprise authority in Sichuan, Anhui, and Zhejiang provinces. The problems that had emerged, maintained Lin, were merely a reflection of the contradictions between the old system and the development of the productive forces. "If we restrict the trial points at the present level or even return to the status quo before the experiments, then perhaps the contradictions will be covered up temporarily, but if the problem is not resolved then even sharper conflicts will burst out sooner or later." Thus, in the face of difficulties, said Lin, "we should enthusiastically forge ahead, continue to advance, and firmly take the road of reform."[32] Sun Xiaoliang, then a graduate student at CASS, argued that the reforms of the previous year had brought about a healthy competition in the economy.[33]

In response, several conservative writers argued strongly that readjustment should take precedence over reform. For instance, one Qin Wen (apparently a pen name) complained that readjustment had not been accomplished effectively because there was no long-term plan defining development needs and appropriate proportions among different sectors of the economy and because decentralization had made it difficult to impose financial control. The existence of different channels for raising funds meant that the state could not adequately control investment. According to Qin, "While some capital construction projects were scrapped according to the plan, the actual work was continued with money transferred from proceeds in the campaign to tap financial potential. While some capital construction projects were given less investment according to plan, loans were provided from other quarters. While the central government decided to scrap certain items, the projects that the localities wanted to build would go unscathed." With so many projects being pursued beyond the control of the state, said Qin, there was an increasing shortage of materials, which could only be made up by tapping the "initiative" of enterprises. But tapping the initiative of enterprises, argued Qin, "leads to a big increase in the number of purchasing agents, adversely affects state plans and the production and maintenance departments concerned, and contributes to still worse imbalances." Qin concluded that "if no effort is made to improve overall financial planning and get those funds that are being used for capital construction under disguised names into the orbit of our planning, the state plans will be adversely affected."[34]

Similarly, two other economic writers, Chen Peizhang and Jiang Zhenyun, sharply refuted the reformist view that the economic management system had brought about the imbalances in the economy and hence that reform was necessary before there could be a meaningful readjustment of the economy. The various imbalances—such as those between agriculture and industry, light industry and heavy industry, and accumulation and consumption—were in their opinion (which echoed Xu Yi's line of thinking) due to the long-standing "leftist" thinking that had set excessively high targets and had emphasized accumulation and heavy industry at the expense of the people's livelihood and other sectors of the economy. In the opinion of Chen and Jiang, it was "impossible" to reform the economic system without first carrying out a thorough readjustment. This meant that at least for the time being, centralization had to be emphasized over decentralization.[35]

The Politics of Implementing Readjustment

The year 1980 was critical in the development of the early economic reforms in the PRC. During the first part of the year, Deng Xiaoping was clearly ascendant, but by the end of the year his power had been clipped and Chen Yun's influence had risen to a new level. Over the course of the year, economic factors, ideological disputes, and international influences converged to bring about this change in the political atmosphere and to slow the pace of economic reform for the next two years.

In his important January 1980 speech "The Present Situation and Tasks," Deng straddled the major economic issue of the day by both endorsing readjustment and pushing for the continuation of reform. Deng said that there had been "great achievements" in the economy over the preceding three years—"especially in 1979"—but noted that there were various "imbalances" in China's economy, including those between agriculture and industry, light and heavy industry, and accumulation and consumption. He acknowledged that the 20 percent increase in the procurement price of agricultural produce had exacerbated the state's fiscal problems and had led to inflationary pressures. Although Deng endorsed the need for readjustment, he also made clear that economic experiments, such as expanding enterprise authority, would continue. It was necessary, he said, to "find a road that both conforms to China's actual conditions and enables us to proceed more quickly and economically."[36]

Deng's determination to pursue reform even while endorsing readjustment was underscored by the Fifth Plenary Session of the Twelfth Central Committee in February 1980, which purged the so-called little Gang of Four—Wang Dongxing, Wu De, Chen Xilian, and Ji Dengkui—added Zhao Ziyang and Wan Li to the Standing Committee of the Politburo, and named Hu Yaobang general secretary of the Central Committee. Having made these changes in leadership, Deng Xiaoping and Chen Yun moved in March to secure greater control over economic policy by replacing the Finance and Economic Commission of the State Council with the Central Finance and Economic Leading Group. This new group strengthened the Deng–Chen coalition, and particularly Chen Yun, at the expense of the Petroleum Group. Although the group was formally headed by Zhao Ziyang, economic policy makers, including the newly promoted Zhao, deferred to Chen Yun, whose close associate Vice Premier Yao Yilin served on the group. Wan Li and Fang Yi, both strongly committed to economic reform, were added to the group. Although Yu Qiuli, still head of the State Planning Commission, and Gu Mu, head of the State Capital Construction Commission, were appointed to the new group, Li Xiannian's departure signaled the waning influence of the Petroleum Group.[37]

At the same time, the expansion of enterprise authority continued. In February, the SEC announced that more than 3,000 industrial enterprises had been given expanded decision-making authority on an experimental basis. The output value of these enterprises accounted for more than 30 percent of China's total industrial output value, and their profits accounted for about 45 percent of the country's industrial profits.[38]

While the Fifth Plenum and the establishment of the Central Finance and Economic Leading Group undermined the strength of the Petroleum Group, those favoring continued large investment in heavy industry continued to resist pressures for further cuts. Speaking to an early March meeting of provincial party leaders and cadres from central economic organs, Li Xiannian reflected the continuing stalemate. On the one hand, said Li, the budget deficits facing Beijing constituted a "hidden peril" in the economy, but on the other hand he declared that the state's capital construction budget had been tightened as far as it could be, and that "it would not do to compress it further." Describing the scale of construction as being "somewhat too large," Li urged the party secretaries to return to their localities and check on extra-budgetary investment in their areas, but he did not set any mandatory targets, thereby inviting them to ignore his instructions.[39]

This deadlock continued at a symposium on long-term planning convened by the State Council from March 30 to April 24, 1980. Deng Xiaoping, Chen Yun, Li Xiannian, Zhao Ziyang, and Yao Yilin all spoke at this meeting, suggesting the importance the leadership attached to it, but the meeting ended in compromise since it endorsed maintaining capital construction expenditures for the next two to three years at the then current level of about 50 billion yuan. None of Deng's, Chen's, or Li's speeches to this meeting have been published, perhaps because their opinions continued to differ.[40]

The turning point in implementing retrenchment appears to have come at a conference on capital construction in May 1980. Shortly thereafter, on June 9, an authoritative editorial in *People's Daily* argued that investment in capital construction continued to exceed the nation's capability, causing shortages in materials and energy as well as hurting the people's livelihood by squeezing the rate of consumption. This editorial was followed during the next two weeks by four more editorials and a Contributing Commentator article, all arguing that it was necessary to impose control over capital construction and "act according to one's capability" (*liang li er xing*), a phase closely identified with Chen Yun and Yao Yilin.[41]

Not long after these editorials appeared, a campaign was launched to criticize the Petroleum Group. This campaign opened with harsh criticism of the expensive 1.5 meter Wuhan rolling mill for which Li Xiannian had been responsible. It then continued by denouncing the lax management that allegedly led to the capsizing of an offshore oil-drilling rig in the Bohai Gulf, known as "Bohai No. 2." In the wake of this campaign, petroleum minister Song Zhenming was forced to issue a self-criticism and relinquish his position; Yu Qiuli was subsequently forced to yield his position as head of the State Planning Commission to Yao Yilin, Chen Yun's long-term associate.

The Changing Political Environment

In early 1980, Deng Xiaoping and Chen Yun appear to have worked well together. The elevation of Hu Yaobang, Zhao Ziyang, and Wan Li at the Fifth Plenum marked a clear political victory for Deng. The replacement of the Finance and Economic Commission of the State Council by the Central Finance and Economic Leading Group, with a significantly revamped membership, marked an important gain for Chen Yun, one that was consolidated with the ouster of Yu Qiuli and the subsequent demise of the Petroleum Group. The decision to grant 3,000 industrial enterprises greater decision-making authority, however, pointed in a very different direction than the May–June decision to implement retrenchment, as the debate over reform and readjustment discussed above made clear. If support for reform was still strong in early 1980, by the end of the year the forces supporting readjustment dominated. This shift was inseparable from the ongoing debates over ideology.

In April, Wei Guoqing, head of the Political Work Department of the People's Liberation Army (PLA), speaking at an army political work conference, raised the issue of "supporting the proletariat and annihilating the capitalists" (*xingwu miezi*). This phrase had originally been used by Deng Xiaoping in 1956 and became an important slogan in the antirightist movement of 1957. Wei Guoqing's use of this phrase in 1980 was directed at the efforts of people around Hu Yaobang to revise the party's policy on intellectuals to allow more intellectual freedom. Wei's speech was particularly authoritative because it had been approved in advance by Deng Xiaoping.[42]

In late May, Li Weihan, a senior party member with responsibility for united front work, had a long talk in which he was able to convince Deng that the primary problem they were then facing was not the liberal thinking of intellectuals but rather the continuation of "feudal" practices within the CCP. The term "feudalism" in Chinese parlance encompasses a range of authoritarian practices including bureaucratism, overconcentration of authority, lifelong tenure for leaders, and the granting of special privileges to high-level cadres. Deng accepted Li's opinion and dropped his previous support for the phrase "support the proletariat and annihilate the capitalists" in favor of a campaign to eliminate feudalism.[43]

Deng's decision to support opposition to feudalism appears to have been directly related to the party's ongoing efforts to draft a resolution on party history. This resolution was intended to make an evaluation of Mao Zedong's contributions and errors, which in turn would legitimize Deng's own leadership. Deng then hoped to institutionalize party rule (and his role in doing so) through a reform of the political system.

The interrelationship between the reevaluation of Mao and the reform of the political structure was apparent in Deng's June 1980 comment on an early draft of the resolution of CCP history. In typically blunt fashion, Deng dismissed it as "no good." The document criticized Mao Zedong in overly harsh and personal terms, but "criticizing Chairman Mao's personal mistakes alone will not solve problems," said Deng. Deng's concern was twofold. On the one hand, he was clearly aware that an overly harsh evaluation of Mao would undermine the legitimacy of the CCP as a whole. As Deng said, "When we write about his mistakes, we should not exaggerate, for otherwise we shall be discrediting Comrade Mao Zedong, and this would mean discrediting our Party and State."[44] On the other hand, Deng wanted the resolution to focus attention on what he considered to be the chief weakness of the CCP, the lack of adequate political structures. As Deng said, "What is most important is the question of systems and institutions. Chairman Mao made many correct statements, but the faulty systems and institutions of the past pushed him in the opposite direction."[45]

Deng elaborated on the need for healthy institutions in his important August 1980 speech "Reform of the Party and State Leadership System." In a well-known passage that takes on particular poignancy in the wake of the

Tiananmen crackdown, Deng reflected that the Cultural Revolution was not a problem of Mao's personal characteristics but of an unsound set of political institutions:[46]

> If these systems are sound, they can place restraints on the actions of bad people; if they are unsound, they may hamper the efforts of good people or indeed, in certain cases, may push them in the wrong direction.... Stalin gravely damaged socialist legality, doing things which Comrade Mao Zedong once said would have been impossible in Western countries like Britain, France, and the United States.

Deng's appeal for political reform, however, did not reflect any wavering of his fundamental and enduring commitment to the framework of a Marxist-Leninist party-state. On the contrary, his approach to political reform, like his approach to ideological and economic reform, was premised on the belief that reform could make these structures strong and viable. Moreover, Deng's organizational approach to problems and his highly disciplinarian personality led him to strongly and angrily reject political activity outside the ideological and organizational controls of the party.

In his speech entitled "The Present Situation and Tasks," at the beginning of 1980, Deng had sharply and extensively criticized some of the posters that had appeared on a wall on Chang'an Boulevard at Xidan (which quickly became known as "democracy wall") in central Beijing during the previous year as disrupting "stability and unity." Deng said, "One must not take such things lightly, thinking that they won't cause disturbances," and added that "when liveliness clashes with stability and unity, we can never pursue the former at the expense of the latter."[47] Similarly in his August speech on political reform, Deng said, "In a big country like ours, it is inconceivable that unity of thinking could be achieved among our several hundred million people or that their efforts could be pooled to build socialism in the absence of a Party whose members have a spirit of sacrifice and a high level of political awareness and discipline, a Party that truly represents and unites the masses of people and exercises unified leadership. Without such a Party, our country would split up and accomplish nothing."[48]

Despite Deng's obvious unwillingness to countenance radical reform, his political needs—ousting Hua Guofeng, reevaluating Mao, and reforming the political structure—necessitated a more open ideological atmosphere. Thus, in commenting on the resolution on CCP history in June, Deng said that the resolution should address the "vestiges of feudalism," albeit "in a proper way."[49] In his August speech on political reform, Deng elaborated on the problem of feudalism, saying that its influence was felt in such diverse areas as the relations between leaders and subordinates and between cadres and masses, as well as in "high-handed work styles" prevailing in industry, commerce, and agriculture.[50] In the revolutionary period and in the early years of the PRC, Deng said, the party had failed to "complete the task of eliminating the surviving feudal influences in the ideological and political fields" and hence it was now necessary to take up this task once again in order to avoid "further losses" to the country and its people. Deng again criticized feudalism three days later in his interview with the Italian journalist Oriana Fallaci. In an unmistakable reference to the upcoming ouster of Hua Guofeng, he responded crisply to a question about Mao's selection of Lin Biao as his successor, saying "For a leader to pick his own successor is a feudal practice."[51]

The campaign against feudal influences was strongly supported by Hu Yaobang and his brain trusters. In June, following Deng's initial comments on feudalism, Hu told a forum on party style that "unhealthy tendencies" within the party were related to "feudal ideology." Feudal ideas, said Hu, were reflected in such practices as the lifelong tenure of cadres, the personality cult, and the pursuit of privileges.[52]

In July a Contributing Commentator article in *People's Daily* followed up on some of these themes. People have exaggerated the role of the individual in history, the article said, and experience had shown that "if we exaggerate the role of a leader to an extreme, a personality cult will emerge."[53] Shortly thereafter, philosophical and economic symposia were held to discuss the elimination of feudal influences in those disciplines.[54] Another *People's Daily* Contributing Commentator article declared:[55]

> To remove the obstacles to the four modernizations drive, it is imperative to fully assess the influence of feudalistic thinking on the social life and particularly intraparty life in our country and to designate as a struggle of strategic significance the elimination of feudalistic thought.

Ruan Ming, then a close associate of Hu Yaobang's, attacked feudal influences by arguing that the underdevelopment of the bourgeoisie in China meant that feudal ideology was never criticized in the way it had been in Europe during the Enlightenment. Reflecting Li Zehou's famous thesis that in modern Chinese history "enlightenment" had been overwhelmed by "salvation," Ruan argued that the May Fourth Movement had been unable to adequately criticize feudalism because "the tasks on the ideological and cultural front receded into the background" as the revolutionary struggle of peasants and workers advanced. As a result, Ruan continued, feudal influences were rife in the economic, political, and social life of the nation; among other things, they lay at the core of the "reactionary ideological framework" of Lin Biao and the Gang of Four.[56]

Similarly, Feng Wenbin, another close associate of Hu Yaobang's, argued in a major article that the "remnant poison of feudalism" had led to many defects in the political system, including the tendency to exaggerate the role of class struggle and rule through "patriarchal leadership." To overcome these tendencies, Feng proposed a number of political reforms, including strengthening the role of the National People's Congress, decentralizing political power to the localities, and reform of the cadre system.[57]

The first half of 1980 was thus a period of intense ideological debate, with Deng first siding with the conservative wing of the party and then shifting to support the more open-minded wing. In the latter half of the year, this more open ideological atmosphere gave way to a much more conservative atmosphere—one that would pave the way for the criticism of "bourgeois liberalism" and the writer Bai Hua in the spring of 1981.

Three issues converged in the latter half of 1980 to bring about this sharp change in the ideological situation: the formation of Solidarity in Poland, the ongoing debate over the evaluation of Mao Zedong, and the continuing efforts of conservatives to implement retrenchment and readjustment in the economy. These three issues were mutually reinforcing. Despite the decision reached in May to implement readjustment and the subsequent ouster of the Petroleum Group, it is unlikely that the retrenchment policies adopted in December 1980 would have been as severe, or the subsequent criticism of economic reformers in 1981 and 1982 as harsh, had developments such as the Solidarity movement and the debate over the evaluation of Mao Zedong not intervened, thereby providing conservatives with powerful issues.

The formation of the independent Polish trade union underscored the "dangers" inherent in political reform. According to Hu Yaobang's associate Ruan Ming, Deng Xiaoping and Hu Yaobang were at first sympathetic to the formation of Solidarity, seeing in it a movement that would weaken the Soviet Union. They also believed that there was no danger that such a movement could gain ground in China.[58] But in early October 1980, Hu Qiaomu wrote a long letter arguing that China could develop a crisis along the same lines as Poland, particularly if political dissidents allied with workers. Hu's letter was printed by the Central Secretariat and circulated to organs of the Central Committee, ministries of the the State Council, and mass organizations.[59] On October 9, Wang Renzhong, then head of the Propaganda Department, agreed with Hu Qiaomu's letter and ordered the Propaganda Department to stop discussing Deng's August speech on political reform. Shortly thereafter, Wang transmitted to the department an instruction on propaganda from Chen Yun. Chen's statement was that "if we do not pay attention to the two issues of propaganda and economics then events like that in Poland could happen in China too."[60] Shortly thereafter, discussion on political reform ceased.

Although Deng had bluntly rejected harsh criticism of Mao in June 1980, the campaign against feudalism in the summer and early fall evidently led some within the party to step up their criticism of Mao's failings.[61] Leaders within the PLA soon reacted harshly to such criticism. In November, PLA veteran general Huang Kecheng gave a long speech in which he lashed out against "some comrades" who had "wantonly vilified Mao Zedong Thought and defamed Comrade Mao Zedong." Giving a long defense of Mao's contributions to the party, especially during the period of the revolutionary struggle, Huang averred, "If anyone insists that some other people were wiser or contributed more [than Mao

Zedong], it would be a mockery to history." Huang's defense of Mao was particularly potent because he had himself been a victim of Mao's, having been purged from his posts for siding with Peng Dehuai at the 1959 Lushan Plenum. In an oblique reference to this experience, Huang said, "we must not be emotional or swayed by personal feelings toward such an important issue. We should consider the issue in light of the fundamental interests of the whole party, the whole country, and the 1 billion people."[62]

Coming six months after Wei Guoqing's comments on "supporting the proletariat and annihilating the bourgeoisie," Huang's speech indicated the strong feelings within the army against "bourgeois liberalization." This resistance to ideological and political reform, combined with residual support for Party Chairman Hua Guofeng, forced delay of the Sixth Plenum, originally scheduled for late 1980, and presaged the criticism of the writer Bai Hua that would appear in the spring of 1981. When the party's resolution on CCP history was finally adopted at the Sixth Plenum in June 1981, it was apparent that the ideological initiative of party intellectuals, particularly those associated with Hu Yaobang, had been blunted. The sharp change in the ideological atmosphere in late 1980 also had a major impact on economic policy.

The Fourth Theoretical Symposium on Fiscal Work

As political tensions were mounting within the party, the Chinese Finance Society, the group that Xu Yi had helped organize, convened the Fourth Theoretical Symposium on Fiscal Work in Kunming on November 26, 1980. Although the basic decision to adopt retrenchment and readjustment policies appears to have been made in May, the speeches made at this symposium harshly criticized not only the policies of the Petroleum Group but also those of reform. It seems apparent that conservative economists were marshaling their resources in order to exert influence on the Central Work Conference that was to be convened the following month.

In his opening remarks to the conference, Chen Rulong, vice minister of finance, warned sharply against budget deficits, which he called the product of "leftist" economic thought. He went on, however, to say that disputes during the previous two years about the relationship between readjustment and reform had resulted in a "failure to adequately recognize the importance and urgency of retrenchment and its energetic implementation."[63] There had been too much talk of market regulation and too little discussion of planned regulation, said Chen, and "even negation of the necessity of administrative intervention." Reform had not been used, as it was supposed to have been, to facilitate (*cu jin*) readjustment, but rather to replace it. As a result, deficits were causing prices to increase, adversely affecting political stability and unity.[64] In his closing remarks on December 6, Chen put it bluntly: "Readjustment is the crux, it is the center, it is everything" (*tiaozheng shi guanjian, shi zhongxin, shi quanju*).[65]

Like Chen, Xu Yi vehemently attacked both overextended construction and excessive expansion of enterprise authority. Pointing to three periods of "reckless advance" in Chinese economic history—the Great Leap Forward, the construction of the Third Front, and Hua Guofeng's 1978 call for "ten Daqings"—Xu excoriated the developmental strategy of the Petroleum Group. The economic structure that they had formed, he said, "took oil, the chemical industry, and heavy industry as central" and "imported large-scale items," rode a "foreign horse," and tried to "cook a meal without rice" (that is, to undertake projects without resources). The continuing "leftist" influence and the fact that "the economy had certain results in 1977" had prevented the leadership from acting to correct this orientation, said Xu, and "our heads again became fevered and forgetting the lesson of the three year 'great leap forward,' we put all of our hopes on oil reserves that had not yet been ascertained for sure."[66] Experience proved that the "thesis that deficits are harmless" (*chizi wuhai lun*), which bolstered this developmental strategy, was "groundless." The accumulating deficits of the prior three years were causing an overly rapid increase in the money supply, bringing about price increases and causing complaints among the people.[67]

As harshly as Xu criticized the policies of the Petroleum Group, he also lashed out against one of his favorite targets, Jiang Yiwei's theory of an "enterprise-based economy." As he put it:[68]

> The goal of reforming the management system of state-run enterprises is to mobilize the productive enthusiasm of people and develop the productive forces. This is absolutely correct. But now some people raise the thesis of an enterprise-based economy (*qiye benwei lun*) and completely depart from state planning, oppose administrative interference, oppose planned regulation, and say that this is the socialist ownership system.

The Central Work Conference

On November 28, two days after the Theoretical Symposium on Fiscal Work began in Kunming, Deng Xiaoping met with Chen Yun and Li Xiannian to discuss a plan for readjusting the economy in 1981. At this meeting, Chen Yun apparently laid out the gist of the talk that he was to give at the Central Work Conference the following month.[69] It was apparently also at this meeting that a final decision was made to implement retrenchment beginning in 1981.[70] That such a decision was made by Deng in consultation with the two senior party leaders who had long been involved in economic policy, without the participation of either the premier, Zhao Ziyang, or the general secretary of the party, Hu Yaobang, suggests the degree to which the most important decisions were centralized in the hands of a few senior leaders.

The meeting among Deng, Chen, and Li coincided with a series of Politburo meetings that stretched out for almost a month, between November 10 and

December 5. It was this series of meetings that took up the important issue of Hua Guofeng's ouster as party chairman and his replacement by Hu Yaobang. According to the communiqué of the session, many leaders, following Deng's speech on reform of the party and state leadership in August, had said that in the four years since the fall of the Gang of Four, and especially in the first two years thereafter, Hua Guofeng had made a number of "serious mistakes" and should be removed from his leadership role. After receiving the "criticism and help" of the Politburo Standing Committee, Hua submitted his request to resign from his positions as party chairman and head of the Central Military Commission to the first session of the Politburo meeting on November 10. The Politburo communiqué stated that:[71]

> In the past four years Comrade Hua Guofeng has done some beneficial work, but he obviously lacks the necessary political ability and organizational ability to be chairman of the Central Committee. That he is incapable of fulfilling the responsibilities of chairman of the Military Commission is known by everyone.

The communiqué also made clear that "many comrades" proposed that Deng take over both of Hua's party positions, "because this is what the masses hope for." Deng declined the offer of party chairman, suggesting Hu Yaobang instead. "As for chairman of the Military Commission, because there is no other appropriate person," said the communiqué, "he [Deng] can bear the responsibility for a while." The Politburo "unanimously" agreed with Deng's views.[72]

Although the communiqué largely discussed the problem of Hua Guofeng, there must have been considerable discussion during the course of the nine sessions about the content of the "Resolution on Some Historical Problems Since the Founding of the PRC," which was also approved "in principle" in draft form by the Politburo and passed to a group of 4,000 cadres for further discussion and final revision.

In late November and early December, Deng Liqun gave a series of four lectures at the Central Party School on "Studying Comrade Chen Yun in Undertaking Economic Work." In these speeches, Deng Liqun apparently not only gave a systematic rendition of Chen Yun's economic thought (lauding Chen as the first to grasp the objective laws of China's socialist revolution and stage of development) but also took on the ideological issues involved in drafting the resolution on CCP history.[73]

On December 16, a ten-day Central Work Conference opened to discuss the implementation of retrenchment and readjustment policies. Major speeches were given by Chen Yun, Zhao Ziyang, and Deng Xiaoping. This conference marked a culmination of two years of efforts by conservative political leaders, bureaucrats, and economists to implement sharp cuts in capital construction and focus primary attention on restoring balance among different sectors of the economy. It is apparent from the leadership speeches at the conference, as well as the attendant press commentary, that the views voiced by people like Xu Yi over the preceding year had been endorsed by the leadership. According to one source, Xu personally gave a report at the conference that was subsequently circulated within the party and which "severely criticized deficit financing and the enterprise-based economy."[74]

Chen Yun's speech to the work conference evinced characteristic concern about political stability, the anxiousness of his colleagues for quick results, excessive reliance on capitalist countries, and the need to maintain centralized control. Warning that the price rises then occurring could bring about political instability, Chen called for freezing prices for at least half a year. Although Chen did not urge a return to a "closed door" policy, his criticism of the use of foreign loans and investment by the Petroleum Group combined fiscal prudence with suspicion of the capitalist system. "Foreign capitalists," he said, "are still capitalists"; they were out to earn profits, not to help China's modernization. He then went on to say that "the reason that I repeatedly urge caution while welcoming foreign capitalists is that some of our cadres are still very naive about this."

In order to control fiscal deficits and inflation, Chen urged a major reduction of both central and local government expenditures. Although not explicitly criticizing the 1980 tax reform that allowed localities to retain greater revenues, he complained that the ratio of central government revenues to total government revenues had "diminished greatly." Chen called for "freezing" the fiscal surpluses of local governments and borrowing some of that surplus for the upcoming year. Defending tightened centralized control, Chen said, "It will not do for such a country as ours not to have this type of centralization, otherwise, things will be chaotic and unfavorable to reform."[75]

Reflecting the conservative ideological atmosphere that had emerged in the fall of 1980, Deng Xiaoping criticized sharply the decline in party discipline and made clear that the tightening of such discipline was a requisite of implementing readjustment. Taking aim at some of the liberal trends within the party, Deng sharply criticized the ideological weakness of many of its members. During the new democratic phase of the revolution, he said, the party "took communist ideology as a guide in all our work," but now, in the socialist period, "some people have had the audacity to criticize such revolutionary slogans as 'Serve the people wholeheartedly,' 'The individual is subordinate to the organization,' and 'Fear neither hardship nor death.'" "What is worse," Deng said, "this preposterous criticism, which should have been rejected, has found sympathy and support among some people in our own ranks. How can a Communist imbued with Party and revolutionary spirit tolerate such things?"[76] Linking tightened political control to the implementation of readjustment policies, Deng said, "If stability and unity are disrupted, readjustment will be out of the question."[77]

Deng's comments pointed to a fundamental dilemma of the economic reform, namely, that tightening control over strictly economic problems, such as the overinvestment in basic construction and the need for increasing central revenues, required tight ministerial and party control. Such controls, however, strengthened the hand of both central bureaucrats and ideological conservatives, which in turn made both economic and political reform more difficult.

The Central Work Conference marked an obvious victory for Chen Yun and his approach to economic development. In contrast to the spring of 1979, when Chen had emphasized the need for increasing market forces within the scope of the planned economy, the emphasis was now clearly on the planned economy and reining in localities and enterprises that were no longer adhering to the plan. In April 1981, the State Council would approve a decision not to extend experiments in expanding the decision-making authority of enterprises; economic reform was on hold at least for a while.[78] Moreover, the Central Work Conference clearly bolstered Chen's position within the leadership. As the Hong Kong magazine *Cheng ming*, then closely aligned with the Dengist wing of the party, commented, Chen Yun "has been put in an unprecedentedly high position."[79] With Chen's preeminence over economic policy reasserted, China's leadership became essentially a diumvirate, with Deng having final say on political matters but Chen having the most important voice on economic affairs. Although Deng and Chen shared many goals, including the economic development of China and the retention of party leadership, their personal styles, their different visions of the future, and their different political resources fashioned the central political rivalry in the decade of reform.

There is no doubt that China faced a number of economic problems in 1980. Central finances were undermined as large budget deficits continued. The commitments made under Hua Guofeng to purchase foreign plants and technology strained China's capacity to meet its debt payments. Problems of local protectionism, duplicative construction, and inflation were associated with previous efforts to give enterprises greater decision-making authority. It nevertheless seems clear that the Central Work Conference went well beyond what was called for in strictly economic terms. Had the conference been called in June, for example (when there seemed to be leadership agreement that retrenchment policies were necessary but before ideological controversies had heated up), it seems unlikely that the cuts in capital construction would have been as severe or the efforts to recentralize economic authority as stringent as they were. Without the conservative ideological tide in the latter part of 1980, the policy shift that the Central Work Conference marked would not have been so sharp. And Chen Yun would not have emerged as strong as he did as he did.

Criticizing Reform

Although the Central Work Conference settled the question of implementing readjustment policies in the short run, there was much disagreement among economists over the long-term direction of reform. In the spring, the State

Council's Economic Structural Reform Office, then headed by Liao Jili, held a discussion on the overall plan for reform. One of the central concepts discussed was that of the "planned commodity economy," an idea that had been bruited about at the Wuxi Conference two years earlier. After the meeting, Xue Muqiao conveyed the discussions to a meeting of provincial leaders, some of whom approved their thrust while others opposed it.[80]

These discussions aroused the sharp opposition of Chen Yun. In the spring of 1981, in the course of talks about the draft of the "Resolution on Some Historical Problems Since the Founding of the PRC," which officially assessed Mao Zedong's role in CCP history, Chen Yun proposed that the formulation adopted at the Spring 1979 Central Work Conference ("in our national economy we can implement the principle of integrating planned regulation and market regulation with planned regulation as primary while at the same time paying full attention to the role of market regulation") be changed to read "it is necessary to implement a planned economy on the basis of the public ownership system, and at the same time bring to bear the role of market regulation." Whereas the earlier formulation had emphasized the role of market forces, this reformulation contrasted the "planned *economy*" with "market *regulation*," making clear that the socialist economy was a planned economy and that the market played only a secondary, regulative role.[81] In late 1981 and early 1982, Chen Yun again intervened to stress the principle of the planned economy as primary and market regulation as supplementary. Meeting with party secretaries from provinces and independent municipalities in December 1981, Chen stressed the need to view the "whole country as a chessboard" and to undertake economic construction according to the plan.[82] Two months later, Chen met with leading members of the State Planning Commission to discuss "how to uphold the planned economy as primary, market regulation as subsidiary." At this meeting, Chen said, "Now planning is not welcomed! Therefore on this first day of the new year, I called the responsible comrades of the State Planning Commission together to talk about this matter."[83] This talk clearly caught the attention of China's economists. Four days later, senior economist Sun Yefang presided over a theoretical conference to discuss the importance of upholding the "planned economy as primary, market regulation as subsidiary."[84]

These repeated interventions to emphasize the role of planning ushered in a period of criticism in which ideas that had been raised and accepted at the Wuxi Conference and afterward were subjected to harsh attack. These attacks can be said to mark the end of the "first wave" of reform. Against the freewheeling intellectual atmosphere that had emerged following the publication of Hu Qiaomu's article "Act in Accordance with Economic Laws" and the reform experiments and justifying arguments promoted by such people as Jiang Yiwei and Lin Ling, there now emerged a conservative backlash that effectively shut off intellectual debate and new explorations of reform, at least for a while.

This backlash had an important basis in the economic problems of the time. The greater decision-making authority and resources given to localities and enterprises had produced problems (as freely admitted and discussed by Sichuan reformer Lin Ling) such as duplicative construction, regional protectionism, and a decline in central revenues. However, the wave of criticism that emerged in 1981 and 1982 was no mid-course correction. Even moderate reformers, such as Liu Guoguang and Xue Muqiao, were subjected to harsh criticism. The criticisms voiced by the economists who rallied to Chen Yun's call were, first and foremost, ideological criticisms. They were not the sort of practical arguments voiced by such economists as Xue Muqiao (such as readjustment being a necessary precondition for carrying out a thoroughgoing reform); rather they articulated a different vision of reform, one that resonated more fully with traditional understandings of "socialism" and placed a much greater emphasis on the role of the plan.

To trace this backlash, it is useful to look briefly at some of the arguments put forward in defense of reform and then at the criticisms of reform.

In October 1980, Liu Guoguang published an article that accepted the policy direction that was about to be endorsed at the Central Work Conference, including the formulation "planned regulation as primary," but which also strongly defended the direction of reform over previous years against accusations that it was either an expedient measure, was wrong, or had deviated from socialism.[85] Some people had resisted the concept of market regulation, wrote Liu. Some, for example, complained that "in thirty years of working in factories, I've never heard of a factory seeking its own livelihood," while others felt that market regulation was useful only as an expedient measure that would allow enterprises that lacked sufficient state orders to tide themselves over the period of readjustment.

Admitting that such problems as duplicative construction, regional protectionism, and corruption had accompanied reforms, Liu sharply rejected the claim that market regulation and competition "caused waste and brought about an anarchic situation."[86] To reject market regulation and return to the old system, Liu argued, would never solve the economic problems facing China; integrating planned regulation and market regulation was an extremely important part of economic reform. "In the final analysis," he said, "this is because at the present stage the socialist economy is not only a planned economy, but also because it fully possesses the characteristics (*tezheng*) of a commodity economy."[87]

Developing a theme he had raised at the Wuxi Conference a year and a half earlier, Liu argued that the board-and-plank style of relating plan and market was "transitional." If it was admitted that the means of production and the means of consumption were all commodities, then it stood to reason that "the production and circulation of all products must follow the principles of the socialist commodity economy and respect the demands of the socialist planned economy, finally becoming a unified, fused entity in which the two types of regulation are intimately integrated and subject to market regulation under the guidance of nonmandatory state plans. I believe that this is the model that in the future our economic structural reform should establish."[88]

Another approach to the issue of integrating plan and market that soon came in for harsh criticism was to identify planning with the macroeconomy and market forces with the microeconomy. For instance, senior economist Xu Dixin wrote, "In the macroeconomy (referring primarily to the direction of development of the overall national economy) it is necessary to implement strict planned management. In the microeconomy (referring primarily to the economic activity of basic-level enterprises) it is necessary to fully bring to bear the role of market regulation."[89]

Before long, economists at the State Planning Commission, the Policy Research Office of the CCP Secretariat (which was headed by Deng Liqun), the Ministry of Finance, and Chinese People's University began leveling sharp attacks against the views of Liu, Xu, and other like-minded economists.[90] One of the harshest and most systematic attacks was written by You Lin, then an economist with the Policy Research Office of the Central Secretariat. You dismissed the "interpenetrating" model proposed by Sun Shangqing and Chen Jiyuan and the "fused" (*jiaoti shi*) model proposed by Liu Guoguang, arguing that a division of the economy into a planned part and a part subject to market regulation (i.e., Chen Yun's board-and-plank model of integration) was an "objective" need of the economy. In his view, the reason for market regulation was the simple fact that it was impossible for the plan to encompass everything, given China's stage of economic development. Because production units were so numerous and dispersed and because 80 percent of the population lived in the countryside and were semi-self-sufficient "the state not only has no need but has no possibility" of including everything in the plan. Moreover, You opposed any expansion of experiments in independent accounting, responsibility for profits and losses, or replacing profits with taxes that would weaken state management of enterprises. As he put it, the state had tried to manage too much in the past and had stifled enterprises in doing so, making reform of the planning system and the use of market forces necessary. But, warned You, one "absolutely cannot go from this to negating the planned economy."[91]

Similarly, Gu Shutang, a member of the State Planning Commission, criticized Liu's views for "inappropriately enlarging the scope of market regulation that is not under the guidance of mandatory state planning so that the production and circulation of all products is included." This "fundamentally negates that mandatory planned regulation is an organic component of the socialist economy."[92] By the same token, the Shanghai economist Gong Xuelin wrote, "What is wrong with this viewpoint is that is does not distinguish primary and secondary with regard to planned regulation and market regulation; the scope of market regulation extends throughout the whole social economy."[93]

The issue of how the planned economy should be "integrated" with market regulation was rooted in different ideological conceptions of socialism. As noted in Chapter 2, Chen Jiyuan and Zhang Zhuoyuan had argued at the Wuxi Conference that "the integration of planning and market is the essential characteristic (*benzhi tezheng*) of the socialist economy." This issue was closely related to the role of mandatory planning and the relationship between mandatory planning and the law of value. He Jianzhang in his paper to the Wuxi Conference had called for gradually replacing mandatory planning with guidance planning, a view developed later by Liu Guoguang and other economists. As Zhao Renwei observed, "These views aroused heated debates."[94]

In particular, Beijing Normal University professor Tao Dayong sharply refuted such views, saying that an economy must be either a commodity economy or a planned economy. According to Tao, "the essential characteristic (*benzhi tezheng*) of the socialist economy can only be the planned economy . . . , [which] belongs to a higher stage of economic formation. To lower the socialist economy to a 'commodity economy' can only be a type of historical retrogression." Tao concluded that "if there is not a planned economy, there can be no socialism to speak of."[95] Similarly, Li Zhenzhong of Chinese People's University wrote, "The essential characteristic of the socialist economy should be the planned economy, not the commodity economy."[96]

Although Deng Liqun had been open-minded with regard to economic issues, particularly rural reform, in the late 1970s, it is clear that his views changed as Chen Yun began to emphasize the need for strengthening planning. As noted above, Deng had given four important lectures on Chen Yun's economic thought in late 1980. It was at the same time that Deng had undertaken to edit Chen Yun's works in three volumes (at the time, only Mao Zedong's writings appeared in five volumes, while the writings of other major party leaders, such as Liu Shaoqi and Zhou Enlai, appeared in only two volumes).[97] In the 1981 criticism of reform, Deng strongly defended mandatory planning as an "essential characteristic" of socialism. At the time, Deng said that "to take mandatory planning as a fundamental characteristic of the socialist planned economy is not a mistake." He also said: "Important industries that affect the lifeline of the national economy are managed by the state, and products that affect the welfare of the people are controlled by the state. Implementing mandatory regulation over this portion that accounts for the majority of total industrial and agricultural output value signifies that our economy is fundamentally a planned economy."[98] Similarly, Xu Yi wrote, "If plans were completely for guidance and reference and did not have to be implemented, then that would not be a real planned economy."[99]

Under pressure from such attacks, Liu and others distanced themselves from their earlier positions. For instance, in late 1981 and again in early 1982, Liu said that he had come to feel that the term "market economy" was inappropriate because it was easy to confuse with capitalism. Moreover, he criticized economic discussions that had taken place during the previous few years for overly emphasizing market regulation and the commodity economy. "To define the socialist economy as a 'planned commodity economy,' " Liu said, "is in fact to base the essential characteristic of the socialist economy on the commodity economy and not on the planned economy. In this way, planning is lowered to nothing more than a type of commodity economy and is not the essential characteristic of the socialist economy."[100] Thus, in the face of harsh criticism, Liu yielded and retracted his earlier views.

The conservative critique of reform that unfolded in 1981 and 1982 had a major impact on the political report presented to the Twelfth Party Congress in September 1982. Although Hu Yaobang appeared to go as far as he could to justify the role of market forces, it was clear that Chen Yun's approach dominated the report. The critical passage read as follows:[101]

> China implements a planned economy on the basis of public ownership. Planned production and circulation are the mainstay of our national economy. At the same time, the production and circulation of some products are allowed to be regulated through the market without being planned; that is to say, in accordance with specific conditions at different times and within the scope determined by the state's unified plan, the law of value is allowed to play a spontaneous regulatory role. This part is *supplementary* to planned production and circulation; it is *subordinate and secondary*, but also necessary and beneficial. The state ensures proportionate and coordinated growth of the national economy by means of comprehensive balance of the planned economy and the supplementary role of market regulation.

In accord with this approach, Hu went on to say that reforms to expand both the decision-making authority of enterprises and the scope of the market had interfered with the state's unified planning, which "is not good for the normal growth of the economy." In the future, he warned, "we must on no account neglect or relax unified leadership through state planning."[102]

The provisions on the economy in Hu Yaobang's report were reinforced by the newly revised State Constitution that was adopted at the Fifth National People's Congress, which ended in early December 1982. According to the constitution, "The state practices economic planning on the basis of socialist public ownership. It ensures the proportionate and coordinated growth of the national economy through overall balancing by economic planning and the supplementary role of regulation by the market."[103]

It was at this time that Chen Yun enunciated his famous "birdcage" thesis. Welcoming visitors to his home, Chen praised the new constitution and said that the relationship between enlivening the economy and economic planning was like that between a bird and a cage: "You mustn't hold the bird in your hands too tightly or it would be strangled. You have to turn it loose, but only within the confines of a cage; otherwise it would fly away."[104]

The three-year period from 1980 to 1982 thus marked a high point in Chen Yun's influence and for his approach to economic development. In the earlier period of 1978–79, when the Dengist coalition was challenging the existing leadership for power, the intellectual atmosphere was relatively more open and ideas favoring extensive, even radical, reform of the economy predominated. By late 1979 and early 1980, however, the conservative wing of the party was mounting an effort not only to bring down the Petroleum Group that had been closely identified with Hua Guofeng's "Great Leap Outward" but also to criticize the ideas of reformers. By taking advantage of such issues as the formation of Solidarity in Poland and intraparty controversy over the evaluation of Mao Zedong, conservatives were able to push their agenda with unprecedented success. Not only was the general ideological atmosphere more conservative after the 1980 Central Work Conference, but economic ideas that had been acceptable two years earlier were criticized. Although conservatives reserved their sharpest polemics for radical reformers like Jiang Yiwei, they also criticized such mainstream reformers as Liu Guoguang, leading Liu to recant his earlier ideas.

The conservative swing taken in Chinese politics and economic policy in late 1980 was more than a rational response to genuine economic difficulties. There is no doubt that there were economic problems at the time—including budget deficits, inflationary pressures, and local protectionism—but it also seems clear that conservatives responded to these problems in a way that maximized their own political influence and reflected their own ideological and economic agenda. Their differences with the Petroleum Group on the one hand and with reform-minded economists (and intellectuals) on the other went deeper than disputes about how to accomplish reform. They had very distinct ideas about the nature of the polity and the economy that they wanted to preserve and develop—and that vision did not include marketization of the economy and radical new departures in ideology.

Aside from the important issues that arose in late 1980, which allowed conservatives to press their agenda, there are other, perhaps more fundamental, reasons why they were successful in slowing reform of the industrial economy whereas they had not been successful in doing so in the countryside. First and foremost, the complexity of the industrial economy, in which so many relationships among suppliers, buyers, creditors, and tax authorities were involved, meant that a factory could not simply be given authority over its own production—as a rural household could—without affecting other interests. Giving enterprises greater decision-making authority and some financial incentive in an economy in which the price structure remained irrational and economic law virtually nonexistent was a recipe for difficulties. When problems inevitably occurred, conservatives could persuasively argue the need for strengthening controls.

Another reason why the conservatives were able to slow the reform of the industrial economy was that it was intertwined in ideological issues in a way in which the rural economy was not—despite the heavy ideological commitment to rural policy issues over the years. This was at least in part because Marxism in general was a philosophy that addressed itself first and foremost to industrial societies. In China, the issue of the relationship between the plan and the market was one that was rooted in the industrial economy in a way that it was not in the rural economy. Reforming enterprises in a way that undermined the plan raised ideological questions that were central to the Chinese understanding of socialism. Rural reform certainly posed sensitive ideological questions, but they were parried first by maintaining collective ownership of the land and second by the great increases that had been recorded in production. Precisely because enterprise reforms necessarily entailed problems, the ideological issues could not be sidestepped so easily.

Enterprise reform thus directly posed critical and sensitive ideological questions at the same time that it inevitably caused economic problems and threatened the fiscal interests of the state. Moreover, because the industrial economy was much more bureaucratized and centralized than the rural economy, central leaders had the capacity to strengthen controls over the industrial economy in a way that they could not do with the rural economy once restrictions on the latter were loosened.

Deng Xiaoping apparently acquiesced in Chen's increasing assertion of dominance over economic affairs in 1980–82, but as the economy improved and as it became apparent that Chen's vision of China in the future clashed with Deng's, conflict between the two leaders became inevitable. This became apparent in 1983–84.

Notes

1. Fang Weizhong, *Zhonghua renmin gongheguo jingji dashiji (1949–1980)*, pp. 639–641 and 677.
2. The terms "retrenchment" and "readjustment" differ technically in that the former refers specifically to cutbacks in capital construction and credit designed to reduce aggregate demand whereas the latter refers to efforts to bring the major proportions of the economy—particularly agriculture, light industry, and heavy industry—into better balance. Retrenchment is nevertheless closely associated with readjustment in part because it is only in periods of overinvestment that sectoral imbalances appear that need to be corrected through retrenchment and readjustment and in part because retrenchment policies are inevitably associated with the strengthening of central controls, which are a necessary first step in carrying out readjustment.
3. On Chen Yun, see David M. Bachman, *Chen Yun and the Chinese Political System.*
4. See Chen's speech to the Eighth Party Congress, "Shehui zhuyi gaizao jiben wancheng yilai de xin wenti" (New Problems Since the Basic Completion of Socialist Transformation).
5. Chen Yun, "Jianshe guimo yao he guoli xiang shiying" (The Scale of Construction Should Be Compatible with National Strength).
6. Fang Weizhong, ed., *Zhonghua renmin gongheguo jingji dashiji (1949–1980)*, p. 620.
7. Wang Zhen, Bo Yibo, Wang Renzhong, Chen Guodong, Zhang Jingfu, and Jin Ming were also members of the commission. See Fang Weizhong, ed., *Zhonghua renmin gongheguo jingji dashiji (1949–1980)*, p. 621.
8. Chen Yun and Li Xiannian, "Guanyu caijing gongzuo gei zhongyang de xin" (Letter to the Central Committee Regarding Finance and Economic Work).

9. Chen Yun, "Jianchi an bili yuanze tiaozheng guomin jingji."

10. Li Xiannian, "Zai zhongyang gongzuo huiyi shang de jianghua" (Speech to the Central Work Conference), p. 358.

11. Chen Yun, "Jingji jianshe yao jiaota shidi" (Economic Construction Must Be Down to Earth).

12. See Xue Muqiao, *Dangqian woguo jingji ruogan wenti* (Some Problems in China's Contemporary Economy); idem., *Woguo guomin jingji de tiaozheng he gaige* (Readjustment and Reform of China's National Economy); Ma Hong, *Shilun woguo shehui zhuyi jingji fazhan de xin zhanlue* (On the New Strategy of China's Socialist Economic Development); and Liao Jili, *Zhongguo jingji tizhi gaige yanjiu* (Studies on China's Economic Structural Reform).

13. "Aim of Socialist Production Must Be Really Understood," *Renmin ribao*, Contributing Commentator, October 20, 1979, trans. FBIS, November 9, 1979, pp. L3–10.

14. Yu Guangyuan, "On the Question Regarding 'The Theory of the Goal of Socialist Economy'," Xinhua, October 22, 1979, trans. FBIS, October 24, 1979, pp. L3–8; and idem, "Tantan 'shehui zhuyi jingji mubiao lilun' wenti" (On the "Theory of Socialist Economic Goals"). See also the discussion held by *Jingji yanjiu* and the Economics Institute of CASS.

15. Xu Yi, "Shehui zhuyi jingji guilu yu shehui zhuyi caizheng de zhineng zuoyong" (Socialist Economic Law and the Functions of Socialist Finance), p. 96.

16. Ibid., p. 97.

17. Ibid., p. 98.

18. Xu Yi, "Sanshi nian lai caizheng lilun yu shijian de fazhan" (The Development of Finance Theory and Practice Over the Past Thirty Years), pp. 10 and 17.

19. Ibid., p. 10.

20. Xu Yi, "Shehui zhuyi jingji guilu yu shehui zhuyi caizheng de zhineng zuoyong," pp. 106–107.

21. Ibid., p. 109.

22. He Jianzhang became increasingly conservative during the decade, taking part in the campaign to criticize spiritual pollution in 1983 and, more infamously, in sharply criticizing "bourgeois liberalization" following the 1989 Tiananmen crackdown. Similarly, Chen Jiyuan and Liu Guoguang tended to hold more conservative economic views in the latter part of the 1980s, although not so conservative as those of He Jianzhang. Nevertheless, all three were prominent supporters of economic reform in the early period.

23. Xu was not the only person to hold such views. See, for instance, Chen Peizhang and Jiang Zhenyun, "Jinjin zhuazhu tiaozheng zhege guanjian" (Firmly Grasp Readjustment, the Crux), *Renmin ribao*, May 27, 1980, p. 5.

24. Xu Yi, "Shehui zhuyi jingji guilu yu shehui zhuyi caizheng de zhineng zuoyong," pp. 100 and 106.

25. Xu Yi, "Lun shuishou de honggan zuoyong" (The Function of Tax Levers), p. 185. See also pp. 187 and 188.

26. Xu Yi, "Shehui zhuyi jingji guilu yu shehui zhuyi caizheng de zhineng zuoyong," p. 110.

27. Xu Yi, "Sanshi nian lai caizheng lilun yu shijian de fazhan," p. 29.

28. Xinhua, January 1980, trans. FBIS, January 15, 1980, pp. L5–6. See also Xu Yi, "Sanshi nian lai caizheng lilun yu shijian de fazhan."

29. Ibid., p. 25.

30. Zhao Ziyang, "Yanjiu xin qingkuang, quanmian guanche tiaozheng de fangzhen" (Study the New Situation and Fully Implement the Principle of Readjustment), *Hongqi*, no. 1 (1980), trans. FBIS, February 20, 1980, p. L3–11.

31. Lin Ling, "Kuoda qiye zizhuquan yu gaige qiye guanli" (Expanding Enterprise Authority and Reforming the Management of Enterprises), *Renmin ribao*, May 9, 1980, p.

5. See also Lin Ling, "Jianli zhuanye gongsi, lianhe gongsi de yuanze he fangfa chutan" (A Preliminary Discussion on the Principles and Methods of Establishing Specialized and Amalgamated Companies), *Renmin ribao*, July 1, 1980, p. 5.

32. Lin Zili, "Woguo jingji tizhi gaige de kaiduan" (The Opening Phase in China's Economic Structural Reform), *Renmin ribao*, April 4, 1980, p. 5.

33. Sun Xiaoliang, "Shehui zhuyi tiaojian xia de jingzheng" (Competition Under Socialist Conditions), *Renmin ribao*, June 23, 1980, p. 5.

34. Qin Wen, "Why Has It Not Been Possible to Scale Down Capital Construction?" *Renmin ribao*, January 31, 1980, p. 5, trans. FBIS, March 3, 1980, p. L18.

35. Chen Peizhang and Jiang Zhenyun, "Jinjin zhuazhu tiaozheng zhege guanjian."

36. Deng Xiaoping, "The Present Situation and Tasks," pp. 231, 234, and 243.

37. Members of the group included Yu Qiuli, Fang Yi, Wan Li, Yao Yilin, and Gu Mu. Their division of labor must have been energy, science and technology, agriculture, finance, and foreign trade, respectively. At the time, the State Economic Commission was established with Yu Qiuli in charge. See Fang Weizhong, ed., *Zhonghua renmin gongheguo jingji dashiji (1949–1980)*, p. 650.

38. Xinhua, February 19, 1980, trans. FBIS, February 20, 1980, p. L11.

39. Li Xiannian, "Jianchi caizheng shouzhi pingheng, lue you jieyu de fangzhen" (Uphold the Orientation of Balancing Revenues and Expenses with a Slight Surplus).

40. Fang Weizhong, *Zhonghua renmin gongheguo jingji dashiji (1949–1980)*, p. 651.

41. See "Doing Everything According to Actual Capabilities Is an Important Principle for Capital Construction—More on the Guiding Principle of Doing Things According to Actual Capabilities," *Renmin ribao*, Editorial, June 9, 1980, trans. FBIS, June 12, 1980, pp. L11–14; "Set Capital Construction on the Right Course, Follow Strict Capital Construction Discipline," *Renmin ribao*, Editorial, June 10, 1980, trans. FBIS, June 19, 1980, pp. L1–5; "Haste Makes Waste—A Third Discourse on the Guiding Principle of Acting According to One's Capability," *Renmin ribao*, Editorial, June 12, 1980, trans. FBIS, June 18, 1980, pp. L15–17; "An Important Principle for Making Plans Is to Leave No Gaps—The Fourth Discourse on the Guiding Ideology of Acting According to One's Capability," *Renmin ribao*, Editorial, June 16, 1980, trans. FBIS, June 16, 1980, pp. L3–5; and "What Should Be Upheld and What Should Be Opposed?—Fifth Discussion on the Guiding Thought of Doing Everything According to Actual Capabilities," *Renmin ribao*, Editorial, June 26, 1980, trans. FBIS, July 9, 1980, pp. L8–11.

42. Ruan Ming, *Deng Xiaoping diguo* (The Empire of Deng Xiaoping), pp. 88–91.

43. Ibid., p. 91.

44. Deng Xiaoping, *The Selected Works of Deng Xiaoping*, p. 287.

45. Deng Xiaoping, "Remarks on Successive Drafts of the 'Resolution on Certain Questions in the History of Our Party Since the Founding of the People's Republic of China'," p. 283.

46. Deng Xiaoping, "Reform of the Party and State Leadership," p. 316.

47. Deng Xiaoping, "The Present Situation and Tasks," pp. 236–237.

48. Deng Xiaoping, "Reform of the Party and State Leadership," p. 324.

49. Deng Xiaoping, "Remarks on Successive Drafts of the 'Resolution on Certain Questions in the History of Our Party Since the Founding of the People's Republic of China'," p. 283. Apparently Deng first raised the question of feudalism in his May 31 speech, but that part of his remarks was deleted by Hu Qiaomu and Deng Liqun when they edited Deng's *Selected Works*. See Ruan Ming, *Deng Xiaoping diguo*, p. 91–93.

50. Deng Xiaoping, "Reform of the Party and State Leadership," pp. 317–318.

51. Deng Xiaoping, "Answers to the Italian Journalist Oriana Fallaci," p. 328. The irony of this remark was that Deng was about to install Hu Yaobang in Hua Guofeng's place, apparently against the opposition of many party leaders. As Teiwes insightfully

pointed out well before Hu's fall, this manuever did not bode well for Hu's future. See Frederick C. Teiwes, *Leadership, Legitimacy, and Conflict in China*, p. 88.

52. Xinhua, June 24, 1980, trans. FBIS, June 25, 1980, pp. L1–2.

53. "Correctly Understand the Role of the Individual in History," *Renmin ribao*, Contributing Commentator, July 4, 1980, trans. FBIS, July 7, 1980.

54. See "National Philosophical Symposium of Party Schools Stresses Elimination of Feudal Ideology as an Important Aspect of the Education of Cadres," *Guangming ribao*, July 6, 1980, p. 1, trans. FBIS, July 18, 1980, pp. L3–4; and Du Haozhi, "Zai jingji lingyu fandui fengjian canyu shi yixiang zhongyao de renwu (Opposing Feudal Remnants Is an Important Task in the Economic Realm), *Jingji yanjiu*, no. 9 (September 1980), pp. 76–80.

55. "Pernicious Influence of Feudalistic Thinking Must Be Eliminated," *Renmin ribao*, Contributing Commentator, July 18, 1980, p. 5, trans. FBIS, July 23, 1980, pp. L10–13.

56. Ruan Ming, "An Important Task on the Ideological Front." See Li Zehou, "Qimeng yu jiuwang de shuangzhong bianzou" (The Dual Transformation of Enlightenment and Salvation).

57. Feng Wenbin, "On the Question of Socialist Democracy," *Renmin ribao*, November 24 and 25, 1980, trans. FBIS, November 26, 1980, pp. L23–30.

58. Ruan Ming, *Deng Xiaoping diguo*, pp. 105–106.

59. Ibid., pp. 106–107.

60. Ibid., p. 108.

61. Fang Yi and Lu Dingyi were particularly outspoken in this regard. See ibid., p. 111.

62. Huang Kecheng, "On Appraisal of Chairman Mao and Attitudes Toward Mao Zedong Thought," Xinhua, April 10, 1981, trans. FBIS, April 13, 1981, pp. K6–17. Huang was speaking at a meeting of the Central Discipline Inspection Commission held in November 1980.

63. Chen Rulong, "Jiaoliu chengguo, tansuo zhenli" (Exchanging Results, Exploring the Truth), p. 3.

64. Ibid., p. 3.

65. Chen Rulong, "Weirao jingji tiaozheng kaizhan lilun yanjiu" (Open Up Theoretical Study Around the Theme of Economic Readjustment), p. 10.

66. Xu Yi, "Dangqian caizheng jingji zhong cunzai de wenti he women de duice" (The Fiscal and Economic Problems Existing at Present and Our Countermeasures), pp. 22–23.

67. Ibid., p. 16. Xu went on to say, "We believe that deficit financing is an inevitable product of the inherent contradictions of the capitalist system. It is both a means to alleviate crisis and a poison (*mei ji*) that will exacerbate crisis. It serves the monopoly capitalist class and is a means of strengthening the exploitation of workers. . . . It is totally incompatible with our socialist system; it is absolutely contrary to the goal of socialist production" (p. 27).

68. Ibid., p. 30.

69. Zhao Ziyang, "Guanyu tiaozheng guomin jingji de jige wenti" (Some Questions in the Readjustment of the National Economy), p. 608.

70. According to Ruan Ming, Chen's advisors argued for reducing economic growth rate to zero or even negative growth and greatly strengthening central control in order to eliminate financial deficits, but Deng would only agree to reduce the growth rate to 4 percent. Ruan Ming, *Deng Xiaoping diguo*, p. 112.

71. "Zhonggong zhongyang zhengzhiju huiyi tongbao" (Communiqué of the Meeting of the Political Bureau of the CCP Central Committee), p. 598.

72. "Zhonggong zhongyang zhengzhiju huiyi tongbao," p. 598. In saying that the Politburo decision was unanimous, the communiqué was not including Chen Yonggui and

Saifuding, who were not even notified of the meeting and were formally dropped from the Politburo at the Sixth Plenum. See ibid., p. 596.

73. Ruan Ming, *Deng Xiaoping diguo*, p. 111.

74. Chen Wenhong, ed., *Tiaozheng qi di Zhongguo jingji—Xu Yi lunwen xuanji* (The Chinese Economy in the Period of Readjustment—Collected Essays of Xu Yi), p. 7.

75. Chen Yun, "Jingji xingshi yu jingyan jiaoxun" (The Economic Situation and the Lessons of Experience).

76. Deng Xiaoping, "Implement the Policy of Readjustment, Ensure Stability and Unity," pp. 348–349.

77. Ibid., p. 351.

78. The "Outline Report of the Symposium on Structural Reform of Industrial Management" was adopted by the State Council on April 1. See Gao Shangquan, *Zhongguo de jingji tizhi gaige* (China's Economic Structural Reform), p. 329.

79. Lo Ping, "Reorganization of the Nucleus of the Chinese Communist Party—The Truth of Hua Guofeng's Resignation and the New Troika," *Cheng ming*, no. 40 (February 1, 1981), pp. 7–9, trans. FBIS, February 2, 1981, p. U4. In Ruan Ming's opinion, "The December 1980 Central Work Conference was a turning point in the retreat of Deng Xiaoping's whole reform line as well as a turning point in growing strength and influence of the Chen Yun clique over politics and economics." See Ruan Ming, *Deng Xiaoping diguo*, p. 115.

80. Author's interviews.

81. On Chen's role in this reformulation, see Deng Liqun, "Zhengque chuli jihua jingji he shichang tiaojie zhi jian de guanxi" (Correctly Handle the Relation Between the Planned Economy and Market Regulation), p. 81. See also Fang Weizhong, "Yi tiao buke dongyao de jiben junze" (A Fundamental Principle that Must Not Be Shaken), pp. 154–155. Liu Guoguang explicitly notes the contrast between the formulations adopted at the Central Work Conference and in the history resolution with earlier formulations. See "Yanjiu he taolun jihua jingji yu shichang wenti de yidian xiangfa" (Some Thoughts on Studying and Discussing the Question of Plan and Market), p. 7. In Chen Yun's 1979 letter, he divided the economy into two parts: the planned *economy* and market *regulation*. See "Jihua yu shichang wenti" (On the Question of Planning and Markets), p. 221.

82. Chen Yun, "Jingji jianshe de jige zhongyao fangzhen" (Several Important Directions in Economic Construction), pp. 275–277.

83. Chen Yun, "Jiaqiang he gaijin jingji jihua gongzuo" (Strengthen and Improve Economic Planning Work).

84. This conference was sponsored by the journal *Caimao jingji*. In addition to Sun, Liu Guoguang, Gui Shiyong, He Jianzhang, Wang Jue, Wu Jinglian, and Li Renjun spoke at it. See *Caimao jingji*, no. 4 (April 1984), for summaries of their remarks. Liu says that Chen had recently "repeatedly" emphasized the question of the planned economy as primary, perhaps suggesting that Chen addressed this issue more than his selected works indicate.

85. Liu Guoguang, "Luelun jihua tiaojie yu shichang tiaojie de jige wenti" (Briefly Discussing Some Questions About Planned Regulation and Market Regulation). Note that in discussing "planned regulation" and "market regulation," Liu is subtly rejecting the superordinate-subordinate relationship inherent in Chen Yun's formulation "planned economy" and "market regulation." Moreover, in his discussion of "planned regulation," it is apparent that Liu has a more market-oriented conception of planning (that is to include guidance planning as well as to make plans more in accordance with the "law of value") than does Chen Yun and his supporters.

86. Liu cited an article by Yang Shikuang as the source of this accusation. Yang's article is a harsh attack on the effort of reform-minded economists to justify competition in socialist societies. In conclusion, he states, "competition is an economic concept that exists under capitalist conditions and private ownership. To employ it under the conditions of socialist public ownership system will not only cause theoretical confusion but will harm practical work." See "Shehui zhuyi jingji zhong yinggai you jingzheng ma?" (Should Socialist Societies Have Competition?).

87. Liu Guoguang, "Luelun jihua tiaojie yu shichang tiaojie de jige wenti," p. 4. Note that Liu, like other writers at this time, has adopted the convention of referring to the "present stage," obviously avoiding the ideological problems surrounding the concept of the "initial stage" of socialism.

88. Ibid., p. 7. The notion of a "fused" (*jiaoti shi*) integration was picked up from Hungarian discussions of reform. See "Sun Yefang tongzhi zhuchi zuotanhui xuexi Chen Yun tongzhi chunjie zhongyao jianghua" (Comrade Sun Yefang Convenes Symposium to Discuss Comrade Chen Yun's Important Spring Festival Talk).

89. Xu Dixin, "Zai guojia jihua zhidao xia chongfen fahui shichang tiaojie de fuzhu zuoyong" (Fully Utilize the Subsidiary Function of Market Regulation Under the Guidance of State Planning), *Shijie jingji zengkan*, no. 4 (1981), quoted in Zhao Renwei, "Shehui zhuyi jingji zhong de jihua he shichang" (Plan and Market in the Socialist Economy), p. 481.

90. In addition to the articles cited below, see Fang Weizhong, "Yi tiao bu ke dongyao de jiben junze," pp. 153–165; Wang Renzhi, "Guanyu jianchi shehui zhuyi jihua jingji de jige wenti" (Several Questions on Upholding the Socialist Planned Commodity Economy), and Wang Renzhi and Gui Shiyong, "Jianchi he gaijin zhilingxing jihua zhidu" (Uphold and Improve the System of Mandatory Planning). Fang, Wang, and Gui were all at the State Planning Commission at the time.

91. You Lin, "Jihua shengchan shi zhuti, ziyou shengchan shi buchong" (Planned Production Is Primary, Free Production is Supplementary), *Jingji yanjiu*, no. 9 (September 1981), pp. 3–9.

92. Gu Shutang and Chang Xiuze, "Lun shehui zhuyi jingji de jihua yu shichang de jiehe" (Integration of Planning and Market in the Socialist Economy), in *Guomin jingji tiaozheng yu jingji tizhi gaige* (Readjustment of the National Economy and Reform of the Economic Structure) (Shandong: Renmin chuban she, 1981), as cited in Zhao Renwei, "Shehui zhuyi jingji zhong de jihua he shichang," p. 481.

93. Gong Xuelin, "Guanyu jihua jingji he shichang tiaojie de jidian kanfa" (Some Views on Planned Economy and Market Regulation), *Shehui kexue*, no. 9 (September 1982), cited in Zhao Renwei, "Shehui zhuyi jingji zhong de jihua he shichang," p. 481.

94. Zhao Renwei, "Shehui zhuyi jingji zhong de jihua he shichang," p. 490.

95. Tao Dayong, "Shi jihua jingji, hai shi shangpin jingji?" (Is It a Planned Economy or a Commodity Economy?), *Guangming ribao*, June 26, 1982, p. 3.

96. Li Zhenzhong, "Ye tan jihua he shichang wenti" (Also Discussing the Question of Plan and Market), *Guangming ribao*, December 26, 1981, p. 3.

97. Ruan Ming, *Deng Xiaoping diguo*, pp. 111–112.

98. Deng Liqun, "Zhengque chuli jihua jingji he shichang tiaojie zhijian de guanxi."

99. Gong Shiqi and Xu Yi, "Jianchi jihua jingji wei zhu, shichang tiaojie wei fu" (Uphold the Planned Economy as Primary and Market Regulation as Supplementary).

100. Liu Guoguang, "Yanjiu he taolun jihua yu shichang wenti de yidian kanfa." A note says that this speech was delivered on October 23, 1981, at a symposium on the question of plan and market. See also "Sun Yefang tongzhi zhuchi zuotanhui xuexi Chen Yun tongzhi chunjie zhongyao jianghua," p. 303.

101. Hu Yaobang, "Report to the Twelfth Party Congress," *Renmin ribao*, September

8, 1982, p. 1, trans. FBIS, September 8, 1982, p. K9. Translation reworded on basis of original, and emphasis added..

102. Ibid. For a discussion of the economic provisions of the report to the Twelfth Party Congress, see Wang Jiye, *Jihua jingji yu shichang jingji tiaojie—xuexi dang de shierda wenjian tihui* (Planned Economy and Market Regulation—Understanding Gained Studying the Documents of the Twelfth Party Congress).

103. Article 15 of the "Constitution of the People's Republic of China," Xinhua, December 4, 1982, trans. FBIS, December 7, 1982, pp. K1–28.

104. Xinhua, December 2, 1982, trans. FBIS, December 3, 1982, pp. K4–5.

4

Comprehensive Reform and the Emergence of Young Economists

The first phase of China's economic reform, from 1978 through 1982, had transcribed an arc, moving from the ideological and economic orthodoxy of the pre-reform days to a period of intellectual vitality and economic experimentation and then back to renewed stress on socialist orthodoxy. Ideological trends and economic reforms did not move in uniformity with each other; there were two cycles of ideological opening and closing (from May 1978 to March 1979 and from the summer to the fall of 1980) in the same period in which economic reform got under way until it was put on hold at the December 1980 Central Work Conference. There was nevertheless a relationship between the two spheres of economic reform and ideological openness. It was, as noted above, precisely the convergence of a new wave of ideological orthodoxy (reinforced by concerns about events in Poland) and increased worry over the economic situation that brought about a two-year period, from December 1980 to the end of 1982, in which heightened economic controls were reinforced by tightened ideological strictures.

This period of economic readjustment and ideological control was to a large extent justified by depictions of serious economic problems that required tight control. By late 1982, however, predictions of continued economic difficulties and slow growth were beginning to wear thin. In fact, the economy was performing better than many had predicted. Industrial production grew in 1982 by 7.7 percent over that of 1981, almost doubling the 4 percent growth rate projected by the plan. Enterprise deficits remained high, reaching a peak of 5.58 billion yuan in 1982, and there was a budget deficit of 2.93 billion yuan. Nevertheless, financial revenues had increased 3 percent over those of the previous year, and the budget deficit was only 2.6 percent of revenues, considerably better than the 11.7 percent figure of 1980.

In the rural areas, the economic results were even more striking. The grain harvest reached 354 million tons, a remarkable 9 percent increase over that of 1981. At the same time, cotton production increased 21.3 percent and oil crops 15.8 percent over those of 1981. Wan Li was understandably ebullient when he addressed the Rural Work Conference in November 1982. "Never have peasants been more delighted and confident than today since the cooperative transformation of agriculture," Wan said.[1] He was particularly proud to report that the per capita average annual income of peasants in the 231 poorest counties of China had risen to 150 yuan. The problem then facing agriculture was that peasants had greatly increased the production of grain, cotton, and cash crops, but the bureaucracy had been slow to respond to these changes. Peasants were having trouble selling their crops, and it was difficult to move goods from one area to another. In order to maintain the momentum of rural reform, it was necessary to further loosen policies to allow the emergence of "specialized households" and to reform the circulation system so that it could keep pace with rural production. In short, the successes of the early phase of rural reform were running up against the limits of extant policy and bureaucratic rigidity.

On January 2, 1983, the CCP promulgated Document No. 1, "Some Questions Concerning the Current Rural Economic Policies." This document declared that the household responsibility system had "saved the stagnating situation in agricultural production," but it also went on to warn that unless the thinking of "quite a few comrades" was changed and certain aspects of the "superstructure" were reformed, the "peasants' rising enthusiasm may be dampened again and the booming rural economy suffocated."[2] It went on to praise the "specialized households" that had emerged in the countryside for "seeking economic results and fully utilizing (their) small financial resources and manpower, thus giving free rein to the role of all types of go-getters in the rural areas and promoting division of specialized production and various forms of economic integration."[3]

The document also called for separating government administration from commune management, thus taking the first step toward the dissolution of communes, and approved the hiring of assistants or taking on of apprentices by specialized households. This was a major step because it raised the question of "hired labor." Shortly after the household production system had been implemented, some peasants began to undertake specialized work of one sort or another, frequently hiring a few people to help out. (Because the term "hire" [guyong] in Marxist terminology implies exploitation, such labor was called by such names as "asked-to-help labor" [qingbang gong].) Such trends stirred a new round of debate in the rural areas, with critics saying that the appearance of hired labor in the countryside was clear evidence of the restoration of capitalism. This debate thus raised sensitive ideological questions, and Chen Yun objected to hired labor while Deng Xiaoping agreed to permit it.[4] It is apparent that by the end of 1982 the development of the rural reforms had acquired a momentum of their own, forcing the central authorities to accept further ideological reform (such as the tacit acceptance of hired labor) and institutional reform (such as allowing individual peasants to engage in the long-distance sale of goods) or risk stifling the newly won prosperity of the rural areas. In short, the development of rural reform was forcing new and broader issues of ideological and institutional change onto the reform agenda. In yielding to the imperatives of continued development of the rural economy, Document No. 1 of 1983 marked an important step forward in the ongoing reform of China's rural economy. It was after this document had been accepted that Yang Yizhen, the party secretary of Heilongjiang Province who had opposed the extension of the household responsibility system, was removed and the system adopted throughout the country.

The promulgation of Document No. 1 set the stage for major new reform initiatives in ideology and party leadership on the one hand and in economic reform on the other. In an important speech in late January 1983, Hu Yaobang launched these initiatives by reemphasizing the urgency of reform and the need to break with old conventions—that is, with the ideological prescriptions of orthodox interpretations of Marxism that had hamstrung efforts to introduce new reforms. At the same time, Hu called for promoting cadres who were bold enough to carry out reform, thus presaging a major turnover in provincial leadership that would take place in 1983 and 1984.[5]

In March 1983, Hu Yaobang presided over the centenary commemoration of Marx's death, giving a keynote address that was a milestone in the history of Marxism-Leninism. Calling Marx not only a great revolutionary but also a "great scientist," Hu drew a portrait of him as an intellectual who conscientiously drew on the diverse heritage of mankind to develop a system of thought, indeed an epistemology, for analyzing social development. This portrait of Marx served to justify new efforts to draw upon the achievements of all societies, socialist and nonsocialist alike, and thereby "develop" Marxism to new heights. Intellectuals were critical in this effort to understand the modern world and direct modernization; they could no longer be looked upon as being apart from the working class and discriminated against as "alien" beings.[6]

Hu's effort to raise the status of intellectuals in Chinese society paralleled a major effort by intellectuals who had close links with Hu to provide a systematic reinterpretation of Marxism that would, in turn, provide a theoretical rationale for reform. The crux of this effort revolved around the concepts of humanism and alienation. Drawing on Marx's earlier writings, particularly his *Economic and Philosophical Manuscripts of 1844*, and on East European discussions, such party intellectuals as Zhou Yang, Su Shaozhi, and Wang Ruoshui tried to formulate an ideological framework that would provide an alternative to the party's reliance on traditional methods of ideological and political orthodoxy for maintaining social control. They tried to develop a comprehensive intellectual approach that would both justify reform and provide a sense of morality and idealism to fill the void left by the jettisoning of Maoist ideology in the late 1970s.[7]

Parallel with Hu's efforts to reform ideology and shake up the party bureaucracy, Zhao Ziyang oversaw the implementation of new steps in economic reform. On February 8, 1983, the State Council took a major step toward implementing urban reform by approving Chongqing as an experimental site for "comprehensive" urban reform. Previously, Shashi and Changzhou had been selected as sites for urban reform experiments; however, the selection of Chongqing marked the first time a major industrial city had been named as a site for comprehensive reform. The idea of selecting Chongqing was promoted by Jiang Yiwei and Lin Ling, who had raised the idea in their April 1982 report on the Capitol Iron and Steel Company. In November 1982, they presented Zhao Ziyang with a proposal on selecting Chongqing as a site for comprehensive reform, which was subsequently approved.[8]

In April 1983 the first stage of the "replacing profits with taxes" (*li gai shui*) reform was approved (though not before an acrimonious dispute with Hu Yaobang over the direction of urban reform). This reform, which was supported by both the Ministry of Finance and Vice Premier Tian Jiyun, marked an effort to satisfy the Ministry of Finance's demand for greater revenue as well as the reformers' demands for greater enterprise autonomy. It was intended as an alternative to the contract responsibility system, and it was only after a great deal of argument that Capitol Iron and Steel was allowed to continue its experiment.[9]

In June 1983, Zhao Ziyang, speaking to the First Session of the Sixth National People's Congress, signaled his disagreement with the direction for economic policy that had been laid out at the Twelfth Party Congress. In contrast to the effort to reinforce state controls over the economy suggested by that document, Zhao called for accelerating economic reform. It was necessary, he said, to reform the planning system and learn to use economic levers, such as prices, taxation, and credit policy, to manage the economy.[10]

The contrast between this new wave of reform and the ideological offensive against economic reform concepts in 1981–82 suggests the depth of tension within the party in the first part of 1983. In the fall, party conservatives were able to persuade Deng Xiaoping of the need for a new effort to criticize unorthodox thinking, and at the Second Plenary Session of the Twelfth Central Committee in October 1983, Deng undercut Hu, his general secretary, by siding with conservatives. There were indeed, he declared, people who loved to discuss the "value of people, humanism, and so-called alienation"; such people were not interested in criticizing capitalism but in criticizing socialism. Such theories had spread, Deng said, because of "lax" leadership on the ideological front. It was necessary to strengthen such leadership because, "[t]he danger of spiritual pollution is great; it can endanger the nation and harm the people."[11]

It was a critical moment in the history of reform. Deng not only decisively rejected the comprehensive approach to reform favored by liberal intellectuals; he did so by siding with the conservatives against Hu Yaobang. Perhaps the approach represented by people like Su Shaozhi and Wang Ruoshui never had a chance. Deng's rejection of their ideas, however, was absolutely consistent with his 1979 speech "Uphold the Four Cardinal Principles" and his other denunciations of liberal ideological trends within the party. Instrumentalist in his orientation, Deng had no interest in the abstract philosophical issues involved in redefining China's ideological framework. Moreover, as Xue-liang Ding has commented, formulating a humanistic, democratic ideological framework conflicted with both the autocratic values the top leadership had inherited from China's Confucian past as well as with their Leninist revolutionary experience. It also would have meant sharp ideological conflict within the party, whereas Deng's whole strategy was to minimize opposition to reform by avoiding contentious ideological issues to the extent possible.[12]

Although Deng's intention in supporting the campaign against spiritual pollution was to stress ideological orthodoxy rather than to slow economic reform, the campaign did nevertheless threaten economic reform by intimidating intellectuals whose support was needed, by postponing reform measures that were already under discussion, by creating doubts about the longevity of China's reform program among overseas investors, and by creating great uncertainty about future policy at the local level, particularly among peasants. The campaign incurred the united opposition of Zhao Ziyang, Hu Yaobang, Wan Li, and Fang Yi, who was head of the State Science and Technology Commission.[13]

In his efforts to persuade Deng to call a halt to the campaign against spiritual pollution, Zhao seized upon the concept of the "new technological revolution," urging people to read Alvin Toffler's *The Third Wave*.[14] The concept of the new technological revolution was well chosen both to respond to the issues raised by party conservatives and to win Deng's support for stopping the campaign against spiritual pollution. Just as the conservatives invoked fears of "national nihilism" to bolster their sense of nationalism, the concept of a new technological revolution raised the specter of international competition to tap a different but similarly powerful vein of nationalistic feeling. Suggesting that the world was again passing China by, Zhao was implicitly appealing to the decades-old fear that China would be extinguished (*wang guo*) if it failed to modernize. At the same time, Zhao was using science, which was more easily accepted by the party leadership as being without class character, as the leading edge in reforming the economic system and more rapidly opening China to the outside world. Moreover, the concept of a new technological revolution pointed to the importance of intellectuals, thus undercutting the campaign against spiritual pollution that was frightening intellectuals.

All of these issues appear to have been designed to appeal to Deng, who strongly believed that China had wasted twenty years in its efforts to modernize. As much as he disliked the liberal intelligentsia, Deng clearly recognized the importance of scientific and technical personnel. When he had first returned to power in 1977, Deng had taken charge of work in the areas of science and education, offering to be the "logistics officer" for China's scientists as they labored toward modernization.

Zhao's appeals succeeded; in November Deng changed course, ordering that the campaign against "spiritual pollution" be wound down, much to the dismay of party conservatives.[15] An authoritative article on "revolutionary humanism," published under the name of Hu Qiaomu, but clearly representing more than Hu's personal views, was published in late January in an effort to lay to rest the ideological issues surrounding humanism.[16]

Comprehensive Urban Reform

As the campaign against spiritual pollution waned in late 1983 and early 1984, the pace of economic reform quickly accelerated. It soon became clear that both in scope and depth the new round of economic reforms would vastly exceed those initiated in the late 1970s. In retrospect, Deng's willingness to accept the campaign against spiritual pollution appears to have been an effort to maintain a course that combined orthodox socialist thought with economic reform. When the ideological currents stirred by that campaign threatened the economic reforms, Deng stopped the campaign. It is only from this time that one can speak of China's reforms as embarking decisively on a course of combining political orthodoxy with economic liberalism, and even after this time, particularly in 1986, political liberals mounted yet another challenge to this pattern.

In the economic reforms adopted in 1984, Deng showed himself willing to move more boldly on the economic front than he had ever done before, sharply rejecting the economic program that had been mapped out under Chen's guidance. Whereas only two years earlier, the Twelfth Party Congress had called for implementing "unswervingly" the principles of "readjustment, reform, consolidation, and improvement" throughout the Sixth Five-Year Plan (i.e., through the end of 1985), the party turned decisively in 1984 away from readjustment and toward reform.

The decision to push ahead with reform thus marked a sharpening of differences between Deng and Chen.[17] Whereas in the late 1970s and early 1980s Deng was generally willing to yield to Chen's greater experience and expertise in the economic realm, by 1984 he clearly viewed Chen's economic thinking as outdated and overly cautious. Deng became determined to push ahead over Chen's objections. Thus, the decision to accelerate comprehensive urban reform marked a deep political split within the party, one that would only intensify in the coming years.

Deng's determination to push ahead with economic reform was no doubt based on the economic situation, which had developed more rapidly and with better results than anyone had anticipated. As noted above, the economy had shown better-than-expected results in 1982. In the following year, the economic news was even better. The output value of industry and agriculture increased by 10.2 percent over that of 1982, to reach 920.9 billion yuan. The grain harvest increased almost 12 percent, reaching a historic high of 396 million tons. The output value of village and township enterprises increased 19 percent to 101.6 billion yuan, and enterprise losses had fallen from 5.6 billion yuan in 1982 to 3.7 billion yuan in 1983, their lowest point up to that date in the Dengist period. State revenues had increased almost 12 percent from those of 1982 (although the bumper harvest led to an official budget deficit of 4.3 billion yuan).[18] Such overwhelmingly positive economic news undercut the credibility of conservatives. Dire warnings about severe economic problems without the long-term maintenance of readjustment policies began to ring hollow. Even many cautious economists believed that China could safely push ahead with comprehensive reform.[19]

Deng dramatized the end of the campaign against spiritual pollution and his determination to make a new push on reform with a dramatic visit to the highly controversial Special Economic Zones (SEZs). Chen Yun had long opposed the establishment of the SEZs, and they had received little support from the center, at least since Hu Qiaomu had severely criticized them for corruption and exemplifying class conflict in February 1982.[20] In late January and early February 1984, Deng visited the Shenzhen and Shantou SEZs in Guangdong and the Xiamen SEZ in Fujian. In Shenzhen, Deng wrote, "The development and experience of the Shenzhen Special Economic Zone prove the correctness of our policy to establish Special Economic Zones," and in the Shekou industrial zone in Shenzhen he endorsed its controversial slogan, "Time is money; efficiency is life."[21] In May, Deng convened a meeting on coastal cities that ended, over Chen Yun's opposition, by recommending that fourteen seaboard cities be opened to foreign investment on terms only slightly more restrictive than those in the SEZs.[22]

The policy of opening to the outside world was conceived of as supporting reform of the urban economy both ideologically and economically. It implied that the import of foreign management methods and the expansion of market forces were ideologically acceptable at the same time that it provided the necessary conditions to attract foreign capital and expand imports of raw and semi-finished materials. Perhaps most important, the expansion of trade that came with the opening to the outside world provided an important stimulus to the domestic economy, allowing its growth rate to rise and thereby providing an economic atmosphere in which reform of the urban economy would be more feasible.

In the first half of 1984, a number of reforms were initiated in several interrelated areas: the delegation of decision-making authority, expansion of enterprise authority, reform of the planning system, and reform of the banking system. This reform program differed little in its conceptual approach from the ideas that had been expounded at the Wuxi Conference in 1979. Its guiding principles remained the "organic integration" of plan and market and the expansion of enterprise authority. What made the reforms of 1984 different from those of 1979 were the improved economic circumstances, the enhanced authority of Deng

Xiaoping (which was related to the success of the economy), and the learning that had occurred as a result of previous pilot projects. Reformers, supported by Deng, had a renewed sense of political confidence and boldly launched reforms that directly affected most if not all aspects of the economy. Gone were the days of tentative experiments in pilot enterprises and cities.

It is worth noting that as this new round of reform was undertaken, China's political leaders and their economic advisors continued to look to East Europe as a model of reform. This was only in part because the East European experience could provide an ideologically acceptable cover for introducing the desired reforms in China; it was also in part because most of China's senior economists remained more comfortable with the vocabulary of socialist political economy. Even many more market-oriented economists would reveal the "scars" of their intellectual upbringing. Neither ideologically nor intellectually was China prepared to make an epistemological break with socialist economics.

The primary model of reform to which Chinese economists looked during this period was that of Hungary. In the late 1970s, the most influential model had been Yugoslavia, but as Chinese economists became more familiar with the experiences of East Europe, they focused increasingly on the Hungarian model. This change in focus reflected a growing familiarity with the dysfunctionalities associated with the Yugoslavian reforms, the influence of Hungarian economists such as Janos Kornai, and the top-down approach taken in the Hungarian reforms. The Hungarian reform program was associated, at least in the minds of Chinese economists, with the drawing up of a comprehensive program and its implementation by the government. This approach was more appealing to leaders trying to maintain the authority of the center than the Yugoslavian model of delegating authority.

As the Chinese economic reform program was being discussed, an economic delegation from CASS visited Hungary in May and June 1983 to study systematically the course of Hungarian reforms. Their research report focused on a number of questions of obvious concern to China: the combining of economic regulation with planning, making the switch from relying primarily on administrative methods to relying on economic methods, the formation of an economic system with diverse forms of ownership, and the relationship between the state on the one hand and enterprises and localities on the other. The CASS group concluded that the Hungarians had been able to attain "obvious achievements" in the course of their reform and that the Hungarian economy had been able to develop in a proportionate manner.[23] In September 1983, the Ministry of Finance sent its own delegation to Hungary, headed by Vice Minister Chen Rulong, and in October a group of Hungarian specialists went to China to provide more details on their reform.[24]

A major thrust of the 1984 reform program—the devolution of administrative authority over enterprises to the provincial and municipal levels and the expansion of enterprise decision-making authority—was foreshadowed by Zhao

Ziyang's March trip to Chongqing. It will be recalled that Zhao, acting on the advice of long-time brain trusters Lin Ling and Jiang Yiwei, had in early 1983 designated Chongqing a site for experimenting with comprehensive economic reform. A year later, Zhao praised the results of the Chongqing experiment and declared that efforts to substitute taxes for profits were important for solving the problem of the relationship between the state and enterprises.[25]

A month after Zhao's trip to Chongqing, a critical symposium was held in Changzhou, one of the first two cities approved for experiments with comprehensive urban reform, to discuss measures for expanding the authority of enterprises. Participants at the meeting were reported to be "strongly discontented" with the restrictions on the decision-making authority of enterprises. Referring to the urban reform experiments of Shashi, Changzhou, and Chongqing, the meeting urged that such work be "accelerated" and that enterprises in selected cities be given greater power to decide on such things as production, marketing, funds, cadres, and wages.[26]

The discussions at Changzhou resulted in the "Provisional Regulations Governing the Further Expansion of the Authority of State-Run Industrial Enterprises," which were subsequently approved by the State Council on May 10, 1984.[27] This ten-point regulation authorized enterprises to plan production and marketing of their products as long as they fulfilled their state-assigned quotas and allowed them to negotiate the prices of their above-quota goods within a 20 percent range of the state-set price. Moreover, to encourage enterprises to upgrade their equipment, the regulations allowed them to keep 70 percent of their depreciation funds.[28] The decision to expand enterprise authority was accompanied by the granting of expanded powers to urban areas on an experimental basis. The Changzhou meeting also resulted in a decision to allow six cities—Dalian, Changzhou, Beijing, Tianjin, Shanghai, and Shenyang—to experiment with the factory-director responsibility system. A month later, when the regulations on expanding enterprise authority were approved, provinces were encouraged to select one or two cities in which to experiment with expanded urban authority. In October, it was reported that fifty-two cities had been given such expanded authority.[29]

The new experiments with the factory-director responsibility system marked the beginning of a campaign to shift managerial responsibility within enterprises from the factory party secretary to the technically more competent factory manager. Since the late 1950s, the effective authority in China's factories had been held by the party secretary, which meant that economic management was a function of the hierarchical party structure. Without breaking this vertical chain there was little chance that enterprises could become "independent commodity producers." As early as 1978, Deng had proposed abolishing party committees in industrial enterprises.[30] In 1980, Deng Xiaoping had talked about this problem in his speech on reform of the party and state leadership system, calling for factory managers to be given primary responsibility for production decisions. The extreme sensitivity of this proposal was indicated by its deletion when Deng's speech was first published in the *Selected Works of Deng Xiaoping* in 1983. (It was subsequently restored when Deng's speech was republished on July 1, 1987, in anticipation of the Thirteenth Party Congress.)[31]

One of the core measures in the 1984 reform program was the second stage of the *li gai shui* (tax-for-profit) reform. On September 18, the State Council approved the Ministry of Finance's proposal for eliminating the distinction, upheld in the first stage of the *li gai shui* reform, between taxes and profits. Starting on October 1, enterprises would pay a basic tax rate (55 percent) based on a limited number of categories of taxes.

At a meeting to discuss implementation of the *li gai shui* reform, Zhao Ziyang called this measure a "prerequisite for accelerating urban economic reform." According to Zhao, "If we do not make a breakthrough in this matter we will be unable to carry out the ten-article provisional regulations on extending the decision-making powers of enterprises." The central idea behind the *li gai shui* reform, Zhao made clear, was to free enterprises completely from administrative interference: "Tax collection will regulate the relations of distribution between the state and enterprises and will create conditions for enterprises to operate independently and assume sole responsibility for their profits and losses."[32] In short, the administrative relationship that had previously bound enterprises and ministries together would be replaced by a simple economic relationship. In this way, the enterprises—the "economic cells" of the economy—would be invigorated.[33]

Parallel to the reform of the enterprise system was an effort to revamp and redirect China's planning system. In October, the State Planning Commission announced that beginning in 1985 the number of industrial products subject to compulsory plans would be reduced from 120 to approximately 60; at the same time, the number of agricultural and sideline products subject to the state's purchasing quotas would be reduced from 29 to less than 10. Enterprises that fulfilled the quotas assigned by the state would be able to sell their above-quota products on the market at prices fluctuating within the limits prescribed by the state.[34] A State Council circular criticized the existing planning system as being overcentralized and too rigid, having too many mandatory plans, neglecting the regulative role of the market, and failing to effectively employ economic means of adjustment.[35]

This was a critical step in the reform of the state planning system. The State Planning Commission did not support this reform, but felt that it had no other choice given the political atmosphere prevailing at the time. Later, it would continue to try to subvert the implementation of this and other economic reforms.[36] Nevertheless, the reform curtailed the power of the State Planning Commission in significant ways. As Hua Sheng and his colleagues have commented, "Now matter how we might evaluate these regulations now, it was quite clear that the traditional planned economy could no longer exist after they had been implemented."[37]

The Decision on Economic Structural Reform

In October 1984, the Third Plenary Session of the Twelfth Central Committee adopted a landmark "Decision on Economic Structural Reform." The promulgation of this document marked a turning point in the Dengist period because it demonstrated, in a way that no previous initiative had, Deng's willingness to split decisively with Chen Yun's approach to economic development. When one lays the text of this document side by side with the arguments that conservative economic bureaucrats such as Xu Yi, Wang Renzhi, Deng Liqun, and You Lin (all of whom were part of Chen Yun's network) had presented in 1981, it becomes apparent what a radical departure from traditional concepts this document represented, even with all of its qualifications. Deng's willingness to support the "Decision on Economic Structural Reform" also contrasted with his rejection the year before of efforts by Hu Yaobang and liberal intellectuals to redefine Marxism; Deng was willing to support ideological breakthroughs, but only those he felt were necessary to support the reform of the economic system.

The drafting of the Third Plenum document began as early as late 1983 or early 1984, and went through seven or eight drafts before being adopted at the plenum. The central issue in debates over the document was the concept of a "commodity economy" (*shangpin jingji*), which conservative economists had continuously rejected.[38] The earlier drafts of the document were cautious, retaining language that stressed the dominance of planning. In June, Deng Xiaoping intervened in discussions about the document and stressed the concept of "building socialism with Chinese characteristics," anticipating his public comments on the same theme in August.[39] During the summer of 1984, drafts of the document were discussed with economists, and several argued strongly that unless the plenum decision contained a strong endorsement of the notion of a "commodity economy" there would be no ideological underpinning for urban reform.

Zhao Ziyang discussed this issue repeatedly with several economists so that he could personally hear their objections and their proposals for change. In August, further arguments over the content of the document were made at the leadership's annual meeting at the seaside resort of Beidaihe. On September 9, Zhao sent a letter to the Standing Committee of the Politburo that included several points. Wending his way carefully through the minefield of ideological dispute, Zhao stated that China would implement a planned economy, not a market economy, and that the major aspects of economic life would be controlled by the state plan.

Zhao went on, however, to argue that planning should be interpreted as meaning not only mandatory planning but also guidance planning and that the direction of reform was to decrease mandatory planning in favor of guidance planning. This was a critical point because it refuted the essential argument put forward by conservative economists in 1981–82 that *mandatory* planning was an *essential characteristic* (*benzhi tezheng*) of socialism. It also endorsed the essential point of the models of "organic integration," "mutual penetration," and "fusion" that had been proposed at the Wuxi Conference and afterward, namely, that plan and market should not exist as two separate realms, relating to each other like "boards" and "planks."

In addition, Zhao argued strongly that the document on economic reform needed to include a defense of the concept "planned commodity economy"—precisely the same terminology that Xue Muqiao had argued for in 1981, provoking Chen Yun's reemphasis on the planned economy.[40]

Zhao's letter was endorsed by the entire Standing Committee of the Politburo, although Chen Yun expressed reservations. In a comment on the document, Chen reportedly wrote: I agree with Zhao, but I would like to point out our practice in the past is not simply copying the Soviet model. We have our own development and very good experience. Now, the only thing we should do is to change it, improve it, and to develop it to comply with the new situation.[41]

Just before the Third Plenum opened, conservatives again launched an assault on reformist policies. In mid-September 1984, the Propaganda Department convened a symposium on literature and art in Shanghai. Conservative leaders, including Hu Qiaomu and Deng Liqun, apparently intended this meeting to be used to reopen criticism of "rightist" trends in the cultural arena. Deng Xiaoping, who no doubt wanted to quash any ideological challenges that might derail his plans for the plenum, quickly dispatched Hu Qili, then the fifty-five-year-old protégé of Hu Yaobang who was in charge of the day-to-day management of the CCP Secretariat, to intervene in the meeting. When He Jingzhi, the conservative deputy head of the Propaganda Department, gave the summation speech on the final day of the symposium, it had a very different tone than his opening address had had only a few days earlier. The audience, apparently primed to hear a sharp attack on rightism, was told that the task for the present and future was to "overcome and prevent the influence of 'leftism' in literary and art circles." The report on the meeting in *People's Daily* specifically highlighted Hu Yaobang's "concern" with the meeting and made clear that literature and art must serve economic construction.[42]

With this challenge defeated, the Third Plenum convened in late October and adopted the "Decision on Economic Structural Reform." The passage of this document marked a breakthrough for reformers, and the intellectual atmosphere, particularly with regard to economic issues, became much more open in its aftermath. There were, of course, compromises and concessions in the document that left reform constantly vulnerable to criticism. The term "planned commodity economy" did not settle arguments over the relationship between plan and market; economists and policy makers alike continued to argue about whether the emphasis should be placed on the "planned" or on the "commodity" part of the formulation. Moreover, the section of the "Decision" that dealt with the commodity economy stated bluntly that "Socialist society practices a planned economy on the basis of public ownership of the means of production. . . . This is one of the fundamental indicators of the superiority of a socialist economy." This terminology seemed to belie the declaration of the "Decision" that planning and the commodity economy formed a "unity."[43]

Political disputes about the "Decision" were apparent. In a lengthy defense of the document, Zheng Bijian, Hu Yaobang's political secretary, criticized conservatives for their long-standing and "erroneous" beliefs that "the economic pattern formed under certain historical conditions" was the only legitimate pattern of socialism and for regarding "all those reforms that run counter to this pattern as heresies or departures from socialism."[44] In an extraordinary speech to a meeting of the Central Advisory Commission that immediately followed the plenum, Deng Xiaoping endorsed the "Decision" as a "very good document" but frankly admitted the concerns of his colleagues. "Some of our comrades," Deng said, "are most worried by whether we will become capitalist. . . . They are afraid of seeing capitalism suddenly looming up after having worked all their lives for socialism and communism, and they cannot stand such a sight."[45]

Emergence of Young Economists

The adoption of the "Decision on Economic Structural Reform" was significant not only for its charting of a new conceptual approach to socialist economics that justified an expansion of the role of market forces, but also because it marked the emergence of new leadership strategies for implementing reforms. Prior to 1984, Zhao Ziyang had been very cautious in his relations with Chen Yun and the established economic bureaucracies that generally reflected Chen's influence. Zhao seemed to recognize and accept his position as a junior player in the management of the economy. Whatever his personal feelings about the retrenchment policies adopted in December 1980, Zhao fully supported them in his speech to the Central Work Conference. In return, Chen Yun praised Zhao for his willingness to speak "Beijing dialect" (that is, to speak for the center rather than for the provinces). In addition, Zhao's support for the tax-for-profit reform of the fiscal system came at least partly from a desire to maintain the support of powerful central ministries, particularly the Ministry of Finance.

With the adoption of the "Decision on Economic Structural Reform," Zhao began to turn away from this strategy. It might be said that he really had no choice in the matter. China's economic planning system, with the exception of the State Economic Commission, remained firmly under the control of conservative economic bureaucrats. The powerful State Planning Commission was headed by Chen Yun's long-time protégé Yao Yilin. Zhao could neither dominate this bureaucratic system (despite being head of the Central Finance and Economic Leading Group) nor demand leadership changes that would allow him to command compliance. Leadership arrangements had been worked out by the senior CCP leadership, especially Deng Xiaoping and Chen Yun, and Zhao had to work within the framework that he had been given. In order to implement economic reform, Zhao had little choice but to begin to find ways to go around the bureaucratic structures, particularly the State Planning Commission and the Ministry of Finance, that were dominated by political rivals.

In looking for new sources of ideas and reform strategies, Zhao turned naturally to some of the people who had been instrumental in thinking about, analyzing, and providing ideas for China's rural reforms. At the same time, a new generation of young economists was emerging from China's economics departments. Many of them were still in college or graduate school. Most of them, like the young intellectuals some ten or fifteen years their senior who had pioneered the rural reforms, were bright, energetic people eager to make contributions to China's reform. As a group, they may have differed from their seniors in being even less attached to the institutions and ideas of the CCP. Whereas those who had pioneered rural reform were genuine pragmatists who understood the difficulties of changing institutional and behavioral patterns, many of this younger generation had a greater impatience to change things than they did an appreciation of the difficulties in doing so. They had perhaps received the best training in economics of any generation since the founding of the PRC—many of them had a mathematical background and all of them had, to some extent, studied Western economics. It might also be said, however, that their training was incomplete; few of them had studied overseas, and it seems that their enthusiasm for Western ideas exceeded their understanding of them.

To organize this new group of young intellectuals, Zhao turned to Chen Yizi, the organizer of the Rural Development Group. Chen took some of his associates from the Rural Development Group and organized the Institute for Chinese Economic Structural Reform (*Zhongguo jingji tizhi gaige yanjiusuo*), known widely in China and abroad simply as the *Tigaisuo* or Economic Reform Institute. The Economic Reform Institute was established under the auspices of the State Commission for Economic Structural Reform (*Guojia jingji tizhi gaige weiyuanhui*), to which it was intended to provide a steady stream of research and analysis for the latter's consideration.

At the same time, Chen organized a group of young economists, based mainly in Beijing, to form the Beijing Association of Young Economists (*Beijing qingnian jingji xuehui*). Zhao's secretary, Bao Tong, became the head of this association, while Chen served as the executive deputy director. Some two hundred young and middle-aged economists were named as directors (*li shi*) of the new group. Within a short time, a journal, the *Forum of Young Economists* (*Zhongguo zhongqingnian jingji luntan*) was founded, and although it was independent of the Economic Reform Institute, it carried many articles by young economists, many of whom were associated in one way or another with the institute. Over the next few years, this journal published some of the most innovative, as well as most controversial, articles by China's young economists.[46]

Together, the Economic Reform Institute and the Association of Young Economists became important organizations for discussing the direction of reform and for researching various problems encountered in the reform process. According to Chen Yizi, the establishment of the two organizations encountered opposition from some older members of the party who thought that the leadership was relying too heavily on young people and that the thinking of these young economists was overly Westernized.[47]

This group of young economists actually began to have an impact on the issues of enterprise and macroeconomic reform even before the establishment of the Economic Reform Institute and the Association of Young Economists. A meeting sponsored by four newspapers—*Economic Weekly*, *Economic Daily*, the *World Economic Herald*, the *China Youth Paper*—and other organizations was held in Moganshan in Zhejiang Province's Deqing County from September 3 to 10, 1984. Formally known as the Academic Symposium of Middle-Aged and Young Economists (*Zhongqingnian jingji kexue gongzuozhe xueshu taolun hui*), the Moganshan Conference, as it came to be known, was supported by the leadership, which paid close attention to its proceedings.[48]

The Moganshan Conference is best remembered for its contribution to price reform. Prior to the meeting, there were two main approaches to the question of price reform. The first, favored by the State Council's Economic, Technical, and Social Development Research Center, which was headed by Ma Hong, was to reform prices in one or two large steps. The second approach, favored by some young economists with good connections to the leadership, was to reform prices in a series of small steps. The advantage of the latter approach lay in its low risk and the fact that the Ministry of Finance would not have to allocate money to support price reform.

When the Moganshan Conference convened, some participants favored one or the other of the price-adjustment schemes then being considered by the leadership. There were, however, a small number of influential participants who argued in favor of radical decontrol of the price system. At that time, a number of young economists, including Hua Sheng, then a graduate student at CASS, discussed the issue of price reform in a meeting that lasted past midnight. The participants in the meeting finally came up with the idea of reforming prices by means of a "dual-track" system; that is, in-plan prices would remain under state control while out-of-plan prices would be allowed to follow the market. The idea was that the prices of marginal goods would regulate the economic behavior by leading producers to know which goods were demanded by the market. At the same time, the market prices of such goods would provide relatively accurate signals of how to adjust prices. The approach embodied in this concept was "deregulation followed by adjustment, and adjustment followed by further deregulation."[49] Bureaucratically, this approach had the advantage of introducing market forces without directly challenging the planned economy.

While the Moganshan Conference was still meeting, a number of young economists met with Zhang Jingfu, the member of the Central Finance and Economic Leading Group who was in charge of price reform. Zhang was persuaded by the dual-track approach and returned quickly to Beijing where he energetically promoted it. The young economists then drafted a document entitled "Consciously Making Use of the Dual-Track System to Reform the Price Mechanism Smoothly," The draft was completed on September 12, 1984; on September 30, Zhao approved it.[50]

Zhao liked the approach. He immediately thought of the situation in coal production, where for years coal produced by local mines had been sold at market prices while coal from state mines had been sold at state-set prices. Moreover, the dual-track approach suited Zhao's political needs and his own economic approach. Zhao liked to lead in accordance with the opportunities— *yinshih lidao*, "guide according to the situation"—and the dual-track approach could minimize opposition from Chen Yun.[51]

Defining a New Approach to Reform

As noted above, the reform approach adopted by China's policy makers in 1984 was based on the set of ideas about expanding enterprise authority and rationalizing the price structure that were rooted in the concepts discussed at the Wuxi Conference in 1979. Although this approach called for giving enterprises greater decision-making authority, it was nevertheless primarily a top-down approach to reform. Reform was to be implemented gradually from the top; how much authority enterprises were to have would be decided primarily by the central authorities. Mainstream economic reformers continued to think in macroeconomic terms and about adjusting the balance between the plan and the market.

The emergence of the young economists brought new categories of thought to the reform process that would eventually have a great impact on the way in which central leaders, particularly Zhao Ziyang, thought about reform. Perhaps because of their experience in the process of rural reform, these economists focused naturally on the basic units of the economy; microeconomic concerns came to dominate their thinking. Partly because of their concern with changing the microeconomic behavior of enterprises, these young economists also focused on the related issues of the rate of economic growth and structural impediments to reform. In addition to bringing new categories of thought to the attention to Chinese economists, they brought the same interest in gathering data that had characterized their work in rural reform. Whatever their shortcomings, these young economists changed forever the way in which Chinese economists thought about economic issues. Even conservative economists would have to bolster their arguments with more data and less reference to the traditional categories of Marxist political economy.

A series of articles that began appearing in the journal *Jingji yanjiu* in the summer of 1985 gives a good sense of the way in which these young economists thought of the Chinese economy as the second wave of reform got under way. Perhaps ironically, these articles were not written by members of the Economic Reform Institute, but rather by the young economists who had remained behind in the Rural Development Research Center. Nevertheless, the subsequent evolution of debates over economic policy made it clear that many of those in the Economic Reform Institute shared the intellectual framework of their former colleagues.

The first and most important in this series of articles was an article entitled "The New Stage of Growth of the Chinese Economy and Rural Development." Primarily drafted by Zhou Qiren, a core member of the Rural Development Group, this article reflected an acute awareness that the Chinese economy had, by the mid-1980s, changed substantially from what it had been in the late 1970s. In particular, the success of the rural reforms meant that the problem of providing basic necessities to China's population had largely been solved. Because the basic food needs of the population had been met, the authors believed that the rapid growth of the agricultural economy could not be sustained. Unless China found a new sector that could spur continued growth, they argued, the high growth rates China had enjoyed in the first half of the decade were bound to decline. Thus, as the title of the article suggested, the Chinese economy was moving into a new stage of growth that presented new problems to China's decision makers.

In order to maintain a high rate of growth, the authors argued, it was necessary to identify another sector of the economy that could replace the dynamism of the rural economy. They identified nonessential consumer goods as the most likely candidate but believed that a fundamental shift of the economic structure was necessary in order to bring this potential into being. Drawing on arguments first articulated in the 1979–80 discussion of the "aims of socialist production," the authors maintained that "industrialization," as traditionally understood, would neither be able to support this structural shift nor resolve the employment pressures that China faced; it was necessary to bring about a new, more labor-intensive industrial structure that would be capable of meeting the demand for nonessential consumer goods. In the future, China would have to look less to such areas as machine building and iron and steel production and more to mining, construction, transportation, and the service industry to provide sufficient employment.[52]

A basic assumption of this article, as well as other articles written by like-minded economists, was that both the necessary structural shift and the reform of the economy could only be developed from the bottom up. In order to do this, it was necessary to have a thorough understanding of the microeconomy. In this, the authors were drawing on their own experience in rural reform as well as on the experience of reformers such as Jiang Yiwei and Lin Ling. Economic analysis and political strategy blended as they tried to find an approach that would make reform politically palatable while avoiding the problems that reform had encountered in the 1979–80 period.

Their belief that reform of the microeconomy was the necessary starting point for overall economic reform led the authors to be very suspicious of any approach that emphasized the use of macroeconomic controls. Writing in a period in which a major outcry followed the rapid expansion of both worker bonuses and the money supply in late 1984, the authors nevertheless argued that "the current problems should not be attributed only to the one problem of macro-control" because "if we exaggerate the problem of macro disequilibrium, policy will be led into adopting short-term measures for restoring macroeconomic balance," an approach that would leave the fundamental structural contradictions of the economy unresolved.

As this argument implied, the authors' suspicion of macroeconomic controls was founded partly on the belief that the use of such controls, particularly those that relied heavily on traditional methods of administrative control, would become a substitute for and inevitably delay more important structural changes. Second, the authors implied that a fundamental structural change of the economy and in the behavior of its microeconomic units could only come about in an environment of relatively rapid growth—an environment that required sustaining a high rate of investment, which ran counter to efforts to exercise macroeconomic control. Third, the authors of "The New Stage of Growth" saw an important positive side to the loss of economic balance implied in looser monetary policies and higher investment rates, namely the sense of urgency that economic problems create. They wrote:

> We ought to see that structural problems can be even more readily resolved in a situation in which gross supply and gross demand are in disequilibrium; there is often no way when the original structure is operating smoothly to make society feel that it is urgent to establish a new structure and mechanism. In this sense, what is most dangerous is not the general disequilibrium or even the "loss of control" within a certain range, but that we will not be able by means of structural reform to grasp the opportunity to change the structure of the national economy at a time of general disequilibrium.

Thus, although they did warn against excessive inflation, the authors' bias was clearly toward a relatively high rate of growth, which they believed could provide both the political and economic environment in which to carry out reform.

Contrary to what one might think given the article's (self-conscious) evocation of Rostow's book *The Stages of Economic Growth* in its title, the model of development that the authors had in mind was based not so much on American *laissez-faire* economics as on the Japanese model of guided development. Although the article does not discuss explicitly the Japanese model, its importance is suggested a number of times. For instance, in discussing the transition from an economy concentrating on the production of essential goods to one developing nonessential goods for the consumer market, the authors pointed out that the situation facing China was similar to that facing Japan at the time of its first consumer revolution in the 1950s.[53] Later in the article, they argued that China faced a number of important choices as it entered the new stage of economic growth and that the experience of many countries—"especially Japan"—proved how important it was to choose correctly which products to develop and in what order.[54] Moreover, in discussing the strategy for changing the old economic system, the authors noted that the most difficult and important problem was to decide what parts of the old structure should be weakened in what order so as to encourage the growth of the self-organizing mechanism of society and thus avoid a "willy-nilly expansion of unorganized strength," since that would make the system unable to cope with the "disintegration effect" and lead to a major recentralization. The authors credited Japan with great success in this area.[55] It is therefore apparent that the model of development in the minds of the authors was based on a notion of guided economic development in which the state would play a very different, but nonetheless important, role than it had in the previous three decades of the PRC.

The assumption that China was entering a new stage of economic growth that would require the rapid expansion of consumer goods was widely shared among a segment of young economists. For instance, Bai Nansheng, who was an early member of the Rural Development Group, argued that after 1982, 90 percent of China's population had had no difficulty in satisfying the basic needs of food and clothing. It followed that China was moving from a stage in which such essential products as food and clothing constituted the bulk of consumption to a stage in which nonessential products would form an increasing proportion of consumption.[56]

Bai further developed this approach in an article that he co-authored with Wang Xiaoqiang, who had been a core member of the Rural Development Research Center and had moved with Chen Yizi to help organize the Economic Reform Institute. Bai and Wang argued that "[a]fter the basic needs of existence are satisfied, the consumption demands and consumption desires of people turn toward diversification (yi fen xing)." They asserted that smaller-scale enterprises that were more responsive to the market would be better able to satisfy this demand for more diversified goods.[57] This argument clearly supported the thesis in Zhou Qiren's article that, in the future, economic development in China would shift away from the traditional manufacturing sector toward smaller industries directed at satisfying consumer demand.

The Debate Over High-Speed Growth

As noted above, "The New Stage of Growth of the Chinese Economy and Rural Development" implicitly assumed that high-speed economic growth was both possible and necessary for rapid economic reform. This was a highly controversial thesis with wide-ranging implications. Chen Yun's approach to economic development had always maintained that the growth rate should be kept within a suitable range; a more rapid rate of development than China's material and financial resources allowed would only result in inflation, waste, and sectoral imbalances. The central authorities would ultimately be forced to use harsh administrative means to slow economic growth, reduce inflationary pressures, and readjust sectoral imbalances—all at great cost to economic efficiency. Chen's ideas were rooted in the workings of the planned economy, in which interest rates and prices were not allowed to rise to reflect relative scarcities.

Although it remained highly controversial at the time, a number of young economists began to challenge Chen's assumptions about slow but steady growth. They argued that China had a surplus production capacity that could support higher growth rates and that transformation of China's economic structure could be accomplished more quickly and at lower cost if growth rates were kept high.

This thesis was argued most vigorously in a highly controversial article by Zhu Jiaming, one of the four gentlemen who had participated in the early discussions on enterprise reform. Zhu presented his views on high-speed development to a conference in Tianjin, and his paper was subsequently published in the journal of the Association of Young Economists. Contrary to the conventional wisdom as well as the then-current political line, Zhu argued vigorously that the economic growth China had experienced in 1984 was not inflationary and that there was good reason to believe that China was entering a period of high-speed economic development not unlike that experienced by Japan in the late 1950s and early 1960s.[58]

What was most eye-catching about Zhu's article was his explicit endorsement of an expansionary monetary policy. In late 1984, China's money supply had rocketed as news of an impending reform of the banking system leaked out. Most economists were shocked by the rapid expansion of the money supply and feared the onset of serious inflationary pressures. In contrast, Zhu boldly proclaimed that "[h]igh-speed growth demands a rapid expansion of the money supply." Warning against a conservative attitude in the determination of monetary policy, Zhu argued that it was important to pay attention not only to the inflation index but also to economic growth rates, trends toward commoditization, and the changing velocity of money. "We should bear in mind," he admonished, that "the simultaneous existence of inflation and economic growth is a typical characteristic of developed and developing countries in periods of high growth." This was an early and bold statement of what conservatives would later denounce as the "thesis that inflation is harmless" (*chizi wuhai lun*). As we shall see, concern over growth rates and inflation remained at the core of macroeconomic debate throughout the period from 1986 to 1988.

Although some young economists supported Zhu's article,[59] others refuted his arguments. One of the latter was Guo Shuqing, then a twenty-nine-year-old graduate student at CASS, who would later collaborate with Wu Jinglian (whose views are discussed in Chapter 5) before moving on to the State Planning Commission. In an article entitled, "The National Economy Cannot Be Forced to Take Off," Guo argued that the changeover from direct economic control to indirect economic control had only just begun, that the industrial structure and product mix remained irrational, and that the speed of technical progress remained far below the level needed for sustained high-speed growth. Under these conditions, maintained Guo, "if we pursue the target of high-speed growth, then it will be very difficult for economic growth to leave the old model and track."[60]

It is apparent that by the end of 1984, China's economic reform had entered a qualitatively different phase. Not only had the focus of reform efforts shifted to the urban economy, but more importantly the decision to accelerate economic reform marked a widening of differences between Chen Yun and Deng Xiaoping. In the late 1970s and early 1980s, Deng had largely acquiesced to Chen with regard to the economy. By 1983–84, Deng was convinced that Chen's economic views were too conservative and that Chen's slow but steady approach to the economy would generate neither the growth rates Deng desired for transforming China into a modern country with "wealth and power" nor the popular support needed to maintain the legitimacy of the government. It is also important to note that if economic reform brought higher growth rates and increased incomes to the people, then Deng's political prestige and power would be enhanced—all the more so for his rejecting Chen Yun's advice.

Moreover, by late 1984 Zhao Ziyang had gained a great deal of confidence in his ability to manage the economy, and it is apparent that he felt it necessary to turn away from the economic bureaucrats who should have been one of his main assets as premier. Such agencies as the State Planning Commission and the Ministry of Finance remained firmly under the control of people loyal to Chen Yun. Rather than trying to wrest control of these bureaucracies from the conservatives, Zhao adopted the less confrontational approach of turning to others for economic advice. This was one of the main functions of the Economic Reform Institute—to provide a source of analysis and policy advice that was independent of the various economic bureaucracies. One of the disadvantages of this approach was that Zhao would never gain dominance over the bureaucratic structure that he headed, and that would influence both his policy choices and his ability to control policy.

The emergence of the young economists and the establishment of the Economic Reform Institute marked the arrival on the Chinese political scene of a group of people who were far less wedded to the old economic order and who viewed the microeconomy rather than the macroeconomy as the key to economic reform. True to their origins in the rural reform, these people believed that there could be no blueprint for reform, that reform had to emerge through the adoption of policies that would permit reform to develop from the bottom up. As a group the young economists and institute members were also less concerned—though not unconcerned, as some have charged—with the issue of inflation, believing that rapid growth and some inflation were necessary to provide room for reform. Such views would bring them into conflict not only with the traditional economic bureaucrats of the State Planning Commission and the Ministry of Finance but also with mainstream reformers like Liu Guoguang and radical reformers like Wu Jinglian (whose views will be discussed in Chapter 5).

Notes

1. Wan Li, "Further Develop the New Phase of Agriculture Which Has Already Been Opened Up," *Renmin ribao*, December 23, 1982, pp. 1, 2, and 4, trans. FBIS, January 4, 1983, pp. K2–20. Wan's speech was delivered on November 5, 1982.
2. "Some Questions Concerning the Current Rural Economic Policies," Xinhua, April 10, 1983, trans. FBIS, April 13, 1983, p. K1.
3. Ibid., p. K4.
4. Author's interview.
5. Xinhua, January 20, 1983, trans. FBIS, January 21, 1983, pp. K1–2. Hamrin, *China and the Challenge of the Future*, pp. 64–65.
6. Hu Yaobang, "The Radiance of the Great Truth of Marxism Lights Our Way Forward," Xinhua, March 13, 1983, trans. FBIS, March 14, 1983, pp. K1–16.
7. Xue-liang Ding, "The Disparity Between Idealistic and Instrumental Chinese Reformers."
8. Jiang Yiwei, "Guanyu zai Chongqing jinxing zonghe gaige shidian de jidian jianyi" (Some Views on Conducting a Comprehensive Reform Experiment in Chongqing). A note identifies this article as co-authored with Lin Ling and as the third part of a proposal submitted to Zhao on November 5, 1982. It does not say what the first two parts were about.
9. Author's interviews. On the arguments over the profit-for-tax system, see Susan L. Shirk, *The Political Logic of Economic Reform in China*, Chapters 11–13.
10. Zhao Ziyang, "Report on the Work of the Government," Xinhua, June 23, 1983, trans. FBIS, June 23, 1983, pp. K14–K15.
11. Deng Xiaoping, "Dang zai zuzhi zhanxian he sixiang zhanxian shang de poqie renwu" (Urgent Tasks for the Party on the Organizational and Ideological Fronts), pp. 25 and 29. Baum traces the first use of the term "spiritual pollution" to Deng Liqun in a speech to the Central Party School on June 4, 1983. See Baum, *Chinese Politics in the Age of Deng Xiaoping*, Chapter 6.
12. Xue-liang Ding, "The Disparity Between Idealistic and Instrumental Chinese Reformers."
13. Ruan Ming, *Deng Xiaoping diguo*, p. 150.
14. Hamrin, *China and the Challenge of the Future*, pp. 75–78. Yue Bing, "New Changes in China's Production Structure,"*Liaowang*, Overseas Edition, no. 14 (April 1986), trans. JPRS-CEA–86–057 (May 9, 1986), pp. 53–56.
15. See, for instance, the article by PLA writer Liu Baiyu, "Adhere to the Four Basic Principles, Eliminate Spiritual Pollution," *Jiefangjun wenyi*, January 1, 1984, trans. FBIS, February 10, 1984, p. K1–4. This article was based on a speech given at a forum on an unspecified date, but it was published after a decision had been made to drop the campaign against spiritual pollution, indicating dissatisfaction with that decision. Liu was active in the campaign to criticize Bai Hua in 1981 and would participate in criticism of reform-minded writers during the campaigns against "bourgeois liberalization" in 1987 and 1989–90.
16. Hu Qiaomu, "On Humanism and Alienation," *Renmin ribao*, January 27, 1984, pp. 1–5, trans. FBIS, February 7, 1984, pp. K1–33.

17. This is not to say that compromises and concessions to Chen's wing of the party were not made. There were many such efforts to make the reform program more palatable to Chen, which ultimately hampered the cohesion and success of the reforms themselves. Nevertheless, there was a fundamental difference between the approach to reform that Chen had championed in the earlier period and that which began to unfold in 1984.

18. Figures on the economy are drawn from Wang Bingqian, "Guanyu yi jiu ba san nian guojia juesuan he yi jiu ba si nian guojia yusuan cao'an de baogao" (Draft Report on the State's Accounts for 1983 and the State's Budget for 1984) and *Zhongguo xiangzhen qiye nianjian, 1978–1987* (Chinese Township and Village Enterprise Yearbook, 1978–1987), p. 572.

19. Author's interviews.

20. Ruan Ming, *Deng Xiaoping diguo*, pp. 133–136.

21. Hamrin, *China and the Challenge of the Future*, p. 82.

22. Ibid., pp. 82–84.

23. "Xiongyali jingji tizhi kaocha baogao" (Investigation Report on the Economic Structure of Hungary), *Jingji yanjiu*, no. 2 (February 1984), pp. 10–21.

24. "Xiongyali caizheng tizhi kaocha" (Investigation of the Hungarian Finance Structure), *Jingji yanjiu*, no. 3 (March 1984), pp. 13–22, 8. The visit of Hungarian specialists to China is mentioned in "Xiongyali jingji tizhi kaocha baogao."

25. Sichuan Radio, March 6, 1984, trans. FBIS, March 8, 1984, p. K7.

26. "Minutes of a Symposium on Experimental Economic System Reform in Selected Cities, Approved by the State Council and Circulated by the State Economic System Reform Commission," *Renmin ribao*, May 21, 1984, pp. 1 and 3, trans. FBIS, June 8, 1984, pp. K12–14.

27. The connection between the Changzhou meeting and the provisional regulations is suggested not only by the similarity in their content but also by the fact that the minutes of the Changzhou meeting were approved by the State Council the same day the regulations were promulgated, suggesting that the minutes were the basis of the regulations. See Gao Shangquan, *Jiunian lai de Zhongguo jingji tizhi gaige* (China's Economic Structural Reform in the Last Nine Years), p. 155.

28. "Provisional Regulations of the State Council on Further Expanding the Decision Making Powers of State-Owned Enterprises," Xinhua, May 11, 1984, trans. FBIS, May 16, 1984, pp. K15–17.

29. The decision to expand the authority of six cities was revealed on April 25, the day the Changzhou meeting ended, suggesting that this was a decision that came out of the Changzhou meeting. See "The System of Offering Greater Decisionmaking Power to Factory Directors Is Being Tested in Six Cities," *Jingji ribao*, April 26, 1984, trans. FBIS, May 8, 1984, p. K7. Authorization for provinces to select cities for experimentation is reported in *Renmin ribao*, Commentator, "Speed Up Comprehensive Urban Reform," June 8, 1984, trans. FBIS, June 12, 1984, pp. K14–15. On the expansion of urban reform experiments to fifty-two cities, see "Experimental Comprehensive Reform of the Urban Economic System Is Being Carried Out in Fifty-Two Cities," *Guangming ribao*, October 16, 1984, p. 1, trans. FBIS, October 23, 1984, pp. K8–9.

30. Xue-liang Ding, "The Disparity Between Idealistic and Instrumental Chinese Reformers," p. 1133.

31. Deng's 1980 speech was photographically reproduced by the Taiwan publication *Chung-kung yen-chiu*, July 15, 1981, permitting comparison with the version in his selected works. According to Xue-liang Ding, Deng had proposed abolishing party committees in industrial enterprises in late 1978. See Xue-liang Ding, "The Disparity Between Idealistic and Instrumental Chinese Reformers," p. 1133.

32. Xinhua, July 7, 1984, trans. FBIS, July 9, 1984; and Beijing Radio, July 7, 1984, trans. FBIS, July 9, 1984, p. K13.

33. "Substitution of Tax Payment for Profit Delivery Is the 'Key' to Urban Reform," *Renmin ribao*, Editorial, September 19, 1984, p. 2, trans. FBIS, September 24, 1984, pp. K16–17. On the compromises made to push the profit for tax reform through in 1984, see Shirk, *The Political Logic of Economic Reform in China*, Chapter 12.

34. "State Planning Commission to Conduct Major Reform of Planning System," *Jingji ribao*, October 6, 1984, p. 1, trans. FBIS, October 11, 1984, pp. K1–2.

35. Xinhua, October 9, 1984, trans. FBIS, October 11, 1984, pp. K4–8. See also "An Important Step for Reforming the Planning System," *Renmin ribao*, Editorial, October 11, 1984, trans. FBIS, October 11, 1984, pp. K2–4.

36. Wang Lixin and Joseph Fewsmith, "Bulwark of the Planned Economy: The Structure and Role of the State Planning Commission."

37. Hua Sheng, Zhang Xuejun, and Luo Xiaopeng, *China: From Revolution to Reform*, p. 105.

38. The term "commodity economy" itself is a compromise term since it shies away from an unambiguous call for a "market economy" (which the Fourteenth Party Congress in October 1992 finally accepted), but it nevertheless implies that the economy as a whole is governed by commodity relationships. In this sense, it goes well beyond the term "market regulation."

39. Deng's comments in June are cited in Lu Zhichao, "Deepening a Scientific Understanding of Socialism," *Guangming ribao*, February 4, 1985, p. 3, trans. FBIS, February 27, 1985, pp. K14–18. Deng's comments are cited on p. K18. For Deng's remarks on building socialism with Chinese characteristics, see Deng Xiaoping, "Jianshe you Zhongguo tese de shehui zhuyi" (Build Socialism with Chinese Characteristics).

40. A partial text of Zhao's letter is included in Hua Sheng, Zhang Xuejun, and Luo Xiaopeng, *China: From Revolution to Reform*, p. 221, fn. 8. Author's interviews.

41. As quoted to the author in an interview. See also the paraphrasing of Chen's comments as reported in Hua Sheng, Zhang Xuejun, and Luo Xiaopeng, *China: From Revolution to Reform*, pp. 221–222, fn. 9. This quote makes clear that reformers were criticizing the Chinese economic system as a rigid import of the Soviet system, whereas conservatives emphasized that there were important differences between the economic systems of China and the Soviet Union.

42. See the report on the meeting in *Renmin ribao*, September 18, 1984, pp. 1 and 3. See also Chi I, "A Dramatic Conference of the CCP Central Committee Propaganda Department," *Cheng ming*, no. 87 (January 1, 1985), trans. FBIS, January 7, 1985, p. W1; and Chao Lu, "No Ideological Education for Three Years; the First Instance of Opposition to Leftism in Literature and Art Circles—The Inside Story of How Deng Xiaoping and Hu Yaobang Straightened Out the Orientation," *Ching-pao yueh-k'an*, no. 90 (January 10, 1985), trans. FBIS, January 23, 1985, pp. W3–7.

43. "Decision of the Central Committee of the Communist Party of China on Reform of the Economic Structure," Xinhua, October 20, 1984, trans. FBIS, October 22, 1984, pp. K1–19.

44. Zheng Bijian and Luo Jingbo, "Deepen Scientific Understanding of Socialism," *Renmin ribao*, November 2, 1984, p. 5, trans. FBIS, November 9, 1984, pp. K2–7.

45. Deng Xiaoping, "A Talk by Deng Xiaoping at the Third Plenary Session of the Central Advisory Commission on October 22, 1984," Xinhua, December 31, 1984, trans. FBIS, January 2, 1985, pp. K1–6.

46. Chen Yizi, *Zhongguo: Shinian gaige yu bajiu minyun*, p. 76.

47. Ibid., p. 77.

48. The following is based on interviews. See also Chen Yizi, *Zhongguo: Shinian gaige yu bajiu minyun*, p. 76.

49. Author's interviews.

50. Author's interviews. For the text of the young reformers' proposal, "Consciously Making Use of the Dual Track System to Reform the Price Mechanism Smoothly," see Hua Sheng, Zhang Xuejun, and Luo Xiaopeng, *China: From Revolution to Reform*, pp. 126–131. This proposal was jointly submitted by Hua Sheng, He Jiacheng, Jiang Yue, Gao Liang, and Zhang Shaojie.

51. Author's interview.

52. Chinese Rural Development Research Group, "Guomin jingji xin chengzhang jieduan he nongcun fazhan" (The New Stage of Growth of the Chinese Economy and Rural Development). *Jingji yanjiu*, no. 7 (July 1985), pp. 13–14.

53. Ibid., p. 7.

54. Ibid., p. 12.

55. Ibid., p. 17.

56. Bai Nansheng, "Wu guo kaishi jinru chao bixupin xiaofei jieduan" (China Begins to Enter the Period of Nonessential Products Consumption), pp. 306–316.

57. Bai Nansheng and Wang Xiaoqiang, "Zhun zhi, yi fen, yu jingji guanli" (Common Quality, Differentiation, and Economic Management). See also Xu Jingan, "Woguo jingji fazhan jinru xin jieduan" (China's Economic Development Has Entered a New Stage).

58. Zhu Jiaming, "Lun woguo zheng jingli de jingji fazhan jieduan" (On the Economic Development Stage Our Country Is Presently Going Through).

59. Sheng Hong and Huang Tieying, "Wei jingji gaosu zengzhang shengbian" (In Defense of High-Speed Economic Development), and Sheng Hong and Zou Gang, "Jingji fazhan guocheng zhong de huobi gongying" (The Money Supply in the Process of Economic Development).

60. Guo Shuqing, Liu Jirui, and Qiu Shufang, "Guomin jingji buneng qiangxing 'qifei'" (The National Economy Cannot Be Forced to Take Off). Another response to Zhu's article came from Yang Mu, then a thirty-nine-year-old doctoral student at CASS's Institute of Industrial Economics, where he studied with Zhou Shulian. See "Lun yingxiang gongye fazhan sudu de yinsu" (Factors Influencing the Speed of Industrial Development).

5

Conservative Criticism and Emerging Fissures Among Reformers

In the wake of the 1984 Third Plenum and the Decision on Economic Structural Reform, reformers worked to create a more open intellectual atmosphere that would support rapid economic reform. At the Fourth National Congress of the Chinese Writers Association in December 1984, Hu Qili delivered a dramatic congratulatory speech to the opening session criticizing "leftist" mistakes the CCP had frequently committed with regard to literature and art. Hu vowed that political labels would no longer be pinned on writers and promised them "freedom of creation."[1] In this more open atmosphere, the Chinese Writers Association elected a new leadership, including such reform-minded writers as Wang Meng, Liu Binyan, and Lu Wenfu.[2] It was perhaps the high point of intellectual relaxation in post-Mao China. Official policy had never gone so far, and it would not go so far again.

This upbeat, even ebullient, ideological atmosphere was reinforced by the publication of Deng Xiaoping's book, *Building Socialism with Chinese Characteristics*, in December 1984. It had been the interview with Deng on building socialism with Chinese characteristics in August 1984 that had signaled Deng's determination to push ahead with reform; the new book, coming just a year and a half after the publication of Deng's *Selected Works*, was intended to provide ideological backing for the implementation of reform.

In addition to Hu Qili's speech and the publication of Deng's book, Zhao Ziyang toured Guangdong Province and the lower Yangzi valley (the area contiguous to Shanghai) in late December 1984, declaring that it was necessary to "accelerate the pace of economic construction in the coastal areas to spur economic development in the interior."[3] Zhao followed this call with a major change in agricultural policy. The three-decade-old state monopoly over the procurement and sale of agricultural produce was to be replaced by a "contract" system that would, it was said, put state-society relations on a more economic and less coercive basis.[4] Shortly thereafter, Vice Premier Tian Jiyun, whom Zhao had brought with him to Beijing from Sichuan, gave a major address outlining the principles to be followed in undertaking price reform. Suggesting caution, Tian urged an incremental approach, "crossing the river by feeling the stones," and "tackling easy" questions first and difficult ones later.[5]

Reflecting the mood of the times, *People's Daily*'s annual New Year's editorial betrayed not the slightest worry about the economic difficulties that would soon slow efforts at reform. It was necessary, the editorial said, to "*accelerate economic development so that the country could become powerful and prosperous and the people better off at a faster pace.*"[6]

The high hope that this upbeat political and ideological atmosphere could be sustained did not last long. Conservatives argued that the relaxation of ideological restraints had gone too far and that too much attention was being paid to the "seamy side" of Chinese society, particularly through press exposés of corrupt behavior. In early February, Hu Yaobang yielded to conservative pressures by giving a speech on journalism in which he declared that "the party's journalism is the party's mouthpiece."[7] Liu Binyan, China's best-known investigative journalist, recalled that he was "bitterly disappointed by the speech." Even though he understood the pressures to which Hu was subject, Liu felt that the speech went too far.[8] In March, Deng Xiaoping backed away from the strong defense of reform that he had made at the October meeting of the Central Advisory Commission (immediately following the Third Plenum) and gave a speech that stressed the need to have "lofty ideals, moral integrity, education, and a sense of discipline." The goal of the reforms, he said, was to bring about "common prosperity," not polarization.[9]

Economic Difficulties and Conservative Criticism

Pressures to pull back on the ideological front were paralleled by growing criticism of the economy. Starting in the spring of 1985 and lasting throughout the year, conservatives took advantage of policy errors and economic problems to criticize repeatedly the reformers' handling of the economy. Their criticisms ranged across three major areas of the economy: the macroeconomy, the policy of opening to the outside world, and agricultural policy. By the end of the year, conservatives were able to slow significantly the pace of reform. The legacy of this period of criticism was not only a wider rift between reformers and conservatives but also sharp differences among reformers themselves. By late 1985 and early 1986, reform-minded economists disagreed with each other almost as much as they did with the conservative wing of the party. These disagreements reflected the very real dilemmas that a partially reformed socialist economic system presented to China's decision makers.

Conservative Criticism of Overheated Economy

The rate of economic and particularly industrial growth had been accelerating throughout 1984, and this trend continued into early 1985. By March, the rate of industrial growth peaked at 23 percent—not only much higher than the approximately 9 percent rate that had been sustained in the 1979–83 period but also significantly above the 14 percent growth rate that had been attained in 1984. Conservatives sharply criticized this high growth rate for creating new imbalances in the economy and implied that the central leadership had been raising unrealistic expectations for continued high-speed growth.

In March, Wang Jiye, the cautious head of the State Planning Commission's Economic Research Institute, argued that the investment and consumption funds were growing too quickly, causing excessive price increases in certain commodities. Unless measures were taken to strengthen macroeconomic control, argued Wang, it would be impossible to bring about a favorable environment for reform.[10]

In May 1985, the very conservative Zuo Chuntai, a former secretary of Li Xiannian, echoed criticisms of reform that had been leveled in the early 1980s. Zuo warned that aggregate demand could only be reduced and a balance between state revenues and expenditures maintained by "strengthening macroeconomic control and readjustment."[11] Similarly, a long article by the editorial department of *Hongqi*, the CCP's theoretical journal, emphasized the importance of the "parts" being subordinate to the "whole," a long-standing theme of conservatives concerned with the loss of economic control.[12]

One of the most powerful criticisms written against the high rate of growth at this time was authored by Xu Yi, the conservative economist who had spearheaded the drive for retrenchment in 1979 and 1980. Writing in *Caizheng*, the journal of the Chinese Finance Society that he had helped found, Xu argued that the money supply had expanded too quickly in 1984, that the rate of growth had exceeded the capabilities of China's national resources, and that the continuing existence and somewhat increased size of the budget deficit were threatening economic stability and inflation. According to Xu, macroeconomic models showed that the rate of growth should be kept to 7.2 percent—well below the 23 percent that had appeared in March.[13]

Xu's article made clear that he was not only concerned with China's economic growth rate, the continuation of fiscal deficits, and other economic problems but was also alarmed by the devolution of economic decision-making authority and the market-oriented approach that lay at the core of reform. Xu was deeply opposed to trends that had expanded the decision-making authority of enterprises and brought about a rapid expansion of extrabudgetary funds. He pointed out that from 1979 to 1983, extrabudgetary funds had increased by an average of 22.7 percent annually, and that whereas they had accounted for only 31 percent of all budgetary funds in 1978, they constituted 80 percent of such funds in 1984.[14] In Xu's view, the excessive expansion of extrabudgetary investments was the primary cause of the overextension of capital construction in 1982 and 1984. "This shows," Xu said, "that if only budgetary funds are under control and extrabudgetary funds cannot be regulated and controlled, then it is impossible to prevent loss of control over investment." Xu's argument pointed to one of the primary problems in reforming socialist economic systems. Unless the devolution of control over funds is balanced by market forces—including ownership reform—there is no incentive for enterprises to control their expenditures.

Xu's advocacy of strengthening macroeconomic controls was based on his conception of socialism as a system that upholds planning and in which the state must play the role of directing the major economic decisions of the society. In apparent response to the kinds of liberal economic views favored by young economists that were discussed in the previous chapter, Xu said that there were "some comrades" in China who argued that the "investment hunger" syndrome of socialist countries was caused by socialist public ownership and that the economy should be adjusted entirely by means of market mechanisms. These views were wrong, said Xu, because socialist countries could in fact master the self-control needed to prevent excessive investment. As Xu put it, "there is no inexorable link between socialist public ownership and the tendency to pursue blindly and compete with each other for higher speed."[15] Moreover, he said that advocates of market regulation "believe that mechanically copying from capitalism can have a miraculous effect on our socialist economy. In fact, this is only an illusion."

One of the issues that most angered Xu and pointed to a fundamental difference between his view (and that of fellow conservatives) and the main thrust of reform was what he called the "distortion of the socialist banking and credit systems." Arguing strongly in favor of maintaining the state's role in directing investment, Xu criticized those who:[16]

> greatly exaggerate the role of cash funds in the adjustment of reproduction and then propose that fiscal distribution be gradually withdrawn from the area of social reproduction. They believe that banks are economic entities, enterprises that manage credit and currency, and that they, too, can operate on the principle of "expanding where profits are good, reducing where profits are meager, and suspending where there are no profits." They further believe that in a certain sense banks can take over part of the functions of the State Planning Commission and the State Economic Commission. I think that these people are wrong.

Criticism of Opening to the Outside

At the same time that conservatives attacked the high rate of economic growth, they also took aim at China's policy of opening to the outside world. Conservatives had long opposed the SEZs and the opening of coastal cities to foreign investment, and they quickly took advantage of the problems that followed the rapid opening of China's coastal areas in 1984. As enterprises competed to avail themselves of the new opening to the international market, they undercut each other's profit margins and imported duplicate machinery. Imports of technology were not well planned, and many enterprises became overly dependent on imported materials. Moreover, because of the structure of China's foreign-trade system, some 80 percent of its export firms were losing money.[17]

The most serious issue that developed in the first part of the year, however, was the sudden decline in China's foreign-exchange reserves. In order to deal with the inflationary potential brought about by the rapid expansion of the money supply in the latter part of 1984, the government encouraged the import of consumer durables that could be sold on the domestic market, thereby soaking up excess currency. Although this buying spree dampened inflationary pressures, it led to a rapid decline in China's foreign-exchange reserves. Between the last quarter of 1984 and the first quarter of 1985, China's reserves fell by almost one-third.[18]

As early as December 1984, conservatives began criticizing the policy of opening to the outside world. At a symposium on world economic issues, the theoretical basis on which the SEZs had been established came under attack. Chinese commentary on the zones had long cited Lenin's New Economic Policy (NEP) to legitimize this departure from Marxist orthodoxy. At the December conference, however, some charged that the NEP was the "product of specific Soviet historical circumstances," and that in theoretical terms Lenin had regarded it as "one step backward from socialism." Moreover, critics charged that "our strategy of 'exchanging markets for technology' may end up by giving away our market but getting no technology."[19]

In February 1985, high-level conservative leaders began to criticize publicly Deng's policy of opening up. It was at that time that Politburo member Hu Qiaomu traveled to Fujian province and criticized as "improper" a slogan in Fuzhou about "getting rich," one that apparently resembled the "Time is money; efficiency is life" slogan that Deng had praised the previous year.[20] Shortly thereafter, Vice Premier Yao Yilin inspected Shenzhen and reportedly told Yuan Geng, the head of that zone's Shekou industrial area, that the SEZs could not continue to depend on "blood transfusions" (i.e., subsidies) from the state and that it was time to "pull the needle."[21]

In a separate trip to Xiamen in June, Hu Qiaomu took his criticism of the zones a step further, evoking their similarities to the foreign enclaves in China's nineteenth-century treaty ports. Hu recalled that the Qing dynasty adopted an "indifferent attitude" toward the concessions, at the expense of "China's legal rights." He suggested that the current Chinese government had already gone too far down the same road by yielding to the "inordinate demands" of foreigners, and he demanded to know why the CCP "is prohibited from public activities" in foreign investment enterprises in the zones. Moreover, Hu charged, foreign businessmen "show no respect" for Chinese unions and "forget even the laws of their own countries when they come to the SEZ's."[22]

Criticism of China's policy of opening to the outside world culminated during the summer of 1985 with the exposure of corruption on Hainan island. An investigation that had been launched in March by the Central Discipline Inspection Commission (CDIC)—headed by Chen Yun—culminated in the publication of a long report that was published in late July. According to the report, cadres in Hainan island were guilty of using an excessive amount of foreign exchange to import some 89,000 foreign automobiles and 2 million television sets with the intention of reselling them for large profits in China's interior. While this import scheme apparently had its origins in loopholes in State Council regulations and the desire to find sources of revenue to finance Hainan's economic construction, the CDIC report detailed an extensive web of corruption extending from the island to Guangdong and elsewhere.[23]

Thus, by the first half of 1985, concerns over economic issues, Chinese sovereignty, and large-scale corruption had combined to fuel a conservative assault on the policy of opening to the outside world that had been unveiled with so much fanfare only a short year before. Deng began to backpedal. In March he ordered that steps be taken to stanch the outflow of foreign exchange, and in June he dramatically declared that the Shenzhen SEZ was only an "experiment," the success of which "remains to be proven."[24] Shortly thereafter, Gu Mu, Secretariat member in charge of the policy of opening to the outside world, announced that China would "give priority" to only four of the fourteen open cities—Shanghai, Tianjin, Dalian, and Guangzhou—and temporarily "slow down" the development of foreign cooperation in the other ten.[25]

Problems in Rural Policy

Throughout the early part of the Dengist period, agriculture had been the brightest spot in China's economic picture. Grain production had increased by a third, from 305 million tons in 1978 to 407 million tons in 1984. The per capita income of the rural population had increased by more than two and a half times in the same period, from 134 yuan to 355 yuan.[26] Reform, development, and prosperity seemed inexorably linked.

The unexpected growth of agricultural productivity strained China's ability to handle it. Storage facilities were overwhelmed and much grain was left in the open to rot; processing capabilities lagged far behind what was needed to deal with such a bountiful harvest. Moreover, China's transportation system was overwhelmed. According to one report, "even if six good trains were dispatched from Jilin each day with a carrying capacity of 2,500 tons each, one whole year would not be enough" to remove the surplus grain.[27]

The most daunting problem in the agricultural sector, however, was the massive subsidies that such harvests required. From 1978 to 1984, subsidies for agricultural products had increased by nearly sixfold, from 5.5 to 30.5 billion yuan. Thus, while agricultural subsidies had been only 4.5 percent of state reve-

Table 5.1

Agricultural Subsidies, 1978 to 1984 (in billions of yuan)

Year	Agricultural Subsidies	As % of State Revenues	Total Price Subsidies	As % of Price Subsidies
1978	5.5	4.5	9.4	58.8
1979	13.1	11.9	18.1	72.2
1980	17.0	15.7	24.3	70.3
1981	20.5	18.9	32.8	62.4
1982	22.6	20.1	31.8	71.0
1983	25.5	20.4	34.2	74.6
1984	30.5	20.3	37.0	82.3

Sources: Qiao Rongzhang, *Jiage butie* (Price Subsidies), pp. 28, 30; State Statistical Bureau, *Statistical Yearbook of China*, 1986, p. 509.

nues in 1978, they were a whopping 20 percent of state revenues in 1984. As a percentage of all price subsidies, agricultural subsidies grew from 58.85 percent to 82.34 percent in the same period (see Table 5.1). Such large subsidies strained state finances, making it difficult for the state either to balance the budget (as demanded by conservatives) or to shift resources to such urgently needed areas as energy and transportation.

The decision to embark on comprehensive urban reform made it urgent to reduce the burdens of grain subsidies. The question was how to do so. Beginning in 1982, members of the Rural Development Group had begun thinking about the abolition of the state's monopoly over the purchase and sale of grain, a system that had been in place since 1953. Rural reformers were hoping to deepen the rural reforms by further commercializing the production and procurement of agricultural produce, thus getting the state out of the business of overseeing production administratively. They undertook two experiments to allow grain prices to float freely, first in Hebei Province and then in Xinjiang. Neither was successful, but the idea of abolishing the state procurement system had been planted.[28]

By late 1984, Zhao was coming under intense pressure to deal with the problems that the bumper harvest of that year had created, particularly the difficulty peasants had in selling their grain and the rising cost of agricultural subsidies, as well as to find funds to support the urban reforms being planned by the leadership. The State Planning Commission and the Ministry of Finance, concerned with the rising subsidies, were particularly strong in their advocacy of measures to control costs.

Thus, in December 1984, Zhao decided to reform the agricultural system by abolishing the three-decade-old state monopoly over the procurement and sale of grain and replace it with a "contract" system. In theory, the peasants would enter into voluntary contracts to sell a specific amount of grain to the state (thus limiting the state's obligation to buy all the grain the peasants produced) for a set price. Peasants would be free to sell the grain that they had not contracted to sell to the state on the free market. With the passage of time, the state would contract to buy successively less grain, and a genuine grain market would develop in the countryside.

This important decision, with wide ramifications for China's countryside, was apparently made without the input of either the Rural Development Institute or the State Council's Rural Development Research Center. Given the difficulties these reformers had experienced in their experiments in Hebei, they would have advised Zhao against such a sudden change had their advice been solicited.[29] Confronted with the very difficult financial situation China was facing, and with bureaucratic pressures from the State Planning Commission and the Ministry of Finance, Zhao went ahead and made the decision to abolish the state procurement and sale monopoly. It seems ironic that the advice of the Rural Development Institute and Rural Development Research Center was not solicited about an issue in which they had an established expertise as well as personal connections with Zhao and other top leaders. Perhaps Zhao felt that by making this decision himself, he could avoid pressures to act in a less drastic fashion.

As it turned out, Zhao's hope of relieving the pressures of excess grain in the countryside and the fiscal problems of the state through a single reform of the agricultural procurement system would bring about new problems and make reformers vulnerable to the charge of neglecting agriculture. The primary reason for the failure of this reform was that it was accompanied by the reinstitution of a unified procurement price for the purchase of grain.[30] In 1979, in order to stimulate grain production, the state had not only raised the price of grain by 20 percent but had also agreed to purchase above-quota grain for 50 percent above the regular grain price. It was this policy that largely accounted for the mounting subsidies faced by the central government. Hoping to lessen the burden on the state, the 1985 reform instituted the so-called inverse 3:7 price ratio, meaning that all state grain procurements would be made at a single unified price calculated as a composite of 30 percent of the former monopoly purchase price plus 70 percent of the former above-quota price. For China as a whole, this worked out to an increase of 1.8 percent in the total amount paid for state grain procurement, but since the cost of agricultural inputs increased by nearly 7 percent in 1985, the result was actually a net 4.9 percent decrease in peasant income for 1985 alone.[31]

Even disregarding the increased costs of agricultural inputs, the effect of the inverse 3:7 ratio on peasant receipts for grain varied from one location to another, depending on the previous grain quota and the amount sold to the state. For instance, the peasants in Jiaxing Prefecture of Zhejiang Province benefited somewhat from the new policy, but those of Jinhua Prefecture of the same province, which had a somewhat lower grain quota than Jiaxing, received less than they had previously received for grain sold to the state.[32]

Similarly, institution of the inverse 3:7 ratio had an adverse effect on peasants in Hengyang city of Hunan Province. In 1983, the average price of commodity grain sold to the state was 34.38 yuan per 100 kilograms (including standard purchases, purchases exceeding the contracted amount, and negotiated purchases). In 1985, under the inverse 3:7 ratio, the average price per 100 kilograms of grain in Hengyang fell to 31.18 yuan, reducing peasant income in the area by a total of 16.7 million yuan.[33] Overall, the price paid to peasants declined in approximately half of China's regions.[34] According to one source, "every jurisdiction reports strongly that the 'inverse 3:7' ratio grain price caused losses for grain farmers."[35]

The adverse impact of the new pricing system was exacerbated by the rising price of grain on the free market. In August 1984, the market price of grain—influenced by the record-breaking harvest of that year—was below the state purchase price. By the spring of 1985, however, as the new contracts were to be signed, the market price had rebounded and was above the contract price.[36] In 1986, grain output was some 10 million tons greater than in 1985, but despite this increase in supply, the market price of grain continued to rise and remained substantially above the state purchase price in 1987.[37]

The differential between the open-market price of grain and the lower price paid by the state for its grain procurements effectively constituted a tax on grain production—and a highly visible one at that. The state had long extracted investment funds through the "scissors effect" (that is, by purchasing agricultural goods from the countryside at a low price and selling industrial goods to the countryside at a high price), but the implementation of the dual-track system "gave the peasants a clear standard of the equal exchange, making the hidden tax on grain production open." Moreover, this "tax" had the perverse tendency to increase when there was a shortage of grain, thus driving up market prices and making the peasants feel the most exploited precisely at the time when increased output was most needed. Thus, this dual-track system gave the peasants a distinct disincentive for meeting contract obligations to the state.[38]

For these reasons, the contract purchase system was unpopular from the outset. Even in early 1985, as the system was first being introduced, there were reports of peasant resistance to it. For instance, peasants in Sichuan Province were reported to be "still watching the rise and fall of grain prices on the market" in late April and not signing contracts "even after stalling for a long time."[39] Similarly, Hunan Province reported that "contracts on the purchase and sale of agricultural products have been signed slowly," and Guangdong Province reported that people had the "mistaken" idea that "they would sign the contracts if they think them suitable and refuse if they are not. This simply will not do."[40] Though the unusually bad weather in 1985 contributed to the 6.9 percent decline in grain production that year, Chinese agricultural experts judged that the primary reason for the decline in production was the combination of the contract purchase system and the inverse 3:7 ratio purchase price.[41]

The continuing problems with grain production touched off one of the fiercest and most interesting policy debates in the course of Chinese economic reform. The essential questions in this debate were whether or not there was a serious problem in the rural economy; if so, who was responsible, and what should be done to address the issue.

An issue that complicated the debate was the role of township and village enterprises. The rapid development of these rural industries was one of the real surprises of the rural reform; no one had anticipated how quickly they would grow or the important economic role they would begin to play by the mid-1980s. In 1978 there had been only 1.5 million rural enterprises employing some 28 million people. In early 1984 the party promulgated its Document No. 4, which strongly supported the development of rural enterprises. That year, the number of rural enterprises exploded: from 1.3 million in 1983 to 6.1 million, and the number of people employed in these enterprises jumped from 32 million to 52 million. In 1985, the number of rural enterprises doubled to 12.2 million and the number of people employed in them grew to more than 69 million.[42]

This explosive growth of rural enterprise drew investment funds, particularly from county governments, that might otherwise have gone into agricultural production precisely at a time when state investment in agriculture was falling. During the period of the Fifth Five-Year Plan (1976–80), state investment in agricultural capital construction totaled 24.6 billion yuan, or 10 percent of total state investment in capital construction. During the period of the Sixth Five-Year Plan (1981–85), state investment in agriculture fell almost 28 percent to 17.8 billion yuan, or 5.2 percent of total state investment in capital construction. Under the Seventh Five-Year Plan period (1986–90), agricultural investment was to receive only 14.7 billion yuan per year—about 3.9 percent—of the 375 billion yuan budgeted for state investment in capital construction, but reports indicated that actual investment was even less than this.[43]

As rural enterprises grew, peasants received a greater proportion of their income from nonagricultural pursuits. Whereas in 1978, 85 percent of all peasant income was derived from agricultural production, by 1985 only 66.3 percent of income came from agriculture. Income from nonagricultural pursuits had grown from 7 percent to 21.7 percent over these seven years.[44] As nonagricultural sources of income became more important, peasant "enthusiasm" for agricultural production declined, and so did household investment in agricultural production. Moreover, as income from agricultural pursuits in general declined in importance, income from grain production declined relative to income from other types of agricultural production. The economic returns from cash crops far exceeded those from grain production.[45]

The problems that emerged in the agricultural sector in 1985, particularly the decline in grain production, placed the members of the Rural Development Institute in a difficult position. Even though they had not advocated the policy measures that had brought about the decline, they had, as noted in the previous chapter, talked about the "relative surplus" in grain production, the shift toward a higher quality diet, and the inevitable slowdown in agricultural growth. Now they were accused of being wildly optimistic about the grain situation and not being sufficiently cognizant of China's future need for grain as its population grew.[46]

Criticisms came from both the left and the right, in the former case from those who felt that the reforms had gone too far and in the latter from those who felt they had not gone far enough. Taking the latter perspective were a number of researchers in the Ministry of Agriculture's Policy Research Office, including Gao Hongbin, Li Qingzeng, and Zhou Binbin. They argued that the lower grain harvests that had begun in 1985 were the result of policy mistakes. The focus of this critique was on the need to create a truly free market, probably including private property, in the rural areas. Gao, Li, and Zhou argued that the crux of the agricultural problem was that as the state had progressively reduced its investment in agriculture over the years, particularly since the start of reform, it had failed to create sufficient incentives to encourage peasant investment to fill the gap. In particular, they argued, continuing uncertainty about the stability of rural policy not only discouraged peasant investment but encouraged consumption. In their opinion, it was a mistake to describe the 1985 decline in grain output and the subsequent slow growth as a change from a period of "supernormal growth" in the early 1980s to a period of "normal growth" after 1985. If the proper incentives were provided, Gao and his colleagues asserted, the high rates of agricultural growth that China had witnessed in the early 1980s could continue. Therefore, it would be more accurate to characterize the slowdown in grain production as marking a turn from "normal growth to subnormal growth." New and more liberal policies were needed.[47]

The criticism by Gao, Li, and Zhou of the idea that grain production was going from "supernormal growth to normal growth" was a reference to a series of articles written by Chen Xiwen, one of the core members of the State Council's Rural Development Research Center. Chen argued that as a heavily populated, land-poor nation, China must exert long-term efforts to promote a steady, but not spectacular, increase in grain production. The rapid growth in grain production in the early 1980s, said Chen, was caused by a one-time release of pent-up energy brought about by the breakup of the overly rigid commune system. Following this spurt of "supernormal" growth, grain production had settled back into a period of "normal" growth characterized by slow but steady increases in output. There were no quick fixes, maintained Chen; the glory days of the early 1980s were gone forever. People should not, Chen argued, "unrealistically follow the illusion that a new document or some policy can change the entire agricultural situation overnight." On the contrary, it was necessary to "consolidate and enlarge the results already achieved by rural economic reform through realistic and even more meticulous work."[48]

Given both budget constraints and the ideological atmosphere of the mid-1980s, there was little chance that the policy recommendations of the Ministry of

Agriculture's Policy Research Office would be accepted. More serious criticism came from the conservative wing of the party. Conservatives (as well as some reformers) focused their attention on the declining rural infrastructure brought on by decreased investment from the state, local collectives, and individuals. They indicted rural policy for neglecting the infrastructure that had been built up over the years and for "living off old capital" (*chi laoben*). According to one writer:[49]

> A substantial number of our more than 80,000 reservoirs are in disrepair and dangerous. Of the existing 80 million horsepower in irrigation and drainage machinery, one-quarter is obsolete. . . . Many of our 2.4 million mechanized wells have reached the end of their service life and need to be replaced; we need to replace 100,000 wells a year.

The decline in such elements of the rural infrastructure, it was alleged, led to a decrease in the number of hectares under irrigation and weakened China's ability to withstand both flood and drought.

Implicit in this conservative critique was that the household responsibility system had exhausted its potential for expanding grain production and that some sort of recollectivization was necessary. The unwillingness or inability of individual households to invest in grain production, the parcelization of land under the responsibility system, and the neglect of the rural infrastructure all indicated to those who held this view that the state must begin to take a firmer hand in the countryside.

The attitude of those who took this approach was summed up by one writer (who was not sympathetic to this conservative viewpoint but appears to have described its proponents' attitude accurately) as follows:[50]

> They believe that the scarcity of China's per capita agricultural natural resources and the backwardness of the agricultural mode of production are two basic reasons why it is difficult for a fundamental change to occur in a short time. Because of this, China will face the difficult economic problem of agricultural supplies being tight for a long time. Based on this perception, those holding this view believe that subjecting the relationship of supply and demand of agricultural produce to the market mechanism, at least for some time to come, is a facile plan not in accordance with China's national characteristics. The social turbulence [that such a change] would bring about definitely could not be compensated by the increased incomes of the peasants.

This conservative critique would be presented powerfully by Chen Yun in September 1985, when he excoriated the party's rural policies at the September conference of party representatives, as discussed below.

Reformist Criticism of High-Speed Growth

Conservatives were not the only ones who had harsh things to say about China's economic policies, particularly the trend toward high-speed growth that emerged in late 1984 and early 1985. One of the sharpest criticisms leveled in that period came from Li Rui, the former secretary of Mao Zedong who had become one of the harshest critics of the old order. In a three-part article that was given prominent play on the front page of *Guangming Daily* in May, Li launched a sharply worded broadside against China's high growth rate. Comparing the atmosphere surrounding the pursuit of a high rate of economic growth in 1985 to that which had prevailed during the Great Leap Forward, Li harshly condemned the role the press had played in the late 1950s in boasting of successes and cheering the "leap." Li pointedly recalled that *People's Daily* had been forced to make an "earnest self-criticism" in 1961 for the role it had played during the leap and suggested that it was again taking the lead in boosting high-speed development. Warning that the rate of economic growth in early 1985 was much too high, Li revealed that "a veteran comrade has reportedly written to the central leading comrades" about the economic consequences of pursuing such a high growth rate.[51]

As harsh as Li's criticisms were, he offered no new ways of responding to the fundamental dilemma facing reformers: effecting reform while preventing the economy from overheating. Despite differences in emphasis, the basic approach of most reform-minded economists from the Wuxi Conference in 1979 through the 1984 reform program was based on the approach of "delegating authority and allowing profits" (*fangquan rangli*). This approach meant giving enterprises more decision-making authority over their production and allowing them to earn and retain profits by selling part of their production on the market. Although this approach was successful in stimulating enterprises to produce more, it did not necessarily make them more efficient. Because the price structure remained distorted and enterprises remained subordinate to administrative organs, giving enterprises greater decision-making authority tended to stimulate investment but distort investment patterns. Enterprises, it was frequently said, were "responsible for profits but not for losses." Soft budget constraints inevitably lead to economic overheating.

In 1985, confronted on the one hand by high-speed growth and on the other by harsh criticisms from conservatives, reformers began to search for new approaches to reform. For the first time since the inauguration of reform, sharply different approaches began to appear within the reform wing of the CCP. In particular, two schools of thought emerged at this time that presented new ways of thinking about reform. One school centered around Wu Jinglian, a senior economist at the State Council's Economic, Technological, and Social Development Research Center; the other centered around the young economists of the Economic Reform Institute.

Both of these groups were willing to give up much of the intellectual framework that had previously guided reform in favor of an acceptance of markets as efficient allocators of scarce resources. Epistemologically, both groups broke with long-held socialist beliefs that markets were inherently "blind" and "anarchistic." This marked an important turning point in the evolution of thinking about reform. No longer were such people thinking in terms of reforming the old system, in the sense of making it work better; they were instead thinking in terms of transforming the old system into something radically new. They disagreed, however, about *how* to transform the system, and this division reflected both their very different beliefs about the capacity of the Chinese government to effect change and their different assumptions about the economy and society they hoped to see in the future. These differences would soon lead to bitter disputes between them.

Wu Jinglian and "Coordinated Reform"

From the emergence of enterprise reform in the late 1970s reform thinking had centered around the notions of giving enterprises greater decision-making authority and providing them with incentives by allowing them to retain a greater percentage of their profits. Beginning in 1985, Wu Jinglian, a senior economist of the State Council's Economic, Technological, and Social Development Research Center, and others began to develop a fundamental critique of this approach, which they saw as advancing along a single axis of "delegating authority and allowing profits." In their opinion, this approach would inevitably lead to the sort of overheated economy China had experienced in late 1984 and early 1985 because it had not paid sufficient attention to creating competitive markets that would force enterprises to behave rationally. In contrast, Wu and his colleagues believed that it was necessary to implement a "coordinated reform" (*peitao gaige*) in which the expansion of enterprise authority would be coordinated with the growth of a market system and the development of an effective macroeconomic control system.

Wu had been born in Nanjing in 1930. Because of illness, he had not begun college until 1950, when he entered the economics department at Fudan University in Shanghai. Politically committed by that time, he immediately joined the New Democratic Youth League, and two years after that joined the CCP. After graduating from Fudan University, he had been sent to the Economics Institute of the CAS, where he came under the influence of the Soviet economist A. Bierman, who was then teaching at Chinese People's University. In the late 1950s, Wu participated in the editing of *On Socialist Economics* (*Shehui zhuyi jingji lun*) under the direction of Sun Yefang and also took part in the writing of textbooks on political economics that was undertaken by a small group led by Yu Guangyuan. In 1968, Wu went with other members of the Philosophy and Social Science Department of CAS to a cadre school in Henan, where he began rethinking socialist economics. When he returned to Beijing, after the fall of the Gang of Four, he participated enthusiastically in criticizing their economic thought.[52]

It is apparent from his writings of the late 1970s and particularly the early 1980s that Wu was heavily influenced by the work of East European economists, particularly W. Brus, Ota Sik, and Janos Kornai. Both Brus and Sik had given a series of widely attended lectures when each had visited China in early 1980 and early 1981, respectively. Kornai did not visit China until 1985, but his writings, and particularly his classic work *Economics of Shortage*, were widely read in China. Wu wrote a long introduction to a compendium of the lectures given by Brus and Sik, reviewing the development of East European economic theory, but the book that it was supposed to preface was never published because of the conservative wave that swept Chinese economics in 1982. It is nevertheless clear from Wu's introduction, which was later published separately, as well as from many of his articles that he found much of value in the writings of East European economists.

One theme to which Wu was particularly attracted in Brus' writings was the argument that successful reform depended on a basic balance among the major economic proportions of a society and a relatively relaxed economic atmosphere (i.e., the relationship between supply and demand being in balance, preferably with supply being somewhat greater than demand). Only under such conditions, argued Brus, would the strains caused by economic reform not lead to serious dislocations and inflation. If such conditions do not obtain, said Brus, then it is first necessary to concentrate efforts on readjustment (rather than reform) to bring them about.[53] Both Brus and Sik believed that in the early stages of economic reform, growth rates and wages must be held down. Besides his attraction to these concepts, Wu also singled out Sik's belief that although the goal of reform is a system in which prices are completely free, this cannot be achieved in a single step. It is instead necessary to go through a process in which prices are first readjusted in accordance with prices calculated according to input-output tables.[54]

In January 1983, Wu left China for a year and a half of study at Yale University. While there, he devoted much of his time to the history and contemporary circumstances of reform in socialist countries.[55] At the same time, he became more familiar with Western economic concepts. Following his return to China in the summer of 1984, Wu's writings evinced new interest in the role of prices in bringing about a rational distribution of economic resources as well as a greater familiarity with monetarist theories.

After returning to China, Wu immediately plunged into debates over the draft of the decision on economic reform that was being prepared for the upcoming Third Plenum. Along with a number of other economists, Wu vigorously supported the idea that China's economy was a "commodity economy."[56] At the same time, he went on a trip to the Northeast to investigate the results of enterprise reform, particularly the ten regulations on expanding enterprise authority. It was around the time of this trip that Wu became concerned that the authority that the reforms were supposed to delegate to enterprises was ending up in the hands of local administrative authorities. In order to avoid this problem, Wu proposed that reform had to proceed along three tracks: reform of the planning system to reduce the scope of mandatory planning, implementation of price reform, and the establishment of effective macroeconomic control.[57] This view was clearly influenced by Wu's understanding of the reform experience in East Europe.

Drawing on Janos Kornoi's concept of "paternalism" (*fuzi quanxi*), Wu argued that in the past, Chinese economists, including himself, had overly emphasized the problem of "enlivening" enterprises and had not paid sufficient attention to the other half of the problem: the tendency of administrative organs to protect the industries subordinate to them.[58] In clear opposition to the economists of the Economic Reform Institute, Wu argued that the problem of the lack of enterprise vitality could not be resolved by looking only at enterprises themselves. The lesson that Kornai—and Wu—drew from the difficulties encountered in the Hungarian reform was that it was necessary to create a competitive market with a rational price structure before launching reform.[59]

Looking at the reform experience in East Europe, Wu concluded that the only way in which to bring about a competitive market was to create a "buyers' market" in which enterprises had to work to meet the demands of their consumers. A buyers' market, however, could not develop in a rapidly expanding economy; on the contrary, only by tightening control over credit and the money supply could one create the necessary "relaxed economic environment" in which to launch reform.[60]

In the first half of 1985, Wu drew on his understanding of the East European reform experience and the problems that he saw developing in the Chinese economy to write a series of articles that criticized the "overheating" of the economy in late 1984 and challenged the approach of those who, like Zhu Jiaming, Sheng Hong, and others, advocated a loose monetary policy and rapid economic growth. In an essay that appeared in February 1985, Wu revisited the discussions about the relationship between reform and readjustment in 1979 and 1980, suggesting that the lesson of that period—that readjustment was necessary to provide a relaxed economic environment for reform—was applicable to the situation in late 1984 and early 1985. Facing increasing demands on state resources, including pressures to rapidly raise people's standard of living and expand the scale of construction, the government had to be aware of the need to preserve the good economic environment that had thus far been achieved through readjustment. In the face of the excess expenditures incurred in the latter part of 1984, it would have to strengthen macroeconomic control.[61]

Wu noted that the incremental reform strategy that had been adopted in China had advantages: it prevented major social disruptions, reduced obstacles to reform, and made reform easier for people to accept. Nevertheless, Wu argued that incremental reform increased the difficulty of maintaining macroeconomic control. He particularly observed that the dual-track price system that had been proposed by young economists whose approach closely paralleled that of the economists of the Economic Reform Institute had created many problems, including loopholes by which enterprises and localities could avoid administrative controls as well as engage in outright corruption. The dual-track system, asserted

Wu, reduced the efficacy of the old control system before a new, effective control system could be developed.[62]

Wu's critique of the approach of the Economic Reform Institute was more explicit in another article written shortly thereafter. In an apparent allusion to the Moganshan Conference, Wu wrote that since the summer of 1984, some economists had been drawing on Keynesian theories to argue that a loose monetary policy would lead to strong demand and great pressure to rapidly expand production. Wu countered that although Keynesian economics is of some use in the West, where demand is generally insufficient, such an approach was not suitable for China because demand there was normally greater than supply. In such a situation, said Wu, a loose monetary policy would only further tighten the economy. Pressing his argument a step further, Wu said that even in Western economics, the appearance of stagflation and lower efficiency had revealed the disadvantages of a loose monetary policy. Observing that the use of a monetarist approach to the money supply had begun with the "Erhard economic miracle" in West Germany after the Second World War, he quoted Milton Friedman as saying, "The so-called Erhard miracle is really very simple. It just removed restrictions on prices and wages and permitted the market to move freely (while) at the same time strictly controlling the quantity of money."[63]

Wu further maintained that although the Chinese economic situation had improved in recent years, it had not yet made a "fundamental turn for the better." The excessive capital construction, the growth of consumption funds, the waste in administrative expenses, and the loss of control over credit and loans as well as over the money supply in the latter part of 1984 were highly disadvantageous to reform, said Wu. In particular, they tended to distort further China's industrial structure by directing scarce investment funds to the processing industries, where the irrational price structure ensured high profits and quick returns. This tendency in turn exacerbated shortages in energy, transport, and raw materials. To counteract such trends, noted Wu, China had been forced to slow the pace of economic reform in general and price reform in particular. China's experience since 1979, he said, showed that "control over accumulation funds and consumption funds cannot be loosened at any time . . . whenever anything out of the ordinary happens, it is necessary to take immediate steps to overcome it."[64]

Wu's emerging critique of the reform strategy that had been implemented in 1984 took more complete form during a symposium convened in July 1985.[65] Referring to a draft document under discussion—probably an early draft of the "Proposal on the Seventh Five-Year Plan" that was to be presented to the Central Committee meeting in the fall of 1985—Wu criticized a sentence that declared, "Enlivening enterprises is the starting point and resting point of urban economic structural reform." While agreeing that enlivening enterprises was a central task of urban economic reform, he argued that the results over the previous year of implementing the policy of "simplifying government and delegating authority" (*jianzheng fangquan*) had not been very good because the concept of simply enlivening enterprises was inadequate to effect reform.

Wu noted that although many Chinese economists were using Kornai's concept of "paternalism" to describe the relationship between the government and enterprises, they were, in his opinion, neglecting an important aspect of this concept. As was generally agreed, paternalism implied that government organs oversee their subordinate enterprises to the degree that they stifle the enterprises' ability to make operational decisions and destroy their incentives to cut costs and meet market needs. This destroyed the "vitality" of the economy. But, added Wu, paternalism also meant that government organs took care of and protected the inefficient enterprises that were subordinate to them. Measures aimed at "loosening restrictions and delegating authority" (*songbang fangquan*), as called for by the approach of enlivening enterprises, addressed only the first half of this problem. Enterprises would be given greater freedom from government organs, but such measures could generate no pressure on enterprises to actually become more efficient. The result would be that enterprises would "bear responsibility for profits but not for losses."[66]

Drawing on East European and Soviet economists' use of the term "mechanism" to describe the complex interrelatedness of economies, Wu argued that unless reform measures were coordinated with each other and implemented with an overall design, their effectiveness would be diminished and it would be difficult to control the results of reform. It was necessary to proceed along three tracks simultaneously. First, it was necessary that enterprises indeed become relatively independent commodity producers responsible for their own profits and losses. Second, there must be a regulated and competitive market system. Third, there had to be a macroeconomic control system that was capable of regulating a commodity economy. These three links were interrelated, Wu argued, and had to be implemented as a "package" (*yi lanzi*). This did not mean they had to be implemented all at once, but that measures for implementing them had to be designed with attention to the order in which they would go into effect. The whole package could thus be implemented over a period of time—such as the period of the Seventh Five-Year Plan—according to a well-designed plan.[67]

Wu soon became the central figure in a what can properly be described as a school of thought—that is, a relatively systematic body of ideas that are held by a number of people over a period of time—that included a number of young economists who had begun to take part in economic discussions over the previous year. Chapter 4 noted Guo Shuqing's sharp response to Zhu Jiaming's 1985 article favoring high-speed economic growth, and many of Guo's ideas paralleled those of Wu, who supervised Guo's dissertation.[68] In the summer of 1985, Guo joined with two other young economists, Luo Jiwei and Liu Jirui, to write a research report on coordinated reform, that was forwarded to the leadership of the State Council. Paralleling Wu's ideas, they argued that China's reform needed to proceed along the three links of expanding enterprise authority, creating a market system, and establishing mechanisms capable of exercising effective indirect macroeconomic control. They also argued that the first steps toward reform should not be too rapid and that the growth rate should be maintained at about 8 percent.[69]

The Economic Reform Institute and the Problem of the Microeconomy

In November 1985, *Jingji yanjiu* published an investigative report conducted by the Economic Reform Institute and based on several previous studies, including two surveys of Chinese industries conducted in February and July 1985. The investigation report, signed by twenty-one economists affiliated with the institute, suggests that there had been some evolution in thinking since the publication in the summer of 1985 of the Rural Development Group's report, "The New Stage of Growth." Whereas the earlier report had played down the threat of inflation and implied that continued large-scale investments were necessary in order to change the structure of production and sustain high-speed economic growth, the Economic Reform Institute's report argued that the threat of inflation was in fact quite serious. The report's analysis of the causes of this threat and the solutions it proposed, however, differed sharply from both the conservatives' call for strengthening the planning system and Wu Jinglian's appeal to combine tight monetary policies with price reform. Whereas the conventional wisdom of the period held that inflation derived from macroeconomic imbalances, particularly the overly rapid expansion of the money supply caused by excessive investments and bonuses, the Economic Reform Institute's report focused on the microeconomic causes of inflation.[70]

According to the report, there were two microeconomic reasons for inflation. First, the lack of labor mobility meant that wage levels were not determined by the market but rather by a mutual competition among enterprises to maintain production in a period of economic growth, which in turn led to a mutual competition among workers over wages (the phenomenon described in Chinese as *panbi*). According to this analysis, profits were unrelated to labor productivity. In their survey of industry, the Economic Reform Institute found fifty-six enterprises with a decline in profits of more than 15 percent annually, but whose labor productivity grew at more than 10 percent per year. At the other extreme, there were forty-three enterprises whose profit rate grew by more than 120 percent per year but whose labor productivity growth was negative. Accordingly the Economic Reform Institute report argued that trying to link wages with profits, as many economists were then proposing, would be a very poor policy.[71]

Second, they further argued that although product prices were being freed, there was no significant market for the means of production (roughly the equivalent of capital goods). With no way for the means of production to flow to those areas in which the returns were the highest, the inevitable result would be inflation.

In addition to these factors, the report argued that with the changeover from state financial allocations to bank loans, the restrictions on allocations were becoming more rigid while those on bank loans were becoming looser. Enterprises had begun using their own capital for bonuses and welfare and were relying on bank loans for capital construction, which, combined with local pressures for continued growth, put great pressure on banks to extend loans. The looser restrictions on bank loans were reflected in the growing number of delinquent accounts. Under these circumstances, the People's Bank of China ultimately had to yield and issue more currency.

Thus, the Economic Reform Institute report viewed the danger of inflation as stemming more from the imperfections in the microeconomy than from the state's failure to exercise sufficient vigilance over the money supply. Their prescription for combating inflation accordingly focused on rapidly and radically extending the reform of the microeconomic system. On the one hand, they argued for opening China's labor markets not only within cities but also between cities and rural areas—a radical departure from the country's two-decade-old system of controlling labor migration, but one that was in full agreement with the suggestion in the Rural Development Research Group's report about the need to change the urban-rural relationship. Doing so, the Economic Reform Institute argued, would hold down wages by stimulating competition for jobs as well as by reducing expectations for future wage increases. In promoting this seemingly improbable change, they argued on the basis of their survey research that a large percentage of workers, particularly younger workers, would be willing to exchange job security and high wages for the chance to find jobs that fit their desires and gave them a chance to develop their abilities. Taking advantage of this psychology, the report asserted, would make the changeover much less turbulent than might otherwise be expected.[72]

On the financial side, the report argued that in the years preceding 1985, there had grown up a significant nongovernmental credit system (*minjian xindai*), consisting primarily of commercial credit (*shangye xinyong*) among enterprises. Commercial credit, according to the figures of the Economic Reform Institute, was already equivalent to 35 percent of bank loans for circulating capital in 1984 and expanded another 42 percent in 1985, becoming an important support of economic activity in China—as well as being a major reason why the economy continued to grow during 1985 despite the implementation of retrenchment policies. The Reform Institute's report argued that the restraints facing enterprises with regard to this nonofficial credit were significantly more rigid than those on bank loans; whether or not one enterprise would extend commercial credit to another enterprise depended on the latter's reputation, and hence, unlike bank loans, such loans had to be repaid on time.[73]

The emergence of this alternative source of funds and the hard restraints associated with it opened the possibility of creating a dual-track system in finance comparable to the one that had been introduced in the price system. The institute's economists therefore argued that encouraging horizontal linkages (*hengxiang lianhe*) among enterprises would harden restraints on them. Like the dual-track price system, which stimulated both production and efficiency by freeing part of the price structure, a dual-track financial system would gradually harden restraints on enterprises as nonofficial credit expanded and official bank credit gradually declined.[74]

This analysis of the causes and remedies of inflation suggests that the views of the Economic Reform Institute economists who worked on this article were not very different from those of the Rural Development Group. This judgment is strengthened when one considers that the article was written in the latter half of 1985, a period in which the government had tightened macroeconomic control to reduce demand, and hence a period in which directly countering government policy would not have been judicious. Taking a contrary tack, the article appears to be playing off the official line by arguing in effect that if inflation represented such a serious danger, then it was preferable to push microeconomic reform than to overly stress macroeconomic control. It therefore seems probable that the authors of the article continued to believe that a relatively rapid rate of economic growth continued to be necessary and that inflation was not as serious a danger to the economy and reform as was delaying reform while imposing macroeconomic control. This interpretation is strengthened by an examination of the analyses produced by economists associated with the Economic Reform Institute on the effect of retrenchment policies in 1986 (see Chapter 6).

Adopting Retrenchment Measures

The emergence of the different perspectives offered by Wu Jinglian and the Economic Reform Institute would lead to sharp disagreement in 1986 and later; in 1985, however, most economists agreed on the need to tighten macroeconomic control. Xue Muqiao, for instance, strongly defended price reform ("Having been in charge of commodity price control," wrote Xue, "I am sure that it is absolutely impossible for the commodity price control departments to set and adjust the prices of hundreds of thousands of commodities") but argued that macroeconomic control needed to be strengthened. Viewing the situation in 1984, Xue warned that the consumption fund had risen too quickly, observing that "in the fourth quarter of last year, especially in December, some units randomly raised wages and freely handed out bonuses and goods seeking thus to raise the wage base and obtain more wages this year." The inflationary impact of this increase on the money supply made both wage and price reform difficult.[75]

More conservative economists urged the tightening of macroeconomic control in even stronger terms. For instance, Shen Liren, an economist at CASS's Economics Institute, said that "we should not fail to see that if the speed of our progress is too fast, it will certainly bring about bad results."[76] Similarly, Liu Hong and Wei Liqun, both of whom were in the State Planning Commission's

Policy Research Office, warned that "recently, the scale of investment in fixed assets was too large, the growth of consumption funds was too violent, granting of credit and loan funds was excessive, and, as a result, certain unstable factors emerged in economic life."[77]

Over the course of 1985, Zhao Ziyang and the State Council held four meetings with provincial governors to discuss ways of controlling capital construction and reducing inflationary pressures. The first, which convened in February, adopted some measures to bring the economy under control. In April, Zhao argued that a method of "slow braking" should be used to gradually reduce the rate of growth and seemed to imply that he would be satisfied if growth could be reduced to approximately the level of 1984, or about 14 percent. Zhao said that the government should not use the means of "sharply braking or carrying out a large readjustment" but should instead gradually reduce the rate of growth to an "appropriate speed."[78]

Zhao's plan to slow the economy gradually gave way to a more vigorous effort to slow economic growth through the use of administrative measures. Although continued pressure from conservatives was one factor in this change, unexpected support for administrative measures from foreign economists was critical in Zhao's change of course. The turning point came at the "Bashanlun Conference" of early September 1985. Formally known as the "International Symposium on Macroeconomic Control," the meeting took its nickname from the Bashan boat on which it convened on the Yangzi River. This meeting was attended by such internationally known scholars as W. Brus, Janos Kornoi, and James Tobin, the Nobel Laureate from Yale University, as well as by economists from CASS and the Chinese Association for the Study of Economic Structural Reform. A major result of the meeting was the conclusion that the transition from a planned economy to a market economy required strong macroeconomic control and that administrative controls were necessary to achieve this. James Tobin was cited as saying emphatically that "even in Western developed countries administrative methods were sometimes more effective than fiscal and monetary methods; therefore, fiscal and monetary methods must be integrated with administrative controls."[79] Zhao Ziyang was reportedly surprised to hear that a well-known Western economist, particularly one in the Keynesian tradition, had suggested the need for administrative controls, and thereafter supported more vigorous action in this regard.[80]

Conference of Party Delegates and Retrenchment

Tensions over the proper rate of growth as well as over broader issues of the relationship between plan and market were reflected in the Conference of Party Delegates that convened in September 1985. Although primarily noted for the large-scale promotion of younger leaders into the Central Committee, the Conference of Party Delegates was also important for adopting the "Proposal on the

Seventh Five-Year Plan." The "Proposal" was an attempt by reformers to set the parameters of the Seventh Five-Year Plan, which was then being drafted under the auspices of the State Planning Commission and would be adopted by the National People's Congress the following spring.[81] One innovation in the "Proposal" was the adoption of Wu Jinglian's formula for a simultaneous advance on the three fronts of enterprise reform, market creation, and macroeconomic control, suggesting that the top leadership of China was beginning to think of reform in new ways. In this sense, the "Proposal" marked the waning of the influence of mainstream reformers like Liu Guoguang and Chen Jiyuan, who had participated in the Wuxi Conference and helped shape the original reform strategy, in favor of a new brand of reform thinking led by Wu Jinglian and like-minded people.

Despite this apparent advance in thinking about economic reform, the policies adopted by the Conference of Party Delegates were those favored by the conservative wing of the party. Chen Yun openly and sharply criticized the performance of the reform program. Chen said that the high growth rate that had prevailed in the early part of the year "cannot be maintained." Drawing a sharp distinction between the guidance planning that had been authorized by the Third Plenum's 1984 Decision on Economic Structural Reform and market regulation—which "blindly allows supply and demand to determine production"—Chen echoed conservative criticisms of reform in the early 1980s, saying that "planning is the essence of macroeconomic control." With regard to the agricultural sector, Chen criticized the rapidity with which rural enterprises were being developed, saying that "the call of 'no prosperity without engaging in industry' is heard much louder than that of 'no economic stability without agricultural development'." Suggesting that this rapid development of rural enterprises had undermined agricultural production in 1985, Chen gave the blunt warning, "without grain there will be chaos" (wu liang ze luan).[82]

Chen's criticisms were incorporated into official policy. The "Proposal on the Seventh Five-Year Plan," which largely endorsed a reform-oriented program, nevertheless stated that the growth rate for the five-year plan period should be maintained at about 7 percent—just as Xu Yi and other conservatives had argued. Moreover, it said that this growth rate had been agreed to "unanimously" by the Politburo Standing Committee, suggesting that, as in 1980, Deng and Chen Yun had come to an agreement and then passed it on to Zhao and the rest of the leadership.[83]

Following the Conference of Party Delegates, controls over credit and investment were further tightened. The decline in agricultural production appears to have been particularly sobering. Without ever publicly acknowledging a change in policy, the contract system that had been introduced with such great fanfare at the beginning of 1985 was gradually tightened to the point that it was as mandatory as the previous unified procurement system. As one article put it, "the unified procurement and sale system was thrown out through the front door and the 'contract system' came in through the window." Peasants complained that "the quantities covered by the contracts are greater than under unified procurement, and the demands on agricultural varieties are stricter."[84] The vulnerability of reformers created by the decline in grain output in 1985 appears to have been reflected in the fact that Zhao never again undertook a major reform initiative in the field of agriculture.

If the incorporation of Wu Jinglian's ideas into the "Proposal on the Seventh Five-Year Plan" marked a step forward in the way the Chinese leadership (particularly Zhao Ziyang) thought about reform issues, it is also important to underscore the degree to which the acceptance of Wu's ideas marked the failure of previous reform thinking. The reform program of 1984 had run into a great deal of trouble: conservatives were subjecting it to withering criticism, and mainstream reformers did not appear to have new ideas that would effectively rebut those criticisms. In short, the political acceptance of Wu's ideas marked the failure of the original conception of reform and the casting about by the leadership for new ideas that could effectively respond both to the real economic problems that had emerged and to the criticisms of conservatives.

Notes

1. Xinhua, December 29, 1984, trans. FBIS, December 31, 1984, pp. K4–6. See also Lo Ping, "The Basic Battle Against 'Leftism' Waged by Hu Yaobang," *Cheng ming*, no. 2 (February 1, 1985), pp. 6–10, trans. FBIS, February 7, 1985, pp. W1–10.

2. Xinhua, January 7, 1985, trans. FBIS, January 8, 1985, p. K4. See also "Liu Binyan and Wu Zuguang Say: 'Writers Should Value and Fully Use Freedom of Creation,'" Zhongguo xinwen she, January 3, 1985, trans. FBIS, January 4, 1985, pp. K6–7; and "Wang Meng Says the Main Purpose of Advocating Freedom in Literary Creation Is to Clear Away 'Leftist' Residue," Zhongguo xinwen she, January 9, 1985, trans. FBIS, January 11, 1985, pp. K7–8.

3. Xinhua, December 25, 1984, trans. FBIS, December 26, 1984, p. K1.

4. See "Zhao Ziyang's Speech at New Year Tea Party Held by the CPPCC Central Committee," *Renmin ribao*, January 2, 1985, p. 1, trans. FBIS, January 9, 1985, pp. K9–11.

5. Tian Jiyun, "Actively and Steadily Carry Out Reform of the Pricing System," *Renmin ribao*, January 8, 1985, pp. 1 and 2, trans. FBIS, January 10, 1985, pp. K2–9.

6. "Work Together with One Heart in Building the Four Modernizations—1985 New Year Message," *Renmin ribao*, Editorial, January 1, 1985, p. 1, trans. FBIS, January 2, 1985, pp. K6–7. Emphasis added.

7. Hu Yaobang, "On the Party's Journalism Work," *Renmin ribao*, April 14, 1985, pp. 1–3, trans. FBIS, April 15, 1985, pp. K1–15.

8. Liu Binyan, *A Higher Kind of Loyalty*, p. 247.

9. Xinhua, March 8, 1985, trans. FBIS, March 11, 1985, pp. K5–6.

10. Wang Jiye, "Problems of the Economic Environment and Macroeconomic Regulation in Structural Reform," *Renmin ribao*, March 18, 1985, p. 171, trans. FBIS, April 2, 1985, pp. K17–22.

11. Zuo Chuntai and Xiao Jie, "Balance of Financial Credits Is an Important Question in Macroeconomic Control," *Renmin ribao*, May 6, 1985, p. 5, trans. FBIS, May 14, 1985, pp. K4–7.

12. Hongqi Editorial Department, "How to Do a Better Job in Departmental Work," Xinhua, January 31, 1985, trans. FBIS, February 1, 1985, pp. K1–10.

13. Xu Yi, "On the Establishment of a Comprehensive Financial System of Macroeconomic Balance," *Caizheng yanjiu*, no. 5 (May 1985), trans. and ed. Joseph Fewsmith,

"The Debate on China's Macroeconomic Situation (II)," pp. 46–68. It should be noted that the figure of 7.2 percent annual growth was what was needed to quadruple China's GNP between 1980 and 2000—the commitment made by Hu Yaobang in his report to the Twelfth Party Congress—suggesting that it was derived more from political calculation than macroeconomic models.

14. Ibid., p. 66.

15. Ibid., p. 49.

16. Ibid., p. 58.

17. Huan Guocang, "China's Opening to the World," *Problems of Communism*, vol. 35, no. 6 (November–December 1986), p.59.

18. According to Chen Muhua, Chinese foreign exchange reserves stood at U.S. $16,674 million in September 1984 and U.S. $14,420 million in December. By the end of March 1985, reserves had fallen to U.S. $11,262 million. See Yeh Chi-jung, "Chen Muhua Received Hong Kong and Macao Reporters This Morning," *Hsin wan pao*, March 31, 1985, p. 1, trans. FBIS, April 1, 1985, pp. W8–9; and Zhongguo xinwen she, July 6, 1985, trans. FBIS, July 8, 1985, p. K20.

19. "On the International Environment of China's Open Door—Summary of Views at the Symposium on World Economics of Young and Middle-Aged Research Workers," *Shijie jingji*, no. 2 (February 10, 1985), pp. 25–29, trans. JPRS-CEA–85–084 (September 19, 1985), pp. 1–8.

20. *Fujian ribao*, February 7, 1985, trans. FBIS, February 26, 1985.

21. *Ming pao*, June 4, 1985, p. 6, trans. JPRS–CEA–85–063 (July 16, 1985), pp. 122–123.

22. "Hu Qiaomu Warns in Xiamen that Foreign Investment Enterprises Are Not Concessions; Their Inordinate Demands Cannot Be Given Tacit Consent," *Ming pao*, June 22, 1985, trans. FBIS, June 24, 1985, p. W8; and "Special Economic Zones Are Not Special Political Zones; China's Laws Must Be Upheld, Says Hu Qiaomu," *Zhongguo fazhi bao*, June 28, 1985, trans. FBIS, July 8, 1985, pp. K18–19.

23. "Investigation Report of the Central Discipline Inspection Commission," Xinhua, July 31, 1985, trans. FBIS, August 6, 1985, pp. P1–8.

24. Xinhua, June 29, 1985, trans. FBIS, July 2, 1985, p. I1.

25. Xinhua, June 29, 1985, trans. FBIS, July 16, 1985, p. D1.

26. This section draws heavily on my "Agricultural Crisis in the PRC," *Problems of Communism*, vol. 37, no. 6 (November–December 1988), pp. 78–93.

27. Wu Shuo, "A Talk on the Second Major Reform of the Rural Economic Structure," *Liaowang*, no. 4 (1985), pp. 16–17, trans. FBIS, February 7, 1985, pp. K19–22.

28. Author's interviews.

29. Ibid.

30. There were also institutional problems that the reform could not overcome. The institution of "contracts" could hardly change the administrative manner in which grain was procured through the level-by-level assignment of quotas; local grain bureaus were in no position to open negotiations with each household. I appreciate Jean Oi calling this to my attention.

31. Hu Changnuan, "Ping jiu nian lai nongchangpin jiage juece de chenggong yu shiwu" (Evaluating the Successes and Failures of the Agricultural Product Policy Over the Past Nine Years), *Nongye jingji wenti*, no. 6 (June 1988), pp.7–11.

32. Ibid.

33. Chinese Academy of Agricultural Sciences, "China Must Not Have Less than 400 Kilograms of Grain Per Capita," *Nongye jishu jingji*, August 1986, pp. 12–15, trans. JPRS-CEA–87–002, (January 12, 1987), 57–62.

34. Hu Changnuan, "Ping jiu nian lai nongchangpin jiage juece de chenggong yu shiwu."

35. Duan Yingbi, "There Must Be Major Reforms in the Grain Marketing System,"

Nongye jingji wenti, no. 11 (November 1986), pp. 37–40, trans. JPRS-CEA–87–023 (March 23, 1987), pp. 67–73.

36. Comprehensive Problems Section of the Development Research Center, "Nongmin, shichang he zhidu chuangxin (Peasants, Markets, and System Renewal) *Jingji yanjiu*, January 1987, pp. 3–16, trans. JPRS-CEA–87–033 (April 16, 1987) no. 1, pp. 23–48.

37. Gao Xiaomeng, "The Question of Grain Prices and Reform of the Circulation Structure," *Liaowang*, May 25, 1987, p. 16, trans. FBIS, June 10, 1987, pp. K21–23. In some places, according to Gao, the price of grain on rural markets rose by more than 10 percent between October and December 1986. "Grain output and grain prices have increased at the same time," Gao said, adding, "This has not happened since 1954." Guo Yuhai, "Several Opinions on the Grain Problem," *Renmin ribao*, May 18, 1987, trans. FBIS, June 2, 1987, pp. K22–24.

38. Comprehensive Problems Section of the Development Research Center, "Peasants, Markets, and System Renewal."

39. Chengdu Radio, April 2, 1985, trans. JPRS-CAR–85–018 (June 10, 1985), pp. 126–127.

40. Changsha Radio, April 2, 1985, trans. FBIS, April 3, 1985, p. P2; and Guangzhou Radio, May 18, 1985.

41. Chinese Academy of Agricultural Sciences, "Problems in Development of a Commodity Economy in Agriculture and Policies for Dealing with Them," *Nongye jingji jishu*, December 1986, pp. 1–5, trans. JPRS-CEA–87–034 (April 20, 1987), pp. 70–80. How much grain output actually declined in 1985 is open to question. Statistics on grain production are less accurate than those for industrial production; several agricultural experts have stated that they deviate from real grain output by at least 5 percent. Moreover, figures on grain production are subject to political influence. For these reasons, some people maintain that grain production did not decrease significantly in 1985.

42. *Zhongguo xiangzhen qiye nianjian, 1978–1987*, pp. 570–571.

43. *Nongye jingji xiaoguo*, no. 2 (April 25, 1987), pp. 2–5, trans. JPRS-CAR–87–014 (July 2, 1987), pp. 65–71. The figures for investment during the Seventh Five-Year Plan period come from Geng Zhi, "Raising the Share and Readjusting the Composition of Agricultural Investment," *Nongye jingji xiaoguo*, no. 6, (December 25, 1986), pp. 1–3, trans. JPRS-CEA–87–043 (May 19, 1987), pp. 78–82. See also Chinese Academy of Agricultural Sciences, "Problems in Development of a Commodity Economy in Agriculture and Policies for Dealing with Them," which gives slightly different figures, indicating that state investment in agricultural construction during the Sixth Five-Year Plan period amounted to 6 percent of total state investment in capital construction.

44. State Statistical Bureau, *Statistical Yearbook of China, 1986*, p. 583.

45. A survey of agricultural returns conducted by the Jiangsu Price Bureau in 1985 recorded the per mu net profits for a variety of agricultural products as follows: grain, 55.71 yuan; oil crops, 64.59 yuan; hemp and similar crops, 231.94 yuan; and vegetables, 323.4 yuan. See Duan Yingbi, "There Must Be Major Reforms in the Grain Marketing System," pp. 67–73.

46. See, for instance, Lu Xueyi, "Dangqian de nongcun xingshi he liangshi wenti" (The Current Rural Situation and the Grain Question). As noted in Chapter 1, Lu was one of the earliest supporters of the household responsibility system, but he apparently never collaborated closely with the Rural Development Institute. His article suggests that by the mid-1980s he was quite critical of the institute's proposals, though he remained a strong partisan of the household responsibility system—something that cannot be said about many of the institute's critics.

47. Economic Growth Study Group of the Policy Research Center under the Ministry of Agriculture, Animal Husbandry, and Fishery, "Changgui zengzhang, yihuo fazhan

chizhi" (Normal Growth [or] Stagnating Development?). Gao, Li, and Zhou are identified as the authors in an endnote. See also Zhou Binbin, Liu Yunzhou, and Li Qingzeng, "Nongcun mianlin de tiaozhan yu xuanze" (The Challenges and Alternatives Facing Agriculture), *Nongye jingji wenti*, no. 12 (December 1986), pp.35–39.

48. Chen Xiwen, "Zhongguo nongcun jingji: Cong chaochanggui zengzhang zhuanxiang changgui zengzhang" (China's Rural Economy: The Change from Supernormal Growth to Normal Growth). Wu Xiang, then deputy director of the Rural Development Research Center, argued along similar lines. See Wu Xiang, "Deepen the Reform and Strengthen the New Structure of the Rural Economy."

49. Shi Bing, "Guanyu nongye xuyao zengjia touru wenti de tansuo" (An Exploration of the Need to Increase Agricultural Inputs), *Nongye jingji wenti*, no. 1 (January 1987), pp. 6–9 trans. JPRS-CAR–87–007 (June 16, 1987), pp. 6–9.

50. Problem Group of the Rural Development Research Group of the State Council, "Zhongguo nongcun jingji tizhi zhongqi (1988–1995) gaige tiyao" (Outline of the Structural Reform of the Chinese Rural Economy in the Medium Term, 1988–1995).

51. Li Rui, "Do Not Blindly Seek a Higher Rate of Development," *Guangming ribao*, May 7, 1985, p. 1, trans. FBIS, May 15, 1985, pp. K10–12; Li Rui, "On Proneness to Boasting and Exaggeration," *Guangming ribao*, May 8, 1985, p. 1, trans. FBIS, May 20, 1985, pp. K12–13; and Li Rui, "Another Discussion on Proneness to Boasting and Exaggeration," *Guangming ribao*, May 9, 1985, p. 1, trans. FBIS, May 20, 1985, pp. K13–15.

52. See Li Jiange, "Jiecheng jian zhi yong, qiusu yi jianxin—Wu Jinglian zhuanlue" (Wholeheartedly and Bravely Seeking Wisdom and Simplicity Among Hardships—A Brief Biography of Wu Jinglian), vol. 5, pp. 544–70.

53. Wu Jinglian, *Jingji gaige wenti tansuo* (Explorations of Chinese Economic Reform), p. 346. It is important to point out that Wu participated in the China Economic Structure Research Group headed by Ma Hong and Sun Shangqing in late 1979 and contributed an article on readjustment to the two-volume study edited by Ma and Sun. See Wu Jinglian, "Jingji tizhi gaige yu jingji jiegou tiaozheng de guanxi" (The Relationship Between Economic Reform and Economic Readjustment).

54. Wu Jinglian, *Jingji gaige wenti tansuo*, pp. 348–349.

55. Li Jiange, "Jiecheng jian zhi yong, qiusu yi jianxin—Wu Jinglian zhuanlue," vol. 5, p. 560.

56. Ibid., p. 561.

57. Ibid.

58. Wu Jinglian, "Women yingdang cong Xiongyali gaige de chengbai deshi zhong qude shenma jiaoshun?" (What Lessons Should We Derive from the Successes and Failures of Hungary's Reform?).

59. In this regard, Wu points out that both Brus and Sun Yefang overlooked the role of the competitive market and that the Hungarian reform had been heavily influenced in the beginning by the idea of expanding enterprise autonomy with a consequent neglect of the market. See "Cong Xiongyali jingyan kan woguo dangqian gaige," (Viewing China's Current Reform from the Perspective of Hungary's Experience).

60. Wu Jinglian, "Women yingdang cong Xiongyali gaige de chengbai deshi zhong qude shenma jiaoshun?" pp. 393–394.

61. Wu Jinglian, "Jingji gaige chuzhan jieduan de fazhan fangzhen he hongguan kongzhi wenti" (The Development Orientation in the Initial Stage of Economic Reform and the Problem of Macroeconomic Control), *Renmin ribao*, February 11, 1985, p. 5.

62. Ibid.

63. Wu Jinglian, "Zailun baochi jingji gaige de lianghao jingji huanjing" (Again Discussing Maintaining a Favorable Economic Environment for Economic Reform), *Jingji*

yanjiu, no. 5 (May 1985), pp. 3–4. See also Wu Jinglian, "Jingji gaige chuzhan jieduan de fazhan fangzhen he hongguan kongzhi wenti."

64. Wu Jinglian, "Zailun baochi jingji gaige de lianghao jingji huanjing."

65. Wu Jinglian, "Danxiang tuijin, haishi peitao gaige" (Advancing on One Front or Coordinated Reform?), pp. 268–278. Internal evidence in the article suggests that the symposium was called to discuss an early draft of the "Proposal for the Seventh Five-Year Plan."

66. Ibid., p. 269.

67. Ibid., pp. 276–277. See also Wu Jinglian, "Jingji jizhi he peitao gaige" (Economic Mechanisms and the Coordinated Reforms), *Hongqi,* no. 5 (March 1, 1986), pp. 19–23.

68. Wu included three articles authored or co-authored by Guo in a collection of articles that outlined and defended this school of thought. See Wu Jinglian, Zhou Xiaochuan, et al., *Zhongguo jingji gaige de zhengti sheji* (The Integrated Design of China's Economic Reform).

69. Guo Shuqing, Luo Jiwei, and Liu Jirui, "Guanyu tizhi gaige zongti guihua de yanjiu" (Research on the Overall Plan for Structural Reform), pp. 25–47. Note also their criticisms of the dual-track system, pp. 41–42.

70. Chinese Economic Structural Reform Institute, "Gaige: Woguo mianlin de tiaozhan yu xuanze" (Reform: The Challenges and Choices Confronting China), *Jingji yanjiu,* no. 11 (November 1985), pp. 3–18.

71. Ibid., p. 8.

72. Ibid., pp. 13–15.

73. Ibid., p. 16.

74. Ibid., pp. 17–18.

75. Xue Xiaohe, "Properly Handle the Two Reforms and Overcome the Two Gusts of Ill Wind—Xue Muqiao on Economic Relations in the Current Year," *Renmin ribao,* March 6, 1985, trans. FBIS, March 8, 1985, pp. K13–17.

76. Shen Liren, "A Discussion on Optimal Speed," *Jingji guanli,* no. 9 (September 1985), pp. 16–19, trans, JPRS-CEA–85–110 (December 17, 1985), pp. 84–91.

77. Liu Hong and Wei Liqun, "On Correctly Handling Several Important Relationships in the Seventh Five-Year Plan," *Jingji yanjiu,* no. 10 (October 1985), pp. 3–9, trans. JPRS-CEA–85–112 (December 20, 1985), p. 5.

78. This is the estimate offered by Chen Wenhong. See Chen Wenhong, *Zhongguo jingji wenti* (China's Economic Problems), p. 4.

79. Cited in Liu Guoguang et al., "Jingji tizhi gaige yu hongguan jingji guanli" (Economic Structural Reform and Macroeconomic Control), *Jingji yanjiu,* no. 12 (December 1985), p. 11.

80. Author's interviews.

81. Hamrin, *China and the Challenge of the Future,* especially pp. 179–183.

82. Chen Yun, "Zai Zhongguo gongchandang quanguo daibiao huiyi shang de jianghua" (Talk to the Conference of Delegates of the Chinese Communist Party).

83. "Proposal of the Central Committee of the Chinese Communist Party for the Seventh Five-Year Plan (1986–90) for National Economic and Social Development," Xinhua, September 25, 1985, trans. FBIS, September 26, 1985, pp. K1–24.

84. Comprehensive Problems Section of the Development Research Center, "Nongmin, shichang he zhidu cuangxin." See also Chinese Academy of Agricultural Sciences, "Problems in Development of a Commodity Economy in Agriculture and Policies for Dealing with Them"; and Lu Wen, "Nongcun jingji fazhan zhong de xin dongtai" (New Dynamism in the Rural Economy), Nongye jingji wenti, no. 11 (November 1987), pp. 3–6.

6

The 1986 Recession and Deepening Debates Over the Course of Reform

Conservative criticism of reform in 1985 clearly slowed the momentum of economic reform in China and put its supporters on the defensive. As the new year began, expectations were low. *People's Daily*'s annual New Year's editorial set the goal for the year modestly as "consolidating, digesting, and supplementing" (*gugong, xiaohua, buchong*) the achievements of the previous two years. Looking toward a brighter future, it called for research and experimentation to prepare for "an important step forward for next year's [1987's] reform."[1]

Contrary to these modest expectations, the new year soon emerged as a turning point in the development of reform. In terms of reform strategy, 1986 was critical because it was the year in which Zhao Ziyang came to adopt the microeconomic reform strategy that had been developed in large measure by the young economists of the Rural Development Group and the Economic Reform Institute. In doing so, Zhao gave up on efforts to design a top-down approach to reform and began to emphasize a bottom-up approach.

This switch stemmed from two considerations. On the one hand, Zhao became increasingly aware of and concerned about the difficulties and risks involved in negotiating and implementing the sort of top-down, "coordinated reform" advocated by Wu Jinglian and others. On the other hand, despite being in charge of all economic reform efforts, Zhao remained unable to dominate the bureaucratic machinery that had overall control over the economy, particularly the State Planning Commission and the Ministry of Finance, and therefore had to find ways of implementing reform that did not depend on the cooperation of such organs. Thus, both the desire to minimize political and economic risks and the need to find a way around the planning apparatus led Zhao to focus on the reform of the microeconomy.

As Zhao turned his attention from the macroeconomy to the microeconomy, his differences with conservative bureaucrats increased. In the early 1980s, Zhao had sought to maintain good relations with Chen Yun, sometimes at the expense of Hu Yaobang. In 1986 Zhao split definitively with Chen's approach; in this pursuit of a separate path to reform lay the seeds of Zhao's own demise three years later.

In early 1986 the first counterattack against the conservative criticism of reform came from Hu Yaobang, not Zhao Ziyang. In 1985, the Hainan incident, the rapid growth of speculative "briefcase companies," and an investigation into the manufacture of fake medicine in Fujian Province (which conservatives had used to remove the reform-minded head of the province, Xiang Nan) had tarred reform as promoting corruption. Hu Yaobang himself may have been vulnerable to this criticism since there were allegations that his son was involved in official profiteering.[2] In January 1986, Hu Yaobang presided over a huge rally of 8,000 cadres (evoking comparisons with the famous 7,000 cadre conference of 1962) called to address the issue of corruption. This meeting showcased some of the new, younger leadership that had been promoted at the Conference of Party Delegates the previous September. Hu Yaobang's protégé Hu Qili, who had just been named to head the Central Secretariat, presided over the meeting. Zhao Ziyang's protégé Tian Jiyun, who had been promoted to vice premier the previous September, gave a speech, as did Wang Zhaoguo, who had been named a member of the Central Secretariat. Li Peng, who had also just been promoted to vice premier, was conspicuous by his absence, suggesting that he was already distancing himself from Hu and Zhao.

The meeting laid down a tough line. Hu Yaobang told the conference that "it is necessary to reinforce law and discipline to ensure that laws are strictly enforced and that lawbreakers are punished."[3] Shortly thereafter, Politburo member Hu Qili reinforced Hu's message, telling a graduation ceremony at the Central Party School that "those who have broken the law should be punished by imprisonment or death" and that it was necessary to "execute one as a warning to a hundred."[4] These warnings were not idle. A special committee headed by Hu Yaobang's associate Qiao Shi was established within the Central Committee to root out corruption. In February, shortly after the establishment of this committee, three sons of high-level cadres were executed.[5] There were soon reports that the children of a number of conservative party leaders, including Peng Zhen, Hu Qiaomu, and Ye Fei, were under investigation, suggesting that Hu Yaobang was targeting his critics.[6] Moreover, the decision to set up a special committee within the Central Committee to tackle this issue appeared to be a challenge to the CDIC, headed by Chen Yun, as the agency of discipline within the party.

At the same time that Hu Yaobang was confronting conservative criticism of corruption, the National Economic Conference met in Beijing. At the conference, many enterprise managers raised the issue of interference by party secretaries and demanded greater freedom. This demand was welcomed by Zhao Ziyang, who sought to make enterprises more independent and more responsive to economic stimuli.[7] A *People's Daily* Commentator article published after the conclusion of the meeting hinted at this effort to strengthen the hand of enterprise managers by stressing the need to improve management.[8]

These two issues—corruption and enterprise management—would fuel renewed pressures for political reform, and by the late spring and early summer of 1986 the issue of political reform would return to the Chinese political scene for the first time since Deng Xiaoping's speech of August 1980. Before the issue of political reform was raised, however, an important debate emerged in February about the rate of industrial growth and continued through April. This debate paralleled in many ways the arguments over high-speed growth that had been voiced in 1985. In contrast to the situation in 1985, however, the advocates of loosening the money supply and stimulating growth rates won the 1986 debate. This was important not only because it rejected the arguments of conservative economic bureaucrats, but also because it provoked a major split within the reform camp. The debates over macroeconomic versus microeconomic approaches to reform, implicit in the previous writings of Wu Jinglian and the Economic Reform Institute, respectively, turned into bitter controversy with recriminations that continued for years.

It was the evolving economic situation that provoked this debate. In late 1985, as noted above, Zhao had acceded to demands to tighten macroeconomic control and slow the growth rate. As a result, China's industrial growth rate began to decline significantly in the fourth quarter of 1985, and by February 1986 the gross value of industrial output had declined to 56.76 billion yuan, down from 74.32 billion yuan in June 1985 and only 0.9 percent higher than in February 1985 (see Table 6.1).

This slow growth rate was alarming. In some regions and some sectors of the economy there were serious declines in output. Inventory rates were high and enterprise losses began to mount. At the same time, central revenues began to decline. This economic performance set off one of the sharpest debates over macroeconomic policy in the history of Chinese reform. On the one hand, some economists argued that since aggregate demand remained greater than aggregate supply, tight control should be maintained over the money supply to counter inflationary pressures. On the other hand, other economists argued that retrenchment policies had been excessive and that supply was lower than demand. Moreover, those associated with this latter school of thought began to question the relevance of macroeconomic policy, other than within a rather broad range, as appropriate either for regulating economic behavior or for promoting reform goals. This argument, closely associated with the Economic Reform Institute, was rooted in different theoretical assumptions as well as in different visions of the goal of economic and social reform. These differences would soon lead to a second debate in 1986 about whether ownership reform or price reform should lead reform.

Debate Over the 1986 Recession

Despite the decline in production in late 1985 and especially in early 1986, many economists continued to argue against loosening monetary controls, believing that continued implementation of retrenchment policies would stabilize or even

Table 6.1

Industrial Output Value, March 1985–March 1986 (in billions of yuan)

Year/Month	Industrial Output Value	Percent Increase Over Same Period of Previous Year
1985		
March	69.57	22.3
April	71.20	24.8
May	72.31	22.5
June	74.32	22.8
July	67.89	20.2
August	67.60	17.4
September	70.30	14.5
October	68.58	11.7
November	70.33	8.7
December	72.24	10.2
1986		
January	68.19	5.6
February	56.76	0.9S
March	73.77	6.0

Source: State Statistical Bureau, *Zhongguo tongji yuebao* (Chinese Statistical Monthly), May 1986, p. 17.

reduce price levels. For instance, Liu Guoguang argued that China's economic system made it necessary to maintain a constant vigil against the loss of macroeconomic control. "[R]igid financial policies," said Liu, "should be combined with rigid monetary policies" so as to "curb excessive demand and create a good economic environment in which supply is slightly greater than demand."[9] Liu's concerns with excess demand were seconded by other economists, including Xue Muqiao and Zhang Zhuoyuan.[10] Moreover, their views were supported by the State Statistical Bureau, which reported that "total social demand exceeds total social supply" in early 1986.[11]

Perhaps the most sophisticated and systematic expression of the viewpoint that demand exceeded supply came in an article written by Wu Jinglian and three other young economists of the State Council's Economic, Technological, and Social Development Research Institute. Arguing against those who believed that the macroeconomic policies adopted in the latter half of 1985 had led to an insufficiency of demand, Wu and his colleagues stated bluntly that "at present, aggregate demand exceeds aggregate supply in our national economy, not the other way around."[12] The effective restraint on economic growth, they believed, came from resource constraints, not an insufficiency of demand.

Wu and his colleagues placed particular emphasis on what they believed was the contradiction between continuing energy shortages and the decentralization of administrative authority. Although energy shortages were a long-standing problem in the Chinese economy, they had become more serious since the fourth quarter of 1984, when "high-speed" economic growth appeared. The lead coefficient of electric power to industrial production from 1954 to 1980 was 1.33 (that is, for every 1 percent increase in the gross value of industrial output, the increase in electric power generated was 1.33 percent). This relationship began to change in the Sixth Five-Year Plan. In the first three years of that plan (1981–83), the coefficient had dropped to about 0.7 and had then fallen to only 0.52 in 1984 and to 0.44 in 1985. In 1985, the shortages in power supply totaled 45 to 50 billion kilowatt hours, or about 12 percent of the total electric power generated that year.[13]

This shortage of energy resources, argued Wu and his colleagues, was being exacerbated by the economic consequences of the administrative and fiscal decentralization that had taken place under the reforms. The problem was twofold. On the one hand, given the irrational price structure and fiscal incentives generated by the 1980 reform of the tax system, the localities had an incentive to invest in processing industries, which have a shorter investment cycle and yield higher profits, thereby fueling high-speed growth and exacerbating energy and supply shortages. The dual-track price system contributed to this misallocation of investment funds because it allowed smaller, locally owned industries to raise the prices of their goods while the output of state-owned enterprises had to be sold at state-set prices. This practice allowed the smaller enterprises to outbid state-owned enterprises for raw materials and to have higher profit margins. Wu pointed to the establishment of more than 200 new small-scale steel rolling mills in Liaoning province in 1984 as a case in point of how the price and fiscal structures had led to a situation in which smaller, less efficient enterprises could thrive at the expense of larger and more efficient, state-owned enterprises.[14]

On the other hand, decentralization had permitted local areas to adopt protective measures, including the closing of borders, levying of exit taxes, and use of administrative means to prevent the outflow of resources. Such restrictions on the internal circulation of goods further decreased the efficiency of resource allocation in the whole economy.[15]

The Critique of Retrenchment Policies

In 1985 such arguments had been persuasive; in 1986 they were not. That they were not was due to a combination of factors, including Zhao Ziyang's political needs, the growing influence of the young economists associated with the Economic Reform Institute, and new ways of thinking about the Chinese economy. Conservative criticism of reform in 1985 threatened to overwhelm the reform agenda that party leaders had put forward in 1984. Unless new ways could be found to push reform forward, there was a real danger that management of the economy would once again fall into the hands of conservative economic bureaucrats. If Zhao were going to establish his own political power, he would have to turn to new ideas for reform—particularly to ideas that could push reform forward without directly challenging the power of the economic bureaucrats.

Coinciding with Zhao's political needs was the growing influence of the young economists associated with the Economic Reform Institute. As noted in Chapter 4, Zhao had begun to turn to these young economists in late 1984 as the CCP was moving toward so-called comprehensive economic reform. By late 1985 and early 1986, these economists had had time to undertake a large number of empirical studies and put forth a growing number of ideas for consideration by the leadership. Many of these ideas broke new ground. It seems safe to say that these young economists were part of a genuine intellectual revolution. However their ideas are ultimately judged, it became impossible to turn back to the old ways of thinking about the economy. With this combination of new ideas and enhanced access to decision makers, the Economic Reform Institute attained a new level of influence in 1986.

As young economists saw the economy in late 1985 and early 1986, there were a number of indicators that it could grow at a faster rate and that retrenchment policies were having a number of negative effects on the economy that were creating difficulties for its reform. For instance, inventory levels in the early part of 1986 were high, suggesting that economic growth could be accelerated without causing serious inflation.[16] At the same time, indicators of economic efficiency pointed to poor results under the retrenchment policies. Net profits per 100 yuan of fixed assets had declined by 3.7 yuan from 1985, reaching their lowest rate in recent years. Labor productivity had increased by less than two percentage points, its lowest increase in recent years; the comparable product cost of state-managed industrial enterprises within the budget had increased by 6.6 percent; realized profits had declined by about 10 percent; and the turnaround rate on circulating funds had increased by 7.3 days. At the same time, the number of deficit enterprises had increased by 40 percent, and the size of deficits had increased by 90 percent. The economic results of commercial enterprises had also declined significantly.[17]

In trying to explain these and other phenomena, young economists began to question the relevance of broad discussions of the relation between "aggregate supply" and "aggregate demand" to the Chinese economy, arguing instead that reform needed to address other, more fundamental problems that could not be ameliorated by tight monetary and credit policies, but which could be exacerbated if such policies were applied too stringently and for too long.

One such effort to reevaluate the economic situation grew out of a survey of Chinese enterprises undertaken in March 1986 by a group of graduate students affiliated with Chinese People's University. This survey, which was conducted independently to avoid ministerial bias, examined more than twenty industrial and mining enterprises in Beijing, as well as basic-level banks. The survey resulted in a report entitled "Looking at the February 1986 Industrial Slide from the Perspective of Enterprises." In order to regularize the efforts of this group, a "Microeconomic Situation Analysis Small Group" (*Weiguan jingji fenxi xiaozu*) was organized, and its efforts to analyze the effects of macroeconomic policies on China's enterprises continue to the present. The theoretical perspective of this group drew on Western concepts of the microeconomic foundation of macroeconomics.[18]

An important conclusion of this work was that the retrenchment policies of 1985 had caused a loss of efficiency. Profits and taxes declined more rapidly than production, the industrial comparable cost of products (a measure of efficiency) rose, the quality of products declined, and both the scope and scale of enterprise losses increased. Contrasting this situation with that in the first half of 1985, the authors concluded that "in a period of economic upsurge, enterprises manifest qualitative development, whereas in a period of economic decline they manifest quantitative decline." They explained this counterintuitive conclusion on the basis of the increased unit costs facing enterprises. Enterprise costs could be reduced in periods of tight money if fixed assets could be traded freely on the market and if labor could circulate freely, but, said the authors of the survey, "the retrenchment policy restricted the policy environment in precisely these areas," making enterprises unable to digest rising unit costs.[19]

A second and perhaps more important conclusion of the survey report was that there was a certain threshold rate of growth below which growth would be inefficient. "Only when the speed of growth reaches this threshold can economic efficiency and the rate of growth develop and increase synchronically. At present, the growth rate is clearly beneath this threshold."[20]

A third conclusion of the report was that an "increment space" was necessary for reform and the structural transformation of the economy. The introduction of the dual-price system, the right to sell out-of-plan products on the market, and the use of bonuses all provided an "increment space"—in the form of the gap between the part of production that was under control of the plan and total production—through which market forces could affect enterprise performance. The adoption of retrenchment policies, argued the survey report, "squeezed out the increment space," thus reducing the efficacy of market forces on the marginal production of enterprises. The structural contradictions of the economy could only be ameliorated, maintained the report, through the process of growth, and the "readjustment of the stock has to be realized through the readjustment of the increment."[21]

The conclusions reached in this study were apparently widely shared by many young economists of the time as well as by Zhao Ziyang. Such arguments reinforced Zhao's own belief that the economy was growing too slowly and that a higher rate of economic growth would facilitate the implementation of reform.

Another effort to understand the economic effects of retrenchment focused on the role of personal savings. This effort was led by Song Guoqing, a graduate of Beijing University who was then head of the Economic Reform Institute's Macroeconomic Policy Division, and Zhang Weiying, a young economist who had received his master's degree at Northwest University in Xian and then joined the Macroeconomic Policy Division at the Economic Reform Institute. In a groundbreaking article published in June 1986, Song and Zhang argued that economic theory in China had long considered personal savings as "compulsory" because they resulted from the shortage of commodities and hence constituted "surplus purchasing power." Viewed from this perspective, increased personal savings were *prima facie* evidence that aggregate demand was in excess of aggregate supply. In contrast, Song and Zhang argued that the simultaneity of the increase in savings with an improvement in market supplies demonstrated that personal savings were not (or not only) compulsory. The implication of this argument was that there had not been, as many economists argued, an "over-distribution" of the national income; the increase in the money supply was not, or not necessarily, inflationary.[22]

Song and Zhang also analyzed the nature of money in China, perhaps the first time this question had been addressed in China. They argued that gross demand was related to the amount of currency in circulation (M1) but not to the scale of credit and currency broadly defined (M2). This distinction was important, because the size of China's M2 in early 1986 suggested the existence of excessive demand but that M1 indicated that demand was insufficient. Moreover, Song and Zhang argued that it was necessary to look at the structure of money, that is, how much money was in the hands of enterprises versus individuals, and how much in the hands of peasants versus urban dwellers. For instance, the much slower velocity of money in rural than in urban areas meant that the decreased rate of growth of rural incomes in 1985 had reduced the overall velocity of money, bringing about a situation of insufficient demand in early 1986.

At the same time, other economists began to focus greater attention on the structural problems in the Chinese economy. They came to the conclusion that controlling the macroeconomy could never solve the deep structural problems that were facing the economy. Perhaps the most sophisticated article to take this approach was written by Deng Yingtao and Luo Xiaopeng of the Rural Development Research Center in 1987.[23] Consciously building on the analysis developed by that group two years earlier, Deng and Luo argued that China's long-standing distorted price structure and rigid administrative system had brought about an irrational distribution of capital assets (only about two-thirds of the country's assets were utilized effectively) that rendered macroeconomic policies ineffective and distorted investment. Because capital assets could not be transferred, new capital outlays often went either to importing or manufacturing equipment that was already present but underutilized in the economy. For instance, the utilization rate of metal-cutting lathes had dropped continually between 1976 and 1985 (from 59.5 percent to 50.3 percent), a decade in which growth rates and monetary policies had fluctuated greatly. This suggested that macroeconomic policies had had no significant effect on microeconomic behavior. Moreover, the number of such lathes had increased from 2.27 million to 3.5 million in the same period; instead of transferring lathes from places where they were underutilized to places where they were needed (thus raising their utilization rate), new lathes were manufactured with funds that could have been directed to other needs.

Moreover, the irrational distribution of capital assets meant that while the production of some goods met demand (and hence constituted "effective supply" [*youxiao gonggei*]), the production of other goods did not meet the demand structure (and hence constituted "ineffective supply" [*wuxiao gonggei*]). If one deducted ineffective supply from total supply, Deng and Luo argued, it was apparent that effective supply was insufficient. Since the implementation of retrenchment policies reduced effective supply more quickly than ineffective supply, a "simplistic" reliance on tightening macroeconomic policies to create a so-called relatively relaxed atmosphere would do more harm than good.

Another effect of the inability to transfer capital assets throughout the economy was the tendency for all enterprises to increase and decrease their investments at the same time. When tight monetary and credit policies were implemented, there was no tendency for efficient industries that were meeting demands to increase their investments, while inefficient industries sold off unneeded capital goods to reduce expenditures, thus effecting a readjustment of capital goods in the economy to more efficient sectors. On the contrary, retrenchment policies hurt efficient industries more than inefficient enterprises, and efficient enterprises tended to grow more slowly than inefficient ones when monetary policies were loosened.

Over time, the structure of capital assets became more and more irrational and the ratio of effective supply to ineffective supply fell. The major accomplishment of readjustment periods—such as those of the early 1960s and the late 1970s and early 1980s—was to correct this maladjustment. But such readjustments had to rely on administrative means and hence could never fundamentally resolve the underlying reasons for the irrational distribution of capital assets. Moreover, as reform had progressed, the amount of investment under the control of the central government had decreased steadily—from 53 percent in 1978 to about 20 percent in 1986—meaning that the central government had less ability to effect a readjustment of the structure of capital assets throughout the country. This meant that the only alternative was to speed up microeconomic reform so that enterprises would have the ability and incentives to direct their investments in a rational direction.

Price Reform Versus Ownership Reform

The very different conceptual frameworks that informed the debate over the 1986 recession also underlay the best-known debate of 1986, that between those who emphasized price reform and those who emphasized ownership reform. This debate emerged directly out of efforts to draw up a comprehensive reform plan that had begun the previous year. Zhao Ziyang accelerated this effort in March

1986 when he spoke at a meeting on economic reform, calling for a coordinated reform of prices, taxes, and finances.[24] Shortly after Zhao's talk, the Leading Group for the Study of Economic Structural Reform (*Jingji tizhi gaige yantao lingdao xiaozu*) was established under Tian Jiyun's leadership.[25] There were two offices under this leading group, one in the State Commission of Economic Structural Reform and the other in the State Council's Economic, Social, and Technological Development Research Center. Wu Jinglian headed up the work in the latter office.[26]

Wu's advocacy of price reform did not mean that he had abandoned the position that he had adopted in 1985 that "relatively independent" enterprises, a competitive market, and an effective macroeconomic regulatory system were all necessary and interrelated, but it does appear to mark an evolution in his thinking, a fleshing out of his previous ideas of how to make the transition from a planned economy to a market economy. As pointed out above, Wu had, since returning from the United States, repeatedly urged that a "relatively relaxed economic environment" was necessary for making the transition to a market economy and that a rational price mechanism was critical to bringing about a rational distribution of resources. In 1986, Wu brought these beliefs together with the idea that a well-designed price reform program, including coordinated reforms of the tax and financial systems, could bring about a relatively rapid transition of the economic system. Such a transition, Wu believed, could overcome the dysfunctions emerging from reform and put economic activity on a rational basis.

Wu's ideas on coordinated reform and price reform appear to have been highly influential between the summer of 1985 and the spring of 1986. As noted above, his idea of carrying out coordinated reform of enterprises, markets, and the macroeconomic control system was incorporated into the "Proposal for the Seventh Five-Year Plan," and his ideas appear to have been central to the reform plan that was being drawn up under Tian Jiyun's auspices in the spring of 1986.[27] Precisely at the time when Wu's ideas appear to have been at the peak of their influence, the logic, coherence, and necessity for implementing such a reform plan was publicly questioned. This challenge came from Li Yining, professor of economics at Beijing University.

Li Yining and Ownership Reform

Li Yining was a graduate of Beijing University's Economics Department, where he had become deeply interested in Western economics but a devotee of Oscar Lange, the well-known advocate of market socialism. Because his ideas were already regarded as too radical, Li, upon graduation, was not permitted to teach and was assigned to the research materials office at Beijing University where he studied and translated many Western economic treatises. During the early years of the Cultural Revolution, which he spent in Jiangxi Province, Li reevaluated his economic thinking, particularly with regard to the economic debates between Frederick Hayek and Oscar Lange that he had studied in college. He came to believe that there were serious weaknesses in Lange's approach, which basically accepted the Soviet economic model. Li came to believe that the Soviet economic model was flawed at its core and needed to be fundamentally negated. In common with many of the philosophers of the time, but unlike most of his economic colleagues, Li began focusing on the problem of man and tried to combine economics with his humanist concerns.[28] With the end of the Cultural Revolution, he began teaching on a full-time basis, being named an associate professor in 1979 and a full professor in 1983. He joined the Communist Party in 1984. It was during this period that he became one of the most prolific and controversial economists in China.[29]

Li's challenge to Wu's ideas came in an article published in *Beijing Daily* on May 19, 1986. In perhaps the best-known sentence to be penned in the course of debate over economic reform, Li wrote, "Economic reform can fail because of the failure of price reform, but its success cannot be determined by price reform but only by ownership reform." Only ownership reform, Li argued, touched on the fundamental problems of interest, responsibility, system, and motivation.[30]

Li became a media star almost overnight. China's news service for overseas Chinese, Zhongguo xinwen she, reported that Li's article had "caught the attention of all circles since its publication." Articles by Li were reprinted in *People's Daily*, *Beijing Daily*, and *World Economic Herald*.[31] *Guangming Daily* published an interview with Li by the well-known writer and reporter Dai Qing.[32]

The content of Li's ideas on ownership reform became clearer as he published a series of articles over the ensuing months. Li argued that prices ultimately reflect ownership of the factors of production and thus, in the final analysis, "prices are the terms of exchange of ownership among people in the market."[33] Thus, unless the ownership system is first reformed, price reform will not, in and of itself, lead to a market equilibrium. Moreover, Li maintained that a rational price system is not something that can be dictated by the government but rather something that must come about through the interaction of independent commodity producers. Thus, said Li, price reform "can only be based on enterprise reform and cannot be the breakthrough point for economic reform."[34]

Whereas Wu Jinglian focused on the creation of a good market environment to achieve economic rationality, Li looked to defining relations of production and power. One writer described the concerns of those who, like Li, emphasized ownership reform as follows:[35]

> They hold that the root cause for the inflated aggregate demand in the second half of 1984 lies in the fact that enterprises did not have a well-defined responsibility for the management of their funds. The enterprises used more state funds without correspondingly undertaking greater economic responsibilities. This has given rise to unfair distribution of funds among enterprises with different fund contributions and a strong impetus among local governments and enterprises to scramble for more funds and credit from higher authorities.

The solution to this problem, in the approach championed by Li Yining, was to define clearly ownership relations and thereby give operational autonomy to enterprises.

Li sought to unify production and power, as was done in the rural economic reforms, by having enterprises—including the critical large and medium-sized corporations—implement a shareholding system. Li saw the ability of enterprises to buy and sell each other's shares as essential to the formation of "enterprise groups" (vertically or horizontally integrated conglomerates) and the development of "horizontal economic ties" (*hengxiang jingji lianhe*). Without a clear definition of ownership relations, the free combination and recombination of economic interests would be difficult or would be controlled by traditional vertical administrative relations, interfering with the rational circulation of factors of production.[36]

To free enterprises from ministerial and other governmental (either central or local) intervention, Li proposed establishing "stock-asset management bureaus" (*guoyou gufen zichan guanli ju*) at various levels to manage government-owned shares of enterprises. These asset management bureaus would be responsible for handling the state's investments in enterprises, purchasing or selling stock as deemed appropriate, and appointing the requisite number of directors to the enterprises' boards of directors. Bureaus would be established on all administrative levels (national, provincial, municipal, and county), but there would be no hierarchical administrative relationships among them. Local bureaus would manage local interests in enterprises just as the national bureau would oversee the state's interests. Li was particularly emphatic that the state's shares not be managed by the traditional ministries, departments, and bureaus. The responsibility of such administrative organs would be limited to deciding developmental plans and policies, harmonizing relations between enterprises, and overseeing the implementation of policies and laws. It would not involve the internal affairs of enterprises.[37]

Different Visions

The difference between Li Yining and Wu Jinglian lay not just in their different assumptions about the relative importance of macro- and microeconomic factors, but rather more fundamentally in their different assumptions about society and the type of social economic system they hoped to bring about. Wu said as much when he wrote, "the basic reason why people have different views over the primary content and measures of reform is that they, in fact, cherish different medium-range and even long-term goals."[38]

The difference in the two economists' thinking was reflected in their assumptions about the state. Wu did not use the term "new authoritarianism," a concept that would be widely discussed beginning in 1988 and which stressed the use of state power to bring about a top-down reform of the economy, but many of his ideas paralleled the ideas of those who advocated this concept.[39] Noting that "we must not imagine that we can attain this [reform] through the spontaneous individual actions of the multitude of the masses without a situation of leadership and organization," Wu argued that the "prestige of the central government is especially critical" and that the government must have a clear recognition and firm grasp of the trend of history and go and mobilize, encourage, and guide the whole body of the people."[40]

Wu's assumption that the state must play a central role in guiding economic reform was closely related to his belief in the centrality of large and medium-sized state-owned enterprises in the economy. As he wrote:[41]

> [Our] country has already established an industrial structure with large and medium-sized enterprises as the backbone. These enterprises cannot grow healthily if there is not a well-developed and extensive market with clear-cut rules. If we were still an agricultural society almost without any large industries, we might still be able to realize modernization by advancing along the long historical path of developing from a primitive commodity economy. However, our nation has now reached a certain developmental stage, and the objective conditions do not allow us this choice. If we choose this [developing from a primitive commodity economy], it implies "introducing into the socialist economy a type of economic mechanism reminiscent of Manchester capitalism of the nineteenth century, in which markets were free from all government interference and small enterprises were dominant." *This implies historical retrogression.*

It was this belief in the centrality of the large and medium-sized state-owned enterprises that led Wu to be highly critical of the reform strategy of "delegating authority and granting benefits" (*fangquan rangli*), which he believed had led to the "perverse" (Wu's term) outcome of invigorating the least modern and most backward sectors of the economy—agriculture and rural industry—while allowing the most modern and best-equipped sectors of the economy to stagnate. It is thus apparent that Wu's vision of "coordinated reform" was premised on strong state action to reinvigorate large and medium-sized state enterprises.

In contrast, Li Yining, like the economists associated with the Economic Reform Institute, was highly skeptical of state planning, regarding it as often doing more harm than good. According to Li, "if planned management is subjective and unscientific, we would rather not have it; and if the government's regulative role is inefficient and confusing, we would rather not have it."[42] Similarly, in contrast to Wu's contemptuous dismissal of the "primitive commodity economy," Li stated that "unscientific government regulation is certainly not needed since it is not as good as market regulation."[43]

Ownership Reform and Political Reform

Li Yining was not the first person in China to raise the issue of ownership reform. As noted above, Dong Fureng had raised this issue as early as 1979. At the same time, Yu Guangyuan's Theory and Methodology Research Group, which had been established in 1979 under the State Council and of which Dong was deputy head (see Chapter 2), had spent considerable time organizing discussions on the issue of ownership. In 1979, the group convened ten symposia on the ownership structure of urban collectives, and in January 1980 it organized the first national meeting on the issue in Shenyang. In October 1979, this group convened a meeting on the ownership structure of the rural collective economy, and the following month it launched a series of biweekly seminars on the state ownership structure.[44] Dong's 1979 article on the ownership system was no doubt a product of these discussions.

The issue of ownership was raised again at a conference of young economists in Tianjin in 1985. At that time, two young economists, Du Xia, then a thirty-seven-year-old lecturer at Nankai University's Economic Research Institute, and Hao Yisheng, a thirty-two-year-old intern with the Tianjin Academy of Social Sciences, argued that ownership reform was critical for successful reform of the economy.[45]

Reflecting the renewed interest in ownership reform that developed in 1985, Dong Fureng published another article on the subject in June of that year, which implicitly criticized the decision on economic reform that had been adopted by the Third Plenum only a short while before. Dong suggested that the decision's emphasis on the separation of ownership and management had sidestepped the harder and more critical question of ownership reform.[46] In November a symposium on ownership reform was held. For the first time, Liu Guoguang argued that reform of the ownership system was necessary. In a paper co-authored with two young economists, Hua Sheng and He Jiacheng, Liu argued that the expansion of consumption funds in late 1984 was ultimately due to the absence of a self-restraining mechanism in enterprises. If enterprises were to be able to respond quickly to changes in macroeconomic policy, then their organization would have to be changed. In order to do this, wrote Liu and his co-authors, "reform of ideas on state ownership is indispensable."[47]

This new emphasis on ownership reform, which was forcefully and predictably rebutted by economists from the State Planning Commission,[48] appears to have been related to renewed interest in political reform, which, as noted above, stemmed directly from the issues of corruption and enterprise management. At the National Economic Conference in January 1986, enterprise managers complained about continual interference by party secretaries in the enterprises. It was said at the time that only 20 percent of managers and party secretaries cooperated fully, another 50 percent had different agendas while nominally cooperating, and the remaining 30 percent had very bad relations.[49] In February, *People's Daily* supported the position of enterprise managers when it reprinted a report on the Yingkou City party committee supporting a reformist enterprise manager against a frivolous lawsuit brought by the party secretary of the enterprise.[50] In March, a *People's Daily* Commentator article took up the issue of relations between enterprise managers and party secretaries. It called for a clear division of responsibility between the two, with the party secretary concentrating on ideological work and party building rather than directing production.[51] This support for the role of factory managers would lead, on October 1, to the implementation of the factory-director responsibility system, in which managers, not party secretaries, were declared to be the "center" of the enterprises.

The issue of corruption was seen as related to the abuse of power both by bureaucrats and by children of high-ranking cadres. The case of Du Guozhen, which was widely publicized by the Chinese media in early 1986, reflected these concerns. Du had passed himself off as having good connections. Bureaucratism and the desire to make use of his "connections" had allowed him to amass over 200 million yuan in ill-gotten gains.[52]

In April 1986, a meeting of provincial governors was called to discuss the factory-director responsibility system. Deng Xiaoping gave a speech at this meeting reiterating the basic themes of his 1980 speech on political reform. On June 20, he gave another speech in which he linked the issue of corruption to political reform. Deng declared that "unconditioned power is the source of all unhealthy tendencies."[53] According to Ruan Ming's account, Deng also addressed the issue on four other occasions, including on June 10, June 28, and September 3. In these speeches Deng implicitly criticized the CDIC for interfering in cases in which it should not and the State Planning Commission for taking back powers that it had delegated.[54]

Just as the factory-director responsibility system, the issue of corruption, and the question of political reform were being raised and debated, the political atmosphere in China became electrified, first by the "Ma Ding" incident and then by new demands for intellectual freedom. In March 1986, the economic paper *Economic Reference* (*Jingji cankao*) criticized as non-Marxist an article by "Ma Ding," the pen-name of Song Longxiang, a young philosopher at Nanjing University, which had originally been published in the central workers' paper *Workers Daily* (*Gongren ribao*) the previous November.[55] Yu Guangyuan, the former deputy director of CASS, quickly came to the defense of Ma Ding, chiding critics for "rashly" criticizing him and advising that discussion of Ma's article be taken "as an opportunity to gain experience in implementing the 'double hundred' policy."[56]

The Ma Ding incident formed the perfect curtain raiser for a flurry of meetings and articles to commemorate the thirtieth anniversary of the enunciation of the "hundred flowers" policy in 1956. These activities were kicked off with an article describing the historical background of the hundred flowers policy by Lu Dingyi, who as head of the Propaganda Department of the CCP had delivered the primary speech articulating the hundred flowers policy in 1956.[57] Lu's article was quickly followed by many others. Yu Guangyuan, who had been head of the science section of the Propaganda Department in 1956, noted that in the first campaign the "good times did not last long" and that now it was necessary to ensure that "the policy will no longer be abolished."[58] Feng Lanrui, an advisor and researcher in CASS's Institute of Marxism-Leninism-Mao Zedong Thought, wrote a strong defense of academic freedom, stating baldly that "democratic centralism cannot be implemented in the academic field." Expressing the tensions that reform-minded intellectuals were then feeling, Feng wrote that "some people are afraid of and disgusted with freedom" and felt that "the mere mention of freedom means 'going in for bourgeois liberalization.' "[59]

At a meeting of academic and literary circles on May 29, attended by CCP Propaganda Department director Zhu Houze, Yu Guangyuan, and international affairs advisor Huan Xiang, "some scholars" maintained that there were two reasons why the double hundred policy (that is, the policy of "letting a hundred flowers blossom and a hundred schools of thought contend") had not been implemented over a long period of time: the proposition that class struggle should be regarded as the guiding principle of building socialism and "some people's wariness of bourgeois liberalization." They pointed out that such thoughts were a "continuation of the leftists' infantile disorder in the history of the world communist movement." Participants at the meeting argued that the "hundred schools of thought should not be reduced to only two"—proletarian and bourgeois—and that the "relationship between Marxism and non-Marxism should not be one between the ruler and the ruled." Linking the effort to maintain intellectual freedom to the emerging discussions on political reform, some participants argued that the implementation of the hundred flowers policy had to be guaranteed by political democracy.[60]

It was into this politically charged atmosphere that Li Yining dropped his manifesto on ownership reform. Li appears to have been quite aware of what he was doing. On the same day that his article on ownership reform appeared in *Beijing Daily*, another article by Li appeared in *People's Daily*. Arguing that intellectual contention was vital to the development of economics, Li sharply criticized conservatives' efforts to dampen the discussion of economics in China. If scholars "regard several formulas and conclusions of the Marxist classics as doctrines that can never be changed or even allow no doubt, no supplement, and no revision," Li wrote, that would "not safeguard Marxism but will distort it." Suggesting the tension existing over economic policy, Li said sarcastically, "We should notice that in work, some persons who can neither do nor suggest anything often become the best qualified persons to blame others in case they think something goes wrong. Of course, this is very abnormal." In order to make economic theory flourish, said Li, it was necessary to completely do away with such an atmosphere and "remove all resistance and interference" in academic discussion. Such an open intellectual atmosphere would inevitably give rise to different schools of thought, but such schools of thought would all be devoted to socialism and should not be considered "arguments between the 'proletarian and Marxist sides' or between the 'Marxist and anti-Marxist blocs.' "[61]

If the emergent atmosphere of free-wheeling intellectual debate went some way toward explaining why Li's ideas received such attention at this time, it also seems likely that Li could count on the help of an old schoolmate, Politburo member Hu Qili, to give his ideas a hearing at the highest levels.[62] Hu Qili, as the Secretariat member in charge of ideology, was the point man in working to change the ideological atmosphere in the spring of 1986, and it may well be that Li's connection with Hu allowed him to judge the time as auspicious for putting forth his ideas.

Ownership Reform as a Critique of Price Reform

The burgeoning mood of relative intellectual freedom in China in 1986 no doubt provided an atmosphere in which the sensitive issue of ownership reform could be raised, but it is also true that Li (as well as the young economists associated with the Economic Reform Institute) had hit on a serious weakness in Wu's approach to economic reform. Unless the relationship between enterprises and administrative bureaucracies could be fundamentally changed, a rapid implementation of price reform, whether or not accompanied by a series of other reforms in the financial and tax areas, was not as likely to bring about the "level playing ground" of rational prices that Wu so much desired as it was to bring about an unprecedented scramble for administrative protection. The very likely outcome of this scramble would be the restoration of the original price parities but at a higher level (*bijia fugui*). In this case, price reform would only result in inflation.

As later studies would show, there were ample grounds for believing that this was the case. One of the most impressive studies of the difficulties of price reform was done by the price group of the State Council's Economic, Technological, and Social Development Research Center under the direction of Tian Yuan. Examining data from 1985, Tian noted that although no large-scale adjustment of prices had been made under state auspices, the pressures from implementation of the dual-track price system caused the price index of heavy industrial products to increase by 11.25 percent. Of the 414 kinds of heavy industrial products, Tian found that the prices of 182 kinds of products had risen by more than 10 percent, and that the prices of 37 products had risen by more than 30 percent—including such basic products as timber (35.28 percent) and pig iron (30.67 percent). Many industries could not or would not absorb such price increases, argued Tian; instead they either passed their increased costs on to consumers in the form of higher product prices or to the government in the form of reduced tax payments. A survey of Jiangsu Province in 1986 found that ex-factory prices had increased by 4.79 percent and that provincial revenues had declined by 12.6 percent as a result of the increased costs that local industries had faced. At the same time, because of the existing tax system, local governments were able to shift losses from price increases to the central government.[63]

The reason for this perverse outcome, in Tian's opinion, lay in the system of administrative control over enterprises. Tian argued that over the first three decades of the PRC, the seriously distorted price system and encouragement of local self-sufficiency had brought about an enterprise structure in which there was not only much duplicative construction but also one in which production costs varied greatly from one region to the next—what Tian called a "ladder-shaped" structure of production costs. Because production costs varied so much from one part of the country to another, it was necessary for financial authorities to establish a revenue system that mirrored the cost structure of enterprises—an "inverse ladder-shaped" structure of taxes.[64]

The production cost and tax structures not only mirrored each other but reinforced each other, said Tian, preventing a rationalization of the price system. Looking at the reaction of local enterprises and governments to the limited price reforms brought about by implementation of the dual-track price system in 1985, Tian concluded in a passage that is worth quoting at length that:[65]

> the long-term distortion of the price system has become an obstacle to its own rationalization; the existing structure of enterprise organization in fact rejects rationalization. The contradictions between the two [the structure of enterprise organization and the rationalization of prices] were fully apparent in the preliminary reform of the prices of industrial products [via the dual-track price system in 1985]. The increase in the prices of the means of production immediately lashed against enterprises. As the costs of the processing industries were increasing, those whose costs were high and had low efficiency were under relatively greater pressure. [However,] the ossified structure of enterprise organization under the prevailing structure excluded the possibility of eliminating backward enterprises; on the contrary, it gave rise to a violent outcry to block price reform. This was especially apparent in those regions and industries where the prices of inputs increased the most. They universally reflected an inability to digest or absorb [the price increases] and strongly demanded that the financial authorities make new arrangements to protect their vested interests. At the same time, there were few instances in which enterprises went bankrupt or stopped production. From this it can be seen that the increase in the prices of energy, raw materials, and transportation fundamentally did not touch the irrational structure of enterprise organization.

It was precisely this mutually reinforcing structure of irrational prices and administrative structures that doomed the price reform plan that was being drawn up under Vice Premier Tian Jiyun's direction. Over the summer of 1986, the State Council received reports that enterprises would not be able to absorb the proposed price increases, suggesting that the result of a comprehensive price reform program would be inflation and reduced revenues to the central government. At the same time, government revenues were falling short of their expected level, giving the central government even less flexibility. In short, the resistance of enterprises and localities to price reform was matched by the central government's fear that its revenues would fall. Under these conditions, the ambitious plans for price reform were trimmed back to an adjustment of the prices of some products. No effort was made to reform the prices of the means of production, the critical link in any attempt to rationalize China's price system.[66]

From this perspective, the key question was not the relative tightness or looseness of monetary policy but rather the ability to break the link between government and enterprise. Both Wu Jinglian and Li Yining agreed that this was the essential link in enterprise reform. Wu believed that it could be accomplished by a well-designed and authoritatively implemented price reform plan that would bring about the market competition necessary to force enterprises to turn their attention from the bureaucracy to the market. Li, in contrast, believed that this was not possible.

Renewed Tension: The Sixth Plenum and the Fall of Hu Yaobang

By the latter part of 1986, economic problems and ideological disputes had brought conflict within the CCP to a new height. Discussions on political reform in the spring and summer had provoked sharp conflict within the party, forcing it to delay adopting measures to promote systematic reform of the political system. Instead, the Sixth Plenary Session of the Twelfth Central Committee, meeting in the fall, adopted a resolution on the construction of "socialist spiritual civilization." The Sixth Plenum resolution stands unique among the documents adopted by the CCP in the Dengist period as the only official effort to hammer out the contentious ideological issues that had divided the party since the inauguration of reform.

In many ways the Sixth Plenum resolution is a surprisingly liberal document. In one of its most significant doctrinal changes, the resolution called for building spiritual civilization "with Marxism as guidance." Four years previously, in Hu Yaobang's report to the Twelfth Party Congress, the party had—in deference to conservative demands—mandated a much higher ideological standard of building spiritual civilization "with communist ideology as its core." The difference between "Marxism" and "communist ideology" on the one hand and between "guidance" and "core" on the other suggested that a less rigid ideological standard would be used in determining policy and in guiding the polity. This loosening of ideological rigidity was paralleled by a distinction between the "common ideal" of building "socialism with Chinese characteristics" and the "ultimate ideal" of building "a communist society that applies the principle 'from each according to his ability, to each according to his needs." Emphasizing the "common ideal" permitted a broader definition of the united front to include "party members and nonparty people, Marxists and non-Marxists, atheists and believers, citizens at home and those living abroad"; it also underscored the difference between the present, initial stage of socialism and the future, advanced stage of communism.

The Sixth Plenum resolution also expanded modestly on the concept of the "initial stage of socialism," foreshadowing the important status that that thesis would attain the following year at the Thirteenth Party Congress. Hinting at the political, economic, and cultural implications of the thesis, the resolution stated that "our country is in the initial stage of socialism. Not only must we implement distribution according to labor and develop the commodity economy and competition, but also for a fairly long period develop diverse economic elements under the premise that public ownership is primary and encourage a part of the people to become wealthy under the goal of common prosperity."[67] This more extensive treatment of the meaning of the initial stage of socialism went well beyond the acknowledgment in the resolution on party history adopted by the Sixth Plenum in 1981 that "even though our socialist system is in the initial stage, there is no question that our party has established a socialist system"—a formulation intended to assert the socialist nature of China's political system rather than elaborate on the need to tolerate a variety of economic, political, and cultural phenomena not suited to a higher stage of socialism.[68]

Such ideological formulations were intended to support the ongoing economic reforms, particularly the rapidly expanding village and township industries and various forms of individual economic activities. However, many parts of the resolution bore the marks of the contentious political atmosphere in which it was drafted. In particular, the document handled the issue of political reform, which had stirred so much controversy over the summer, with great circumspection. The resolution simply stated that "in urging reform of the political structure, as it has done of late," the Central Committee aims to "take a step further in extending socialist democracy and improving the socialist legal system." Eschewing mention of concrete steps to be taken, the document stated only that the Central Committee will "work out plans" so that political reform could proceed "step by step and with proper guidance."

Moreover, the issue that was about to burst over the political scene—"bourgeois liberalization"—also stirred acrimonious debate both at the Beidaihe session that hammered out the final draft of the document and at the Sixth Plenum itself. Under pressure from conservative party leaders including Wang Zhen, Peng Zhen, Bo Yibo, Hu Qiaomu, and Deng Liqun, Hu Yaobang finally compromised and included a sentence strongly condemning bourgeois liberalization. Lu Dingyi, the former head of the Propaganda Department, strongly opposed including this condemnation, pointing out that the issue of liberalization (*ziyouhua*) had first been raised by the Soviet Union in opposition to China's hundred flowers policy in 1956. Lu spoke three times at the Beidaihe meeting on this issue and then voiced his opposition twice more at the Sixth Plenum itself.[69]

It is said that Hu Yaobang made a critical mistake in these discussions. When Lu Dingyi argued on the floor of the Sixth Plenum that the sentence condemning bourgeois liberalization be removed from the document, Hu agreed with Lu. In so doing, he exceeded the bounds of his authority and crossed Deng Xiaoping, who was in attendance. Shortly thereafter, Deng countermanded Hu, demanding that the sentence be left in the document. Hu had violated a central code in the political conduct of party leaders, namely, an unspoken understanding of when to speak and how far to go on a given issue. By going too far and then being contradicted by Deng, Hu lost enormous prestige and authority in the party and raised renewed questions about his capability to head the party.[70]

Given these acrimonious debates, it is no wonder that the official communiqué of the session omitted the standard reference to party unanimity—the first time in the Dengist period that a plenum or congress document had done so. The omission pointed to the mounting tensions within the party, tensions that soon exploded as students took to the streets in the largest public demonstrations since the Cultural Revolution (at least until the much larger student movement two years later). On November 6, 1986, students at Chinese Science and Technology University in Hefei, Anhui, demonstrated to protest the party's refusal to allow some people onto the ballot for the local people's congress election. In early December the protest had spread to Shanghai as 50,000 students took to the streets of that city.[71]

When Hu Yaobang resisted responding forcefully against the students, conservatives within the party publicly displayed their discontent. On December 28, Hu Qiaomu, Deng Liqun, Wang Zhen, Bo Yibo, and Song Renqiong met with a traditional storyteller who was famous for his rendering of the classic *Romance of the Three Kingdoms*. Wang praised the storyteller for "raising our national dignity and sense of pride," contrasting his efforts favorably with "some people" who "advocate national nihilism, debase, and negate China, and call for the complete Westernization of China." Similarly, Bo warned that the policy of opening to the outside world and studying the advanced science and technology of foreign nations should not cause Chinese to "belittle" themselves or to "consider all things foreign to be better than in China." "We must not think," he said, "that 'the moon in foreign countries is fuller than in China.' "[72]

Finally, on December 30, Deng Xiaoping gave a speech on opposing bourgeois liberalization that became the text of the New Year's editorial in *People's Daily*. A full-fledged campaign against bourgeois liberalization ensued, and Hu Yaobang's days as party secretary were numbered. Deng's children reportedly spent much of January 4 trying to change their father's mind, but to no avail.[73] Deng had become dissatisfied with his heir apparent and determined to use this occasion to remove him.

According to Ruan Ming's account, at the "party life" meeting that was called to criticize Hu Yaobang, party elder Bo Yibo read out a letter that Zhao Ziyang had written in 1984 criticizing Hu Yaobang.[74] In addition, Zhao made a brief statement telling Hu, "You are an old red army man and I greatly respect you and generally accept what you say. However, your interference in the work of the State Council has made it so that I cannot work."[75]

Zhao's letter, if there was one, and his criticism of Hu at the meeting no doubt reflected the tensions that had built up between the two leaders since the early 1980s. As early as 1982, Zhao and Hu had clashed seriously over the contract responsibility system of economic management (see Chapter 7). With Deng

Liqun's support, Zhao had persuaded Deng Xiaoping to decree that Zhao was in charge of the economy; Hu was not to interfere.[76] Hu, however, loved to travel throughout the country, expressing the ambition to visit all of China's more than 2,000 counties. Typically local leaders would use the occasion of Hu's visits to petition for special favors, and Hu, desirous of displaying his largess and his authority, would frequently approve such requests, causing those who worked with Zhao endless problems in trying to figure out how to satisfy Hu's promises without upsetting their own plans for reform and the management of the economy. For instance, Hu was an ardent supporter of efforts to plant trees and grass in the Northwest to create a greenbelt for protection of the environment. This was a good and necessary policy, but it was also expensive and diverted scarce resources from other uses.[77]

In similar fashion, Hu promised minority areas that their subsidies would be increased by 10 percent per year. Again this was important for the areas involved, but it pinched the budget for other things. In 1983, Hu traveled to the Southwest, urging that per capita incomes be increased by 100 yuan within two or three years. These kinds of actions irritated Zhao and those around him. They saw Hu's actions as arbitrary, a sort of Great Leap Forward campaign-style support for development that clashed with their own vision of a systematic program of reform. In the case of Hu's promises to the Southwest, Zhao sent people to follow in Hu's wake, finding out what he had promised and trying to persuade local leaders that Hu's promises had been unrealistic, and then writing a report on what should be done. It then fell to Du Runsheng, who had good relations with both Zhao and Hu, to try to find a face-saving way to get Hu to retreat from his promises.[78]

The tensions between Zhao and Hu not only reflected their policy differences and their very different personalities (Hu having a more passionate, even romantic personality while Zhao was a more cerebral, rational thinker) but also the inherent conflict between the role of the general secretary and that of the premier, particularly in an age of economic reform. Although running the party and setting the ideological tone remained important tasks for the party head, Hu could not simply delegate management of the economy to Zhao without being seen as superfluous to the party's most important task. Thus, even though Deng Xiaoping had directed that Zhao, not Hu, was in charge of economic reform, Hu continued to intervene in economic work by demanding that party groups in the State Council ministries report periodically to the Secretariat.[79] Such interventions clearly angered Zhao, who felt that they undermined his own authority.

Whatever the tensions between the two leaders, Zhao's role in Hu's downfall remains the focus of much attention and criticism. In all probability Zhao could not have saved Hu given the opposition from conservative party elders and Deng Xiaoping, though some maintain that Zhao might have been able to persuade Deng to change his mind.[80] It does seem likely that Zhao, frustrated over years of conflict with Hu, was willing to allow Hu to fall and did not want to rouse conservatives' suspicions by coming to Hu's defense. In acting in this manner, Zhao was able to succeed Hu as general secretary of the party, although it seems that Zhao badly underestimated the strength of conservatives in the party and thought that he could handle them.

The fall of Hu Yaobang in January 1987 marked the end of a year in which conflict over party affairs, including corruption and intellectual freedom, overlapped with deep debates about economic strategy and the need for political reform. Tensions about ideological issues, present since the beginning of reform, culminated in the fierce debates over the Sixth Plenum resolution and the subsequent ouster of Hu Yaobang. These inner-party tensions were coming to a head precisely as difficulties in economic reform were forcing a reappraisal of strategy, leading many reform-minded economists to look to increasingly radical solutions to China's problems. Both radical price reform and ownership reform represented full-scale assaults on the planning system as it had theretofore existed.

The recession of 1986 provoked new debate about macroeconomic policy as economic conservatives urged the strengthening of central controls to reduce inflationary pressures and maintain "balance," while the young economists around Zhao urged a loosening of monetary policy in order to enhance the influence of market forces in the economy. At the same time, the reform wing of the party began to factionalize as traditional reformers, such as Liu Guoguang, were left behind and new and more radical reformers came to the fore. The emergence of more radical reformers, however, did not mean the formation of a new consensus but rather yet deeper disagreements as they divided between those like Wu Jinglian, who urged a combination of tight monetary control and radical price reform, and those like Li Yining and the Economic Reform Institute, who were convinced that Wu's proposals would exacerbate inflation and that ownership reform was a necessary prerequisite of fundamental reform. It was a split that from the outside seemed unnecessary and destructive; both Wu Jinglian and Li Yining readily admitted that price reform and ownership reform were necessary components of a thoroughgoing reform. It was a combination of the particular political situation facing China at the time and the different visions of China's society in the future that drove economists who should have worked together apart, and led in later years to bitter polemics.[81]

The inability to forge a consensus on a reform program in 1986, including the increasing politicization of macroeconomic policy and heightened debate about how to proceed with reform, foreshadowed the policy conflicts that would lead to Zhao Ziyang's fall from power in 1988.

Notes

1. "Let the Spirit of the Foolish Old Man Fill the Divine Land—1986 New Year Message," *Renmin ribao*, Editorial, January 1, 1986, p. 1, trans. FBIS, January 2, 1986, pp. K1–2.

2. Author's interviews.

3. Hu Yaobang, "Central Organs Must Set an Example for the Whole Country," Xinhua, January 10, 1986, trans. FBIS, January 13, 1986, pp. K1–22.

4. Xinhua, January 18, 1986, trans. FBIS, January 21, 1986, pp. K1–3.

5. The most prominent of the three was Hu Xiaoyang, son of Hu Lijiao, then head of Shanghai's People's Congress. See *Wen wei po,* February 18, 1986, p. 7, trans. FBIS, February 19, 1986, pp. W1–2.

6. Among those allegedly under investigation were Hu Shiying, son of Hu Qiaomu; Fu Yan, daughter of Peng Zhen; Ye Zhifeng, daughter of Ye Fei; and Liu Shikun, son-in-law of Ye Jianying. See Lo Ping, "Two Shocking Cases," *Cheng ming,* no. 105 July 1, 1986), pp. 6–7, trans. FBIS, July 10, 1986, pp. W1–3; and Lo Ping, "Doubts as to Whether Tigers Are Butchered to Cover Up Things," *Cheng ming,* no. 103 (May 1, 1986), pp. 8–10, trans. FBIS, May 14, 1986, pp. W1–7.

7. Author's interviews. Although Hu Yaobang generally supported political reform, he did not apparently support Zhao's initiative in giving factory managers greater responsibility because the party organization—that is, Hu's constituency—opposed this change. Two years later, when Zhao was in charge of the party, he similarly found it difficult to promote political reform without undermining his own position.

8. "Make a Success of Enterprise Management," *Renmin ribao,* Commentator, January 20, 1986, p. 1, trans. FBIS, January 30, 1986, pp. K4–5. See also the comments of Lu Dong, minister of the State Economic Commission, at the meeting, Xinhua, January 11, 1986, trans. FBIS, January 15, 1986, pp. K6–7.

9. Liu Guoguang, "A Brief Talk on Macroeconomic Control," *Guangming ribao,* January 4, 1986, p. 3, trans. FBIS, January 22, 1986, pp. K8–11.

10. Zhang Zhuoyuan and Bian Lishi, "Price System Reform Must Be Carried Out Step by Step and in Coordination with Other Reforms," *Jingji ribao,* February 8, 1986, p. 3, trans. FBIS, February 28, 1986, pp. K3–8. Xue Muqiao's views are cited in *China Daily,* April 5, 1986, p. 4.

11. Guo Wenru and Yang Zejun, "Consumption Funds Have Increased Too Rapidly, Macroeconomic Control Needs Strengthening," *Renmin ribao,* February 12, 1986, p. 5, trans. FBIS, February 21, 1986, pp. K9–11. *Renmin ribao* identifies the authors as being with the State Statistical Bureau.

12. Wu Ji, Zhang Junkuo, Yue Bing, and Li Jiange, "Lun jingji zengzhang de youxiao yueshu" (On the Effective Restraint on Economic Growth), *Jingji yanjiu,* no. 6 (June 1986), p. 22. Wu Ji is Wu Jinglian's pen name. See also Wu Jinglian, Li Jiange, Ding Ningning, and Zhang Junkuo, "The Key to Bringing About a Benign Cycle in the National Economy," *Jingji ribao,* January 4, 1986, pp. 1 and 3, trans. FBIS, January 14, 1986, pp. K15–18.

13. Wu Ji et al., "Lun jingjie zhengzhang de youxiao yueshu," pp. 20–21.

14. Ibid., p. 21.

15. Ibid., p. 21.

16. See the important article by the Macroeconomic Research Office of the Economic Reform Institute, "1986 niandu xingshi fenxi" (An Analysis of the Economic Situation in 1986), translated in Bruce Reynolds, ed., "The Debate Over China's 1986 Recession," *Chinese Economic Studies* (Spring 1986), pp. 3–23. This article argues that the level of production in 1986 was below the potential production capacity and hence that there was room for stimulating the economy to a certain extent. It also argued that retrenchment policies would exacerbate, not alleviate, the gap between supply and demand. In conclusion, it labeled ideas calling for continuing retrenchment policies in the hope of eliminating inflation as "impetuous" and "harmful."

17. Figures are from Zou Gang et al., *Zhongguo weiguan jingji fenxi* (Analysis of

China's Microeconomy), pp. 37–38.

18. Ibid., pp. I–II.

19. Ibid., p. 19.

20. Ibid., pp. 16–17.

21. Microeconomic Situation Analysis Group, "Jinsuo de jingji zengzhang: 1986 nian shang ban nian weiguan jingji fenxi baogao" (Economic Growth Under Retrenchment—A Report on the Analysis of the Microeconomic Situation in the First Half of 1986), translated in Gary Zou, ed., "The Debate on China's Macroeconomic Situation (I)," *Chinese Economic Studies* (Winter 1989–90), pp.79–80.

22. Song Guoqing and Zhang Weiying, "Guanyu hongguan pingheng yu honguan kongzhi jige lilun wenti" (Theoretical Questions Concerning Macroeconomic Balances and Macroeconomic Control), *Jingji yanjiu*, no. 6 (June 1986), pp. 25–35.

23. Deng Yingtao and Luo Xiaopeng, "Lun zongliang fenxi he zongliang zhengce zai woguo jingji lilun yu shijian zhong de juxianxing" (The Limitations of Gross Quantity Analysis and Gross Quantity Policies in China's Economic Theory and Practice), *Jingji yanjiu*, no. 6 (June 1987), pp. 3–16.

24. Xinhua, March 16, 1986, trans. FBIS, March 17, 1986, pp. K9–11. See also the report on Tian Jiyun's opening address to the session, Xinhua, March 10, 1986, trans. FBIS, March 12, 1986, pp. K10–12. Shortly after the session closed, the State Council promulgated the "Regulations Governing Several Questions on Further Promoting Lateral Economic Ties," Xinhua, March 23, 1986, trans. FBIS, April 1, 1986, pp. K1–6. The effort to promote horizontal economic ties was promoted by two editorials. See "Zhua hengxiang lianxi, cu jingji tizhi gaige" (Grasp Horizontal Economic Cooperation, Promote Reform of the Economic Structure), *Renmin ribao*, Editorial, March 31, 1986, p. 1; and "Chongpo tiaokuai fenlie cai neng fazhan shengchanli" (Productive Forces Can Only Be Developed by Breaking Through Administrative Barriers), *Renmin ribao*, Editorial, April 18, 1986, p. 1.

25. Author's interviews.

26. Ibid.

27. It is at least clear that Wu fully endorsed the reform scheme that was drawn up. He later wrote that the reform scheme designed in the spring of 1986 for the early stage of the Seventh Five-Year Plan was "very possibly a feasible design" and that "both theoretical analysis and the experience of past practice show that with the support of certain macroeconomic policies it will not be too difficult to implement this reform scheme," See Wu Jinglian, "Guanyu gaige zhanlue xuanze de ruogan sikao" (Some Thoughts on the Choice of Reform Strategy), *Jingji yanjiu*, no. 2 (February 1987), p. 6.

28. This effort resulted in a book, *Tizhi, mubiao, ren—jingjixue mianlin de tiaozhan* (Structure, Goal, and Man—The Challenge Facing Economics), which was published by Heilongjiang renmin chuban she (Harbin) in 1986.

29. On Li's life, see He Li, " 'Ren' de yanjiu—jingji yanjiu de zuigao zengci—Li Yining zhuanlue" (The Study of 'Man,' the Highest Level of Economic Research—A Biography of Li Yining).

30. Li Yining, "Gaige de jiben silu" (The Basic Train of Thought for Reform), *Beijing ribao*, May 19, 1986, p. 3.

31. Xu Kong, "Independent Thinker of China's Economic Reform—On Li Yining, Professor of Beijing University," Zhongguo xinwen she, May 28, 1986, trans. FBIS, June 10, 1986, pp. K2–4.

32. Dai Qing, "Jingji tizhi gaige de guanjian shi suoyuozhi gaige—fang Li Yining" (The Crux of Economic Structural Reform Is Ownership Reform—An Interview with Li Yining), *Guangming ribao*, August 4, 1986, p. 2.

33. Li Yining et al., "1988–1995 nian wo guo jingji tizhi gaige gangyao" (Outline for Economic Structural Reform in 1988–1995), p. 90.

34. Ibid., p. 91.

35. Xiao Jie, "Diversified Views on the Focus of Economic Reform in the Seventh Five-Year Plan Period," *Shijie jingji daobao*, January 6, 1986, p. 3, trans. FBIS, January 15, 1986, pp. K11–14.

36. Li Yining, "A Conception of Reform of the Ownership System in Our Country," *Renmin ribao*, September 26, 1986, p. 5, trans. FBIS, October 22, 1986, pp. K5–11.

37. Li Yining, "Suoyouzhi gaige he gufen qiye de guanli" (Ownership Reform and the Management of Joint-Stock Enterprises), part 2, *Zhongguo jingji tizhi gaige*, no. 1 (January 1987), p. 25.

38. Wu Jinglian, "Guanyu gaige zhanlue xuanze de ruogan sikao," p. 6.

39. Discussions on "new authoritarianism" (*xin quanwei zhuyi*) started among Shanghai intellectuals in 1986 and became public in late 1988. Wu did not join the debate over new authoritarianism, although his ideas appear to put him firmly within that school of thought. While there were different versions of new authoritarianism, the basic approach was to emphasize that the creation of a modern, commodity (market) economy required a strong, authoritarian hand at the top. The idea was that economic liberalization must precede political democratization. See Stanley Rosen and Gary Zou, eds., "The Chinese Debate on the New Authoritarianism," *Chinese Sociology and Anthropology*, nos. 1–4 (Winter 1990–91, Spring 1991, Summer 1991, and Fall 1991).

40. Wu Jinglian et al., "Jingji tizhi zhongqi gaige guihua gangyao" (Outline Plan for Mid-Term Economic Structural Reform), p. 203.

41. Wu Jinglian, "Guanyu gaige zhanlue xuanze de ruogan sikao," p. 7. Wu borrows the quote from Kornai's description of Hungarian economic debates. Emphasis added.

42. Zhongguo xinwen she, June 30, 1986, trans. FBIS, July 7, 1986, pp. K13–15.

43. Li Yining, "Jingji tizhi gaige de guanjian shi suoyouzhi" (The Crux of Economic Structural Reform Is the Ownership System), *Guangming ribao*, August 4, 1986, p. 2.

44. *Zhongguo baike nianjian, 1980*, p. 292.

45. Du Xia and Hao Yisheng, "Tiaozheng suoyouzhi jiegou shi chengshi jingji gaige de guanjian suozai" (Readjusting the Structure of Ownership Is the Critical Point in Urban Economic Reform). Contrary to the prevailing opinion both at that time and later, Du and Hao took the position that ownership reform should combine management and ownership. Why is it, they ask, that state enterprises are not as good as collective enterprises? It is because state enterprises do not combine the interests of the owners with the interests of managers as well as collective enterprises do, and they in turn do not do it as well as private enterprises.

46. Dong Fureng, "Guanyu zengqiang quanmin suoyouzhi qiye huoli de wenti" (The Problem of Strengthening the Vitality of Enterprises Owned by the Whole People), *Jingji yanjiu*, no. 6 (June 1985), pp. 3–12.

47. Liu Guoguang, "Certain Problems Concerning the Reform of the System of Ownership—Outline of a Speech Delivered at an Academic Symposium on the System of Ownership on November 30, 1985," *Jingji yanjiu*, no. 1 (January 4, 1986), p. 3, trans. FBIS, January 14, 1986, pp. K23 and K26. Although Liu advocates reform of the ownership system in this article, he does not propose any concrete measures for bringing this about, so his ideas on ownership reform remain undefined.

48. See, for instance, Fan Maofa, Xun Dazhi, and Liu Xiaping, "Gufenzhi bushi quanmin suoyouzhi de fangxiang" (Shareholding Is Not the Direction for Enterprises Owned by the Whole People), *Jingji yanjiu*, no. 1 (January 1986), pp. 17–22. The authors were affiliated with the Planned Economy Institute under the State Planning Commission.

49. Author's interviews.

50. See Zhao Fu, "Give Firm Support to Reforms," and the accompanying report

"Yingkou City CCP Committee Correctly Handles a 'Lawsuit Brought by a Party Secretary Against a Plant Director'," both in *Renmin ribao*, February 13, 1986, p. 2, trans. FBIS, February 26, 1986, pp. K1–3.

51. "Ideological Work Needs Cooperation Between Party Secretaries and Factory Directors," *Renmin ribao*, Commentator, March 7, 1986, p. 2, trans. FBIS, March 14, 1986, pp. K4–5.

52. *Renmin ribao* published two Commentator articles on Du. See "What Is Shown by the Career Rise and Arrest of 'Du, the God of Fortune'?" *Renmin ribao*, December 30, 1985, p. 1, trans. FBIS, January 7, 1986, pp. K1–2; and "The Harm Done by Bureaucratism as Viewed from Economic Crime," *Renmin ribao*, January 26, 1986, p. 2, trans. FBIS, January 28, 1986, pp. K1–2.

53. Cheng Hsiang, "Tentative Analysis of Discussions Concerning Reform of the Political Structure," part one, *Wen wei po*, July 21, 1986, p. 2, trans. FBIS, July 24, 1986, pp. W1–3.

54. Ruan Ming, *Deng Xiaoping diguo*, pp. 177–179. Ruan does not mention Deng's remarks of April or June 20.

55. For Ma's original article, see Ma Ding, "Ten Major Changes in China's Economics," *Gongren ribao*, November 2, 1985, trans. FBIS, May 22, 1986, K3–11. On the course of the controversy, see Hsiao Chung, "The 'Ma Ding Case' Which Shocks CCP Theorists," *Cheng ming*, no. 103 (May 1, 1986), pp.14–15, trans. FBIS, May 8, 1986, pp. W3–6; Lo Ping, "A Counterattack on the Conservatives Criticizing Zhao," *Cheng ming*, no. 103 (May 1, 1986), trans. FBIS, May 12, 1986, pp. W3–7; and Hou Su-hao, "Public Indignation Aroused by the 'Ma Ding Incident' Leads to Intervention by Hu Yaobang," *Kuang chiao ching*, no. 164 (May 16, 1986), pp.15–17, trans. FBIS, May 21, 1986, pp. W1–4.

56. Yu Guangyuan, "Discussion of Ma Ding's Article Should Be Taken as an Opportunity to Gain Experience in Implementing the 'Double Hundred' Policy," *Shijie jingji daobao*, April 21, 1986, trans. FBIS, May 12, 1986, pp. K8–10. During this incident, a deputy director of CASS' World Politics and Economy Institute wrote a report to criticize the bourgeois liberal tendencies of young economists in general and the Economic Reform Institute in particular. Hu Qiaomu forwarded the report to Zhao Ziyang without comment, and Zhao defended young economists by saying that it was not the time to set constraints on them but rather to encourage them. Author's interviews.

57. Lu Dingyi, "Historical Review of 'A Hundred Flowers Blooming and a Hundred Schools of Thought Contending'—in Commemoration of the Thirtieth Anniversary of the 'Double-Hundred Policy'," *Guangming ribao*, May 7, 1986, p. 1, trans. FBIS, May 27, 1986, pp. K8–10.

58. Yu Guangyuan, "The Thirtieth Anniversary of the Setting Fourth of the 'Double Hundred' Policy," *Renmin ribao*, May 16, 1986, p. 5, trans. FBIS, June 2, 1986, pp. K1–8.

59. Feng Lanrui, "Academic Work Cannot Flourish Without Freedom and Democracy," *Shijie jingji daobao*, May 26, 1986, p. 5, trans. FBIS, May 12, 1986, pp. K8–10.

60. Beijing domestic service, June 13, 1986, trans. FBIS, June 20, 1986, pp. K7–17.

61. Li Yining, "Contention in Economics and Flourishing Economics," *Renmin ribao*, May 19, 1986, p. 5, trans. FBIS, May 20, 1986, pp. K1–4.

62. On the relationship between Li and Hu, see Chen Wenhong, *Zhongguo jingji de luxiang* (The Path of the Chinese Economy), p. 97.

63. Tian Yuan, "Jiage gaige yu chanquan zhidu zhuanhuan" (Price Reform and the Changeover in the Property Rights System), *Jingji yanjiu*, no. 2 (February 1988), pp. 14–15.

64. Ibid., p. 15.

65. Ibid.

66. Ibid., p. 13.

67. "Resolution of the Central Committee of the Communist Party of China on the Guiding Principles for Building a Socialist Society with Advanced Culture and Ideology," Xinhua, September 28, 1986, trans. FBIS, September 29, 1986, pp. K2–13. The use of the term "economic elements" (*jingji chengfen*) was also significant. The term *chengfen* (elements) was applied to different forms of economic ownership during the transition phase (*guodu shiqi*) to socialism in the early years of the PRC. Following the socialist transformation, nonsocialist forms of economic ownership were referred to as "forms" (*xingshi*), a usage followed in all official documents of the Dengist period prior to the Sixth Plenum resolution. By using the term *chengfen*, the resolution was implying a previously unrecognized equality between different forms of ownership.

68. "Resolution on Certain Questions in the History of Our Party Since the Founding of the People's Republic of China," Xinhua, June 30, 1981, trans. FBIS, July 1, 1981, pp. K1–38. Note that Hu Yaobang's report to the Twelfth Party Congress extended this modestly by adding that in the initial stage of socialism, "material civilization is not well developed," See "Hu Yaobang's Report to the Twelfth Party Congress," Xinhua, September 7, 1982, trans. FBIS, September 8, 1982, p. K12.

69. Ruan Ming, *Deng Xiaoping diguo*, pp. 183–185.

70. Author's interviews.

71. The student demonstrations were widely reported in the Chinese and Western media in December 1986. See, for instance, the reports in FBIS, December 22, pp. O1–14.

72. Xinhua, December 28, 1986, trans. FBIS, December 30, 1986, pp. K6–8.

73. Han Shanbi, *Deng Xiaoping zhuan* (Biography of Deng Xiaoping), vol. 3 (1978–1988), p. 177. Ruan Ming, *Deng Xiaoping diguo*, p. 191.

74. Ruan Ming, *Deng Xiaoping diguo*, p. 191. Whether there was such a letter, when it was written, and what it said are all in dispute among Chinese intellectuals. Some say that if there was such a letter it could not have directly criticized Hu's work because Zhao did not have the right to demand the removal of senior officials such as Hu; that authority remained in the hands of party elders. Others say that there was a letter but that it was written in the fall of 1986. Still others maintain that there was no letter at all, that Zhao's only criticism of Hu came in his oral comments at the "party life" meeting. Clarification of what did or did not happen will obviously have to wait to a later time. Author's interviews.

75. As quoted to me by someone who heard these words from a participant in the meeting. Author's interviews. Zhao's brief statement contrasted with the five-hour lecture that Deng Liqun gave at the meeting. See Ruan Ming, *Deng Xiaoping diguo*, pp. 168–172.

76. Author's interviews.

77. Ibid.

78. Ibid.

79. Ibid.

80. Ibid.

81. See the three-part critique of Wu Jinglian's position by Hua Sheng, Zhang Xuejun, and Luo Xiaopeng, "Ten Years of Reform: Review, Reflection, and Prospects," which appeared in *Jingji yanjiu*, nos. 9, 11, and 12 (September, November, and December 1988), trans. JPRS-CAR–89–004 (January 11, 1989), pp. 16–45; JPRS-CAR–89–024 (March 23, 1989), pp. 16–37; and JPRS-CAR–89–036 (April 26, 1989), pp. 4–24. See also the response by Shi Xiamin and Liu Jirui, "An Economist Must Primarily Respect History and Facts—Commenting on 'Ten Years of China Reform (Review)'," which appeared in *Jingji yanjiu*, no. 2 (February 1989), pp. 11–33, trans. JPRS-CAR–89–064 (June 22, 1989), pp. 5–29.

7

The End of the Zhaoist Era

The campaign against "bourgeois liberalization" that was unleashed in late 1986 was directed primarily against ideological trends that were deemed incompatible with Marxism and party rule, but party conservatives soon tried to turn it to include economic issues as well. One of those who was most vociferous in this effort was Peng Zhen, the conservative head of the NPC Standing Committee.

Throughout 1986, before the campaign against bourgeois liberalization had begun, Peng had repeatedly challenged the efforts of reformers. For instance, in January 1986 Peng went to Zhejiang Province to investigate Wenzhou, where the rapid development of private business aroused conservatives' ire. In a speech to Zhejiang University, Peng stressed upholding the fundamental theory of Marxism-Leninism.[1] In September, Peng used his position as head of the NPC Standing Committee to delay passage of a bankruptcy law that the State Council and Central Secretariat clearly backed (the legislation was subsequently passed the following spring).[2] In October, Peng gave another speech in which he sharply criticized those who questioned the correctness of the fundamental principles (*jiben yuanli*) of Marxism and considered Marxism "outdated." In November he signaled his dissent from the just-passed resolution of the Sixth Plenum. In contrast to the resolution's emphasis on the common ideal, Peng declared that "the communist ideal was, is, and always will be a source of strength and a spiritual pillar for us communists and advanced elements. If we abandon this supreme ideal, we will lose our source of strength and our spiritual pillar and consequently our bearings as well. How could this not be a real problem?"[3] Peng concluded that there were "some people who wanted to go toward bourgeois democracy, as if the moon in bourgeois democratic society were brighter than our sun."[4]

With the inauguration of the campaign against bourgeois liberalization, Peng was soon joined by other conservatives. Among them was Jiang Liu, the education head at the Central Party School, who challenged Zhao's formulation of the "two basic points" (i.e., that economic reform and opening up on the one hand and the four cardinal principles on the other hand had constituted the two basic points of the party's line since the 1978 Third Plenum). According to Jiang, the four cardinal principles constituted the "key link" (*gang*), while reform and opening up only constituted the "mesh" (*mu*) (a formulation that self-consciously harkened back to Mao's demand to regard class struggle as the key link [*gang*]).[5] The implication was that economic reform (the mesh) had to be constructed on the foundation of socialist principles (the key link). In April 1987, Peng Zhen echoed this thesis, saying "Uphold the four cardinal principles. . . . Grasp this key link and one grasps the fundamentals."[6]

At the same time, Deng Liqun raised a distinction between what was said and what was done. According to Deng, people were upset that they could only criticize the advocates of bourgeois liberalization and not the cadres who were engaged in such liberalization.[7] The latter obviously referred to those around Zhao Ziyang who were engaged in economic reform.

In the face of this challenge, Zhao worked both quickly and adroitly—and with Deng Xiaoping's strong support—to curtail and then to end the campaign against bourgeois liberalization. Even before Hu Yaobang's resignation as general secretary, Zhao's secretary Bao Tong, who would be sentenced to seven years in prison following the Tiananmen incident, published an article in *People's Daily* entitled "The Young Horse of Socialism, the Old Horse of Capitalism, and Other Related Matters." Developing the thesis that China was in the initial stage of socialism, Bao argued that the economic foundation of China's socialism was weak and still contained many "feudal vestiges." Pointing to the political rationale of this argument, Bao said that once it was acknowledged that China was in the initial stage of socialism, "many ideological questions can be readily solved."[8] Bao's article was followed by another by Chen Junsheng, then secretary general of the State Council. Chen stressed the need both to effect reform and opening up and to uphold the four cardinal principles.[9]

In late January 1987, the party promulgated its "Document No. 4," which outlined the limits of the campaign against bourgeois liberalization. According to the document, the campaign was to be "protracted"—indicating that there was no need to carry it out in an intense manner—and that it was necessary to "refrain from linking the struggle with the politics of economic reform, rural policies, science and technology research, the exploration of the style and skill in literature and art, and people's daily life." Warning that it was necessary to guard against the practice of criticizing rightist errors with "leftism," the document stated that it was "imperative to take the line, principles, and policies since the Third Plenary Session of the Eleventh CCP Central Committee as the criteria."[10]

In February, Zhao presided over a meeting of the drafting committee of the report that was to be presented to the Thirteenth Party Congress and expressed the view that the theory of the initial stage of socialism could "fully answer all questions." Then on March 13, Zhao took another step by publicly endorsing, in a speech to a national meeting of directors of propaganda departments, the thesis that China was in the initial stage of socialism. Adhering to this recognition would prevent both leftist and rightist errors, Zhao declared. On March 18, Zhao addressed a letter to Deng, which Deng later approved, summarizing the discussions of the drafting group and endorsing the thesis of the initial stage of socialism.[11] Shortly thereafter, China's newspaper for intellectuals, *Guangming Daily*, began a special column for discussion of the thesis.

At the same time, plans for political structural reform, which had been shelved in late 1986, were put back on the agenda.[12] Speaking to the Standing Committee of the Chinese People's Political Consultative Committee (CPPCC) on March 15, Zhao stated without elaboration that "our political structural reform is in the planning stage, and we are studying a concrete program (*juti fangan*) for this reform."[13] A week later, Deng Xiaoping told Canadian Governor-General Jeane Sauve that a program (*shexiang*) for political reform was under consideration for the Thirteenth Party Congress.[14]

Conservative leaders, angered by this progressive whittling away of the campaign against bourgeois liberalization, convened a meeting in Zhuo County, Hebei Province, from April 6 to 12. Sponsored by the party theoretical journal *Hongqi*, the central paper *Guangming Daily*, and the conservative literary journal *Wenyi lilun yu piping* (Literature and Art Theory and Criticism), the meeting was called "to solicit articles on combating bourgeois liberalization."[15] At the meeting, He Jingzhi, deputy head of the Propaganda Department, declared that "we should not be blindly optimistic in the struggle against bourgeois liberalization" and called for "getting organized and joining hands in a broader way."[16] Similarly, Xiong Fu, the editor-in-chief of *Hongqi*, criticized the situation in theoretical circles and literature and art, saying that "contemporary young people have been poisoned both intensively and extensively by bourgeois liberalization to a very distressing extent."[17] The factional nature of the meeting was underscored by the failure of the party paper *People's Daily* to even report the meeting.

The Zhuo County meeting marked a turning point. When Deng heard reports on the meeting he realized that he had an opportunity to act promptly and strongly to refute the conservative ideologues and prepare the way for the Thirteenth Party Congress. Meeting with Spanish Socialist Workers Party leader Alfonso Guerra on April 30, Deng defined the party line since the 1978 Third Plenum as "reform and opening up"—a significant departure from the formula that had been used since the beginning of the year (and which was later revived), when Zhao had defined the party line as consisting of the two basic points of upholding the four cardinal principles on the one hand and reform, opening up, and enlivening the economy on the other. The implication of Deng's revision was that it was time to emphasize reform, not the four cardinal principles. Although Xinhua did not report it, Deng made this implication explicit in his talk with Guerra, saying that leftism was the "main danger" facing the party.[18]

This criticism of leftism—barely hinted at in these first public comments—was soon incorporated in party policy in a major inner-party speech given by Zhao Ziyang on May 13. In striking contrast to He Jingzhi's assessment only a month earlier, Zhao maintained that "great changes have taken place in the political and ideological spheres" and that the trend toward bourgeois liberalization had been "curbed." While stating that the struggle against bourgeois liberalization had to be "deepened," Zhao made clear that this deepening should be done only by means of "positive education." Moreover, he accused unnamed people of holding "erroneous views," such as believing that the existing economic situation was very poor and that there was no need to effect political reform or opening to the outside world.

In addition, Zhao, in an apparent allusion to Deng Liqun, charged that some people desired to "smash" the boundaries laid down in Document No. 4 so that "the struggle against bourgeois liberalization can be extended to the economic sphere." Speaking harshly, Zhao asked rhetorically, "Who would be responsible for the chaos if the current [economic] policies were interpreted as liberalization?"[19]

Zhao's speech was followed by a meeting of theorists and journalists which pointed out that the media "should publicize the socialist nature of the reforms of the last few years and the correctness and stability of our current policies."[20] Perhaps disappointed with the response to Zhao's speech, the Propaganda Department held a second meeting in June, which clearly set a Dengist tone as "many comrades" emphasized that "poverty is not socialism" and "the fundamental task of socialism is to develop productivity."[21]

By July it was apparent that the reform wing of the party had staged a remarkable comeback from the political turmoil of the winter. On July 1 (the anniversary of the founding of the CCP), *People's Daily* republished Deng's 1980 speech "On Reform of the Party and State Leadership Structure"—even restoring the section on the factory-director responsibility system that had been deleted when Deng's selected works were published in 1983. An accompanying *People's Daily* editorial made clear that reform—including political reform—would be the main theme of the Thirteenth Party Congress.[22] And on July 9, Zhao Ziyang's May 13 speech was finally published, suggesting that opposition to publishing it had been overwhelmed.

Implementing the Contract Responsibility System

Even as Zhao was dealing with the political fallout of the campaign against bourgeois liberalization, including attacks on his economic reforms, he was pushing ahead with a package of economic reforms that was intended to modify the relationship between the state and enterprises and between the party organization and the managers of enterprises. Indeed, Zhao's ability to press ahead with this agenda suggests the very strong backing he had from Deng Xiaoping in this period. Deng had no tolerance for student activists and little taste for the theoretical arguments of sophisticated intellectuals, but he was equally determined not to allow the campaign against bourgeois liberalization to disrupt the economic reforms he sought.

Nevertheless, Zhao's position was very difficult. As noted above, conservatives were charging that the source of bourgeois liberalization lay in the economy. At the same time, the economic situation facing Zhao was no less difficult. Ever since the implementation of the second stage of the tax-for-profit reform (the *li gai shui* reform) in 1984, the profits and taxes of enterprises had declined month by month, squeezing the revenues of the state.

One reason for this decline was the impact of reforms on large and medium-sized state-owned enterprises. First, reforms had increased the costs of such enterprises. The increase in the state procurement price of agricultural products as well as the decrease in the number of materials allocated at state-set prices via mandatory state plans had increased the costs of enterprises' raw materials. At the same time, circulation and transportation costs increased. In addition, the replacement of state-allocated funds with bank loans had increased the cost of funds (even if such funds were still cheap, with loans being repaid before taxes). Moreover, large and medium-sized state-owned enterprises were facing increasingly stiff competition from the large number of collective and village and township enterprises that had thrived under the reforms.[23]

Not only did their increased production costs reduce the profits of large and medium-sized state-owned enterprises, but as the central government took measures to slow the industrial growth rate in late 1985 and early 1986, the number of deficit enterprises began to increase. In 1985, enterprise losses topped 4 billion yuan, an 18.3 percent increase over the previous year, and in 1986 such deficits increased by another 78.7 percent to reach 7.2 billion yuan. At the same time, the profits of profit-making enterprises declined in 1986 from 98.5 billion to 95 billion yuan.[24]

The contradiction between the increasingly difficult financial situation of large and medium-sized state-owned enterprises and the state's need for a steady and increasing source of revenues made it difficult both to reform these enterprises and to proceed with economic reform as a whole. As one article put it, "If the large and medium-sized enterprises find it more and more difficult to engage in production and other operations, it will inevitably strain the state's financial strength, *making it necessary for the state to eventually reinforce the role of the old structure*, which will increase the difficulty of future reform."[25] In short, the concern was that unless ways were found to reform large and medium-sized state-owned enterprises so as to increase state revenues and decrease industrial losses, the pressures on the government were such that they would force efforts to strengthen planning. There was indeed much truth to Zhao's frequently invoked metaphor comparing reform to a boat being rowed against the current: "If it doesn't move forward, it moves backward."

Zhao's approach to economic reform in 1987 can be seen as a direct response to the problems and arguments that had arisen in the wake of efforts to formulate a comprehensive price reform program. Zhao had become convinced not only that the scheme was infeasible bureaucratically but that the microeconomic basis of Chinese society could not sustain a rapid reform of the price system without generating high inflation. Unless the relationship between the enterprise and the state bureaucracy was changed in fundamental ways so that the "paternalistic" bond between them was broken, it would be impossible to implement thorough-going price reform. In short, the arguments presented by Li Yining and many of the young economists associated with the Economic Reform Institute had convinced Zhao that reform first had to be approached from the microeconomic basis of society.

Even as debate over comprehensive price reform continued to rage in 1986, Zhao had begun to look at a series of measures to support greater decision-making authority for enterprises. As discussed in Chapter 6, Zhao had begun raising the issue of the factory-director responsibility system in early 1986. With the support of the State Economic Commission, the State Council approved that system in September 1986 along with two other sets of regulations on party committees in enterprises and workers' congresses.[26] Despite ambiguities in the regulations and differences in their interpretation, it was clear that their intent was to shift power from party secretaries to factory directors.[27] In 1988 these measures would culminate in the promulgation of an "Enterprise Law" that sought to further define the autonomy of enterprises.

In casting about for ways to keep the boat of reform moving forward in late 1986, Zhao had been convinced that the program for comprehensive price reform was both politically and economically untenable and that it was necessary to turn attention to the microeconomic basis of society in order to provide a foundation for long-term reform. However, ownership reform, the logical approach to addressing the problems of the microeconomy, remained too ideologically sensitive and involved too many practical difficulties to be adopted as the major thrust of reform at that time.

It was under these conditions that Zhao turned to the contract responsibility system (*chengbao jingying zeren zhi*). The contract responsibility system was not new. As discussed in Chapter 3, Jiang Yiwei and Lin Ling had helped draft the first formal contract for the Capitol Iron and Steel Plant in Beijing in 1982. Capitol Iron and Steel had prospered under the contract responsibility system, becoming a model and a forceful advocate for it. The increased revenues and taxes of Capitol Iron and Steel had made a believer of the Beijing Municipal CCP Organization, which became a strong supporter of both Capitol Iron and Steel and the contract responsibility system. At the same time, Jilin province began to adopt this system on a fairly large scale.[28]

In late 1982 and early 1983, when Zhao was out of China on a state visit to Africa, Hu Yaobang gave an important speech on the contract responsibility system. Hu, supported by Vice Premier Wan Li, wanted to introduce into the cities the methods that had been used with such success in the rural reforms. As part of this effort to introduce the contract responsibility system, Hu Qili, Hao Jianxiu, and Wan Li visited Tianjin in mid-February. Finding support among local cadres, Wan praised the experience of Capitol Iron and Steel, saying it had shown that as soon as the contract responsibility system was introduced, the economy became enlivened (*yibao jiuling*).[29] When Zhao returned from Africa, he was angry at this interference in what he considered to be his area of responsibility. Zhao, who favored the tax-for-profit reform, pushed the Ministry of Finance to accelerate its drafting of regulations for substituting taxes for profits.[30] Zhao also appealed to Deng, asking for support in his own responsibility to manage the reform of the economy. Deng ruled in Zhao's favor, saying that Zhao was in charge of the economy and that Hu should not interfere.[31]

When the tax-for-profit reform was adopted in two stages in 1983 and 1984, the contract responsibility system faded from the scene. Capitol Iron and Steel was allowed to continue with the system only after long argument. In Jilin Province, the system was cut back, but provincial authorities continued to support it and it revived. In late 1985, the system as it was being implemented in Jilin was criticized, and in 1986 it was basically abandoned. The worsening financial situation at the end of 1986, however, prompted calls for its revival.[32]

The basic idea behind the contract responsibility system was to give enterprises greater decision-making authority and reduce administrative interference in the running of enterprises by making the state-enterprise relationship contractual.[33] The state would be guaranteed revenues and the enterprise would be allowed to keep revenues in excess of specified amounts.

There were two basic reasons why interest in the contract responsibility system revived in late 1986. The first was financial. As noted above, the tax-for-profit system had not worked out as hoped; for twenty-two straight months, revenues from enterprises had declined. There was an urgent need to find a way to shore up central finances. The second was political. Zhao needed to keep the momentum of reform going or he would be forced to yield ground to conservatives. When efforts to formulate a comprehensive reform of the price system collapsed, there was an urgent need to find another program to keep reform moving. The contract responsibility system fit the bill.[34] Its adoption thus marked more the appearance of reform than the reality.

Zhao began arguing on behalf of the contract responsibility system in late 1986. During a late November trip to the city of Wuhan, Zhao, accompanied by Vice Premier Li Peng, had a meeting with managers of the Wuhan Automobile Engine Plant, the Wuhan Chemical Machinery Plant, the No. 1 State-Run Cotton Mill, and the No. 461 Plant—all enterprises that had experimented with the contract responsibility system. Zhao praised their experience, saying that the main reason for their success was that "the self-operation of the enterprises has genuinely separated ownership from operation rights of enterprises, improved the manager responsibility system, and given more powers to managers in business operations."[35]

Early in 1987, Zhao toured Beijing and Shanghai and argued that it was "imperative" for large and medium-sized enterprises to implement the contract responsibility system. In February the State Council endorsed the contract responsibility system at a national governor's work meeting, and in March Zhao publicly announced the policy decision to support the system in his report to the National People's Congress.[36] The support of enterprises and localities for the new system can be judged by how quickly it spread. By July, just over half of China's large and medium-sized enterprises had adopted the system, while by December, over 80 percent had implemented it.[37]

Several versions of the contract responsibility system were adopted simultaneously, the most widely implemented being known as the "two guarantees and one link." Enterprises working under this system guaranteed to deliver a specified amount of taxes and profits to the state and to fulfill the technological transformation projects approved by the state under the Seventh Five-Year Plan. The "one link" referred to setting the amount of total salaries and wages according to the amount of realized profits and taxes.[38] This system was simpler to implement than the complex scheme of competitive bidding called for by Hua Sheng and his colleagues under the asset responsibility system (discussed below), though the latter system was implemented on an experimental basis in some enterprises.[39] As Yu Guangyuan put it, "the contract responsibility system provides a simple method, and everyone from top to bottom knows how to calculate in light of this method. Therefore the contract system is suited to the characteristics of the initial stage of socialism and to the low educational and socialization levels."[40]

Economists were sharply divided in their opinion of the contract responsibility system. Those who, like Wu Jinglian, had argued for a rapid reform of the price system opposed the contract responsibility system because it accepted the existing price structure and could make more difficult the future implementation of price reform (since price reform would affect every contract in the country).[41]

Among those who supported the contract responsibility system, opinion was divided between some who saw the system as a long-term policy and others who saw it as a transitional system. The first school of thought was championed by Zhou Guanwu, the head of Capitol Iron and Steel; Yang Peixin, a senior economist with the State Council's Economic, Technological, and Social Development Research Center; and He Jianzhang, then a member of the Industrial Economics Institute at CASS. Such people argued that because the price system was irrational and could not be straightened out in a short period, the only practical way to deal with the situation was to fix separate contracts for each enterprise. This would reduce administrative interference in the management of enterprises and make them the primary entities for future investment ("expanded reproduction"). Those who felt this way also had a political agenda. In their view, the contract responsibility system could effect the separation of ownership and management but not affect the ownership system. They saw the contract responsibility system as opposed to the shareholding system, which they believed was the equivalent of privatization.[42]

In contrast, a number of young economists began to study the contract responsibility system as an alternative both to proposals for "comprehensive reform" and to problems with implementing ownership reform and the shareholding system. On December 24, 1985, five young economists—Hua Sheng, He Jiacheng, Zhang Xuejun, Luo Xiaopeng, and Yong Bianzhuang—presented a paper on "The Theoretical Basis and Initial Design for Implementing the Asset-Responsibility System in State-Owned Enterprises" at the Ninth Symposium on the National Economy.[43] The basic idea of their proposed "asset responsibility system" was to introduce competitive bidding into contracting for enterprises. Bidding would, they hoped, simulate the market and arrive at a reasonable evaluation of an enterprise's assets.

These people were attracted to the idea of the asset responsibility system because they believed on the one hand that reform could not be accomplished by the sort of coordinated reforms that Wu Jinglian and others favored, and on the other hand that proposals for instituting the shareholding system were not practical under the conditions then prevailing. They agreed that the problems of the preceding years had shown that "economic structural reform is not one single act or a set of mutually coordinated acts, but an arduous and prolonged historical process."[44] On the other hand, they argued that allowing other forms of ownership to grow up alongside state-owned enterprises enabled the former to reap rich profits, "producing disparities in social income and unrest among the people." When shareholding reforms were introduced within the state-owned economy, there were often problems with public assets being used for private ends and an expansion of consumption funds.[45] In short, neither coordinated reforms nor ownership reform held out prospects of countering the problems that reform had encountered in its first years.

In the opinion of Hua and his colleagues, the problem of reform stemmed from the fact that there was no "personified representative" (*rengehua daibiao*) of the enterprise and because the relationship between the state and the enterprise was obscure. In their opinion, changes in macroeconomic policy, including the freeing of prices, were insufficient to bring about a healthy market mechanism. It was necessary to "reconstruct the microeconomic base." As they wrote:[46]

> If we neglect the restructuring of the microeconomic foundation while transforming the model of economic operation, then no matter how skillful the design of the model of market functions and the regulation of market mechanisms, there will certainly be breakdowns in the operation or it will be utterly impossible for the models to operate. This is the major experience gained in the great victory in the initial battle of rural reform and is also the basic cause of the difficulties in carrying out our urban reform.

There was a fundamental difference in the approach of such economists and older economists, such as Yang Peixin and He Jianzhang, who argued on behalf of the contract responsibility system. The model of the contract responsibility system that Yang, He, and others constantly referred to was Capitol Iron and Steel. A central feature of the Capitol Iron and Steel model was that in the contract between the state and the enterprise, the enterprise was represented by the whole body of workers (represented by the workers' congress) rather than by its manager(s) as individuals or a group. Precisely the opposite was the case in the proposal made by Hua and his colleagues. In their minds, one of the virtues of the contract responsibility system was that it could demarcate a separate "entrepreneurial stratum" with its own separate interest. They maintained that it was necessary for an entrepreneurial stratum to have a separate interest, linked to the performance of the enterprise, precisely because only such a clearly demarcated group could restrain the constant pressures for wage increases.[47]

The views of Hua Sheng and his colleagues received support from young economists within the State Economic Commission. A Young Economists Research Group was set up within the commission in the summer of 1986. The group was headed by Ren Kelai, son of the strongly reformist former Guangdong party secretary Ren Zhongyi, who was then serving as director of the Policy Analysis Division at the State Economic Commission. Ren's group produced a report on the contract responsibility system entitled "An Investigation of the Question of Deepening Enterprise Reform," which was read and approved by "leading comrades" of the State Council in April 1987. The report was too late to influence the basic decision to introduce the contract responsibility system, but it may have had an influence on thinking about the system and how it might evolve in the future. In an interview, Ren argued that the problem with the contract responsibility system as it had previously been implemented (and was then being implemented) was that since it was always the factory director or manager who knew the most about the factory, they were always able to get the better of any bargain with the state. Paralleling the arguments of Hua Sheng and his colleagues, Ren argued that the practice of inviting tenders in determining the basic quota for a contract could introduce a competitive mechanism into the contract responsibility system.[48]

Zhao's decision in 1986–87 to adopt the contract responsibility system marked an important turning point in the evolution of reform policy. When the Third Plenum decision on economic reform was adopted in 1984, most reformers thought that reform could bring about a rationalized economic system in about five years. At first, they sought to do so by adopting the dual-track price system; by 1985–86, they were casting about for a plan that would allow the implementation of sweeping reforms in a package. By 1987, Zhao was convinced that the economic and political risks of such a course were too great. The adoption of the contract responsibility system reflected a belief that the transition to a marketized economic system was going to take longer than had originally been hoped. By December 1987, Zhao was quite explicit about how far he had moved away from the consideration of a comprehensive price reform package. "Price reform might take a longer time than anticipated," he told the Central Party School. It was necessary first to place emphasis on improving the "operating mechanisms" of enterprises, a measure that would create a "good environment" for other reforms, including price reform.[49]

The Great International Cycle

Zhao's other major economic initiative for 1987 was a program for rapidly expanding the role of village and township enterprises in the Chinese economy by allowing them to participate in the "great international cycle" (*guoji da xunhuan*). The theory of the great international cycle was proposed by Wang Jian and Pei Xiaolin, two young economists with the Economic Planning Institute of the State Planning Commission, as a solution to a fundamental dilemma facing China's economic reform: that both the pressure to transfer surplus labor out of the agricultural sector (an estimated 180 million people by the year 2000) and the need to upgrade China's aging industrial plant required vast investments. With limited funds to address these pressing needs, it appeared that modernization would be a slow process. The theory of the great international cycle proposed to escape this dilemma by rapidly expanding China's village and township industries, particularly along the coast, so that they could absorb the labor being transferred out of the agricultural sector. The village and township enterprises could take advantage of this inexpensive labor to increase vastly China's exports. The foreign exchange earned could then be used to buy technology on the international market, speeding the modernization of China's traditional industries. Moreover, the present was said to be an opportune time to embark on this process because a number of labor-intensive industries were being transferred from the developed and newly industrialized nations to the developing nations. By taking advantage of this shift, China could hope to enter the great international cycle on a large scale, thereby resolving its problems of employment and limited capital.

Wang Jian had begun thinking in terms of the great international cycle during the preparations for the Thirteenth Party Congress. At that time he participated in the drafting of background materials for the section on strategic development in Zhao's report, and this participation caused him to think systematically about policy prescriptions that could meet the policy needs of Zhao and extricate China from the difficult economic dilemmas it was facing. With the help of Pei Xiaolin, Wang came up with the idea of the great international cycle and drafted a report on it. This report was published in Xinhua's internal reference publication in August 1987. Undoubtedly vetted among Zhao's policy advisors, Wang's proposal landed on Zhao's desk while the Thirteenth Party Congress was in session. Only a few days later, Zhao, displaying his characteristic tendency to enthusiastically subscribe to new and bold ideas, endorsed Wang's proposal, saying, "I think it makes sense."[50]

Wang's ideas struck a responsive cord with Zhao, who had long supported the development of China's Special Economic Zones and the opening up of the coastal areas. Shortly after the close of the party congress, Zhao embarked on an inspection tour first of China's southeastern provinces and then, a month later, of the lower Yangzi Valley. These trips were not only intended to give the general secretary a firsthand understanding of conditions in the Southeast and build support for the new policy but also to alleviate doubts that had already surfaced about the strategy of the great international cycle. As *Wen wei po* put it, Zhao wanted to gather more information about the great international cycle, since "a number of different opinions arose after this strategy was proposed."[51]

Whatever doubts had been expressed to the general secretary, Zhao firmly endorsed the basic theses of the great international cycle strategy during his tour. While in Fujian, he stated that:[52]

> In the past, Fujian relied on the domestic market and processed raw materials from the interior. Now it seems that this will lead Fujian nowhere. We always say that China is a big country with abundant natural resources. Actually this is not so. China is not a large country abounding in natural wealth. On the contrary, natural resources constitute a major factor conditioning China's Four Modernizations. Therefore, China should seize the current opportunity, take part in international competition, and push the coastal areas into the international market.

Zhao went on to endorse the idea of putting "both ends on the outside" (*liang tou zai wai*), with coastal enterprises importing the raw materials they need and exporting the finished products. He also said that if the coastal areas could develop their economies into export-oriented economies, their development would certainly bring along that of the central and western parts of China.[53]

The speed with which Zhao endorsed the great international cycle strategy suggests the very real economic and political pressures facing the new general secretary. From January 1987 until the Thirteenth Party Congress met in September, Zhao had retained his position as premier while acting concurrently as general secretary of the party. As the congress approached, four candidates for premier were suggested: Li Peng, Tian Jiyun, Wan Li, and Hu Qili. Zhao, of course, supported Tian, then a vice premier whom Zhao had brought with him to Beijing from Sichuan, where Tian had been in charge of finances. Zhao objected to Wan Li, with whom he had never gotten along well, and Hu Qili was eliminated because he did not have enough experience in economic matters. Eventually, Li Peng, then the vice premier in charge of industry, was chosen not only because he had economic experience, but also because he had the support of party conservatives and therefore would help maintain a balance of forces at the top. Zhao apparently felt that he could dominate the less experienced and less capable Li.[54]

Moving from head of the State Council to head of the party posed problems for Zhao. As premier, he had headed both the Central Finance and Economic Leading Group and the State Council. When he became general secretary, Zhao retained the former post but had to give up his institutional control over the latter. Li Peng was hardly willing to subordinate himself to Zhao, looking instead to conservative party leaders including Chen Yun for support. Zhao wanted to maintain control over economic policy through his position as head of the Central Finance and Economic Leading Group, but this group, despite being an organ of the Central Committee of the CCP, did not have the institutional authority to impose decisions on the State Council. When Zhao had headed both the State Council and the leading group, the top leadership felt obliged to attend meetings of the latter. After Zhao lost the premiership, leaders such as Yao Yilin no longer felt they had to attend in person, but could send deputies instead.[55]

Zhao's rapid endorsement of the concept of the great international cycle was thus an effort to maintain the initiative in economic policy. He apparently believed that by using his position as head of the Central Finance and Economic Leading Group, he could publicize ideas and generate support for continued reform. However, his effort to continue to set the agenda for economic reform failed. As it turned out, no ministry of the State Council ever formally endorsed proposals for implementing the great international cycle; the propaganda campaign that surrounded the concept masked the fundamental weakness of Zhao's position.[56]

From Zhao's perspective, one attractive feature of the great international cycle was that it offered a way in which to maintain rapid development of the economy without either putting further strains on China's basic industries or fueling inflationary pressures. By encouraging village and township enterprises to import and export on a large scale, Zhao apparently hoped to reduce pressures on domestic resources, particularly energy and raw materials. This would permit the economy to continue to develop rapidly, thereby satisfying demands for growth and consumption, as well as stimulating the growth of fiscal revenues for the state, without exacerbating inflationary pressures. At the same time, because the development of village and township enterprises would rely mostly on local funds, the state could harbor its scarce financial resources for the benefit of key projects.

Economically, the strategy of the great international cycle would accelerate the shift from large state-owned enterprises to small-scale enterprises in the central-eastern and southeastern parts of China. Suggesting his frustration with the state sector, Zhao pointed out that "under the existing economic conditions in China, it is difficult to invigorate the large and medium-sized enterprises in one fell swoop." In contrast, he lauded village and township enterprises at length, calling their organization and management "extremely good." Such enterprises, he said, took responsibility for their own profits and losses right from the beginning. In an implicit but nonetheless pointed comparison with the state sector, Zhao noted that village and township enterprises "grow up in a market environment. Only those that survive the competition can grow."[57]

This shift meant a turning away from efforts to invigorate backbone enterprises toward the development of local enterprises that would be "collective" in nature, if not private. In effect, the adoption of the great international cycle strategy implied an effort to accelerate the transformation of the ownership structure of Chinese industry. At the same time, it would undermine China's central bureaucracies by making an "end run" around them.

In short, the great international cycle strategy had the advantage of undermining Zhao's conservative opponents within the regime who were arguing that China's rapid development was straining its resources and increasing inflationary pressures. Such opponents wanted precisely the opposite strategy of restraining the pace of development of village and township industries, promoting the development of energy and transportation resources, and devoting greater resources to backbone enterprises. This group called for slowing the rate of China's development and revitalizing the economy on the basis of the state-owned sector rather than by discarding it. Wang's policy paper presented an elegant argument for accelerating development rather than restricting it; it thus matched Zhao's political desire to avoid the policy prescriptions being advocated by his conservative opponents and the political effects that would stem from them.

Pressures to Retrench

From the foregoing discussion, it is apparent that the policies of the contract responsibility system and the strategy of the great international cycle were intended to avoid pressures from conservatives and keep reform moving forward; the alternative was to adopt retrenchment measures and strengthen central controls over the economy. In other words, Zhao's reform program in 1987 was in large part a defensive effort to ward off pressures to abandon reform. In late 1987 and early 1988, new pressures mounted that would lead Deng to intervene decisively in the policy-making process in favor of a program of radical price reform, followed by the collapse of the reform program itself, at least until it could be resurrected in the post-Tiananmen period. These pressures centered around the three issues of inflation, corruption, and mounting enterprise losses.

The issue of inflation in a reforming socialist economy is by no means a simple one, and Chinese economists were sharply divided over both the causes and remedies for inflation. In general, their views on inflation fell into three categories. First, some economists held that the factors that led to inflation in 1986 and 1987 were essentially the same as in previous periods of inflation: an expansion of the consumption fund caused by excessive investment, overextended credit, and an overly rapid increase in the money supply. In short, they argued that aggregate demand exceeded aggregate supply.

Those who held this view could be further subdivided into two schools. On the one hand were the conservatives who had been arguing throughout the decade that tightening state controls, especially over investment, was the only way to prevent inflation. On the other hand were mainstream reformers like Liu Guoguang, who wanted to move to a market-oriented economy but believed that an extended period of economic retrenchment was necessary in order to wring inflationary pressures out of the economy. Such economists not only believed, as Liu has stated, that "the basic reason for inflation is the 'overheated' investment and 'overheated' consumption of recent years, creating a demand[-driven] inflation," but had also concluded that inflationary pressures in the Chinese economy were deep-seated and abiding.[58]

Falling into the second category were economists like Wu Jinglian, who continued to argue that comprehensive price reform was the key to solving inflation but that it was necessary to adopt strong retrenchment policies first in order to bring about a "relaxed" economic environment. The difference between Wu's approach and that of mainstream reformers like Liu Guoguang was that Wu believed that retrenchment measures should be sharp but brief, whereas Liu saw the need for maintaining them over an extended period of time. In Wu's opinion, maintaining retrenchment measures for a long period would allow problems in the economy to accumulate and make future reform more difficult.

The third approach was that taken by many young economists, including those associated with the Economic Reform Institute. These economists argued that inflation was not primarily due to excessive investment and an excessive demand in the economy but rather to other factors such as China's distorted production structure. For instance, Chen Zhao, director of the International Banking Office under the Banking Department of the Central Finance and Banking Institute, argued that inflation was due in large measure to the frictions generated by rapid changes in consumption patterns versus slow changes in the structure of production, and to the coexistence of the low rate of agricultural growth after 1985 with the high rate of industrial growth. Similarly, Cheng Xiaonong, director of the Comprehensive Studies Department of the Economic Reform Institute, argued that increases in food prices in 1987 reflected periodic fluctuations in agricultural production. He maintained that China's agricultural production fluctuated once every four to five years and that changes in market prices were the main reason for the fluctuations. Cheng argued that pig raising became very profitable in the mid-1980s because bumper harvests had sharply driven down the cost of feed grain. Thus, pork production was at a peak just when grain production fell in 1985, and the subsequent shortage of feed grain made peasants sharply reduce their pork production. This occurred exactly at the time that urban consumers were enhancing their diets and demanding more pork. The decline in pork production therefore coincided with an increase in demand, fueling price increases for pork in 1987.[59]

Those who viewed the causes of inflation as primarily structural believed that retrenchment measures would on the one hand fail to alleviate the basic causes for inflation (perhaps leading to a new and worse cycle of inflation in the future, when retrenchment policies were eased), and on the other hand undermine reform by reimposing various administrative measures. For such people, inflation was an important but nevertheless a secondary concern.

In January, Zhao convened at least two meetings to discuss the economic situation. He was convinced that the economic situation was not as bad as Li and other conservative leaders maintained and that reform could continue in the new year. Reflecting these discussions, He Jiacheng and Zhang Xuejun, two young scholars then affiliated with CASS, wrote an article that argued that macroeconomic controls had in fact been tightened effectively during 1987 and that "total domestic demand in our country was brought under effective control." Directly criticizing the approach taken at the economic work conference, He and Zhang observed that "Some comrades have indiscriminately blamed the expansion of consumption and the expansion of aggregate social demand for intensifying the contradiction between supply and demand. This is an obviously incorrect view."[60]

When the Second Plenary Session of the Thirteenth Central Committee convened in March 1987, Zhao made a strong effort to seize the initiative on economic affairs and thus rebut Li Peng's effort to take control of the economy. As premier, Li was in a position to supervise the economy and thus undermine the authority of the general secretary, much as Zhao had done to Hu Yaobang. Macroeconomic policy inevitably became the battleground for their struggle.

In his speech to the plenum, Zhao echoed the optimistic evaluation of the economy in 1987 offered by He and Zhang. He told the session that "China's economic situation [in 1986] was fine" and argued that the existing economic situation would allow China to combine rapid growth with economic efficiency.[61] In saying this, Zhao seemed to be accepting the argument that a certain degree of inflation was inevitable, perhaps even desirable. He also seemed concerned that the adoption of retrenchment measures would end his hopes of building on the successes of the Thirteenth Party Congress to implement wide-ranging, market-oriented reforms during the year.

Following the Second Plenum, the tight controls on the money supply were loosened in an apparent effort to promote growth. But precisely at the time that Zhao was taking steps to accelerate growth, signs that the economy was already overheated were beginning to mount. In the first quarter of the year, prices increased by 13 percent.[62] At the same time, enterprise losses, which normally decreased when the rate of economic growth increased, continued upward from their already high level of 1986. Moreover, whereas the money supply usually decreased in the early part of the year as peasants and workers spent the money they had earned from the harvest and from their year-end bonuses, very little cash came back in early 1987, and in May, usually a month in which large quantities of funds were absorbed, the money supply actually expanded.[63] At the Second Plenum, Yao Yilin and Li Peng had strongly advocated curtailing the growth rate, but Zhao had dismissed their pessimistic views.[64]

Moreover, precisely at the time that Zhao was trying to spur economic growth to provide an atmosphere for rapid economic reform, widespread resentment over corruption was mounting. According to one estimate, the aggregate difference between the state-set price of capital goods and the negotiated price at which they were actually sold amounted to 200 billion to 300 billion yuan annually. Figuring conservatively that 20 percent of this difference was illicitly siphoned off, the authors suggested that corrupt profits amounted to 20 billion to 40 billion yuan annually.[65]

Conservatives argued that reform had brought corruption and demanded greater emphasis on ideology to deal with the issue. It was apparently in this context that Zhao made his comment, subjected to ruthless criticism since June 1989, that a certain degree of corruption was unavoidable in the course of reform. Conservatives were not the only ones offended by corruption within the party and society. At the early April meeting of the Chinese People's Political Consultative Conference, the well-respected senior economist Qian Jiaju scathingly denounced corruption to the hearty applause of his colleagues. Qian said, "Honest people can barely make a living, whereas opportunists and the corrupt live in abundance and are envied by others. Nothing corrupts the moral climate in society more than this."[66]

Qian's views expressed widespread dissatisfaction in Chinese society. In March members of the Economic Reform Institute were shocked to see the results of their own survey of public opinion. Not only were people opposed to further price reform, but they were turning away from reform in general.[67] Whether in economic or political terms, no time could have been worse for the launching of radical reform. But that is just what Deng Xiaoping proceeded to do.

Deng and the Push for Comprehensive Price Reform

It was in the atmosphere described above that Deng intervened decisively in the policy-making process to push for comprehensive price reform. In early May 1987, in a meeting at his home, Deng called for completing price reform in three to five years.[68] On May 15, he hinted at his determination to move forward with radical reform when he met with Argentine President Raul Alfonsin. Deng told Alfonsin: "Now our policy of upholding reform and opening up is not being restricted but is advancing another step. This is risky, and there may be twists and turns and even mistakes. However, we should meet stormy waves head-on while striving to avoid big mistakes."[69]

Four days later, on May 19, when there was still no response from the Politburo Standing Committee, Deng began campaigning publicly on behalf of radical price reform.[70] Meeting with North Korean Defense Minister O Chin-u, Deng declared that "China's price reform is a courageous action. It is necessary to take certain risks, but the center has confidence that this matter can be done well."[71] On May 24, when meeting with David Rockefeller, Deng declared that it was necessary to cross through the "dangerous pass" of price reform; this pass, he said, "cannot be gone around." On June 3, in a meeting with participants of an international symposium on "China and the World in the 1990s," Deng was even more emphatic. Saying that China had the necessary conditions for comprehensive price and wage reform and that "short-term pain is better than long-term pain," Deng demanded that "we must now be determined to take the risk" of price reform.[72]

This emphasis on "braving the wind and waves" and a "comprehensive" approach to price reform, and the observation that "a short pain is better than a long pain" provide strong evidence that Deng had decided to reject the approach of people like Li Yining and the young economists of the Economic Reform Institute—whose views had been largely adopted by Zhao—in favor of Wu Jinglian's approach.

Given China's situation, Wu's approach of comprehensive price reform offered many advantages. First and foremost, by eliminating the dual-track system, price reform could undermine one of the primary causes of corruption—the rent-seeking behavior of officials making use of the difference between in-plan and out-of-plan prices. It will be recalled that in 1986, Hu Yaobang had attempted to deal head-on with the issue of corruption by ordering the arrests of a number of children of high officials. Deng wanted to avoid the sort of open clash that Hu's actions had precipitated, and radical price reform seemed to be a way to attack corruption without paying a high political price for doing so. In short, Deng was intervening in economic issues in order to deal with a political problem.

Second, price reform, at least as it was apparently envisioned by Deng, sidestepped the issue of ownership reform.[73] The apparent hope was that the price system could be reformed and the economy made more efficient without raising the ideologically sensitive and politically contentious issue of ownership reform.

Deng's decision to intervene in favor of radical price reform may also have been influenced by the concept of "new authoritarianism" that young intellectuals had begun discussing since1986. This concept drew heavily on the experience of other East Asian nations, particularly Taiwan, South Korea, and Singapore, to argue that modernization required a benevolent but dictatorial hand at the top. Such a hand could resolve the conflict among the societal interests that had become such a prominent part of the Chinese landscape by imposing from the top a solution that would ultimately be beneficial to all. Dictatorship could be used to promote economic reform, particularly price reform, which societal interests would otherwise stymie. This notion apparently appealed to Deng.[74]

Finally, there was the personality of Deng. Comprehensive price reform had the benefit of being a simple solution that appeared to be the answer to multiple problems, including corruption, economic reform, and social conflict over group interests. It did not call for the patient development of markets or for confronting the most contentious ideological issue of the day—ownership reform. It also had the benefit of seeming to be a dramatic step forward in reform. For at least two years, Deng had been urging Zhao to speed up the pace of reform.[75] Price reform appealed to Deng, who was getting impatient with the pace of reform and increasingly aware of his mortality. Propaganda for price reform in the spring frequently mentioned that the time for it was right because senior leaders such as Deng were still around; reform could take advantage of his prestige and authority.

Li Tieying, then the youngest member of the Politburo and the son of veteran revolutionary Li Weihan, was apparently critical in persuading Deng to push ahead with price reform. Following the Thirteenth Party Congress, Li had replaced Zhao Ziyang as head of the State Commission on Economic Structural Reform. Li apparently hoped to use this position to promote his own interests. He understood the political problems confronting Deng and saw Wu Jinglian's ideas on price reform as a way of solving them.[76]

Confronted with Deng's strong advocacy of price reform, Zhao had little choice but to endorse Deng's ideas, hoping to fold in his own ideas behind Deng's leadership. From May 30 to June 1, Zhao presided over a meeting that was originally designated an "enlarged Politburo meeting" but was then transformed into the Ninth Plenary Session of the Politburo.[77] It was at this meeting that Zhao gave a talk on establishing the so-called new order of the socialist commodity economy and at which the Politburo endorsed the need for a comprehensive and systematic plan for price and wage reform.[78] According to the official report of the meeting, "reform is risky, but not advancing is retreating; if we retreat there is no way out."[79]

The "new order of a socialist commodity economy" suggested by Zhao was a ten-point proposal to carry out price and wage reform, improve enterprise productivity, improve the macroeconomic environment, deal with problems of corruption, and improve ideological and political work.[80] According to Zhao, freeing the prices of most commodities could result in a 50 percent increase in prices over the next five years.[81] Zhao pointed out that "in Brazil prices increase 15 percent a month and 70 percent a year—how can people live there? Why can't we live [with similar price increases]?"[82] The implication was that since China could adopt mechanisms such as wage indexation to deal with inflation, fear of inflation was not a sufficient reason to put off reform. Zhao's speech also reflected the influence of the "new authoritarianism." Zhao said, "I feel that students taking to the streets is not good. Students took to the streets in 1986 because the pace of reform was not fast. The students support reform. They took to the streets then to support reform. This time it was not like this. Some students wanted to pull us down. We should have preparations against turmoil (*dongluan*). Our attitude toward demonstrations is first, we don't fear them, and second, they should be suppressed. We should strengthen basic-level work, make legal preparations; we need a law for emergency situations."[83]

The Politburo agreed in principle that "the reform of the price and wage systems needs comprehensive thought and a systematic plan" and that it was necessary to "fix coordinated (*pei tao*) reform measures," but it did not endorse a specific decision to effect price reform right away. Nevertheless, the Politburo did endorse the approach long advocated by Wu Jinglian, and Wu reportedly received the congratulations of his fellow economists.[84] Whatever his initial reaction, Wu quickly developed doubts about the course of policy. Although he had long advocated comprehensive price reform, he had always argued that it should be preceded by the adoption of tight monetary and fiscal controls to bring about a "buyers' market" in which price reform could be introduced. On May 27, even before the Politburo meeting, Wu had a vehement argument with Zhao in which he opposed the price reform program on the grounds that the economic environment was inflationary.[85]

Although Zhao decided that he had to support price reform, he was fully aware of its risks and continuously tried to integrate his ideas on enterprise reform with price reform. This was apparent in his speech at the Ninth Plenary Session of the Politburo on the new order of the socialist commodity economy in which he stressed the need to raise enterprise efficiency. During his June 14–21 trip to the provinces of Shanxi and Shaanxi, Zhao returned to this theme:[86]

> The main reason reform of the price and wage systems is difficult to withstand is that our society has a poor ability to withstand the impact of this reform. This ability is primarily dependent on the economic results of enterprises. Both the resolution of financial difficulties of enterprises and elimination of price hike factors depend on improving economic results of enterprises. *Society would have no ability to withstand the impact of price and wage reform if enterprises are not reformed first.* . . . In the final analysis, reform of the price and wage systems depends on improving economic results of enterprises. Once the economic results of enterprises are improved, there will be more leeway to maneuver price and wage reform.

The following month, in a visit to the Northeast, Zhao again stressed that the forthcoming reform must concentrate not only on prices and wages but on enterprise efficiency. He warned that price reform alone could result in a new round of inflation, with price parities remaining unchanged. Therefore, he said, "we cannot consider the price issue merely from the angle of price reform."[87]

Shortly after the Thirteenth Party Congress, and long before Deng intervened on behalf of radical price reform, the State Commission for Economic Structural Reform had asked nine units to formulate proposals for reform over the next eight years. The proposals were drafted by most of the major schools of thought that had been debating with each other over the previous years, including those of Wu Jinglian, Li Yining, Liu Guoguang, the Economic Reform Institute, the State Planning Commission, and a group from Chinese People's University headed by Wu Shuqing, the conservative vice president of the university who would be tapped as president of Beijing University in the wake of the June 1989 crackdown.

In late May and early June, the participants in these studies met at the Jingxi Hotel in Beijing to discuss their proposals. As this meeting was taking place, Deng, in his meeting with the internal symposium on "China and the World in the 1990s," made his strongest statement to date on price reform, saying that the party had already decided to undertake radical price reform, even though no such decision had been made.[88] Attending the meeting was An Ziwen, the party secretary of the State Commission for Economic Structural Reform, who was caught off guard by Deng's announcement. The next morning An hurried to the Jingxi Hotel to advise the participants that they had to make their proposals under the assumption of radical price reform.

The Economic Reform Institute, which was not in favor of radical price reform, withdrew its proposal. The other eight proposals were subsequently published in a volume entitled *Major Ways of Thinking About Chinese Reform*.[89] Strikingly, despite An's admonition, which forced the economists meeting at the Jingxi Hotel to couch their proposals in the language of radical reform so as to fit the existing political mood, none of the proposals endorsed Deng's vision of launching comprehensive price reform in the immediate future. Wu Jinglian, whose proposal was the most radical in that it called for a fundamental transformation of the economic system within four years, nevertheless warned that it was necessary to take "forceful measures" to curb aggregate demand and provide the necessary conditions for radical reform.[90] Li Yining called for two years of "perfecting and developing" the contract responsibility system before implementing the shareholding system on a widespread basis during the two subsequent years. Only after that did Li foresee the radical readjustment of prices.[91]

Most striking, however, was that the proposals of Liu Guoguang, Wu Shuqing, and the State Planning Commission all called for a lengthy period of price stabilization. Liu had been one of the central figures in the mainstream approach to reform through the late 1970s and early 1980s, but his influence had waned as that of others, such as Wu Jinglian, Li Yining, and the economists of the Economic Reform Institute had become more prominent in reform circles in the period from 1985 to 1988. At this time, Liu appears to have made a conscious decision to cast his lot with the conservatives. Liu argued that the greatest danger to the economy stemmed from the "overheating" that had developed since 1984 and said that it was only possible to "advance on the basis of stability." He maintained that in a tense economic environment, such as China had been experiencing, "a comprehensive reform plan, including price reform, can in no way be effective." Accordingly, he called for a three-year period in which measures to stabilize the economy would be emphasized.[92] This was perhaps the first public endorsement of the idea of improvement and rectification (*zhili zhengdun*) that would be adopted at the party plenum in the fall.

The proposal made by the State Planning Commission gently turned aside Deng's call for price reform by saying, "if we give priority to one area, neglecting the others, not only will we not accelerate the progress of the overall economic reform, but new gaps will appear and reform and development will encounter new obstacles."[93] In the commission's view, it would take eight years or "a little longer" to "fundamentally establish and develop the framework of a new structure of a planned commodity economy"—considerably longer than the three to five years for which Deng had been calling.

The most openly conservative of the eight published proposals was that by Wu Shuqing. This proposal was quite pessimistic about the conditions facing China over the following eight years. Citing population pressure, employment pressure, unstable development of grain production, increasingly tight supplies of raw materials, and severe shortage of capital, Wu and his group argued that it was necessary not to set hopes too high. During the next eight years, they said, "we will not be able truly to establish the basic framework of the new structure; rather, we will only be able to create the underlying conditions for the eventual establishment of the basic framework of the new structure."[94]

It was thus apparent that China's most influential economists were universally pessimistic about radical price reform in the immediate future, although they differed greatly among themselves about how to implement reform. Also apparent was that a significant number of influential economists, including Liu Guoguang, Wu Shuqing, and the technocrats of the State Planning Commission, were not only pessimistic about price reform but were implicitly criticizing the policy direction being set by Zhao Ziyang. All of them argued for a period of economic stabilization.

Nevertheless, the Politburo meeting that convened on June 1 approved Deng's plans for radical price reform. Ironically, Yao Yilin, the conservative head of the State Planning Commission, was put in charge of drawing up a price reform program. Over the following two months, Yao progressively watered down the proposal for radical price reform until it was devoid of content. While Yao was still engaged in this process, in late July, Chen Yun intervened in the policy-making process by giving a personal instruction to Yao that it was time to "improve" (*zhili*) and "readjust" (*zhengdun*) the economy.[95]

The Beidaihe Meetings

Price reform was the central topic on the agenda for the annual meeting of the CCP leadership at the seaside resort of Beidaihe, which got under way on July 20.[96] Zhao presided over a three-hour-long forum on "the forming and developments of markets" on July 20, and then, in apparent frustration at the hostile reception to his ideas, left the meeting on a tour of the Northeast. He visited Heilongjiang Province from July 22 to 26, and then went to Jilin on July 26, to Shenyang on July 27, and finally returned to Beijing on July 28.[97]

The seaside session was apparently stormy. Only five days before the leadership convened in Beidaihe, Deng had reiterated his strong support of radical price reform: "We are not afraid of stormy waves but will pass all the hurdles braving the wind and the waves."[98] In the face of such statements, conservative leaders could not directly challenge the need for price reform, but they could argue that the economic situation required that its implementation be delayed. As

a result of such arguments, the meetings broke off on July 28 for "further studies."[99] One of the efforts at such "further study" may well have been the Six-
teenth Executive Meeting of the State Council, which convened from August 5
to 9.

There were indications that Deng was seeking a compromise. In an obvious
reference to Deng, the PRC-owned Hong Kong press reported that "one authoritative figure" had declared, "We must be bold and take risks in our reforms but
also stress a scientific approach."[100] The PRC-owned Hong Kong press expressed open concern about this apparent backing away from radical reform. The
Beidaihe meetings, it said, had been "unable to come to any conclusion or draw
up any plan regarding the questions of price reform and economic development."
As a result, "many people are worried whether the orientation of China's reforms
will be affected."[101]

The apparent disruption of the Beidaihe meeting, the concession offered by Deng,
and the State Council executive meeting—which undoubtedly viewed price reform
less benignly—all suggest that fundamental disagreements over policy were taking
their toll. Nevertheless, when the Politburo convened its Tenth Plenary Session in
Beidaihe from August 15 to 17, it issued a surprisingly strong endorsement of price
and wage reform. According to the official Xinhua report of the session, the meeting
declared that "prices and wage reforms are the key to the entire economic reforms"
and called the implementation of such reforms an "all-out intensification" of reform.
The meeting also defined the "general orientation" of price reform as one of "letting
the state control the prices of a few important commodities and labor services and
decontrolling the prices of the majority of commodities and subjecting them to market
regulation"—a formulation that echoed the one set out by Zhao Ziyang two months
earlier in his speech on the establishment of the new order of the socialist commodity
economy.[102]

Unfortunately, the report of the Politburo meeting in *People's Daily* did not
reflect the reality. In fact, there was no price reform program. Yao Yilin had
diluted the program to the point at which it called only for the readjustment of a
few prices over a period of two to three years.[103] Moreover, the Beidaihe meeting made the enactment of radical reform of any sort impossible by ordering the
Central Finance and Economic Leading Group to cease functioning, thus depriv-
ing Zhao of his only institutional control over the economy.[104]

From Reform to Readjustment

Within two weeks after the Politburo's apparent endorsement of radical price
reform, policy turned sharply toward a series of retrenchment measures designed
to control inflation. The critical shift came at the August 30 meeting of the State
Council. That meeting played down the importance of price reform, declaring
that it was a "long-term goal" that could be attained only "after strenuous efforts
of five years or a little longer." In contrast to the Politburo's emphasis on reform

measures for 1989 being of vital significance, the State Council said that the steps to be taken toward price reform in 1989 would be "not large." The primary goal, it said, would be to make the increase in prices "obviously lower" than in 1988. In addition, it reiterated the slogan of "stabilizing the economy and deepening reform"—the slogan Li Peng had advanced the previous December.[105] In was not until September 2 that a meeting of the Politburo Standing Committee endorsed these price-stabilization measures.[106]

The shift within two weeks from the endorsement of radical price reform to the adoption of measures for economic stabilization marked the most dramatic reversal of official policy in the Dengist period. It was brought about by the wave of bank withdrawals and panic buying that swept China in August, following the Politburo's announcement of comprehensive price reform. As one report put it, the Politburo's announcement had been "misunderstood"; fearing rapid price increases, people withdrew their money from banks and rushed to purchase durable consumer goods as a hedge against inflation.[107]

The Central Work Conference and the Third Plenum

A seven-day Central Work Conference was held from September 15 to 21; the decision to convene such a meeting was apparently taken at the Tenth Plenary Session of the Politburo in August.[108] Zhao Ziyang chaired the session, and Yao Yilin gave an explanation of the "price reform" scheme, which was really the plan for economic stabilization.[109] According to one report, "one relatively unanimous view" expressed at the work conference was that inflation had to be brought down. Clearly criticizing the approach of Zhao Ziyang, this view held that "in the past some held the view that a mild degree of inflation could stimulate production, but the practice of the past few years has proved this unworkable." The report stated further that "an important task" of the conference was to determine how the "economic retrenchment scheme" proposed by the State Council at the beginning of September could be "firmed up for every province, municipality, autonomous region, and department."[110]

The ensuing Third Plenary Session of the Thirteenth Central Committee, which convened September 26 to 30, confirmed how radically the policy direction had shifted since the Beidaihe meetings. The communiqué issued by the session declared that the "focus" of reform work for the next two years would be on "reforming the economic environment and rectifying the economic order"—code words for sharply curtailing demand to fight inflation and for cracking down on various commercial abuses that were blamed both for fostering corruption and fueling inflation. Although the communiqué called for paying close attention to enterprise reform in 1989, and particularly to efforts to further separate government administration from enterprise management and improve the contract responsibility system, it also made clear that "all work must be subordinate" to the goal of reducing price increases.[111]

Laying out the intellectual rationale for the adoption of retrenchment policies was Liu Guoguang, who gave a speech entitled "Face Inflation Squarely." Liu's speech apparently stressed that the inflationary situation in 1988 had stemmed from 1986, when monetary controls were loosened after the 1985 retrenchment, and argued that a major downturn in production could be avoided if resources were properly directed to bottleneck areas such as transportation, agriculture, and energy. In order to retrench, Liu was quoted as saying, "we can only rely on intensifying administrative means in this period."[112]

Deng Xiaoping strongly backed the new emphasis on economic stabilization. Having been convinced by the outcry that arose after the panic buying of August, Deng shifted his position radically. Instead of calling for "braving the wind and the waves" as he had in July, he now demanded that the economic situation be stabilized. In his report to the plenum, Zhao cited Deng's "recent" assertion that "macroeconomic control should show that the central authorities mean what they say" and that "we would rather be strict than casual, even if it means that we have to be a bit excessive."[113] Reflecting Deng's new determination to be tough in the face of inflation, a *People's Daily* editorial on September 28 called for relying on the party's "political superiority" (i.e., party discipline) to stabilize the economy.[114]

Zhao's speech to the session—which was not released by Xinhua until a month later—was the least "Zhaoist" speech that Zhao had delivered in recent years, indicating the degree to which he had lost influence over the direction of economic policy. In what may have been a reference to the disputes about inflation and policy that had surfaced at the Second Plenum in February, Zhao said self-critically, "If we had paid close attention to this problem [inflation] early this year, the current situation would have been better. We took note of this problem and tried to tackle it a little too late." More importantly from a policy standpoint was Zhao's admission that the basic assumptions that had guided policy earlier in the year were wrong. "The outstanding problems in economic life," he now declared, "are noticeable inflation and an excessive rise in commodity prices. The root causes for this situation are the overheated economy and aggregate demand outstripping aggregate supply. Aggregate demand has outstripped aggregate supply for years. At a time when new structures are replacing old ones, we still cannot solve this problem by setting up new mechanisms."

In accordance with this revised estimation of the problems facing China, Zhao laid out a series of policy measures—consistent with those already adopted by the State Council—to improve the economic environment and rectify the economic order. Zhao further declared that the dual-track price system, which earlier in the year had been viewed as a primary cause of corruption and which the price reform policy was intended to abolish, "should not be abolished in a short time." His speech did reaffirm the overall goal of reform as stated by the August Politburo meeting—that the prices of a small number of major commodities and labor services should be set by the state while the prices of the overwhelming majority of commodities should be open to market regulation—but postponed efforts to implement this goal. Zhao expressed this by saying, "China's actual situation shows we can only gradually proceed with decontrolling prices and letting the market regulate them."[115]

It was no doubt necessary to adopt retrenchment measures of some sort in the fall of 1988. Deng's price reform program had been ill conceived and ill timed; inflation in the major cities had reached some 30 percent by August, and the panic buying in the latter part of August suggested an economy spiraling out of control. The retrenchment measures adopted in the fall, however, were aimed not merely at restoring price stability but rather at enhancing state control over the economy and "correcting" the imbalances created by reforms. In the eyes of party conservatives, reform policies had created a number of "biases" in the economy: the economy was tilted too far in favor of the coastal provinces; it favored small, non-state enterprises (particularly township and village enterprises) at the expense of large, state-owned enterprises; it was becoming overly dependent on the outside world at the expense of self-reliance (and importing too many goods that competed with China's domestic industries), and it permitted the excessively rapid growth of processing industries, thereby causing bottlenecks in the supply of energy, raw materials, and transportation. Such biases disrupted the balance of the economy and, in the views of conservatives, made "proportional" growth impossible; they also led to large budget deficits and high inflation.[116]

Conservatives also deplored the devolution of authority and the increasingly close connections between local authorities and local enterprises that had evolved in the course of reform and which would later be criticized as the "feudal lord economy" (*zhuhou jingji*). According to this argument, which was not without a basis in reality, economic reform, rather than delegating authority to the enterprises as intended, had delegated it primarily to the localities at the same time that it had given the localities a distinct economic self-interest. This had brought about a condominium of interest between the localities and local enterprises that had led to regional protectionism and politically weakened the ability of the state to exercise control. At the same time, the devolution of authority, combined with an irrational price system that rewarded investment in processing industries while punishing investment in basic industries, created a distorted production structure that exacerbated bottlenecks.[117]

The conservative critique of reform, then, called for reversing the various biases that had emerged in the late 1980s by reducing the growth rate to about 6 percent, reducing inflationary pressures by cutting investment, readjusting the industrial structure through administrative measures and the enforcement of an industrial policy, slowing the growth of village and township enterprises while giving preferential treatment to large and medium-sized state-owned enterprises, and recentralizing to at least some degree economic authority in Beijing.

The adoption of a state industrial policy in March 1989 reflected this conservative agenda and was intended to provide a long-term policy framework for the retrenchment measures that had been adopted the previous fall. Conservative economists had argued for some time that China's industrial structure was distorted in favor of processing industries to the neglect of basic industries. The industrial policy reflected this view in stating that:[118]

> The major problems are excessive production capacity in processing industries and inadequate capacity in the fields of agriculture, energy, raw materials, communications and transport, and other basic industries; excessive production capacity in common processing industries and inadequate capacity in high-level processing industries; irrational industrial layout in regions which cannot make full use of their own advantages; dispersal of industrial organizations; poor centralization in production; a low level of specialization; and poor links and coordination among various enterprises.

In other words, the state's industrial policy was intended to strengthen centralization in industry, bring about a redistribution of China's industrial plant throughout the country, restrict "common" processing, and concentrate on the development of "bottleneck" industries such as energy and transportation. In order to accomplish these goals, the state industrial policy intended to use a combination of financial and administrative means: financial means to direct investment toward critical areas and administrative means to strengthen industrial centralization and restrict the production of oversupplied goods. The intention to rely primarily on administrative measures, rather than market forces, to readjust China's economy was apparent in the policy's declaration that "the State Planning Commission will organize the implementation of, and be responsible for, explaining this decision."[119]

The shift in authority over economic policy from Zhao Ziyang to Li Peng, as head of the State Council, thus brought to the fore a very different conception of economic reform and the role of the state. It is no wonder that reform-minded economists and enterprise managers began to worry aloud about the future of reform. Beijing University economics professor Xiao Zhuoji, for example, warned that government intervention would not solve the problems facing the Chinese economy. He stated that excessive reliance on administrative measures threatened a restoration of the old administrative order, and that such a restoration would further distort prices and exacerbate the gap between supply and demand. The ensuing damage to reform, Xiao said, would be "an even more serious problem to solve than inflation."[120]

Similarly, Li Yining, perhaps predictably, applauded the decision to postpone price reform but warned that retrenchment could lead to stagflation. For Li, the primary problem facing China was not one of excessive demand, as the policy of retrenchment presumed, but one of inadequate supply. Thus, Li warned that "an excessive cut in bank credits will hinder enterprises' normal production and management," leading to a slower growth of supplies and an expanding gap between supply and demand. "We must clearly bear in mind," Li said, "that increasing supply is the basic measure for stabilizing the market," and the basic way to increase supply was to clarify property rights and turn enterprises into economic entities bearing sole responsibility for their profits and losses.[121]

At a forum held at the Capitol Iron and Steel Plant in December 1988, enterprise managers complained that the various decrees of the State Council were taking back powers previously delegated to enterprises and were in violation of the Enterprise Law that was supposed to guarantee the rights of enterprises. They expressed fear that such measures would "control enterprises to death" and that output would decline and financial revenues fall off. "If the center does not quickly correct this," warned the forum, "the highly concentrated old system will be restored and the achievements of reform will be destroyed in a day."[122]

Such fears reflected the enormous political tensions that were building up in the fall and winter of 1988–89. Zhao's loss of authority became evident at the Third Plenum, and there were rumors that he would be replaced as general secretary at the next plenum. In late 1988 and early 1989 a spate of articles appeared extolling Mao Zedong, marking the beginning of a "Mao Zedong craze" (*Mao Zedong re*). The newfound popularity of Mao was a complex social and political movement that combined popular rejection of the contemporary leadership with conservative condemnations of reformers.[123] In December, a conversation between the political theorist Yan Jiaqi and Wen Yuankai, a well-known scientist and reform thinker at the University of Science and Technology, expressed the sense of frustration and fear for the future shared by many intellectuals:[124]

> Wen: China's reform currently faces three choices. The first is to stop and await our fate. But if reform stops, then it will sink deeper and deeper into a bog. The second choice, which is what it appears we are currently doing, is to "back up the car," hoping to back out of the bog and find a new way out. . . . We have already seen Poland and Czechoslovakia retreat for several years and try to start out again from the original starting point. This is frightful. What I am currently exploring is the third choice, whether it is possible to keep going forward, go through the crisis and get out of the bog so that the words "deepening the reform" do not become empty. I worry that the current readjustment, "improving the economic environment and rectifying the economic order," will completely wash out "deepening of reform."

> Yan: I believe a major problem facing China is that we cannot again allow the sort of improper use of power that led to the removal of Khrushchev and Liu Shaoqi. . . . The reason that people feel that China is currently in a crisis is related to this understanding. . . . At that time, some people extended [criticism] of "Hai Rui Dismissed from Office" to Peng Zhen to Liu Shaoqi, resulting in the "Great Cultural Revolution." At present, some people want to extend such a little thing as [the criticism of the highly controversial television series] River Elegy, thus causing a large storm."

The fears of Yan and Wen would prove to be all too well founded. In particular, Yan's intimation that Zhao Ziyang would be removed as Liu Shaoqi had been two decades earlier seemed to reflect, perhaps unintentionally, his sense that the CCP's tradition of merciless struggle was about to be engaged once again. Conflict over economic policy was central in driving China's political leadership to the edge of the abyss; with the development of the student and popular movement in the spring of 1989, conflict within the party became irreconcilable. Then the logic of total victory took over, with tragic results for the people of China.[25]

Notes

1. Ding Wang, " 'Fei ma' yu 'shou ma' zhi zheng" (The Struggle Between "De-Marxification" and "Holding onto Marxism"), *Chao liu*, no. 2 (April 15, 1987), p. 30; and Zhou Zuyou, "Peng Zhen Inspects Zhejiang University," *Renmin ribao*, January 30, 1986, p. 1.

2. In his closing remarks to the session of the Standing Committee, Peng stated that "all legislation should be in accordance with the Constitution" and that "laws must not contradict each other"—an apparent reference to the provision of the Constitution that states that "citizens of the People's Republic of China have the right as well as the duty to work," See Xinhua, September 5, 1986, trans. FBIS, September 8, 1986, pp. K1–2. On the Secretariat's backing, see "The Bankruptcy System May First Be Carried Out in Enterprises," *Renmin ribao*, Commentator, August 28, 1986, pp. 1, trans. FBIS, September 2, 1986, pp. K16–17.

3. Peng Zhen, "Speech at the Joint Group Meeting of the Eighteenth Session of the NPC Standing Committee Discussing the 'Resolution of the Communist Party of China on the Guiding Principles for Building a Socialist Spiritual Civilization," Xinhua, November 26, 1986, trans. FBIS, December 1, 1986, pp. K9–13.

4. Cited in Ding Wang, " 'Fei ma' yu 'shou ma' zhi zheng."

5. Ruan Ming, *Deng Xiaoping diguo*, p. 206.

6. *Guangming ribao*, April 5, 1987, p. 1. See also Liu Ming, "Zhonggong baoshou shili paochu zuoqing gangling" (The Conservative Forces of the CCP Throw Out a Leftist Program), *Ching-pao yueh-k'an*, no. 6 (June, 1987), pp. 34–38.

7. Ruan Ming, *Deng Xiaoping diguo*, pp. 206–207.

8. Bao Tong, "The Young Horse of Socialism, the Old Horse of Capitalism, and Other Related Matters," *Renmin ribao*, January 5, 1987, p. 5, trans. FBIS, January 13, 1987, pp. K9–13.

9. Chen Junsheng, "Uphold the Four Cardinal Principles in the Course of Reform and Opening," Xinhua, January 11, 1987, trans. FBIS, January 12, 1987, pp. K12–21.

10. According to Ruan Ming, Deng Liqun drafted a version of Document No. 4, but Zhao's secretary, Bao Tong, drafted an alternate version, which Zhao sent to Deng Xiaoping for approval before presenting it to the Secretariat. Ruan Ming, *Deng Xiaoping diguo*, pp. 204–205.

11. Zhongguo xinwen she, November 4, 1987, trans. FBIS, November 4, 1987, p. 2.

12. *Wen wei po*, August 25, 1987, reported that there had been about a two-month hiatus in the work of political structural reform. See FBIS, August 25, 1987, p. 6.

13. Xinhua, March 15, 1987, trans. FBIS, March 16, 1987, p. K4.

14. Xinhua, March 19, 1987, trans. FBIS, March 23, 1987, p. J3.

15. See the report on the meeting in *Guangming ribao*, May 23, 1987, p. 1.

16. "In an Internal Speech, He Jingzhi Calls for Vigilance Against Carrying Out the Antiliberalization Drive in a Superficial Way," *Chiu-shi nien-tai*, no. 6 (June 1, 1987), pp. 28–29, trans. FBIS, June 15, 1987, pp. K9–12.

17. "In an Internal Speech, Xiong Fu Talks on the Integration of Literature and Art Circles and Other Circles in Practicing 'Liberalization'," *Chiu-shih nien-tai*, no. 6 (June 1, 1987), pp. 30–32, trans. FBIS, June 9, 1987, pp. K7–11.

18. Chen Tean, "Deng Xiaoping Meets Guerra, Points Out that China's First Goal of Construction May Be Reached Ahead of Schedule," *Renmin ribao*, May 1, 1987, p. 1, trans. FBIS, May 1, 1987, p. G3. AFP, April 30, 1987, FBIS, May 4, 1987, p. G2.

19. Zhao's speech was not published immediately, but the main points were incorporated in a pair of *Renmin ribao* editorials that appeared on May 17 and 22. Zhao's speech was later published by *Renmin ribao* on July 9. See "Speech at a Meeting of Propaganda, Theoretical, Press, and Party School Cadres," Xinhua, July 8, 1987, trans. FBIS, July 8, 1987, pp. K1–8.

20. Xinhua, May 23, 1987, trans. FBIS, May 26, 1987, p. K2.

21. Xinhua, June 9, 1987, trans. FBIS, June 11, 1987, p. K4.

22. "Place the Reform of the Political Structure on the Agenda," *Renmin ribao*, Editorial, trans. FBIS, July 1, 1987, pp. K1–3.

23. Song Chun, Wen Li, Liu Heng, and Jing Guiliang, "Duli hesuan gongye qiye kuisun yuanyin" (The Reasons Industrial Enterprises with Independent Accounting Incur Deficits), pp. 56–60.

24. Fang Weizhong and Wu Jiajun, eds., *Gongye qiye kuisun diaocha yanjiu* (Investigation and Study of Losses in Industrial Enterprises), p. 1.

25. Li Shiyi and Gao Qinglin, "The Keynote of China's Economic Reform This Summer—Large and Medium-Sized State Enterprises Begin to Implement the Contract System," *Liaowang*, Overseas Edition, no. 24 (June 15, 1987), pp. 3–4, trans. JPRS-CAR–87–023 (July 22, 1987), pp. 27–31. Emphasis added.

26. "Regulations Governing the Work of Factory Directors of State-Owned Industrial Enterprises," "Work Regulations for Grass-Roots Organizations of the CPC in State-Owned Industrial Enterprises," and "Regulations on Workers' Congresses of State-Run Industrial Enterprises," All three regulations were adopted on September 15, 1986, and went into effect on October 1, 1986. They were, however, not published by Xinhua until January 11, 1987. The first two are translated in FBIS, February 4 and 5, 1987, and the third is translated in JPRS-CEA–87–019 (March 16, 1987).

27. That different party leaders interpreted the documents quite differently is apparent from the following statements. According to Deng Liqun, "The plant director responsibility system does not mean that our party no longer controls the cadres," In contrast, Yuan Baohua, the vice director of the State Economic Commission, stated that "the director is fully responsible for the enterprise. He is responsible not only for building the material foundation but also the spiritual foundation of the enterprise. Furthermore, the director exercises decision-making power and directing power by himself," See Wan Maohua, "Deng Liqun Expresses Views on Hunan's Two Civilizations," *Hunan ribao*, trans. JPRS-CPS–87–013 (March 26, 1987), p. 131; and Beijing Radio, August 25, 1987, trans. FBIS, August 26, 1987, p. 18.

28. Du Haiyan, "Chengbaozhi: guoyou qiye tizhi gaige de chushi xuanze" (The Contract Responsibility System: An Initial Choice for the Restructuring of State Enterprises), *Jingji yanjiu*, no. 10 (October 20, 1987), pp. 10–18.

29. Author's interviews. Hu's speech was not publicized in the Chinese media, but extensive coverage of the experience of Capitol Iron and Steel reflected Hu's push. See Dong Kenong and Zhang Zhongwen, "The Way Must Not Be Blocked—Second in a Series of Reports on the Capitol Iron and Steel Company," *Guangming ribao*, December

22, 1982, p. 2, trans. FBIS, January 6, 1983, pp. K2–4; idem., "A Trench—Third in a Series of Reports on the Capitol Iron and Steel Company," *Guangming ribao*, December 25, 1982, p. 2, trans. FBIS, January 6, 1983, pp. K4–5; Wu Xinmin, "For the Workers to Become Masters of the House Is the Key to Creating a New Situation in an Enterprise—Zhou Guanwu, Party Secretary of the Capitol Iron and Steel Company, Talks About the Economic Responsibility System," *Gongren ribao*, December 24, 1982, pp. 1, 2, trans. FBIS, January 6, 1983, pp. K5–8; and "Popularize the Business Responsibility System Adopted by Retail and Service Trades—Third Discussion on Stopping the Practice of 'Eating From the Same Big Pot'," *Renmin ribao*, Editorial, January 20, 1983, p. 1.

30. Shirk, *The Political Logic of Economic Reform in China*, pp. 239–241.

31. Ibid., p. 345; author's interviews.

32. Du Haiyan, "Chengbaozhi: guoyou qiye tizhi gaige de chushi xuanze,"

33. See Zuo Mu's comment that the contract responsibility system has changed the previous relationship between enterprises and their responsible departments from a hierarchical relationship of higher and lower "into a relationship between equal partners in the commodity economy," Zou Mu, "On the Contracted Management Responsibility System," *Renmin ribao*, June 15, 1987, p. 5, trans. FBIS, June 24, 1987, p. K24.

34. Susan Shirk has argued that Zhao's adoption of the contract responsibility system was related to Hu Yaobang's fall from power; that Zhao wanted to take over Hu's clientalist network by promoting the system. I can find no evidence to support this interpretation. Zhao began promoting the contract responsibility system in November 1986, nearly two months before Hu fell.

35. Hubei Radio, November 30, 1986, trans. FBIS, December 22, 1986, p. K24. Before going to Hubei, Zhao, Li, and Deng Liqun had stopped in Hunan, where Deng had told leaders of the Xiangtan Iron and Steel Plant, "You Can Study and Refer to the Experiences of the Capitol Iron and Steel Company," Hunan Radio, November 28, 1986, trans. FBIS, December 22, 1986, p. K22.

36. Li Shiyi and Gao Qinglin, "The Keynote of China's Economic Reform This Summer—Large and Medium-Sized State Enterprises Begin to Implement the Contract System.

37. Xinhua, July 17, 1987, trans. FBIS, July 20, 1987, p. K18; and Zhongguo xinwen she, December 8, 1987, trans. FBIS, December 17, 1987, p. 22.

38. Other forms of the contract responsibility system included: (1) Progressive increases in the contract for delivery of profits. Under this system, the amount of taxes an enterprise paid to the state was fixed, but the amount of profits turned over increased annually at a stipulated progressive rate. (2) Percentage sharing of profits in excess of the contracted base figure of profits (or taxation target) for delivery to the state. Under this system, a base figure for profits to be handed over to the state was set; profits in excess of this base figure would then be divided on á percentage basis. (3) Profit contracting or loss contracting by enterprises making small profits or incurring outright losses. (4) Industries and trades contracting for input and output. Under this system, the state set the level of retained profits and investment requirements and allowed the enterprises to carry them out. This system was adopted in eight industries and trades: petroleum, coal, petrochemicals, metallurgy, nonferrous metals, railroads, posts and telecommunications, and civil aviation. In addition, experiments were being conducted in six cities and towns in the enterprise operation responsibility system. Under this system, enterprises paid a tax of 55 percent on their "basic profit," Profits in excess of this figure were taxed at a reduced 30 percent rate. See Lu Dong, "Chengbao jingying shi gaohuo dazhongxing qiye de youxiao tujing" (Operation on a Contract Basis Is an Effective Way to Invigorate Large and Medium-Sized Enterprises), *Hongqi*, no. 9 (May 1, 1987), pp. 21–24; and Zou Mu, "On the Contracted Management Responsibility System.

39. The asset responsibility system was apparently first tried out in Wuhan in November 1986. See Xinhua, November 13, 1986, trans. FBIS, November 14, 1986, pp. 4–5. According to Lu Dong, in 1987 the asset-responsibility system was being implemented on an experimental basis in several factories in Shenyang and Chongqing. See Lu Dong, "Operation on a Contract Basis Is an Effective Way to Invigorate Large and Medium-Sized Enterprises."

40. Yu Guangyuan, "My Views on the Contract System," *Shijie jingji daobao*, October 5, 1987, p. 10, trans. FBIS, October 28, 1987, p. 31. Yu delivered this speech at a forum on the theory and practice of the contract responsibility system held at the Capitol Iron and Steel Plant on August 31, 1987.

41. Wu Jinglian, "Guanyu gaige zhanlue xuanze de ruogan sikao," pp. 3–14.

42. See, for instance, He Jianzhang, "Seriously Improve and Develop the Contract System," *Jingji yanjiu*, no. 4 (April 1989), pp. 28–36, trans. JPRS-CAR–89–083 (August 9, 1989), pp. 8–17; Yang Peixin, "On Upholding and Perfecting the Enterprise Contract System," *Jingji yanjiu*, no. 3 (March 1990), pp. 44–50, trans. JPRS-CAR–90–048 (July 5, 1990), pp. 48–54; and Zhou Guanwu, "On the Contract System," *Jingji quanli*, no. 3 (March 1986), pp. 6–10, trans. JPRS-CEA–86–066 (June 4, 1986), pp. 22–30.

43. *Jingjixue zhoubao*, January 5, 1986, p. 4. This report was subsequently expanded and published in two parts in *Jingji yanjiu*. The first part was called "Transfer of the Economic Operational Model—Problems and Train of Thought on Further Reforming the Economic System" and the second part was called "The Reconstruction of the Microeconomic Base—More on Problems and Train of Thought on Further Reforming the Economic System," See *Jingji yanjiu*, no. 2 (February 1986), pp. 3–11, and no. 3 (March 1986), pp. 21–28, respectively. At the time, according to *Jingji yanjiu*, Hua Sheng and He Jiacheng were at CASS's Economics Institute; Zhang Xuejun was with the Economic Readjustment Office of the State Council; Luo Xiaopeng was with the Rural Development Research Center of the State Council; and Yong Bianzhuang was with CASS's Financial, Trade, and Material Economic Research Institute. Their ideas were later expanded into book form. See Enterprise Structure Group of the Chinese Academy of Social Sciences, *Zichan jingying zerenzhi* (The Asset Responsibility System). The main authors of this book, according to the note inside the front cover, were He Jiacheng and Du Haiyan. Those who assisted in researching and writing the book were Hua Sheng, Zhang Xuejun, Luo Xiaopeng, Yong Bianzhuang, Guo Jiping, Yuan Gangming, Zhang Xiaomeng, Wang Hongling, Liu Xiaoxuan, and Wei Hui. This is the most comprehensive published discussion of the asset responsibility system.

44. Hua Sheng, He Jiacheng, Zhang Xuejun, Luo Xiaopeng, and Yong Bianzhuang, "The Reconstruction of the Microeconomic Base—More on Problems and Train of Thought on Further Reforming the Economic System," *Jingji yanjiu*, no. 3 (March 1986), pp. 21–28, trans. JPRS-CEA–86–073 (June 17, 1986), pp. 16–29.

45. Ibid., p. 18.

46. Hua Sheng, He Jiacheng, Zhang Xuejun, Luo Xiaopeng, and Yong Bianzhuang, "Transfer of Economic Operational Model—Problems and Train of Thought on Further Reforming the Economic System," *Jingji yanjiu*, no. 2 (February 1986), pp. 3–11, trans. JPRS-CEA–86–068 (June 9, 1986), pp. 1–17.

47. This argument stirred great controversy in China, and after Tiananmen, it evoked vehement condemnation. An early indication of the controversy was published in *Hongqi* in May 1987. Feng Baoxing, who was with the Jilin Provincial Economic and Technological Research Center, noted that "some comrades" thought that the contracting party should be entrepreneurs and business executives, while others believed that contracts should be undertaken collectively by enterprise staff and workers. Sharply rejecting the former position, Feng writes, "the view that there should be a separate class of entrepre-

neurs with their own special interests and that these interests should be independent of the interests of the state, that is, the owner of the enterprises' property and assets, and those of enterprise staff and workers is questionable as far as the nature of the system of ownership by the whole people is concerned," See Feng Baoxing, "Dui chengbao jingying zerenzhi jige wenti de tantao" (Discussing Several Questions Concerning the Contract Management Responsibility System), *Hongqi*, no. 10 (May 16, 1987), pp. 25–28.

48. Dai Yuqing, "Chongfen renshi chengbao zerenshi de yiyi; guojia jingwei qingnian jingji yanjiu xiaozu zuzhang Ren Kelei tong jizhe tanhua" (State Economic Commission's Young Economists Research Group Leader Ren Kelei Interviewed on Significance of Contract Responsibility System), *Renmin ribao*, August 7, 1987, p. 2.

49. Xinhua, December 18, 1987, trans. FBIS, December 21, 1988, pp. 20–21.

50. On the origins of the idea of the great international cycle, see Li Delai, "Xin de zhongda xuanze" (A New and Important Decision), *Jingji ribao*, January 5, 1988, p. 1; and Wang Jian, "Develop an Externally Oriented Economy to Speed Up the Transformation of Our Industrial Structure," *Zhongguo qinggongye jingji*, no. 4 (April 1988).

51. Liu Jui-shao, "Why Is There 'Secrecy' Over Zhao Ziyang's Inspections?" *Wen wei po*, February 25, 1988, p. 2, trans. FBIS, February 25, 1988, p. 11.

52. Zhongguo xinwen she, January 7, 1988, trans. FBIS, January 11, 1988, p. 27.

53. Ibid.

54. Author's interviews; Ruan Ming, *Deng Xiaoping diguo*, p. 218.

55. Author's interviews.

56. Ibid.

57. Xinhua, January 22, 1988, trans. FBIS, January 25, 1988, p. 10. It should be noted that following Zhao's trips to the south, he wrote a 12,000 character report entitled "The Question of Strategy for Economic Development of the Coastal Regions," which was approved by Deng Xiaoping on January 23, 1988. Deng wrote on Zhao's report, "I fully agree. We must in particular pursue this with great boldness and speed up our pace; we must not bungle this chance," See *Ta kung pao*, March 1, 1988, p. 1, trans. FBIS, March 1, 1988, p. 10.

58. Economic Institute, Chinese Academy of Social Science, "Zhongguo jingji tizhi zhongqi (1988–1995) gaige shexiang" (The Midterm Reform [1988–1995] of China's Economic Structure).

59. These views are summarized in Cheng Wanquan, "Wujia shangzhang de yuanyin ji pingyu wujia de duice" (Causes of Commodity Price Rises and Measures for Stabilizing Commodity Prices), *Renmin ribao*, April 8, 1988, p. 4. Cheng's focus on the reason for price increases in foodstuffs was because 65 percent of China's 1987 inflation rate of 7.2 percent was attributed to the increase in food costs. See Cheng Xiaonong and Huang Yuncheng, "Price, Income, and Inflation," *Jingji yanjiu*, no. 5 (May 1988), pp. 3–9, trans. JPRS-CAR–88–039 (July 22, 1988), pp. 31–38. See also Zhao Ziyang, "Report to the Second Plenary Session of the Thirteenth Party Congress," *Renmin ribao*, March 21, 1988, trans. FBIS, March 21, 1988, p. 21. In addition to economic reasons, some intellectuals attributed inflation to the lack of political democracy, which they believed permitted the abuse of power that drove prices up. For instance, Su Shaozhi and Wang Yizhou asked rhetorically, "Who has the capability of pushing up the price levels in our entire economic life by such a large margin and on such a large scale?" In their view, "Only those medium and large state-owned enterprises and the so-called 'government profiteers,' who are supported by the administrative bureaucratic system, and possess a large quantity of resources and information can do so, because their products, product mix, and productive capability can influence the entire society and economy," Similarly, Fang Gongwen, deputy editor-in-chief of *Guangming ribao*, stated that "the most important reason for inflation was that party organizations and governments at all levels have lacked

democracy in their work, and that we have lacked mechanisms for exercising control over power," See Su Shaozhi and Wang Yizhou, "Crisis and Thought—On the Current Situation and Next Step of Reform in China," *Shijie jingji daobao*, October 24, 1988, p. 7, trans. FBIS, November 15, 1988; and *Ta kung pao*, December 25, 1988, p. 1, trans. FBIS, December 29, 1988.

60. He Jiacheng and Zhang Xuejun, "China's Economic Situation in 1987," *Shijie jingji daobao*, February 8, 1988, p. 3, trans. FBIS, March 4, 1988, pp. 21–23. This article cites the theory of periodic fluctuations in agriculture developed by Cheng Xiaonong, making clear the authors' acceptance of his explanation of inflationary pressures in 1987.

61. *Renmin ribao*, March 21, 1988, trans. FBIS, March 21, 1988, pp. 20–21.

62. Chuang Ming, "Zhao Ziyang wei jian xin zhixu tichu shitiao" (Zhao Ziyang Raises Ten Points for Creating a New Order), *Ching-pao yueh-k'an*, no. 7 (July 1988), p. 25.

63. In a typical year, several tens of billions of yuan normally returned to the treasury between February and May. Between January and April 1987, however, only some 20 million yuan had returned (*hui long*) to the treasury, and in May the state issued some 4 billion yuan of currency (in May 1986 the state had recovered 7.5 billion yuan). Ibid., p. 23.

64. Ibid., p. 24.

65. Economic Situation Analysis Group of the Economic Institute, Chinese Academy of Social Sciences, "Near-Term Measures for Freeing Reform from Its Current Difficulties," *Jingji yanjiu*, no. 7 (July 1989), pp. 3–12.

66. "Qian Jiaju Discusses Prices, Reform, and Social Mood," *Wen wei po*, April 4, 1988, trans. FBIS, April 12, 1988, p. 39.

67. Author's interviews.

68. Li Tieying conveyed this message to the State Commission for Economic Structural Reform on May 7, 1988. See Xiaonong Cheng, "A Radical Reform and Its Miscarriage in the Summer of 1988."

69. *Renmin ribao*, May 16, 1988, p. 1.

70. Xiaonong Cheng writes that there was a meeting of the Politburo in mid-May that adopted several points on economic reform but failed to address the issue of radical price reform. See Xiaonong Cheng, "A Radical Reform and Its Miscarriage in the Summer of 1988."

71. *Renmin ribao*, May 20, 1988, p. 1.

72. *Renmin ribao*, June 4, 1988, p. 1.

73. Li Tieying, who actively supported Deng's approach to price reform and may have been critical in persuading Deng to adopt it, believed that price reform could form a perfect market economy without private ownership. See Xiaonong Cheng, "A Radical Reform and Its Miscarriage in the Summer of 1988."

74. On new authoritarianism, see Stanley Rosen and Gary Zou, "The Road to Modernization in China Debated: The Origins, Development and Decline of the Neoauthoritarianism and Direct Democracy Schools."

75. Author's interviews.

76. Xiaonong Cheng notes that Li Tieying spoke to young economists about comprehensive price reform twice in late March and early April. Deng apparently first advocated price reform in a meeting with Li on May 5, and it was Li who relayed Deng's comments to the State Commission on Economic Structural Reform on May 7. See Xiaonong Cheng, "A Radical Reform and Its Miscarriage in the Summer of 1988."

77. The PRC-owned Hong Kong paper *Wen wei po* originally declared that the session was an "enlarged meeting of the Politburo" and went on to point out that "it is relatively rare" for the CCP to convene such a meeting, the previous such meeting being the one on January 16, 1987, that accepted Hu Yaobang's resignation. That report also stated that the session was to be a two-day affair, suggesting that it was later extended. Two days later, *Wen wei po* reported that the meeting was originally convened as an

enlarged meeting of the Politburo, but that some people later felt that, because of the comparison to the Hu Yaobang affair, to designate the meeting as such would "strain the atmosphere," See Liu Jui-shao, "Enlarged Meeting of the CCP Political Bureau Decides on Tough Action on Prices and Other Problems," *Wen wei po*, May 31, 1988, p. 1, trans FBIS, May 31, 1988, p. 19; and Liu Jui-shao, "A Meeting at a Crucial Moment—An Insider Account on the CCP Central Committee Political Bureau Meeting," *Wen wei po,* June 2, 1988, trans. FBIS, June 2, 1988, p. 31.

78. Chuang Ming, "Zhao Ziyang wei jian xin zhixu tichu shitiao," pp. 22–27.

79. *Renmin ribao*, June 2, 1988, p. 1.

80. Chuang Ming, "Zhao Ziyang wei jian xin zhixu tichu shitiao," pp. 22–27.

81. As the *Ching-pao yueh-k'an* account of Zhao's speech notes, inflation in May 1988 had already reached 18 percent, making Zhao's prediction of a 50 percent increase over five years rather optimistic.

82. Chuang Ming, "Zhao Ziyang wei jian xin zhixu tichu shitiao," p. 25.

83. Ibid., p. 26.

84. Ibid., p. 27.

85. Author's interviews.

86. Xinhua, June 23, 1988, trans. FBIS, June 27, 1988, p. 37. Emphasis added.

87. "Zhao Ziyang Talks About Price Reform in Liaoning," *Wen wei po*, August 3, 1988, p. 1, trans. FBIS, August 3, 1988, p. 9.

88. Although the published account in *Renmin ribao* does not make this clear, Deng apparently was explicit that a decision to move ahead with radical price reform had already been made. See Xiaonong Cheng, "A Radical Reform and Its Miscarriage in the Summer of 1988."

89. State Commission for Economic Structural Reform, *Zhongguo gaige da silu* (Major approaches to Chinese Reform). For an abridged translation, see Joseph Fewsmith, ed. and trans., "China's Midterm Economic Structural Reform, 1988–1995," *Chinese Law and Government*, vol. 22, no. 4 (Winter 1989–90).

90. Fewsmith, ed. and trans., "China's Midterm Structural Reform, 1988–1995," p. 27.

91. Ibid., pp. 45–52.

92. Ibid., pp. 60 and 62.

93. Ibid., p. 98.

94. Ibid., p. 75.

95. Xiaonong Cheng, "A Radical Reform and Its Miscarriage in the Summer of 1988."

96. Cheng Hsiang, "Beidaihe Conference Begins Today and Prices and Wages Are the Focus of Discussion," *Wen wei po*, July 20, 1988, p. 2, trans. FBIS, July 20, 1988.

97. Liu Jui-shao, "Viewing the Beidaihe Meeting in Light of Zhao Ziyang's Activities," *Wen wei po*, August 5, 1988, p. 1, trans. FBIS, August 5, 1988; and Heilongjiang Radio, July 26, 1988, trans. FBIS, August 1, 1988, p. 50.

98. *Renmin ribao*, July 16, p. 1.

99. Liu Jui-shao, "Beidaihe Conference Said to Have Concluded a Few Days Ago," *Wen wei po*, August 1, 1988, p. 1, trans. FBIS, August 1, 1988, pp. 29–30.

100. Ibid.

101. Liu Jui-shao, "Will China's Reforms Be Affected?—Thoughts on the Beidaihe Conference," *Wen wei po*, August 2, 1988, p. 1, trans. FBIS, August 2, 1988, p. 8.

102. *Renmin ribao*, August 24, 1988, p. 1.

103. Xiaonong Cheng, "A Radical Reform and Its Miscarriage in the Summer of 1988."

104. Author's interviews.

105. *Renmin ribao*, August 31, 1988, p. 1.

106. *South China Morning Post*, September 3, 1988, p. 1, trans. FBIS, September 6, 1988, p. 36.

107. Bao Xin, "Improve the Economic Environment for Reform, Straighten Out the Economic Environment," *Liaowang*, Overseas Edition, September 12, 1988, p. 1, trans. FBIS, September 21, 1988, pp. 28–29. See also "Bayue de qishi" (Enlightenment Gained in August), *Liaowang*, Commentator, no. 39, September, 26, 1988, p. 1, trans. FBIS, October 3, 1988; and AFP, September 21, 1988, trans. FBIS, September 21, 1988, p. 24.

108. Bao Xin, "Improve the Economic Environment for Reform, Straighten Out the Economic Environment."

109. Ibid.

110. Cheng Hsiang, "Central Work Conference Underway in Beijing," *Wen wei po*, September 19, 1988, p. 2, trans. FBIS, September 19, 1988, p. 20.

111. "Communiqué of the Third Plenary Session of the Thirteenth CCP Central Committee," Xinhua, September 30, 1988, trans. FBIS, September 30, 1988, pp. 18–19.

112. *Ming pao*, January 27, 1989, p. 8, trans. FBIS, September 19, 1988, p. 20.

113. Zhao Ziyang, "Report to the Third Plenary Session of the Thirteenth CCP Central Committee," Xinhua, September 26, 1988, trans. FBIS, October 28, 1988, pp. K1–8.

114. "Give Play to Our Political Superiority," *Renmin ribao*, Editorial, September 28, 1988, p. 1, trans. FBIS, September 28, 1988, pp. 29–30. The importance of this editorial is indicated by the fact that it was issued while the Third Plenum was still in session, something that is highly unusual.

115. Zhao Ziyang, "Report to the Third Plenary Session of the Thirteenth CCP Central Committee."

116. Many conservative critiques of the economy appeared in the months following Tiananmen. See, for instance, Problem Group of the Research Center of the State Planning Commission, "Tizhi zhuanhuan shiqi de hongguan tiaokong" (Macroeconomic Regulation and Control in the Period of Structural Transformation), *Jingji yanjiu*, no. 5 (May 1989), pp. 11–21; Wang Mengkui, "Dangqian jingji xingshi he xuyao yanjiu de yixie wenti" (The Present Economic Situation and Some Problems That Need to Be Studied), *Jingji yanjiu*, no. 12 (December 1989), pp. 23–30; and Dai Yuanchen, "Baochi shidu jingji zengzhanglu he caiqu 'gonggei lue dayu xuqiu' de fan zhouqi duice" (Maintain an Appropriate Rate of Economic Growth and Adopt the Counter Cyclical Policy of "Supply Being a Little Greater than Demand"), *Jingji yanjiu*, no. 11 (November 1989), pp. 3–13.

117. See, for instance, Wang Huning, "Zhongguo bianhua zhong de zhongyang he difang zhengfu de guanxi: zhengzhi de hanyi" (The Changing Relations Between the Central and Local Governments: The Political Implications), *Fudan xuebao*, no. 5 (May 1988), pp. 1–8; and Shen Liren and Dai Yuanchen, "Woguo 'zhuhou jingji' de xingcheng ji qi biduan he genyuan" (The Formation of the "Feudal-Lord" Economy in China: Its Origins and Harm), *Jingji yanjiu*, no. 3 (March 1990), pp. 12–19, 67.

118. *Renmin ribao*, March 18, 1989, pp. 4, 5, trans. FBIS, March 31, 1989, p. 40.

119. Ibid., p. 44.

120. *Shijie jingji daobao*, September 26, 1988, p. 14; and *Shijie jingji daobao*, November 21, 1988, p. 2.

121. Li Yining, "Deepening Reform and Increasing Supply Is a Basic Measure for Stabilizing the Market," *Renmin ribao*, September 16, 1988, p. 5, trans. FBIS, September 29, 1988, pp. 38–41.

122. *Shijie jingji daobao*, December 26, 1988, p. 14.

123. See, for instance, Zhang Yufeng's reminiscences of Mao's later years, which appeared in eleven parts starting on December 26, Mao's birthday, in *Guangming ribao*, trans. FBIS, January 27, 1989, pp. 16–19; and January 31, 1989, pp. 30–37. See also Wang Lingshu, "Ji Dengkui on Mao Zedong," *Liaowang*, Overseas Edition, nos. 6–7 (February 6–13, 1989), trans. FBIS, February 14, 1989, pp. 22–26; and Ye Yonglie's controversial interview with Wang Li, "Wang Li bing zhong da ke wen" (Wang Li, Who Is Ill, Answers His Guest's Questions), *Ta kung pao*, January 3, 4, 5, 6, and 7, 1989.

124. Gao Yu, "Zhongguo ruhe du nanguan, gaige chulu zai nali?—Yan Jiaqi yu Wen Yuankai de duihua" (How Can China Pass the Difficult Gate, Where Is the Way Out for Reform?—A Conversation Between Yan Jiaqi and Wen Yuankai), *Ching-pao yueh-k'an*, no. 12 (December 1988), pp. 18–24.

125. The way in which the protest movement interacted with leadership politics is superbly analyzed by Tsou in "The Tiananmen Tragedy."

Conclusion: Reflections on Chinese Politics in the Era of Reform

The preceding chapters, which have traced the emergence and development of economic ideas and policies in the late 1970s and 1980s, have demonstrated the complexity of the reform process, a process that encompasses the desires and pressures of society (particularly peasants and enterprises), mid-level political actors (particularly in the case of rural reform), quasi-official policy advisors (such as the Rural Development Group), bureaucratic organs and policy groups (such as the State Planning Commission, the State Economic Structural Reform Commission, and the Economic Structural Reform Institute), and the power considerations of elite actors.

In the Western literature on China in the reform era, there has in recent years been a general tendency to focus on the levels below that of elite politics, either on bureaucratic politics,[1] the provincial leadership and the Central Committee,[2] local politics,[3] or societal interests.[4] These perspectives have benefited from the greater access that Western scholars have enjoyed in China in recent years and have greatly enriched our understanding of the complexity of the political process in China. This study has tried, implicitly at least, to build on the understandings gained in such studies and to link such bureaucratic and societal processes to an understanding of elite politics. One insight gained from this study—and it is certainly not a new one—is the degree to which reform policies are propelled, constrained, and warped by the political dynamic at the top of the regime.

The case for elite politics as central to the reform process is perhaps clearest at the beginning of the reform period. The legitimacy of the Hua Guofeng government was sustained by loyalty to Maoist thought (the "two whatevers"), rapid industrialization via import substitution (the "great leap outward" strategy of the so-called Petroleum Group), and a rural policy that combined the seemingly uncombinable: the Dazhai model of self-reliance with a plan to mechanize agriculture in ten years. It may well be that Deng Xiaoping and the "veteran cadres" group (those purged during the Cultural Revolution) could have ousted Hua and returned to power on the basis of their raw political strength, but it is apparent that they chose not to. Establishing their own legitimacy with a comprehensive ideological and economic program was seen as essential to securing power and presiding over their own preferred policies. Political rivalry and ambition had much to do with the transfer of power during this period (not only the competition between Deng Xiaoping and the wing of the party represented by Hua Guofeng but also that between Chen Yun and the Petroleum Group), but it seems inescapable that power and policy went together.

So frequently do we speak in terms of the "de-Maoification" and "de-ideologization" of the reform period—and there is no question that ideology has held a less central place in the reform period than in the preceding Maoist period—that we neglect the central role that ideological formulations played in the establishment of Dengist rule and in the evolution of politics during the decade and more since the Third Plenum of 1978.

Perhaps the first ideological battle was an implicit one. The rural reforms that Wan Li promoted and protected in Anhui not only undermined the policies advocated by Ji Dengkui and Chen Yonggui, they made an implicit argument about the stage of socialist development in China and the appropriate level of social organization. When raised to an explicit theoretical level—that China was in the stage of "undeveloped socialism" or the "initial stage of socialism"—the proposition was controversial, but when raised at the practical policy level in the form of rural reform, the argument and the results were hard to refute.

Hu Qiaomu's 1978 speech on building the economy in accordance with economic laws was similarly an important ideological statement. Again, it is worth emphasizing that this speech was drawn up not by economists but by Marxist-Leninist theoreticians. They were not only concerned with the economic efficacy of their proposals but also, and primarily, with the ideological defensibility of their proposals. Unless the theoretical revisions they were making could be accepted by the party, there was little hope for reforming the economy even if they had political power.

The best known of the ideological assaults on Hua Guofeng's power—the discussion on practice as the sole criterion of truth—directly tackled Hua's ideological claim to power. Again, the interesting fact is that those who were acting to oust Hua felt that they had to anchor their assault on power in an ideological statement of principles. Raw power was not enough.

Together, the early rural reforms in Anhui, Hu Qiaomu's speech on economics, and the discussion on practice as the sole criterion of truth laid out a full-fledged campaign platform for the incoming Dengist coalition, one that presented a statement of ideological principles and a set of economic policies that would characterize the Dengist period, however debated and battered they came to be in the course of implementation.

Although many economic ideas of the Dengist coalition harkened back to the Eighth Party Congress of 1956 and the early experiments with the household responsibility system, particularly those undertaken in the wake of the Great Leap Forward, one has to wonder how rapidly and how radically reform policies would have been pushed had the Dengists not had to define their own policy preferences in the course of a struggle for power. Certainly the defeat of the "whateverists" cleared the political battlefield for the early implementation of reform.

If elite politics helped define the Dengist program and set the stage for the implementation of the early reforms, it is also apparent that elite competition played an important role in the way reforms were and were not implemented in the course of the 1980s. The most important division in this regard, as discussed in the Introduction, was that between Chen Yun and Deng Xiaoping. In retrospect at least, conflict between the two leaders seems inevitable. Deng was the "core" of the party's leadership, but Chen Yun was the party leader most experienced and most respected for his understanding of economics. Deng, not unlike Mao Zedong before him, sought the rapid development of the economy. The goal of "wealth and power" was a manifestation of Deng's nationalistic passion; modernizing the economy and restoring China to its "rightful" position in the world community would secure Deng's place in China's history and indeed accord him an even higher place than Mao. But Deng's drive for rapid economic development also derived from his need to enhance his own legitimacy. In turning his back on traditional Chinese understandings of Marxism, Deng had to demonstrate that he could produce results. Deng's desire for rapid economic growth, however, conflicted with Chen Yun's long-standing understanding of socialist economic development, which called for continuous and proportional economic growth centered around the state-owned economy.

In reviewing the decade from 1978 to 1989, it is apparent that Chen Yun's and Deng Xiaoping's prestige have waxed and waned in inverse proportion to each other. Whenever economic growth has accelerated, Deng's authority within the political system has waxed strong, and whenever the economy has run into difficulties, Chen Yun's position has become more important. Chen Yun's authority was greatest following the 1980 Central Work Conference that implemented readjustment policies and after the collapse of Deng's ambitious and misguided effort to implement comprehensive price reform in 1988. Deng's authority was at its height in the mid-1980s, particularly in 1984 when there was a record-setting agricultural harvest and the industrial economy grew by an impressive 14 percent. The elaborate National Day celebrations on October 1, 1984, were a paean to Deng Xiaoping, and the student banner that said familiarly "How are you, Xiaoping?" (*Xiaoping, nin hao*) reflected Deng's prestige and authority.

The 1984 "Decision on Economic Structural Reform," as pointed out in Chapter 4, was a watershed in the relations between the two leaders. Prior to that

time, whatever differences existed between them (and there were serious differences over such issues as the SEZs and the hiring of labor), conflict was nevertheless confined within certain limits. The passage of the Third Plenum decision,
with its emphasis on a "planned commodity economy," broke those limits and
accelerated the downward spiral in relations between the conservative and reformist wings of the party.

As pointed out in the previous chapters, there was an important structural
aspect in this division. Chen Yun's bureaucratic strength lay in his control over
the comprehensive ministries of the State Council, particularly the State Planning Commission and the Ministry of Finance. In order to pursue reform, Zhao
Ziyang, clearly with Deng's support, had to find ways of going around such
ministries and curtailing their authority, all the while trying to minimize their
opposition.

Political competition at the top of the system and the array of bureaucratic
structures constrained the options available to Zhao. Reformers had to design
strategies that advanced economic goals, minimized bureaucratic opposition, and
were politically palatable to party elders. It is no wonder that by the late 1980s,
many participants and observers alike felt that the reforms were beset by insolu-
able contradictions; Wen Yuankai's observation that it seemed as if reform had
landed in a bog with no easy way out was shared by reformers and conservatives
alike—though they drew very different conclusions about how to proceed.

One of the mysteries in the development of reform is why Deng Xiaoping
acquiesced in Chen Yun's continued dominance of such bureaucratic centers of
power as the State Planning Commission. From the perspective of an outside
observer, this arrangement appears to have hamstrung Zhao from the outset.
Why would Deng select Zhao as premier but not allow him to dominate the
bureaucratic apparatus that he was nominally in charge of? Perhaps another way
of putting this question is, why did Deng not go the extra step and curtail Chen
Yun's influence?[5]

This is a difficult question that in many ways cuts to the heart of the Chinese
political system. It was apparent by 1984 if not earlier that there were mounting
tensions in the relationship between Deng and Chen. Deng's strategy, however,
appears to have been to curtail progressively Chen's influence but not to precipi-
tate a final split with Chen (what Tsou would call a struggle for total victory).
Many reasons suggest themselves for this "struggle without total victory." One is
certainly that Chen never posed a direct threat to Deng. Chen was willing to
acquiesce in Deng's role as the "core" of the party, apparently because he lacked
the ambition or ability to replace Deng in that role. Chen also never publicly
challenged Deng once Deng had declared his opinion on a matter. In other
words, no matter how much Chen may have disagreed with Deng on one policy
matter or another, Chen always played by the rules of the game as they were
understood by the CCP elite and never precipitated a showdown. In the absence
of such a challenge, Deng had little cause to force Chen's ouster.

A second and perhaps more subtle reason was that Chen and his control over the planning apparatus always provided a "safety valve" that permitted Deng to experiment with more daring and far-reaching reforms. As long as Chen and his supporters were in place, Deng knew that whatever went wrong he could always fall back on the tried and true methods of administrative control. This limited the risks that Deng was taking, even if it undermined the very reform efforts he was making. From Deng's perspective, to oust Chen and his supporters meant giving up the assurance that there was someone who could save the situation if economic problems began to spin out of control.

Third, in terms of exercising power, there were advantages for Deng in a "divide-and-rule" strategy. If Deng had acted decisively against the conservative wing of the party, his own influence in the system would have been reduced because he would not be needed to mediate between conservatives and reformers. Deng, of course, did the same thing with regard to the reform wing of the party by allowing a rivalry between Hu Yaobang and Zhao Ziyang to continue for years.

Finally, one has to consider what Tang Tsou has called "the balance between the marginal utility of the next increment of power and the marginal cost of gaining it";[6] in other words, whether Deng felt that the power he could accrue by ousting Chen was worth the political price he would have to pay to obtain it. In this regard, Deng's calculation that it was not worth the price was undoubtedly correct. A decisive struggle between Chen and Deng would have deeply divided the party and would have had unknowable social ramifications—and would have done so before the scars left over from the Cultural Revolution had healed.

If the political competition between Deng and Chen in the decade following the inauguration of reform can be characterized as an implicit struggle between two lines but nevertheless a struggle without total victory, this does not mean that the party's tradition of struggling for total victory had no influence on the evolution of politics during this period. The competition to define the party line was projected onto the next generation as a struggle for succession developed. Although this struggle was certainly present when Hu Yaobang was general secretary, it developed in earnest after his ouster in January 1987. Zhao Ziyang moved into Hu's position as head of the party, but a clear political rival, Li Peng, took over as premier. With a conservative in place as the head of the State Council, debates over macroeconomic policy became deeply politicized.

It is useful to recall briefly the situation in early 1988 when conservatives, led by Premier Li Peng and Vice Premier Yao Yilin, called for a tightening of macroeconomic control to reduce inflationary pressures. Their appeal, however, was not only for tightening monetary policy; behind it, as Zhao was certainly aware, lay a conservative critique of Zhao's management of the economy and a demand that he yield authority over economic matters to conservatives. Li and Yao were also acting at a time when Zhao had given up the premiership to became general secretary of the CCP. To yield to Li and Yao would rapidly erode what remained of Zhao's authority over the economy; in order to preserve his political position, Zhao took a chance that rapid economic growth would not result in unacceptably high inflation. Perhaps, if Deng had not intervened with the issue of price reform in the spring of 1988, Zhao would have won his gamble.

The point of this example is that the debate over macroeconomic policy was inextricable from the contention for power. By early 1988, conservatives realized clearly the difficulty of Zhao's position, and they acted to put him in a yet more difficult position. Long-standing differences had accumulated; there was a sense that end game was approaching. Zhao could not respond simply to the question of inflationary pressures because macroeconomic policy was politicized. It was necessary to respond first to the political challenge and only then to the economic issue. Li and Yao were not seeking accommodation, they were seeking power.

In the four years since Tiananmen it is apparent that economic reform has continued, suggesting perhaps that the conservatives who sought Zhao's ouster desired something less than "total victory." Although it is not possible here to describe in detail the complex and fascinating political maneuvering in the period that has followed Tiananmen, even a broad sketch of the course of events suggests that the CCP's tradition of seeking total victory remains relevant to an understanding of Chinese politics.

The evidence from the period immediately following Tiananmen suggests that conservatives were able to dominate the economic agenda to a degree they had not been able to achieve since the early 1980s. Their agenda was not, as some commentary in the West held, to return to the supposed golden era of the 1950s, but they did, as suggested at the end of Chapter 7, have a very different vision of economic development. It was not a vision that was completely adverse to economic reform or the use of economic measures—as the conservatives' use of value-guaranteed savings deposits and higher short-term interest rates demonstrated. Nevertheless, the conservative vision clearly called for strengthening the position of the plan vis-à-vis the market, the position of the central authorities vis-à-vis the localities, and the role of large, state-owned industry (which they dubbed the "national team" [guojia dui]) vis-à-vis smaller-scale industry (which was dubbed the "local team" [difang dui]).

Although Zhao Ziyang was made the scapegoat for the difficulties the economy had encountered, there is little question that the target of conservative ire was Deng Xiaoping. Conservatives lacked the power to oust Deng and no doubt lacked the desire to split the party decisively by trying to do so, but they did have the desire to constrain Deng and reduce his authority over the economy. Like skilled players of Chinese chess (weiqi), they occupied positions and tried to deny Deng maneuverability. Following the bloody suppression of the protest movement, Deng's prestige within the party plummeted and conservatives took advantage of his weakened position to dominate economic policy as well as other areas of the polity.

Deng's political retreat was very much reflected in his acquiesence to the conservative economic agenda in the summer of 1989.[7] Only a year after he had been promoting radical price reform, Deng echoed conservative demands for increasing investment in basic enterprises and curtailing the rapid growth of village and township enterprises. On June 9, 1989, in his speech to the martial law troops, Deng said, "I am in favor of putting the emphasis on basic industry and agriculture.... We should work for more electricity, more railway lines, more public roads, and more shipping."[8] A week later, in a speech to the Politburo, Deng yielded to conservative pressures, saying that it was all right to shut down inefficient or wasteful village and township enterprises—the same sector of the economy that he had lauded in 1984 as a "large army appearing suddenly over the horizon."[9]

Deng's statement was clearly a concession to the persisting demands of state-owned industries, which had long complained that they could not compete effectively because township and village industries were vying with them for scarce inputs, thereby increasing their costs. In other words, Deng yielded to conservative demands that state-owned industries be given a breather in which they could catch up.

This policy direction was reinforced in January 1990, when a Production Commission was established under the State Planning Commission to oversee the implementation of a so-called double guarantee system. Under this system the state would guarantee the supply of materials to enterprises in return for their guaranteeing fulfillment of their production tasks, including the payment of profits and taxes to the state as well as the delivering of finished products for unified distribution. First adopted for 50 key enterprises in the heavily industrialized Northeast, the system was soon extended to some 234 key enterprises throughout China.[10]

Another indicator of conservative dominance over China's economic agenda was the boldness with which conservatives felt free to change the wording of Deng's remarks to military commanders on June 9, 1989. Deng had told the commanders, "We should continue to uphold the integration of the planned economy with the market economy." But, when the text of Deng's remarks was published by *People's Daily* on June 28, the term "market economy" had been changed to "market regulation." This change in terminology exactly paralleled the terminology used in 1981 when, at the behest of Chen Yun, the resolution on CCP history was revised to read, "it is necessary to implement a *planned economy* on the basis of the public ownership system, and at the same time bring to bear the role of *market regulation*" (see Chapter 3). It is indeed suggestive of Deng's loss of authority in the period immediately after Tiananmen that he could not get his own remarks released without such a critical revision.[11]

When Jiang Zemin delivered his major address on the eve of China's fortieth anniversary on October 1, 1989, his discussion of the relationship between the "planned economy" and "market regulation" echoed the conservative criticism of reform in the period from 1980 to 1982. Reflecting Chen Yun's approach to the economy, Jiang declared that "the ability to purposefully develop the national economy in a planned and proportionate way is a sign of the superiority of the socialist system and a basic feature of the socialist economy." Accordingly, Jiang emphasized the "proper" centralization of the economy, stressed the guiding role of state plans, and called for prioritizing state investment in accordance with the state plan.[12]

Perhaps the nadir of Deng's influence was reached in the winter of 1989–90. In the fall of 1989, Deng had acquiesced in the adoption of a conservative economic line but worked to minimize conservative ideological rhetoric by stressing that the economy remained the focus of the party's work. Thus, an October 10 editorial in *People's Daily*, apparently intended to set the tone for the impending Fifth Plenary Session of the Thirteenth Central Committee, quoted Deng as saying, "In the case of China, the overriding priority is stability. Without a stable environment, nothing can be accomplished and even our past achievements could be lost." The editorial then went on to define economic work as the "central link," suggesting in good Dengist fashion that economic work is the linchpin of political stability.[13]

It began to look as if Deng might be able to repeat his feat of 1987—again ousting a general secretary, focusing attention on the economy, and regaining the political initiative—but as communism crumbled throughout Eastern Europe, the conservative wing of the CCP began to openly, if still implicitly, challenge Deng's leadership and policy agenda. One of the harshest attacks was launched by Wang Renzhi, head of the Propaganda Department, in a speech to the Central Party School on December 15. In that speech, Wang argued—contrary to Deng's long-standing approach—that stability could only be built on the basis of unified, Marxist ideology; only then could economic construction be accomplished without deviating from the proper socialist orientation. According to Wang:[14]

> Historical experience and harsh reality at home and abroad show us that the existence and rampancy of the ideological trend of bourgeois liberalization is the biggest destabilizing factor. Only by criticizing and struggling against the ideological trend of bourgeois liberalization to enable people to achieve unity in thinking and action on the basis of the party's line will we be able to consolidate and develop the political situation of stability and unity and to promote the smooth development of socialist construction and the smooth implementation of reform.
>
> In other words, economic work could only be accomplished on the basis of a continued and unremitting criticism of bourgeois liberalization.

The frustration and virulent opposition of conservatives to efforts by the Deng Xiaoping wing of the party to refocus attention on economic work was evident in a February 1990 article in *People's Daily* that was reprinted from the conservative literary journal *Literary Theory and Criticism*. The article, written by the conservative literary figure Chen Daixi, accused Zhao Ziyang and his think tanks of using "all kinds of dirty tricks with the most malicious motives" to suppress the Zhuo County meeting in April 1987. However, as discussed in Chapter 7, it was really Deng Xiaoping who had used the meeting in Zhuo County to mount an attack on the "left" and prepare the political atmosphere for the Thirteenth Party Congress. It was thus apparent that the authors were criticizing Deng.[15]

Mounting such a direct, though implicit, challenge to Deng's ability to set China's political agenda was unprecedented in the post-1978 period and reflected Deng's own political weakness in the aftermath of Tiananmen—which was compounded by the demise of communism in Eastern Europe. Moreover, the events of late 1989 and early 1990 make it clear that Deng's political opponents were willing to use the political momentum that they had gained in the wake of Tiananmen to push an economic and political agenda quite distinct from that of Deng's. In short, they worked to undermine Deng's authority, establish a different political line, and thereby secure the succession.

Deng, however, was not willing to acquiesce in his own demise. By the fall of 1990, it was apparent that Deng was fighting back vigorously, though with only limited success. It was only after the failure of the coup in the Soviet Union that Deng was able to decisively shift the balance of forces in Beijing. With his dramatic trip to the Shenzhen SEZ in January 1992, Deng was able to regain the political initiative—though not without meeting considerable opposition from party conservatives. However, by the time the Fourteenth Party Congress met in October, it was evident that Deng had won a tremendous personal victory. The political report of the congress gave unprecedented prominence to Deng Xiaoping's "theory of building socialism with Chinese characteristics" and endorsed his proposal to build a "socialist market economy."[16] In short, elite politics and the effort to defeat opposing views through the articulation of political lines remains important for understanding post-Tiananmen China as it was for comprehending political conflict in the preceding decade.

Now, more than four years after Tiananmen, it is apparent that economic reform in China has regained its momentum (though the very momentum of growth and change is creating new problems). Far from turning back the pages of history, as so many commentators—both Chinese and foreign—feared at the time, economic, social, political, and actuarial forces are driving a pace of change that exceeds in breadth and depth anything seen in the years before Tiananmen. In 1988, approximately 50 percent of China's prices were set by market forces; five years later, that figure has risen to about 80 percent. China's opening to the outside world has not only continued but accelerated as total foreign trade has grown from U.S. $80 billion to U.S. $165 billion in that same five-year period.

The combination of economic reform, economic prosperity, and generational transition is bringing about a transformation of the Chinese political system that promises to exceed any change since the Communist revolution in 1949. There are interesting intimations that the Chinese political system is beginning to respond to the political pressures from below in ways that it has not previously responded in the past four decades. In elections for provincial governor in the winter of 1992–93, for instance, there were at least two instances in which the party-designated candidate was defeated by a nominee of the delegates. The trend of delegate-nominated candidates defeating the party-nominated candidate emerged in 1986 with the revision of the electoral law when several party-nominated candidates were defeated at the deputy-governor level. The defeat of party-nominated candidates for governor, however, marks the first time this assertion of local interests is known to have occurred at such a high level. Similarly, at least some of the delegates to the first session of the Eighth National People's Congress in the spring of 1993 were elected by the delegates to local conferences over the party-designated candidates. A particularly notable example of this sort was the election of Lei Yu, who was party secretary of Hainan at the time of the scandal surrounding the import and resale of tens of thousands of automobiles. In 1991, Lei won election as vice governor of Guangxi province and in early 1993 was elected over the party's choice as a delegate from Guangxi to the Eighth National People's Congress.[17]

Such trends hint at accumulating pressures in the Chinese political system that may result in far more extensive changes as Deng Xiaoping and other elders pass from the scene. Such changes, however, will not necessarily be in a democratic direction. Conflict within the CCP remains high, and the tensions between centralization and decentralization could weaken or destroy the political system. Moreover, as this book has argued, there is a long tradition within China, and particularly within the CCP, of ignoring procedures in the pursuit of power. Nevertheless, the passing of the generation that made the revolution, the rapid growth of market forces and non-state enterprises, the growing wealth of the population, and the pressures to contain the forces that could destroy China may yet pave the way for the institutionalization and politics of compromise that have for so long been lacking. Perhaps such cautious optimism may yet prove warranted.

Notes

1. See Lieberthal and Oksenberg, *Policy Making in China: Leaders, Structures, and Processes*; Lieberthal and Lampton, eds., *Bureaucracy, Politics, and Decision Making in Post-Mao China*; and David M. Lampton, ed., *Policy Implementation in Post-Mao China*.

2. Shirk, *The Political Logic of Economic Reform in China*.

3. See, for instance, Jean Oi, *State and Peasant in Contemporary China*, and idem, "Fiscal Reform and the Economic Foundations of Local State Corporatism in China."

4. See, for instance, Kelliher, *Peasant Power in China*; Rosenbaum, ed., *State and Society in China*; and White, *Riding the Tiger*.

5. The following discussion draws heavily on personal correspondence with Tang Tsou.

6. Personal communication from Tang Tsou.

7. Careful analysis of the period following Tiananmen needs to take account of both

Deng's weakness and his strength. Although it took Deng a long time—until after his highly publicized trip to the South in January 1992—before he could again set the policy agenda of China, he clearly retained the ultimate power to decide critical personnel issues. On May 31, 1989, Deng delivered a speech to Li Peng and Yao Yilin in which he explained his decision to promote Jiang Zemin to general secretary and Li Ruihuan to the Politburo Standing Committee, saying that "If we present a lineup which the people think is a rigid, conservative body [i.e., composed of people like Li and Yao] which cannot reflect China's future, there will still be a lot of trouble in the future." See "Deng Xiaoping's Speech to Li Peng and Yao Yilin," *Tung Fang Jih Pao*, July 14, 1989, trans. FBIS, July 17, 1989, pp. 15–17.

8. Deng Xiaoping, "Speech by Deng Xiaoping Made While Receiving Cadres of the Martial Law Units in the Capitol at and Above the Army Level on June 9, 1989, Rearranged According to Records," *Renmin ribao*, June 28, 1989, trans. FBIS, June 27, 1989, pp. 8–10, and June 29, 1989, p. 13.

9. Deng Xiaoping, "Di san dai lingdao jituan de dangwu zhi ji" (The Present Urgent Tasks of the Leadership Group of the Third Generation), p. 312.

10. The 50 enterprises targeted in the Northeast accounted for 47.2 percent of the total industrial output value of all in-budget industrial enterprises in the Northeast and for some 90 percent of the profits and taxes delivered to the state from those industries. See Xinhua, January 25, 1990, trans. FBIS, January 30, 1990. On the extension of the double guarantee system to 234 enterprises, see *China Daily*, March 14, 1990, trans. FBIS, March 16, 1990, pp. 27–28.

11. See the comparison between the version of Deng's speech read over Beijing Radio on June 27 and that published in *Renmin ribao* the following day in FBIS, June 29, 1989, p. 13. In the wake of the Fourteenth Party Congress decision to build a "socialist market economy," Chinese commentators have highlighted this effort to distort Deng's words. See "First Installment of the Inside Story on Deng Xiaoping's Strong Efforts to Defend 'market'," *Wen wei po*, February 11, 1993, trans. FBIS, February 12, 1993, p. 11.

12. "Report by Jiang Zemin, General Secretary of the CCP Central Committee, on Behalf of the CCP Central Committee and State Council," Beijing Television Service, September 29, 1989, trans. FBIS, October 2, 1989, pp. 17–27.

13. "Weihu anding tuanjie zhege daju" (Maintain the Overall Situation of Stability and Unity), *Renmin ribao*, Editorial, October 10, 1989, p. 1.

14. Wang Renzhi, "Guanyu fandui zichan jieji ziyouhua" (On Opposing Bourgeois Liberalization), *Renmin ribao*, February 22, 1990, pp. 1–3.

15. Yi Ren (pseud.), "Zhuozhou huiyi de qianqian houhou" (Before and After the Zhuozhou Meeting), *Renmin ribao*, February 14, 1990, p. 3.

16. Jiang Zemin, "Work Report." Beijing Television Services, October 12, 1989, trans. FBIS, October 13, 1989, pp. 23–43.

17. Zhongguo xinwen she, March 19, 1993, trans. FBIS, March 23, 1993, pp. 26–27.

Bibliography

I. Books and Articles

"Aim of Socialist Production Must Be Really Understood." In *Renmin ribao*, Contributing Commentator, October 20, 1979, pp. 1, 2, trans. FBIS, November 9, 1979, pp. L3–10.

An Gang et al. "Zhongguo nongye zhenxing youwang" (There Is Hope for the Vigorous Development of Chinese Agriculture). In *Renmin ribao*, July 9, 1981, p. 2.

Anhui Provincial Federation of Philosophy and Social Science, ed. *Shelian tongxun* (Bulletin of the Federation). 1983.

Bachman, David M. *Chen Yun and the Chinese Political System.* Berkeley: Institute of East Asian Studies, 1985.

Bai Nansheng. "Wu guo kaishi jinru chao bixupin xiaofei jieduan" (China Begins to Enter the Period of Nonessential Products Consumption). In Chinese Economic Structural Reform Institute, ed., *Zhongguo: fazhan yu gaige (1984–1985, shou zhuan)*, pp. 306–316.

Bai Nansheng and Wang Xiaoqiang. "Zhun zhi, yi fen, yu jingji guanli" (Common Quality, Differentiation, and Economic Management). In *Jingji yanjiu*, no. 6 (June 1985):67–71.

"The Bankruptcy System May Be First Carried Out in Enterprises." In *Renmin ribao*, Commentator, August 28, 1986, p. 1, trans. FBIS, September 2, 1986, pp. K16–17.

Bao Tong. "The Young Horse of Socialism, the Old Horse of Capitalism, and Other Related Matters." In *Renmin ribao*, January 5, 1987, p. 5, trans. FBIS, January 13, 1987, pp. K9–13.

Bao Xin. "Improve the Economic Environment for Reform, Straighten Out the Economic Environment." In *Liaowang*, Overseas Edition, September 12, 1988, p. 1, trans. FBIS, September 21, 1988, pp. 28–29.

Baum, Richard. *Chinese Politics in the Age of Deng Xiaoping.* Forthcoming, Princeton University Press.

"Bayue de qishi" (Enlightenment Gained in August) *Liowang*, Commentator, no. 39, September 26, 1988, p. 1, trans. FBIS, October 3, 1988.

"Be Bold in Destroying the Old and Creating the New." In *Renmin ribao*, Commentator, February 25, 1984, trans. FBIS, February 27, 1984, pp. K8–10.

Bernstein, Thomas. "From Anti-Leftism to Household Farming: A Limited Breakthrough." Unpublished manuscript.

Chang, Parris H. *Power and Policy in China.* 2d ed. University Park, PA: The Pennsylvania State University Press, 1978.

Chao Lu. "No Ideological Education for Three Years; the First Instance of Opposition to Leftism in Literature and Art Circles—The Inside Story of How Deng Xiaoping and Hu Yaobang Straightened Out the Orientation." In *Ching-pao yueh-k'an*, no. 90 (January 10, 1985), trans. FBIS, January 23, 1985, pp. W3–7.

Chen Junsheng. "Uphold the Four Cardinal Principles in the Course of Reform and Opening." Xinhua, January 11, 1987, trans. FBIS, January 12, 1987, pp. K12–21.

Chen Peizhang and Jiang Zhenyun. "Jinjin zhuazhu tiaozheng zhege guanjian" (Firmly Grasp Readjustment, the Crux). In Renmin ribao, May 27, 1980, p. 5.

Chen Rulong. "Jiaoliu chengguo, tansuo zhenli" (Exchanging Results, Exploring the Truth). In Chinese Finance Society, ed., Dangqian caizheng wenti—disice quanguo caizheng lilun taolunhui wenxuan, pp. 1–4.

———. "Weirao jingji tiaozheng kaizhan lilun yanjiu" (Open Up Theoretical Study Around the Theme of Economic Readjustment). In Chinese Finance Society, ed., Dangqian caizheng wenti—disice quanguo caizheng lilun taolunhui wenxuan, pp. 5–12.

Chen Tean. "Deng Xiaoping Meets Guerra, Points Out that China's First Goal of Construction May Be Reached Ahead of Schedule." In Renmin ribao, May 1, 1987, p. 1, trans. FBIS, May 1, 1987, p. G3.

Chen Wenhong. Zhongguo jingji de luxiang (The Path of the Chinese Economy). Hong Kong: Kuang chiao ching ch'u pan she, 1989.

———. Zhongguo jingji wenti (China's Economic Problems). Hong Kong: Kuang chiao ching ch'u pan she, 1989.

Chen Wenhong, ed. Tiaozheng qi di Zhongguo jingji—Xu Yi lunwen xuanji (The Chinese Economy in the Period of Readjustment—Collected Essays of Xu Yi). Hong Kong: Shu-kuang t'u-shu kung-ssu, 1984.

Chen Xiwen. "Zhongguo nongcun jingji: Cong chaochanggui zengzhang zhuanxiang changgui zengzhang" (China's Rural Economy: Turning from Supranormal Growth to Normal Growth). In Jingji yanjiu, no. 12 (December 1987):23–32.

Chen Yizi. "Nongcun de shouguang, Zhongguo de xiwang" (Rural Radiance, China's Hope). In Chinese Rural Development Research Group, ed., Nongcun, jingji, shehui, vol. 1, pp. 33–53.

———. Zhongguo: Shinian gaige yu bajiu minyun (China: Ten Years of Reform and the Democratic Movement of 1989). Taipei: Lien-ching ch'u pan she, 1990.

Chen Yun. Chen Yun wenxuan (1956–1985) (The Selected Works of Chen Yun, 1956–1985). Beijing: Renmin chuban she, 1986.

———. "Jianchi an bili yuanze tiaozheng guomin jingji" (Readjust the National Economy in Accordance with the Principle of Proportionality). In Chen Yun, Chen Yun wenxuan (1956–1985), pp. 226–231.

———. "Jianshe guimo yao he guoli xiang shiying" (The Scale of Construction Should Be Compatible with National Strength). In Chen Yun, Chen Yun wenxuan (1956–1985), pp. 40–49.

———. "Jiaqiang he gaijin jingji jihua gongzuo" (Strengthen and Improve Economic Planning Work). In Chen Yun, Chen Yun wenxuan (1956–1985), pp. 278–280.

———. "Jihua yu shichang wenti" (The Question of Planning and Markets). In Chen Yun, Chen Yun wenxuan (1956–1985), pp. 220–223.

———. "Jingji jianshe de jige zhongyao fangzhen" (Several Important Directions in Economic Construction). In Chen Yun, Chen Yun wenxuan (1956–1985), pp. 275–277.

———. "Jingji jianshe yao jiaota shidi" (Economic Construction Must Be Down to Earth). In Chen Yun, Chen Yun wenxuan (1956–1985), pp. 236–240.

———. "Jingji xingshi yu jingyan jiaoshun" (The Economic Situation and the Lessons of Experience). In Chen Yun, Chen Yun wenxuan (1956–1985), pp. 236–240.

———. "Qingpu nongcun diaocha" (Rural Investigations in Qingpu). In Chen Yun, Chen Yun wenxuan (1956–1985), pp. 161–181.

———. "Shehui zhuyi gaizao jiben wancheng yilai de xin wenti" (New Problems Since the Basic Completion of Socialist Transformation). In Chen Yun, Chen Yun wenxuan (1956–1985), pp. 1–14.

————. "Zai Zhongguo gongchandang daibiao huiyi shang de jianhua" (Talk to the Conference of Delegates of the Chinese Communist Party). In Chen Yun, *Chen Yun wenxuan (1956–1985)*, pp. 303–307.

Chen Yun and Li Xiannian. "Guanyu caijing gongzuo gei zhongyang de xin" (Letter to the Central Committee Regarding Finance and Economic Work). In Chen Yun, *Chen Yun wenxuan (1956–1985)*, pp. 224–225.

Cheng Hsiang. "Beidaihe Conference Begins Today and Prices and Wages Are the Focus of Discussion." In *Wen wei po*, July 20, 1988, p. 2, trans. FBIS, July 20, 1988, p. 15.

————. "Central Work Conference Underway in Beijing." In *Wen wei po*, September 19, 1988, p. 2, trans. FBIS, September 19, 1988, p. 20.

————. "Tentative Analysis of Discussions Concerning Reform of the Political Structure" (part one). In *Wen wei po*, July 21, 1986, p. 2, trans. FBIS, July 24, 1986, pp. W1–3.

Cheng Wanquan. "Wujia shangzhang de yuanin ji pingyi wujia de duice" (Causes of Commodity Price Rises and Measures for Stabilizing Commodity Prices). In *Renmin ribao*, April 8, 1988, p. 4.

Cheng Xiaonong. "A Radical Reform and Its Miscarriage in the Summer of 1988." Forthcoming in Carol Lee Hamrin and Suisheng Zhao, eds., *Deng's China: Dynamics of the Political Process* (Armonk, NY: M.E. Sharpe, forthcoming).

Cheng Xiaonong and Huang Yuncheng, "Price, Income, and Inflation," *Jingji yanjiu*, no. 5 (May 1988), pp. 3–9, trans. JPRS-CAR–88–039 (July 22, 1988), pp. 31–38.

Cheng Zhensheng. "Not Claiming Credit for Oneself, Not Putting the Blame on Others— Learning From Li Xiannian's Lofty Moral Character." In *Qiushi*, no. 15 (August 1, 1992):24–25, trans. FBIS, September 24, 1992, pp. 31–33.

Chi I. "A Dramatic Conference of the CPC Central Committee Propaganda Department." In *Cheng ming*, no. 87 (January 1, 1985), trans. FBIS, January 7, 1985, p. W1.

Chinese Academy of Agricultural Sciences. "China Must Not Have Less than 400 Kilograms of Grain Per Capita." In *Nongye jishu jingji*, August 1986, pp. 12–15, trans. JPRS-CEA–87–002 (January 12, 1987), pp. 57–62.

————. "Problems in Development of a Commodity Economy in Agriculture and Policies for Dealing with Them." In *Nongye jishu jingji* December 1986, pp. 1–5, trans. JPRS-CEA–87–034 (April 20, 1987), pp. 70–80.

Chinese Academy of Social Sciences, Materials Office, ed. *Shehui zhuyi jingji zhong jihua yu shichang de guanxi* (The Relationship Between Plan and Market in the Socialist Economy). 2 vols. Beijing: Zhongguo shehui kexue chuban she, 1980.

Chinese Academy of Social Sciences, Rural Development Institute, ed. *Nongye shengchan zerenzhi lunwenji* (Essays on the Rural Production Responsibility System). Beijing: Renmin chuban she.

Chinese Economic Structural Reform Institute. "Gaige: Women mianlin de tiaozhan yu xuanze" (Reform: The Challenges and Choices Confronting China). In *Jingji yanjiu*, no. 11 (November 1985):3–18.

Chinese Economic Structural Reform Institute, ed. *Zhongguo: fazhan yu gaige (1984– 1985, shou zhuan)* (China: Development and Reform, 1984–1985, vol. 1). Beijing: Zhonggong dangshi ziliao chuban she, 1987.

Chinese Finance Society, ed., *Dangqian caizheng wenti—disice quanguo caizheng lilun taolunhui wenxuan* (Current Fiscal Problems—Essays from the Fourth National Symposium on Finance Theory). Beijing: Zhongguo caizheng jingji chuban she, 1981.

Chinese Rural Development Research Group. "Guomin jingji xin chengzhang jieduan he nongcun fazhan" (The New Stage of Growth of the Chinese Economy and Rural Development). In *Jingji yanjiu*, no. 7 (July 1985):3–18.

————. *Guomin jingji xin chengzhang jieduan he nongcun fazhan* (The New Stage of Growth of the Chinese Economy and Rural Development). Hangzhou: Zhejiang renmin chuban she, 1987.

————, ed. *Baochan daohu ziliao xuan* (Selected Materials on the Household Responsibility System). 2 vols. nd. np.

————, ed. *Nongcun, jingji, shehui* (Countryside, Economy, Society). Vol. 1. Beijing: Zhishi chuban she, 1985.

"Chongpo tiaokuai fenlie cai neng fazhan shengchanli" (Productive Forces Can Only Be Developed by Breaking Through Administrative Barriers). In *Renmin ribao*, Editorial, April 18, 1986, p. 1.

Chuang Ming. "Zhao Ziyang wei jian xin zhixu tichu shitiao" (Zhao Ziyang Raises Ten Points for Creating a New Order). In *Ching-pao yueh-k'an*, no. 7 (July 1988):22–27.

Communiqué of the Fifth Plenary Session of the Eleventh Central Committee of the Communist Party of China." Xinhua, February 29, 1980, trans. FBIS, February 29, 1980, pp. L1–6.

Communiqué of the Third Plenary Session of the Thirteenth CPC Central Committee." Xinhua, September 30, 1988, trans. FBIS, September 30, 1988, pp. 18–19.

Comprehensive Problems Section of the Development Research Center. "Nongmin, shichang, he zhidu chuangxin" (Peasants, Markets, and Systems Renewal). In *Jingji yanjiu*, no. 1 (January 1987):3–16, trans. JPRS-CEA–87–023 (March 23, 1987), pp. 67–73.

Conference Secretariat, ed. *Gaige shidai de tansuo* (Explorations in the Era of Reform). Tianjin: Renmin chuban she, 1985.

"Constitution of the People's Republic of China." Xinhua, December 4, 1982, trans. FBIS, December 7, 1982, pp. K1–28.

"Correctly Understand the Role of the Individual in History." In *Renmin ribao*, Contributing Commentator, July 4, 1980, trans. FBIS, July 7, 1980.

Dai Qing. "Jingji tizhi gaige de guanjian shi suoyuozhi gaige—fang Li Yining" (The Crux of Economic Structural Reform Is Ownership Reform—An Interview with Li Yining). In *Guangming ribao*, August 4, 1986, p. 2.

Dai Yuanchen. "Baochi shidu jingji zengzhanglu he caiqu 'gonggei lue dayu xuqiu' de fan zhouqi duice" (Maintain an Appropriate Rate of Economic Growth and Adopt the Counter Cyclical Policy of "Supply Being a Little Greater Than Demand"). In *Jingji yanjiu*, no. 11 (November 1989):3–13.

Dai Yuqing. "Chongfen renshi chengbao zerenzhi de yiyi; guojia jingwei gingnian jingji yanjiu xiaozu zuzhang Ren Kelei tong jizhe tanhua" (State Economic Commission's Young Economists Research Group Leader Ren Kelei Interviewed on Significance of Contract Responsibility System). In *Renmin ribao*, August 7, 1987, p. 2.

Dangdai Zhongguo jingji xuejia lu (Contemporary Chinese Economists). Guangzhou: Guangdong renmin chuban she, 1988.

"Decision of the CCP Central Committee on Some Problems in Accelerating Agricultural Development (Draft)." In *Zhanwang*, no. 417 (June 16, 1979) and no. 418 (July 1, 1979), trans. FBIS, August 31, 1979, pp. L22–37.

"Decision of the Central Committee of the Communist Party of China on Reform of the Economic Structure." Xinhua, October 20, 1984, trans. FBIS, October 22, 1984, pp. K1–19.

Deng Liqun. "FangRi guilai de sisu" (Thoughts Upon Returning from Japan). In Deng Liqun, Ma Hong, Sun Shangqing, and Wu Jiajun, *FangRi guilai de sisu* (Thoughts Upon Returning from Japan), pp. 1–19. Beijing: Zhongguo shehui kexue chuban she, 1979.

———. "Guanyu jingji wenti de diaocha yanjiu" (On Investigating Economic Problems). In You Lin, Zhao Shaoping, and Wang Mengkui, eds., *Jingji gaige wencong, di yi ji* .

———. "Zai Zhongguo nongcun fazhan wenti yanjiu zu taolun hui shang de jianghua" (Talk at the Symposium of the Chinese Rural Development Research Group,). In Chinese Rural Development Research Group, ed., *Nongcun, jingji, shehui*, vol. 1, pp. 1–7.

———. "Zhengque chuli jihua jingji he shichang tiaojie zhi jian de guanxi" (Correctly Handle the Relation Between the Planned Economy and Market Regulation). In Hongqi, ed., *Jihua jingji yu shichang tiaojie wenti (di yi ji)*, pp. 79–83.

Deng Xiaoping. "Answers to the Italian Journalist Oriana Fallaci." In Deng Xiaoping, *The Selected Works of Deng Xiaoping*, p. 328.

———. "Dang zai zuzhi zhanxian he sixiang zhanxian shang de poqie renwu" (Urgent Tasks for the Party on the Organizational and Ideological Fronts). In Deng Xiaoping, *Jianshe you Zhongguo tese de shehui zhuyi (zeng ding ben)*, pp. 20–33.

———. *Deng Xiaoping wenxuan (1938–1965)* (Selected Works of Deng Xiaoping, 1938–1965). Beijing: Renmin chuban she, 1983.

———. *Deng Xiaoping wenxuan*, vol. 3. Beijing: Renmin chuban she, 1993.

———. "Deng Xiaoping's Speech to Li Peng and Yao Yilino." In *Tung fang jih pao*, July 14, 1989, trans. FBIS, July 17, 1989, pp. 15–17.

———. "Di san dai lingdao jituan de dangwu zhi ji" (The Present Urgent Tasks of the Leadership Group of the Third Generation). In *Deng Xiaoping wenxuan*, vol. 3, pp. 309–314.

———. " 'Full Text of Gists' of Deng Xiaoping's Speech to Members of the New Politburo Standing Committee." In *Tung fang jih pao*, July 15, 1993, p. 6, trans. FBIS, July 18, 1993, pp. 13–15.

———. "Guanyu nongcun zhengce wenti" (On Question of Rural Policy). In *Deng Xiaoping wenxuan, (1938–1965)*, pp. 275–277.

———. "Implement the Policy of Readjustment, Ensure Stability and Unity." In Deng Xiaoping, *The Selected Works of Deng Xiaoping*, pp. 348–349.

———. "Jianshe you Zhongguo tese de shehui zhuyi" (Build Socialism with Chinese Characteristics). In Deng Xiaoping, *Jianshe you Zhongguo tese de shehui zhuyi (zeng ding ben)*, pp. 45–49.

———. *Jianshe you Zhongguo tese de shehui zhuyi (zeng ding ben)* (Build Socialism with Chinese Characteristics [Enlarged Edition]). Hong Kong: Sanlian shudian, 1987.

———. "The Present Situation and Tasks." In Deng Xiaoping, *The Selected Works of Deng Xiaoping*, pp. 224–258.

———. "Reform of the Party and State Leadership System." In Deng Xiaoping, *The Selected Works of Deng Xiaoping*, pp. 302–325.

———. "Remarks on Succesive Drafts of the 'Resolution on Certain Questions in the History of Our Party Since the Founding of the People's Republic of China'." In Deng Xiaoping, *The Selected Works of Deng Xiaoping*, pp. 276–296.

———. *The Selected Works of Deng Xiaoping*. Beijing: Foreign Language Press, 1984.

———. "Speech by Deng Xiaoping Made While Receiving Cadres of the Martial Law Units in the Capital At and Above the Army Level on June 9, 1989, Rearranged According to Records." In *Renmin ribao*, June 28, 1989, trans. FBIS, June 27, 1989, pp. 8–10, and June 29, 1989, p. 13.

———. "A Talk by Deng Xiaoping at the Third Plenary Session of the Central Advisory Commission on 22 October 1981." Xinhua, December 31, 1984, trans. FBIS, January 2, 1985, pp. K1–6.

———. "Zenyang huifu nongye shengchan" (How Can Agricultural Production Be Restored?). In Deng Xiaoping, *Deng Xiaoping wenxuan (1938–1965)*, pp. 304–309.

Deng Yingtao, He Weiling, Luo Xiaopeng, et al. "Lun zhanlue yanjiu" (On Strategic Research). In Chinese Rural Development Research Group, ed., *Nongcun, jingji, shehui*, vol. 1, pp. 261–286.

Deng Yingtao and Luo Xiaopeng. "Lun zongliang fenxi he zongliang zhengce zai woguo jingji lilun yu shijian zhong de juxianxing" (The Limitations of Gross Quantity Analysis and Gross Quantity Policies in China's Economic Theory and Practice). In *Jingji yanjiu*, no. 6 (June 1987):3–16.

Ding Wang. " 'Fei ma' yu 'shou ma' zhi zheng" (The Struggle Between "De-Marxification" and "Holding onto Marxism"). In *Chao liu*, no. 2 (April 15, 1987):30.

Ding, Xue-liang. "The Disparity Between Idealistic and Instrumental Chinese Reformers." In *Asian Survey*, vol. 28, no. 11 (November 1988):1117–1139.

Documents Research Office of the Central Committee of the Chinese Communist Party. *Sanzhong quanhui yi lai zhongyao wenxian xuanbian* (Important Documents Since the Third Plenum). 2 Vols. Beijing: Renmin chuban she, 1982.

"Doing Everything According to Actual Capabilities Is an Important Principle for Capital Construction—More on the Guiding Principle of Doing Things According to Actual Capabilities." In *Renmin ribao*, Editorial, June 9, 1980, trans. FBIS, June 12, 1980, pp. L11–14.

Domes, Jurgen. "The Pattern of Politics." In *Problems of Communism*, vol. 23, no. 5 (September–October 1974):21–22.

Dong Fureng. "Guanyu woguo shehui zhuyi suoyouzhi xingshi wenti" (The Form of Socialist Ownership in China). In *Jingji yanjiu*, no. 1 (January 1979):21–28.

———. "Guanyu zengqiang quanmin suoyouzhi qiye huoli de wenti" (The Problem of Strengthening the Vitality of Enterprises Owned By the Whole People). In *Jingji yanjiu*, no. 6 (June 1985):3–12.

Dong Kenong and Zhang Zhongwen. "The Way Must Not Be Blocked—Second in a Series of Reports on the Capitol Iron and Steel Company." In *Guangming ribao*, December 22, 1982, p. 2, trans. FBIS, January 6, 1983, pp. K2–4.

———. "A Trench—Third in a Series of Reports on the Capitol Iron and Steel Company." In *Guangming ribao*, December 25, 1982, p. 2, trans. FBIS, January 6, 1983, pp. K4–5.

Du Haiyan. "Chengbaozhi: guoyou qiye tizhi gaige de chushi xuanze" (The Contract Responsibility System: An Initial Choice for the Restructuring of State Enterprises). In *Jingji yanjiu*, no. 10 (October 20, 1987):10–18.

Du Haozhi. "Zai jingji lingyu fandui fengjian canyu shi yixiang zhongyao de renwu" (Opposing Feudal Remnants Is an Important Task in the Economic Realm). In *Jingji yanjiu*, no. 9 (September 1980):76–80.

Du Runsheng. "Guanyu nongye shengchan zerenzhi" (On the Agricultural Responsibility System). In Du Runsheng, *Zhongguo nongcun jingji gaige* (China's Rural Reform). Beijing: Zhongguo shehui kexue chuban she, 1985, pp. 1–7.

Du Xia and Hao Yisheng. "Tiaozheng suoyouzhi jiegou shi chengshi jingji gaige de guanjian suozai" (Readjusting the Structure of Ownership Is the Critical Point in Urban Economic Reform). In Conference Secretariat, ed., *Gaige shidai de tansuo*, pp. 167–181.

Duan Yingbi. "There Must Be Major Reforms in the Grain Marketing System." In *Nongye jingji wenti*, no. 11 (November 1986):37–40, trans. JPRS-CEA–87–023 (March 23, 1987), pp. 67–73.

Economic Daily, ed., *Zhongguo dangdai jingji xuejia zhuanlue* (Biographies of Contemporary Chinese Economists). Vols. 1 and 5. Shenyang: Renmin chuban she, 1986 and 1990.

Economic Growth Study Group of the Policy Research Center under the Ministry of

Agriculture, Animal Husbandry, and Fishery. "Changgui zengzhang, yihuo fazhan chizhi" (Normal Growth [or] Stagnating Development?). In *Jingji yanjiu*, no. 9 (September 1987):48–55.

Economic Institute, Chinese Academy of Social Sciences. "Zhongguo jingji tizhi zhongqi (1988–1995) gaige shexiang" (The Midterm Reform [1988–1995] of China's Economic Structure). In State Commission for Economic Structural Reform, ed., *Zhongguo gaige da silu*, pp. 58–89.

Economic Situation Analysis Group of the Economic Insitute, Chinese Academy of Social Sciences. "Zouchu kunjing de jinqi duice" (Near-Term Measures for Freeing Reform from Its Current Difficulties). In *Jingji yanjiu*, no. 7 (July 1989):3–12.

Editorial Committee on the History of Agricultural Cooperativization in Heilongjiang. *Heilongjiang nongye hezuo shi* (History of Agricultural Cooperativization in Heilongjiang). Beijing: Zhonggong dangshi ziliao chuban she, 1990.

Editorial Department, *Jingji yanjiu*, ed. *Jianguo yilai shehui zhuyi jingji lilun wenti zhengming (1949–1984)* (Debates about Theoretical Problems in Socialist Economics Since the Establishment of the PRC, 1949–1984). 2 vols. Beijing: Zhongguo caizheng jingji chuban she, 1985.

Enterprise Structure Group of the Chinese Academy of Social Sciences. *Zichan jingying zerenzhi* (The Asset Responsibility System). Beijing: Jingji kexue chuban she, 1987.

"Experimental Comprehensive Reform of the Urban Economic System Is Being Carried Out in Fifty-Two Cities." In *Guangming ribao*, October 16, 1984, p. 1, trans. FBIS, October 23, 1984, pp. K8–9.

Fan Maofa, Xun Dazhi, and Liu Xiaping. "Gufenzhi bushi quanmin suoyouzhi de fangxiang" (Shareholding Is Not the Orientation for Enterprises Owned by the Whole People). In *Jingji yanjiu*, no. 1 (January 1986):17–22.

Fang Weizhong. "Yi tiao buke dongyao de jiben junze" (A Fundamental Principle that Must Not Be Shaken). In Hongqi, ed. *Jihua jingji yu shichang tiaojie wenji (di yi ji)*, pp. 153–55.

———. ed. *Zhonghua renmin gongheguo jingji dashiji (1949–1980)* (Record of Major Economic Events in the People's Republic of China, 1949–1980). Beijing: Zhongguo shehui kexue chuban she, 1984.

Fang Weizhong and Wu Jiajun, eds. *Gongye qiye kuisun diaocha yanjiu* (Investigation and Study of Losses in Industrial Enterprises). Beijing: Jingji guanli chuban she, 1989.

Feng Baoxing. "Dui chengbao jingying zerenzhi jige wenti de tantao" (Discussing Several Questions Concerning the Contract Management Responsibility System). In *Hongqi*, no. 10 (May 16, 1987):25–28.

Feng Lanrui. "Academic Work Cannot Flourish Without Freedom and Democracy." In *Shijie jingji daobao*, May 26, 1986, p. 5, trans. FBIS, May 12, 1986, pp. K8–10.

Feng Wenbin. "On the Question of Socialist Democracy." In *Renmin ribao*, November 24 and 25, 1980, trans. FBIS, November 26, 1980, pp. L23–30.

Fewsmith, Joseph. "Agricultural Crisis in the PRC." In *Problems of Communism*, vol. 37, no. 6 (November–December 1988):78–93.

———. "The Dengist Reforms in Historical Perspective." In Brantly Womack, ed., *Contemporary Chinese Politics in Historical Perspective*, pp. 23–52.

———. "Reform, Resistance, and the Politics of Succession." Forthcoming in *China Briefing, 1994*. New York: Asia Society, 1994.

———. "Special Economic Zones of the PRC." In *Problems of Communism*, vol. 35, no. 6 (November–December):78–85.

———, ed., "The Debate on China's Macroeconomic Situation (II)." In *Chinese Economic Studies*, vol. 23, no. 6 (Spring 1990).

————, ed. and trans. "China's Midterm Economic Structural Reform, 1988–1995." In *Chinese Law and Government*, vol. 22, no. 4 (Winter 1989–90).

Fewsmith, Joseph, and Gary Zou, eds. "China's Coastal Development (I)." In *Chinese Economic Studies*, vol. 25, no. 1 (Fall 1991).

————. "China's Coastal Development (II)." In *Chinese Economic Studies* (Spring 1992).

"First Installment of the Inside Story in Deng Xiaoping's Strong Efforts to Defend 'Market'." In *Wen wei po*, February 11, 1993, trans. FBIS, February 12, 1993, p. 11.

"Gaige de shidai de tansuo" (Explorations in the Age of Reform). In *Zhongqingnian jingji luntan*, no. 2 (June 1985):4–12.

Gao Shangquan. *Jiunian lai de Zhongguo jingji tizhi gaige* (China's Economic Structural Reform in the Last Nine Years). Beijing: Renmin chuban she, 1987.

————. *Zhongguo de jingji tizhi gaige* (China's Economic Structural Reform). Beijing: Renmin chuban she, 1991.

Gao Xiaomeng. "The Question of Grain Prices and Reform of the Circulation Structure." In *Liaowang*, May 25, 1987, p. 16, trans. FBIS, June 10, 1987, pp. K21–23.

Gao Yu. "Zhongguo ruhe du nanguan, gaige chulu zai nali?—Yan Jiaqi yu Wen Yuankai de duihua" (How Can China Pass the Difficult Gate, Where Is the Way Out for Reform?—A Conversation Between Yan Jiaqi and Wen Yuankai). In *Ching-pao yueh-k'an*, no. 12 (December 1988):18–24.

General Section. "Guanyu 'Zhongguo nongcun fazhan wenti yanjiu' diyi jieduan de gongzuo yijian" (Views on the First Stage Work on "Studies on China's Rural Development Problems"). In Chinese Rural Development Research Group, ed., *Nongcun, jingji, shehui*, vol. 1, pp. 27–28.

Geng Zhi. "Raising the Share and Readjusting the Composition of Agricultural Investment." In *Nongye jingji xiaoguo*, no. 6 (December 25, 1986):1–3, trans. JPRS-CEA–87–043, May 19, 1987, pp. 78–82.

"Give Play to Our Political Superiority." In *Renmin ribao*, Editorial, September 28, 1988, p. 1, trans. FBIS, September 28, 1988, pp. 29–30.

Goldman, Merle. "Hu Yaobang's Intellectual Network." In *The China Quarterly*, no. 126 (June 1991):219–242.

Gong Shiqi and Xu Yi. "Jianchi jihua jingji wei zhu, shichang tiaojie wei fu" (Uphold the Planned Economy as Primary and Market Regulation as Supplementary). In *Jingji yanjiu*, no. 6 (June 1982):3–9.

Gong Yuzhi. *Sixiang jiefang di xin qidian* (A New Starting Point for the Emancipation of the Mind). Changsha: Hunan renmin chuban she, 1988.

"Guanyu jinyibu jiaqiang he wanshan nongye shengchan zerenzhi de jige wenti" (Several Issues Concerning Further Strengthening and Perfecting the Production Responsibility System in Agriculture). In Wang Jiye and Zhu Yuanzhen, eds., *Jingji tizhi gaige shouce*, pp. 73–76.

Guo Chongyi. "Zeren daohu de xingzhi ji qi youguan wenti" (The Nature of Devolving Responsibility to the Household and Related Questions). In Chinese Rural Development Reseach Group, ed., *Baochan daohu ziliao xuan* (Selected materials on the household responsibility system), pp. 15–25.

Guo Shuqing, Liu Jirui, and Qiu Shufang. "Guomin jingji buneng qiangxing 'qifei' " (The National Economy Cannot Be Forced to Take Off). In *Zhongqingnian jingji luntan*, no. 3 (1985):74–76.

Guo Shuqing, Luo Jiwei, and Liu Jirui. "Guanyu tizhi gaige zongti guihua de yanjiu" (Research on the Overall Plan for Structural Reform). In Wu Jinglian, Zhou Xiaochuan, et al., eds., *Zhongguo jingji gaige de zhengti sheji*, pp. 25–47.

Guo Wenru and Yang Zejun. "Consumption Funds Have Increased Too Rapidly, Macroeconomic Control Needs Strengthening." In *Renmin ribao*, February 12, 1986, p. 5, trans. FBIS, February 21, 1986, pp. K9–11.

Guo Yuhai. "Several Opinions on the Grain Problem." In *Renmin ribao*, May 18, 1987, trans. FBIS, June 2, 1987, pp. K22–24.

Halpern, Nina. "Information Flows and Policy Coordination in the Chinese Bureaucracy." In Kenneth Lieberthal and David M. Lampton, eds., *Bureaucracy, Politics, and Decision Making in Post-Mao China*, pp. 125–148.

——. "Making Economic Policy: The Influence of Economists." In *China's Economy Looks Toward the Year 2000, Volume 1: The Four Modernizations*. Washington, DC: U.S. Government Printing Office, 1986, pp. 132–46.

Hamrin, Carol Lee. *China and the Challenge of the Future*. Boulder, CO: Westview Press, 1990.

Hamrin, Carol Lee, and Suisheng Zhao, eds. *Deng's China: Dynamics of the Political Process*. Armonk, NY: M.E. Sharpe, forthcoming.

Han Shanbi. *Deng Xiaoping zhuan* (Biography of Deng Xiaoping). 3 vols. Hong Kong: East and West Culture Co., 1988.

Harding, Harry. "Competing Models of the Chinese Communist Policy Process: Toward a Sorting and Evaluation." In *Issues and Studies*, vol. 20, no. 2 (February 1984):13–36.

"The Harm Done by Bureaucratism as Viewed from Economic Crime." In *Renmin ribao*, January 26, 1986, p. 2, trans. FBIS, January 28, 1986, pp. K1–2.

"Haste Makes Waste—A Third Discussion on the Guiding Principle of Acting According to One's Capability." In *Renmin ribao*, Editorial, June 12, 1980, trans. FBIS, June 18, 1980, pp. L15–17.

——. *China's Second Revolution*. Washington, DC: Brookings Institution, 1987.

He Jianzhang. "Seriously Improve and Develop the Contract System." In *Jingji yanjiu*, no. 8 (August 1989):28–36, trans. JPRS-CAR–89–083 (April 20, 1989), pp. 8–17.

——. "The Shareholding System Is Not the Orientation for State Enterprise Reform." In *Guangming ribao*, October 17, 1987, p. 3, trans. FBIS, October 29, 1987, pp. 38–40.

——. "Woguo quanmin suoyouzhi jingji jihua guanli tizhi cunzai de wenti he gaige fangxiang" (The Problems of the Structure of Planned Management in China's System of Ownership by the Whole People and the Direction of Reform). In Chinese Academy of Social Sciences, Materials Office, ed., *Shehui zhuyi jingji zhong jihua yu shichang de guanxi*, vol. 1, pp. 74–95.

He Jiacheng and Zhang Xuejun. "China's Economic Situation in 1987." In *Shijie jingji daobao*, February 8, 1988, p. 3, trans. FBIS, March 4, 1988, pp. 21–23.

He Li. " 'Ren' de yanjiu—jingji yanjiu de zuigao zengci—Li Yining zhuanlue" (The Study of 'Man,' the Highest Level of Economic Research—A Biography of Li Yining). In Chinese Economic Daily, ed., *Zhongguo dangdai jingji xuejia zhuanlue*, vol. 5, pp. 571–604.

Hongqi, ed., *Jihua jingji yu shichang tiaojie wenji (di yi ji)* (Essays on the Planned Economy and Market Regulation), vol. 1. Beijing: Hongqi chuban she, 1983.

Hongqi Editorial Department. "How to Do a Better Job in Departmental Work." Xinhua, January 31, 1985, trans. FBIS, February 1, 1985, pp. K1–10.

Hou Su-hao. "Public Indignation Aroused by the 'Ma Ding Incident' Leads to Intervention by Hu Yaobang." In *Kuang chiao ching*, no. 164 (May 16, 1986):15–17, trans. FBIS, May 21, 1986, pp. W1–4.

Hsiao Chung. "The 'Ma Ding Case' Which Shocks CPC Theorists." In *Cheng ming*, no. 103 (May 1, 1986):14–15, trans. FBIS, May 8, 1986, pp. W3–6.

Hsu, Robert C. *Economic Theories in China, 1979–1988*. Cambridge, UK: Cambridge University Press, 1991.

Hu Changnuan. "Ping jiu nian lai nongchangpin jiage juece de chenggong yu shiwu" (Evaluating the Successes and Failures of the Agricultural Product Price Policy Over the Past Nine Years). In *Nongye jingji wenti*, no. 6 (June 1988):7–11.

Hu Qiaomu. "Act in Accordance with Economic Laws, Step Up the Four Modernizations." Xinhua, October 5, 1987, trans. FBIS, October 11, 1978, pp. E1–22.

———. "On Humanism and Alienation." In *Renmin ribao*, January 27, 1984, pp. 1–5, trans. FBIS, February 7, 1984, pp. K1–33.

"Hu Qiaomu Warns in Xiamen that Foreign Investment Enterprises Are Not Concessions; Their Inordinate Demands Cannot Be Given Tacit Consent." In *Ming pao*, June 22, 1985, trans. FBIS, June 24, 1985, p. W8.

Hu Qili. "The Historic Mission of the Chinese Working Class in the Present Age." Xinhua, April 30, 1986, trans. FBIS, May 2, 1986, pp. K2–10.

Hu Yaobang. "Address when Meeting the Italian Communist Party." Xinhua, June 21, 1986, trans. FBIS, June 23, 1986, pp. G10–13.

———. "Central Organs Must Set an Example for the Whole Country." Xinhua, January 10, 1986, trans. FBIS, January 13, 1986, pp. K1–22.

———. "On the Party's Journalism Work." In *Renmin ribao*, April 14, 1985, pp. 1–3, trans. FBIS, April 15, 1985, pp. K1–15.

———. "The Radiance of the Great Truth of Marxism Lights Our Way Forward." Xinhua, March 13, 1983, trans. FBIS, March 14, 1983, pp. K1–16.

———. "Report to the Twelfth Party Congress." In *Renmin ribao*, September 8, 1982, p. 1, trans. FBIS, September 8, 1982, pp. K1–30.

"Hu Yaobang's Report to the Twelfth Party Congress." Xinhua, September 7, 1982, trans. FBIS, September 8, 1982, p. K12.

Hua Guofeng. "Unite and Strive to Build a Modern, Powerful Socialist Country." Xinhua, March 6, 1978, trans. FBIS, March 7, 1978, pp. D1–37.

Hua Sheng, He Jiacheng, Zhang Xuejun, and Luo Xiaopeng. "Reform Is Facing a Major Turning Point in Strategy." In *Shijie jingji daobao*, October 10, 1988, p. 15, trans. FBIS, October 27, 1988, pp. 29–31.

Hua Sheng, He Jiacheng, Zhang Xuejun, Luo Xiaopeng, and Yong Bianzhuang. "The Reconstruction of the Microeconomic Base—More on Problems and Train of Thought on Further Reforming the Economic System." In *Jingji yanjiu*, no. 3 (March 1986):21–28, trans. JPRS-CEA–86–073 (June 17, 1986), pp. 16–29.

———. "Transfer of the Economic Operational Model—Problems and Train of Thought on Further Reforming the Economic System." In *Jingji yanjiu*, no. 2 (February 1986):21–28, trans. JPRS-CEA–86–068 (June 9, 1986), pp. 1–17.

Hua Sheng, Zhang Xuejun, and Luo Xiaopeng. "Ten Years of Reform: Review, Reflection, and Prospects." In *Jingji yanjiu*, nos. 9, 11, and 12 (September, November, and December 1988), trans. JPRS-CAR–89–004 (January 11, 1989), pp. 16–45; JPRS-CAR–89–024 (March 23, 1989), pp. 16–37; and JPRS-CAR–89–036 (April 26, 1989), pp. 4–24.

———. *China: From Revolution to Reform*. London: Macmillan, 1993.

Huan Guocang. "China's Opening to the World." In *Problems of Communism*, vol. 35, no. 6 (November–December 1986):59–77.

Huang Kecheng. "On Appraisal of Chairman Mao and Attitudes Toward Mao Zedong Thought." Xinhua, April 10, 1981, trans. FBIS, April 13, 1981, pp. K6–17.

Huntington, Samuel P., and Joan M. Nelson. *No Easy Choice: Political Participation in Developing Countries*. Cambridge, MA: Harvard University Press, 1976.

"Ideological Work Needs Cooperation Between Party Secretaries and Factory Directors." In *Renmin ribao*, Commentator, March 7, 1986, p. 2, trans. FBIS, March 14, 1986, pp. K4–5.

"An Important Principle for Making Plans Is to Leave No Gaps—The Fourth Discourse on the Guiding Ideology of Acting According to One's Capability." In *Renmin ribao*, Editorial, June 16, 1980, trans. FBIS, June 16, 1980, pp. L3–5.

"An Important Step for Reforming the Planning System." In *Renmin ribao*, Editorial, October 11, 1984, trans. FBIS, October 11, 1984, pp. K2–4.

"In an Internal Speech, He Jingzhi Calls for Vigilance Against Carrying Out the Anti-liberalization Drive in a Superficial Way." In *Chiu-shi nien-tai*, no. 6 (June 1, 1987):28–29, trans. FBIS, June 15, 1987, pp. K9–12.

"In an Internal Speech, Xiong Fu Talks on the Integration of Literature and Art Circles and Other Circles in Practicing 'Liberalization'." In *Chiu-shih nien-tai*, no. 6 (June 1, 1987):30–32, trans. FBIS, June 9, 1987, pp. K7–11.

"Investigation Report of the Central Discipline Inspection Commission," Xinhua, July 31, 1985, FBIS, August 6, 1985, pp. K18–19.

Jiang Yiwei. *From Enterprise-Based Economy to Economic Democracy*. In English and Chinese. Beijing: Beijing zhoubao chuban she, 1988.

———. *Jingji tizhi gaige he qiye guanli ruogan wenti de tantao* (An Exploration of Several Problems in Economic Structural Reform and Enterprise Management). Shanghai: Renmin chuban she, 1985.

———. "Qiye benwei lun" (On an Enterprise-Based Economy). In Jiang Yiwei, *Jingji tizhi gaige he qiye guanli ruogan wenti de tantao*, pp. 3–35.

———. "Shougang zai gaige zhong kuabu qianjin" (Capitol Iron and Steel Company Taking Large Steps in Reform). In Jiang Yiwei, *Jingji tizhi gaige he qiye guanli ruogan wenti de tantao*, pp. 102–112.

———. "Tentative Discourse on the Principle of All-Round Material Benefits." In *Renmin ribao*, July 14, 1980, p. 5, trans. FBIS, July 22, 1980, pp. L10–15.

Jiang Yiwei and Lin Ling. "Cong Shoudu gangtie gongsi kan tizhi gaige" (Looking at Structural Reform from the Perspective of the Capitol Iron and Steel Company). In Jiang Yiwei, *Jingji tizhi gaige he qiye guanli ruogan wenti de tantao*, pp. 89–101.

———. "Guanyu zai Chongqing jinxing zonghe gaige shidian de jidian jianyi" (Some Views on Carrying Out an Experiment in Comprehensive Reform in Chongqing). In Jiang Yiwei, *Jingji tizhi gaige he qiye guanli ruogan wenti de tantao*, pp. 150–159.

Jiang Zemin. "Work Report." Beijing Television Service, October 12, 1989, trans. FBIS, October 13, 1989, pp. 23–43.

"Jiechuan 'baochan daohu' de zhen mianmu" (Expose the Real Face of the Household Responsibility System). In *Renmin ribao*, November 2, 1959, reprinted in Chinese Rural Development Reseach Group, ed., *Baochan daohu ziliao xuan*, pp. 291–295.

Kelliher, Daniel. *Peasant Power in China: The Era of Rural Reform, 1979–1989*. New Haven: Yale University Press, 1992.

Kong Qian. "Comment on 'Opposing the Bureaucratic Class'." In *Jiefangjun bao*, February 9, 1981, trans. FBIS, February 10, 1981, pp. L1–3.

Lampton, David M. "Chinese Politics: The Bargaining Treadmill," *Issues and Studies* 23, no. 3 (March 1987):11–41.

———, ed. *Policy Implementation in Post-Mao China*. Berkeley and Los Angeles: University of California Press, 1987.

Lardy, Nicholas R. *Foreign Trade and Economic Reform in China, 1978–1990*. Cambridge, UK: Cambridge University Press, 1992.

———. "Is China Different? The Fate of Its Economic Reform." In Daniel Chirot, ed., *The Crisis of Leninism and the Decline of the Left: The Revolutions of 1989*. Seattle: University of Washington Press, 1991, pp. 147–162.

Lardy, Nicholas R., and Kenneth G. Lieberthal, eds. *Chen Yun's Strategy for Develop-*

ment: A Non-Maoist Alternative. Trans. Mao Tong and Du Anxia. Armonk, NY: M.E. Sharpe, 1983.

"Let the Spirit of the Foolish Old Man Fill the Divine Land—1986 New Year Message." In *Renmin ribao,* Editorial, January 1, 1986, p. 1, trans. FBIS, January 2, 1986, pp. K1–2.

Li Delai. "A New and Important Decision." In *Jingji ribao,* January 5, 1988, p. 1.

Li Jiange, "Jiecheng jian zhi yong, qiusu yi jianxin—Wu Jinglian zhuanlue" (Wholeheartedly and Bravely Seeking Wisdom and Simplicity Among Hardships—A Brief Biography of Wu Jinglian). In Economic Daily, ed. *Zhongguo dangdai jingji xuejia zhuanlue,* vol. 5, pp. 544–570.

Li Rui. "Another Discussion on Proneness to Boasting and Exaggeration." In *Guangming ribao,* May 9, 1985, p. 1, trans. FBIS, May 20, 1985, pp. K13–15.

———. "Do Not Blindly Seek a Higher Rate of Development." In *Guangming ribao,* May 7, 1985, p. 1, trans. FBIS, May 15, 1985, pp. K10–12.

———. "On Proneness to Boasting and Exaggeration." In *Guangming ribao,* May 8, 1985, p. 1, trans. FBIS, May 20, 1985, pp. K12–13.

Li Shiyi and Gao Qinglin. "The Keynote of China's Economic Reform This Summer—Large and Medium-Sized State Enterprises Begin to Implement the Contract System." In *Liaowang,* Overseas Edition, no. 24 (June 15, 1987):3–4, trans. JPRS-CAR–87–023 (July 22, 1987), pp. 27–31.

Li Xiannian. "Dui jingji tiaozheng gongzuo de jige yijian" (Several Views on the Work of Economic Readjustment). In Li Xiannian, *Li Xiannian wenxuan,* pp. 419–422.

———. "Jianchi caizheng shouzhi pingheng, lue you jieyu de fangzhen" (Uphold the Orientation of Balancing Revenues and Expenses with a Slight Surplus). In Li Xiannian, *Li Xiannian wenxuan,* pp. 410–415.

———. *Li Xiannian wenxuan* (The Selected Works of Li Xiannian). Beijing: Renmin chuban she, 1989.

———. "Zai quanguo jihua huiyi de jianghua" (Talk at the National Planning Conference). In Li Xiannian, *Li Xiannian wenxuan,* pp. 395–409.

———. "Zai zhongyang gongzuo huiyi shang de jianghua" (Speech to the Central Work Conference). In Li Xiannian, *Li Xiannian wenxuan,* pp. 343–378.

Li Yining. "A Conception of Reform of the Ownership System in Our Country." In *Renmin ribao,* September 26, 1986, p. 5, trans. FBIS, October 22, 1986, pp. K5–11.

———. "Contention in Economics and Flourishing Economics." In *Renmin ribao,* May 19, 1986, p. 5, trans. FBIS, May 20, 1986, pp. K1–4.

———. "Deepening Reform and Increasing Supply Is a Basic Measure for Stabilizing the Market." In *Renmin ribao,* September 16, 1988, p. 5, trans. FBIS, September 29, 1988, pp. 38–41.

———. "Gaige de jiben silu" (The Basic Train of Thought for Reform). In *Beijing ribao,* May 19, 1986, p. 3.

———. "Jingji tizhi gaige de guanjian shi suoyouzhi" (The Crux of Economic Structural Reform Is the Ownership System). In *Guangming ribao,* August 4, 1986, p. 2.

———. "Suoyouzhi gaige he gufen qiye de guanli" (Ownership Reform and the Management of Joint-Stock Enterprises). In *Zhongguo jingji tizhi gaige,* no. 12 (December 1986):25–28; no. 1 (January 1987):24–25, 29; and no. 2 (February 1987):50–52.

———. *Tizhi, mubiao, ren—jingjixue mianlin de tiaozhan* (Structure, Goal, and Man—The Challenge Facing Economics). Harbin: Heilongjiang renmin chuban she, 1986.

Li Yining et al. "1988–1995 nian wo guo jingji tizhi gaige gangyao" (Outline for Economic Structural Reform in 1988–1995). In State Commission for Economic Structural Reform, ed., *Zhongguo gaige da silu,* pp. 90–128.

Li Yunhe. " 'Zhuan guan zhi' he 'baochan daohu' shi jiejue shenei zhuyao maodun de hao banfa" (The "Specialized Management System" and the Household Responsibility System Are Good Methods to Solve the Important Contradictions Within the Commune). In *Zhejiang ribao*, January 27, 1957, reprinted in Chinese Rural Development Reseach Group, ed., *Baochan daohu ziliao xuan*, pp. 235–242.

Li Zehou. "Qimeng yu jiuwang de shuangzhong bianzou" (The Dual Transformation of Enlightenment and Salvation). In Li Zehou, *Zhongguo xiandai sixiang shi lun* (Essays on the History of Contemporary Chinese Thought). Beijing: Dongfang chuban she, 1987, pp. 7–49.

Li Zhenzhong. "Ye tan jihua he shichang wenti" (Also Discussing the Question of Plan and Market). In *Guangming ribao*, December 26, 1981, p. 3.

Liao Jili. *Zhongguo jingji tizhi gaige yanjiu* (Studies on China's Economic Structural Reform). Beijing: Zhongguo caizheng jingji chuban she, 1985.

Lieberthal, Kenneth G. "The 'Fragmented Authoritarianism' Model and Its Limitations." In Kenneth G. Lieberthal and David M. Lampton, eds., *Bureaucracy, Politics, and Decision Making in Post Mao-China*, pp. 1–30.

Lieberthal, Kenneth G., and David M. Lampton, eds. *Bureaucracy, Politics, and Decision Making in Post-Mao China*. Berkeley and Los Angeles: University of California Press, 1992.

Lieberthal, Kenneth, and Michel Oksenberg. *Policy Making in China: Leaders, Structures, and Processes*. Princeton: Princeton University Press, 1988.

Lin, Cyril L. "The Reinstatement of Economics in China Today." in *The China Quarterly*, no. 85 (1981):1–48.

Lin Ling. "Guanyu jingji gaige zhong de jige wenti" (Several Problems in Economic Reform). In Lin Ling, *Zhongguo jingji tizhi gaige de tansuo*, pp. 45–61.

―――. "Jianli zhuanye gongsi, lianhe gongsi de yuanze he fangfa chutan" (A Preliminary Discussion on the Principles and Methods of Establishing Specialized and Amalgamated Companies). In *Renmin ribao*, July 1, 1980, p. 5.

―――. "Jingji tizhi gaige de lianghao kaiduan" (A Good Start in Economic Structural Reform). In Lin Ling, *Zhongguo jingji tizhi gaige de tansuo*, pp. 11–19.

―――. "Kuoda qiye zizhuquan yu gaige qiye guanli" (Expanding Enterprise Authority and Reforming the Management of Enterprises). In *Renmin ribao*, May 9, 1980, p. 5.

―――. "Sichuan jingji tizhi gaige tichulai de xin keti" (New Problems Brought Out by Sichuan's Economic Structural Reform). In Lin Ling, *Zhongguo jingji tizhi gaige de tansuo*, pp. 217–238.

―――. *Zhongguo jingji tizhi gaige de tansuo* (Explorations of China's Economic Structural Reforms). Chongqing: Chongqing chuban she, 1986.

―――. "Zhongguo jingji tizhi gaige zai Sichuan de shiyan" (The Experiments with Chinese Economic Structural Reform in Sichuan). In Lin Ling, *Zhongguo jingji tizhi gaige de tansuo*, pp. 205–216.

―――. ed., *Sichuan jingji tizhi gaige* (Economic Structural Reform in Sichuan). Chengdu: Sichuan shehui kexue chuban she, 1984.

Lin Zili. "Woguo jingji tizhi gaige de kaiduan" (The Opening Phase in China's Economic Structural Reform). In *Renmin ribao*, April 4, 1980, p. 5.

Liu Baiyu. "Adhere to the Four Basic Principles, Eliminate Spiritual Pollution." In *Jiefangjun wenyi*, January 1, 1984, trans. FBIS, February 10, 1984, pp. K1–4.

Liu Binyan. *A Higher Kind of Loyalty*. New York: Random House, 1990.

"Liu Binyan and Wu Zuguang Say: 'Writers Should Value and Fully Use Freedom of Creation." Zhongguo xinwen she, January 3, 1985, trans. FBIS, January 4, 1985, pp. K6–7.

Liu Chengrui, Hu Naiwu, and Yu Guanghua. "Jihua he shichang xiang jiehe shi woguo jingji guanli gaige de jiben tujing" (Integration of Planning and Market Is the Fundamental Path of China's Economic Management Reform). In Chinese Academy of Social Sciences, Materials Office, ed., *Shehui zhuyi jingji zhong jihua yu shichang de guanxi*, vol. 1, pp. 215–235.

Liu Guoguang. "A Brief Talk on Macroeconomic Control." In *Guangming ribao*, January 4, 1986, p. 3, trans. FBIS, January 22, 1986, pp. K8–11.

———. "Certain Problems Concerning the Reform of the System of Ownership—Outline of a Speech Delivered at an Academic Symposium on the System of Ownership on November 30, 1985." In *Jingji ribao*, no. 1 (January 4, 1986): 3, trans. FBIS, January 14, 1986, pp. K21–26.

———. "Luelun jihua tiaojie yu shichang tiaojie de jige wenti" (Briefly Discussing Some Questions About Planned Regulation and Market Regulation). In *Jingji yanjiu*, no. 10 (October 1980):3–11.

———. "Yanjiu he taolun jihua jingji yu shichang wenti de yidian xiangfa" (Some Thoughts on Studying and Discussing the Question of Plan and Market). In *Caimao jingji*, no. 2 (February 1982):6–8.

Liu Guoguang and Wang Ruisun. "Restructuring the Economy." In Yu Guangyuan, ed., *China's Socialist Modernization*, pp. 71–146. Beijing: Foreign Language Press, 1984.

Liu Guoguang and Zhao Renwei. "Lun shehui zhuyi jingji zhong jihua yu shichang de guanxi" (The Relationship Between Plan and Market in the Socialist Economy). In Chinese Academy of Social Sciences, Materials Office, ed. *Shehui zhuyi jingji zhong jihua yu shichang de guanxi*, vol. 1, pp. 53–73.

———. "Shehui zhuyi jingji zhong jihua he shichang xiang jiehe de biranxing" (The Inevitability of Integrating Plan and Market in the Socialist Economy). In *Jingji yanjiu*, no. 5 (May 1979):46–55.

Liu Guoguang et al. "Jingji tizhi gaige yu hongguan jingji guanli" (Economic Structural Reform and Macroeconomic Control). In *Jingji yanjiu*, no. 12 (December 1985): 3–19.

Liu Hong and Wei Liqun. "On Correctly Handling Several Important Relationships in the Seventh Five-Year Plan." In *Jingji yanjiu*, no. 10 (October 1985):3–9, trans. JPRS-CEA–85–112 (December 20, 1985), pp. 1–14.

Liu Jui-shao. "Beidaihe Conference Said to Have Concluded a Few Days Ago." In *Wen wei po*, August 1, 1988, p. 1, trans. FBIS, August 1, 1988, pp. 29–30.

———. "Enlarged Meeting of the CCP Political Bureau Decides on Tough Action on Prices and Other Problems." In *Wen wei po*, May 31, 1988, trans. FBIS, May 31, 1988, p. 19.

———. "A Meeting at a Crucial Moment—An Insider Account of the CCP Central Committee Political Bureau Meeting." In *Wen wei po*, May 31, 1988, trans. FBIS, May 31, 1988, p. 19.

———. "Viewing the Beidaihe Meeting in Light of Zhao Ziyang's Activities." In *Wen wei po*, August 5, 1988, p. 1, trans. FBIS, August 5, 1988, p. 18.

———. "Why Is There 'Secrecy' Over Zhao Ziyang's Inspections?" In *Wen wei po*, February 25, 1988, p. 2, trans. FBIS, February 25, 1988, p. 11.

———. "Will China's Reforms Be Affected?—Thoughts on the Beidaihe Conference." In *Wen wei po*, August 2, 1988, p. 1, trans. FBIS, August 2, 1988, p. 8.

Liu Ming. "Zhongguo baoshou shili paochu zuoqing gangling" (The Conservative Forces of the CCP Throw Out a Leftist Program). In *Ching-pao yueh-k'an*, no. 6 (June 1987):34–38.

Lo Ping. "The Basic Battle Against 'Leftism' Waged by Hu Yaobang." In *Cheng ming*, no. 2 (February 1, 1985):6–10, trans. FBIS, February 7, 1985, pp. W1–10.

———. "A Counterattack on the Conservatives Criticizing Zhao." In *Cheng ming*, no. 103 (May 1, 1986), trans. FBIS, May 12, 1986, pp. W3–7.

———. "Doubts as to Whether Tigers Are Butchered to Cover Up Things." In *Cheng ming*, no. 103 (May 1, 1986):8–10, trans. FBIS, May 14, 1986, pp. W1–7.

———. "Reorganization of the Nucleus of the Chinese Communist Party—The Truth of Hua Guofeng's Resignation and the New Troika." In *Cheng ming*, no. 40 (February 1, 1981):7–9, trans. FBIS, February 2, 1981, pp. U1–6.

———. "Two Shocking Cases." In *Cheng ming*, no. 105 (July 1, 1986):6–7, trans. FBIS, July 10, 1986, pp. W1–3.

Lu Dingyi. "Historical Review of 'A Hundred Flowers Blooming and a Hundred Schools of Thought Contending'—in Commemoration of the Thirtieth Anniversary of the 'Double Hundred Policy'." In *Guangming ribao*, May 7, 1986, p. 1, trans. FBIS, May 27, 1986, pp. K8–10.

Lu Dong. "Chengbao jingying shi gaohuo dazhong xing qiye de youxiao tujing" (Operation on a Contract Basis Is an Effective Way to Invigorate Large and Medium-Sized Enterprises). In *Hongqi*, no. 9 (May 1, 1987):21–24.

Lu Wen. "Nongcun jingji fazhan zhong de xin dongtai" (New Dynamism in the Rural Economy). In *Nongye jingji wenti*, no. 11 (November 1987):3–6.

Lu Xueyi. "Danggian de nongcun xingshi he liangshi wenti" (The Current Rural Situation and the Grain Question). *Zhongguo nongcun jingji*, no. 6 (June 1986): 1–3.

———. *Lianchan chengbao zerenzhi yanjiu* (Studies on the Production Responsibility System). Shanghai: Renmin chuban she, 1986.

Lu Xueyi, Jia Xinde, and Li Lanting. "Baochan daohu wenti yingdang chongxin yanjiu" (The Question of the Household Responsibility System Should be Restudied). Reprinted in Chinese Rural Development Reseach Group, ed. *Baochan daohu ziliao xuan*, vol. 1, pp. 26–33.

Lu Xueyi and Wang Xiaoqiang. "Baochan daohu de youlai he jinhou de fazhan" (The Origins of the Household Responsibility System and Its Future Development). In *Nongcun, jingji, shehui*, vol. 1, pp. 54–68.

Lu Zhichao. "Deepening a Scientific Understanding of Socialism." In *Guangming ribao*, February 4, 1985, p. 3, trans. FBIS, February 27, 1985, pp. K14–18.

Ma Ding. "Ten Major Changes in China's Economics." In *Gongren ribao*, November 2, 1985, trans. FBIS, May 22, 1986, pp. K3–11.

Ma Hong. *Shilun woguo shehui zhuyi jingji fazhan de xin zhanlue* (On the New Strategy of China's Socialist Economic Development). Beijing: Zhongguo shehui kexue chuban she, 1982.

Ma Hong and Sun Shangqing, eds. *Zhongguo jingji jiegou wenti yanjiu* (Studies on the Chinese Economic Structure). 2 vols. Beijing: Renmin chuban she, 1981.

Macroeconomic Research Office, Economic Structural Reform Institute. "1986 niandu jingji xingshi fenxi" (An Analysis of the Economic Situation in 1986). Translated in Bruce Reynolds, ed., "The Debate Over China's 1986 Recession." In *Chinese Economic Studies* (Spring 1988):3–23.

"Make a Success of Enterprise Management." In *Renmin ribao*, Commentator, January 20, 1986, p. 1, trans. FBIS, January 30, 1986, pp. K4–5.

"Mianxiang gaige shijian, tansuo jingji lilun" (Face the Practice of Reform, Explore Economic Theory). In Conference Secretariat, ed., *Gaige shidai de tansuo*, pp. 536–549.

Microeconomic Situation Analysis Group. "Jinsuo de jingji zengzhang: 1986 nian shang ban nian weiguan jingji fenxi baogao" (Economic Growth Under Retrenchment—A Report on the Analysis of the Microeconomic Situation in the First Half of 1986). Translated in Gary Zou, ed., "The Debate on China's Macroeconomic Situation (I)." In *Chinese Economic Studies* (Winter 1989–90):71–88.

"Minutes of a Symposium on Experimental Economic System Reform in Selected Cities, Approved by the State Council and Circulated by the State Economic System Reform Commission." In *Renmin ribao*, May 21, 1984, pp. 1 and 3, trans. FBIS, June 8, 1984, pp. K12–14.

Nathan, Andrew J. *Chinese Democracy*. New York: Alfred A. Knopf, 1985.

———. "A Factionalism Model for CCP Politics." In *The China Quarterly,* no. 53 (January–March 1973):34–66.

"National Philosophical Symposium of Party Schools Stresses Elimination of Feudal Ideology as an Important Aspect of the Education of Cadres." In *Guangming ribao*, July 6, 1980, p. 1, trans. FBIS, July 18, 1980, pp. L3–4.

Naughton, Barry. "The Third Front: Defence Industrialization in the Chinese Interior." In *The China Quarterly*, no. 115 (September 1988):351–386.

———. "Sun Yefang: Toward a Reconstruction of Socialist Economics." In Carol Lee Hamrim and Timothy Cheek, eds., *China's Establishment Intellectuals*, pp. 124–154. Armonk, NY: M.E. Sharpe, 1986.

Office of the Economic Structural Reform Group of the State Council Finance and Economic Commission. "Guanyu jingji tizhi gaige de chubu yijian" (Preliminary Ideas on the Overall Reform of the Economic Management System). In Chinese Economic Structural Reform Commission, ed., *Zhongguo jingji tizhi gaige guihua ji (1979–1987)* (Compendium of Chinese Economic Structural Reform Plans, 1979–1987). Beijing: Zhongyang dangxiao chuban she, 1988, pp. 22–36.

Oi, Jean. "Fiscal Reform and the Economic Foundations of Local State Corporatism in China." In *World Politics*, vol. 45, no. 1 (October 1992):99–126.

———. *State and Peasant in Contemporary China*. Berkeley and Los Angeles: University of California Press, 1989.

"On the International Environment of China's Open Door—Summary of Views at the Symposium on World Economics of Young and Middle-Aged Research Workers." In *Shijie jingji*, no. 2 (February 10, 1985):25–29, trans. JPRS-CEA–85–084 (September 19, 1985), pp. 1–8.

Peng Zhen. "Speech at the Joint Group Meeting of the 18th Session of the NPC Standing Committee Discussing the 'Resolution of the Communist Party of China on the Guiding Principles for Building a Socialist Spiritual Civilization'." Xinhua, November 26, 1986, trans. FBIS, December 1, 1986, pp. K9–13.

"Pernicious Influence of Feudalistic Thinking Must Be Eliminated." In *Renmin ribao*, Contributing Commentator, July 18, 1980, p. 5, trans. FBIS, July 23, 1980, pp. L10–13.

Pi Shuyi. "Without Reform, There Would Be No Way Out." In *Renmin ribao*, April 25, 1992, pp. 1–2, trans. FBIS, May 11, 1992, p. 19.

"Place the Reform of the Political Structure on the Agenda." In *Renmin ribao*, Editorial, July 1, 1987, trans. FBIS, July 1, 1987, pp. K1–3.

"Popularize the Business Responsibility System Adopted by Retail and Service Trades— Third Discussion on Stopping the Practice of 'Eating From the Same Big Pot'." *Renmin ribao*, Editorial, January 20, 1983, p. 1, trans. FBIS, January 21, 1983, pp. K6–8.

Problem Group of the Research Center of the State Planning Commission. "Tizhi zhuanhuan shiqi de hongguan tiaokong" (Macroeconomic Regulation and Control in the Period of Structural Transformation). In *Jingji yanjiu*, no. 5 (May 1989):11–21.

Problem Group of the Rural Development Research Group of the State Council. "Zhongguo nongcun jingji tizhi zhongqi (1988–1995) gaige tiyao" (Outline of the Structural Reform of the Chinese Rural Economy in the Medium Term, 1988–1995). In State Commission for Economic Structural Reform, ed., *Zhongguo gaige da silu*, pp. 241–266.

"Proposal of the Central Committee of the Chinese Communist Party for the Seventh Five-Year Plan (1986–90) for National Economic and Social Development." Xinhua, September 25, 1985, trans. FBIS, September 26, 1985, pp. K1–24.

"Provisional Regulations of the State Council on Further Expanding the Decision Making Powers of State-Owned Enterprises." Xinhua, May 11, 1984, trans. FBIS, May 16, 1984, pp. K15–17.

"Qian Jiaju Discusses Prices, Reform, and Social Mood." In Wen wei po, April 4, 1988, trans. FBIS, April 12, 1988, pp. 36–40.

Qiao Rongzhang. Jiage butie (Price Subsidies). Beijing: Zhongguo wujia chuban she, 1990.

Qin Wen, "Why Has It Not Been Possible to Scale Down Capital Construction?" In Renmin ribao, January 31, 1980, p. 5, trans. FBIS, March 3, 1980, p. L18.

Qu Anzhen and Zhu Yushan. "Chen Yun on Party Style." In Jiefang ribao, May 15, 1991, p. 6, trans. FBIS, May 23, 1991, pp. 40–42.

"Quanguo nongcun gongzuo huiyi jiyao" (Outline of the National Rural Work Conference). In Renmin ribao, April 6, 1982.

"Regulations Governing Several Questions on Further Promoting Lateral Economic Ties." Xinhua, March 23, 1986, trans. FBIS, April 1, 1986, pp. K1–6.

"Regulations Governing the Work of Factory Directors of State-Owned Industrial Enterprises." Xinhua, January 11, 1987, trans. FBIS, February 5, 1987, pp. 19–25.

"Regulations on the Work in Rural People's Communes." In Issues and Studies, vol. 15, no. 8 (August 1979):100–112, and vol. 15, no. 9 (September 1979):104–115.

"Regulations on Workers' Congresses of State-Run Industrial Enterprises." Xinhua, January 11, 1987, trans. JPRS-CEA–87–019 (March 16, 1987), pp. 97–102.

"Report by Jiang Zemin, General Secretary of the CCP Central Committee, on Behalf of the CCP Central Committee and State Council." Beijing Television Service, September 29, 1989, trans. FBIS, October 2, 1989, pp. 17–27.

"Resolution of the Central Committee of the Communist Party of China on the Guiding Principles for Building a Socialist Society with Advanced Culture and Ideology." Xinhua, September 28, 1986, trans. FBIS, September 29, 1986, pp. K2–13.

"Resolution on Certain Questions in the History of Our Party Since the Founding of the People's Republic of China." Xinhua, June 30, 1981, in FBIS, July 1, 1981, pp. K1–38.

Rosen, Stanley, and Gary Zou. "The Road to Modernization in China Debated: The Origins, Development and Decline of the Neoauthoritarianism and Direct Democracy Schools." Unpublished manuscript.

———. eds. "The Chinese Debate on the New Authoritarianism." In Chinese Sociology and Anthropology, nos. 1–4 (Winter 1990–91, Spring 1991, Summer 1991, and Fall 1991).

Rosenbaum, Arthur Lewis, ed. State and Society in China: The Consequences of Reform. Boulder, CO: Westview Press, 1992.

Ruan Ming. Deng Xiaoping diguo (The Empire of Deng Xiaoping). Taipei: Shih-pao ch'u-pan kung-ssu, 1991.

———. "An Important Task on the Ideological Front." In Lilun yu shijian (Theory and Practice), no. 9 (August 28, 1980), trans. FBIS, September 11, 1980, pp. L64–73.

" 'Sanji suoyou, dui wei jichu' yinggai wending" ("Three-Level Ownership with the Production Team as the Foundation" Should Be Stabilized). In Renmin ribao, March 15, 1979, p. 1.

Schwartz, Benjamin. In Search of Wealth and Power: Yen Fu and the West. Cambridge, MA: Harvard University Press, 1964.

Secretarial Section. "Zhongguo nongcun fazhan wenti yanjiu jihua tigang (cao'an)" (Outline of the Research Plan on China's Rural Development, Draft). In Chinese Rural Development Research Group, ed., *Nongcun, jingji, shehui*, vol. 1, pp. 23–24.

Selden, Mark. *The Political Economy of Chinese Development*. Armonk, NY: M.E. Sharpe, 1993.

"Set Capital Construction on the Right Course, Follow Strict Capital Construction Discipline." In *Renmin ribao*, Editorial, June 10, 1980, trans. FBIS, June 19, 1980, pp. L1–5.

Shapiro, Judith, and Liang Heng. *After the Nightmare*. New York: Alfred A. Knopf, 1986.

Shen Liren. "A Discussion on Optimal Speed." In *Jingji guanli*, no. 9 (September 1985):16–19, trans. JPRS-CEA–85–110 (December 17, 1985), pp. 84–91.

Shen Liren and Dai Yuanchen. "Woguo 'zhuhou jingji' de xingcheng ji qi biduan he genyuan" (The Formation of the 'Feudal-Lord' Economy in China: Its Origins and Harm). In *Jingji yanjiu*, no. 3 (March 1990):12–19, 67.

Sheng Hong and Huang Tieying. "Wei jingji gaosu zengzhang shengbian" (In Defense of High-Speed Economic Development). In Chinese Economic Structural Reform Institute, ed., *Zhongguo: fazhan yu gaige (1984–1985, shou zhuan)*, pp. 380–389.

Sheng Hong and Zou Gang. "Jingji fazhan guocheng zhong de huobi gongying" (The Money Supply in the Process of Economic Development). In *Zhongqingnian jingji luntan*, no. 1 (January 1987):40–46.

Shi Bing. "Guanyu nongye xuyao zengjia touru wenti de tausuo" (An Exploration of the Need to Increase Agricultural Inputs). In *Nongye jingji wenti*, no. 1 (January 1987), trans. JPRS-CAR–87–007 (June 16, 1987), pp. 6–9.

Shi Xiamin and Liu Jirui. "An Economist Must Primarily Respect History and Facts—Commenting on 'Ten Years of China's Reform (Review)'." In *Jingji yanjiu*, no. 2 (February 1989):11–33, trans. JPRS-CAR–89–064 (June 22, 1989), pp. 5–29.

Shirk, Susan L. *The Political Logic of Economic Reform in China*. Berkeley and Los Angeles: University of California Press, 1993.

Shougang zhubian hua chengbao (Major Changes in Capitol Iron and Steel Company Under the Contract Responsibility System). Beijing: Renmin chuban she, 1989.

"Special Economic Zones Are Not Special Political Zones; China's Laws Must Be Upheld, Says Hu Qiaomu." In *Zhongguo fazhi bao*, June 28, 1985, trans. FBIS, July 8, 1985, pp. K18–19.

"Speech at a Meeting of Propaganda, Theoretical, Press, and Party School Cadres." Xinhua, July 8, 1987, trans. FBIS, July 8, 1987, pp. K1–8.

"Speed Up Comprehensive Urban Reform." In *Renmin ribao*, Commentator, June 8, 1984, trans. FBIS, June 12, 1984, pp. K14–15.

Solinger, Dorothy J. *From Looms to Lathes: China's Industrial Policy in Comparative Perspective*. Stanford, CA: Stanford University Press, 1991.

"Some Questions Concerning the Current Rural Economic Policies." Xinhua, April 10, 1983, trans. FBIS, April 13, 1983, pp. K1–13.

Song Chun, Wen Li, Liu Heng, and Jing Guiliang. "Duli hesuan gongye qiye kuisun yuanyin" (The Reasons Industrial Enterprises with Independent Accounting Incur Deficits). In Fang Weizhong and Wu Jiajun, eds., *Gongye kuisun diaocha yanjiu*, pp. 50–78.

Song Guoqing and Zhang Weiying. "Guanyu hongguan pingheng yu hongguan kongzhi jige lilun wenti" (Theoretical Questions Concerning Macroeconomic Balances and Macroeconomic Control). In *Jingji yanjiu*, no. 6 (June 1986):25–35.

Song Guoqing, Zhang Weiying, and Cheng Xiaonong. "Hongguan jingji taolun zhong de ruogan lilun fenqi" (Some Theoretical Divisions in Discussions on the Macroeconomy). In *Jingji yanjiu*, no. 4 (April 1987):3–14.

Stalin, Joseph, *Economic Problems of Socialism in the U.S.S.R.* New York: International Publishers, 1952.

State Commission for Economic Structural Reform, ed. *Zhongguo gaige da silu* (Major Ways of Thinking About Chinese Reform). Shenyang: Renmin chuban she, 1988.

"State Planning Commission to Conduct Major Reform of Planning System." In *Jingji ribao*, October 6, 1984, p. 1, trans. FBIS, October 11, 1984, pp. K1–2.

"Study Well the Documents and Grasp the Key Link." Editorial published jointly by *Renmin ribao, Hongqi,* and *Jiefangjun bao*, February 7, 1977, trans. FBIS, February 7, 1977, pp. E1–3.

Su Shaozhi and Feng Lanrui. "Wuchan jieji qude zhengquan hou de shehui fazhan jieduan wenti" (The Question of Developmental Stages Following the Proletariat's Attainment of Political Power). In *Jingji yanjiu*, no. 5 (May 1979):14–19.

Su Shaozhi and Wang Yizhou. "Crisis and Thought—On the Current Situation and Next Step of Reform in China." In *Shijie jingji daobao*, October 24, 1988, p. 7, trans. FBIS, November 15, 1988.

"Substitution of Tax Payment for Profit Delivery Is the 'Key' to Urban Reform." In *Renmin ribao*, Editorial, September 19, 1984, p. 2, trans. FBIS, September 24, 1984, pp. K16–17.

Sun Qimeng and Xiong Zhiyong. *Dazhai hongqi de shengqi yu duoluo* (The Rise and Fall of the Red Flag of Dazhai). Zhengzhou: Henan renmin chuban she, 1990.

Sun Shangqing. "Guanyu jiazhi guilu zuoyong wenti taolunhui de choubei qingquang he-huiyi de kaifa" (The Preparations for and Opening of the Symposium on the Role of the Law of Value). In Chinese Academy of Social Sciences, Materials Office, ed., *Shehui zhuyi jingji zhong jihua yu shichang de guanxi*, vol. 2, pp. 770–773.

Sun Shangqing, Chen Jiyuan, and Zhang Zhuoyuan. "Shehui zhuyi jingji de jihuaxing yu shichangxing xiang jiehe de jige lilun wenti" (Several Theoretical Questions of Integrating the Planned and Market Natures of the Socialist Economy). In Chinese Academy of Social Sciences, Materials Office, ed., *Shehui zhuyi jingji zhong jihua yu shichang de guanxi*, vol. 1, pp. 96–125.

———. "Zai lun shehui zhuyi jingji de jihuaxing yu shichangxing xiang jiehe" (Another Discussion of Integrating the Planned and Market Natures of the Socialist Economy). In Chinese Academy of Social Sciences, Materials Office, ed., *Shehui zhuyi jingji zhong jihua yu shichang de guanxi*, vol. 1, pp. 126–148.

Sun Xiaoliang. "Shehui zhuyi tiaojian xia de jingzheng" (Competition Under Socialist Conditions). In *Renmin ribao*, June 23, 1980, p. 5.

Sun Yefang. "Ba jihua he tongji fang zai jiazhi guilu de jichu shang" (Place Planning and Statistics on the Foundation of the Law of Value). In Sun Yefang, *Sun Yefang xuanji*, pp. 117–129. Taoyuan: Shanxi renmin chuban she, 1984.

———. "Jianchi yi jihua jingji wei zhu shichang tiaojie wei fu" (Uphold Taking the Planned Economy as Primary and Market Regulation as Supplementary). In *Caimao jingji*, no. 5 (May 1982):1–2.

"Sun Yefang tongzhi zhuchi zuotanhui xuexi Chen Yun tongzhi chunjie zhongyao jianghua" (Comrade Sun Yefang Convenes Symposium to Discuss Comrade Chen Yun's Important Spring Festival Talk). In Hongqi, ed., *Jihua jingji yu shichang tiaojie wenji (di yi ji)*, p. 301.

"The System of Offering Greater Decisionmaking Power to Factory Directors Is Being Tested in Six Cities." In *Jingji ribao*, April 26, 1984, trans. FBIS, May 8, 1984, p. K7.

Tan Zongji and Zheng Qian, eds., *Shinianhou de pingshuo* (An Evaluation Ten Years Later). Beijing: Zhonggong dangshi ziliao chuban she, 1987.

Tang Zongkun. "Jiazhi guilu, shichang jizhi he shehui zhuyi jihua jingji" (The Law of Value, the Market Mechanism, and the Socialist Planned Economy). In Chinese Academy of Social Sciences, Materials Office, ed., *Shehui zhuyi jingji zhong jihua yu shichang de guanxi*, vol. 1, pp. 149–180.

Tao Dayong. "Shi jihua jingji, hai shi shangpin jingji?" (Is It a Planned Economy or a Commodity Economy?). In *Guangming ribao*, June 26, 1982, p. 3.

Teiwes, Frederick C. *Leadership, Legitimacy, and Conflict in China.* Armonk, NY: M.E. Sharpe, 1984.

Tian Jiyun. "Actively and Steadily Carry Out Reform of the Pricing System." In *Renmin ribao*, January 8, 1985, pp. 1 and 2, trans. FBIS, January 10, 1985, pp. K2–9.

Tian Yuan. "Jiage gaige yu chanquan zhidu zhuanhuan" (Price Reform and the Change-over in the Property Rights System). In *Jingji yanjiu*, no. 2 (February 1988):11–18.

"Tiaodong nongmin jijixing de yixiang youli cuoshi" (An Effective Measure for Arousing the Enthusiasm of Peasants). In *Renmin ribao*, May 20, 1979, p. 2.

Tsou, Tang. *The Cultural Revolution and Post-Mao Reforms: A Historical Perspective.* Chicago: University of Chicago Press, 1986.

———. "Political Change and Reform: The Middle Course." In Tang Tsou, *The Cultural Revolution and Post-Mao Reforms: A Historical Perspective*, pp. 219–258.

———. "Prolegomenon to the Study of Informal Groups in CCP Politics." In Tang Tsou, *The Cultural Revolution and Post-Mao Reforms: A Historical Perspective*, pp. 95–111.

———. "The Responsibility System in Agriculture." In Tang Tsou, *The Cultural Revolution and Post-Mao Reforms: A Historical Perspective*, pp. 95–111.

———. "The Tiananmen Tragedy." In Brantly Womack, ed., *Contemporary Chinese Politics in Historical Perspective*, pp. 265–327.

Wan Li. "Further Develop the New Phase of Agriculture Which Has Already Been Opened Up." In *Renmin ribao*, December 23, 1982, pp. 1, 2, and 4, trans. FBIS, January 4, 1983, pp. K2–20.

———. "Zai shengwei gongzuo huiyi shang de jianghua" (Talk at a Work Meeting of the Provincial Party Committee). In Wang Gengjin et al., eds., *Xiangcun sanshi nian*, vol. 2, p. 386.

Wan Maohua. "Deng Liqun Expresses Views on Hunan's Two Civilizations." In *Hunan ribao*, trans. JPRS-CPS–87–013 (March 26, 1987), p. 131.

Wang Bingqian. "Guanyu yi jiu ba san nian guojia juesuan he yi jiu ba si nian guojia yusuan cao'an de baogao" (Draft Report on the State's Accounts for 1983 and the State's Budget for 1984). In *Zhongguo jingji nianjian*, 1984, pp. 23–29.

Wang Gengjin et al., eds. *Xiangcun sanshi nian: Fengyang nongcun shehui jingji fazhan shilu (1949–1983 nian)* (The Countryside Over Thirty Years: A Veritable Record of Fengyang's Social-Economic Development, 1949–1983). 2 vols. Beijing: Nongcun duwu chuban she, 1989.

Wang Huning. "Zhongguo bianhua zhong de zhongyang he difang zhengfu de guanxi: zhengzhi de hanyi" (The Changing Relations Between the Central and Local Governments: The Political Implications). In *Fudan xuebao*, no. 5 (May 1988):1–8.

Wang Jian. "The Correct Strategy for Long-Term Economic Development—Concept of the Development Strategy of Joining the 'Great International Cycle'." In *Jingji ribao*, January 5, 1988. Translated in Joseph Fewsmith and Gary Zou, eds., "China's Coastal Development (I)." In *Chinese Economic Studies* (Fall 1991):7–15.

———. "Develop an Externally Oriented Economy to Speed Up the Transformation of Our Industrial Structure." In *Zhongguo qinggongye jingji*, no. 4 (April 1988). Translated in Joseph Fewsmith and Gary Zou, eds., "China's Coastal Development (II)." In *Chinese Economic Studies* (Spring 1992):36–42.

Wang Jiye. *Jihua jingji yu shichang tiaojie—xuexi dang de shierda wenjian tihui* (Planned Economy and Market Regulation—Understanding Gained from Studying the Documents of the Twelfth Party Congress). Beijing: Zhongguo caizheng jingji chuban she, 1983.

———. "Problems of the Economic Environment and Macroeconomic Regulation in Structural Reform." In *Renmin ribao*, March 18, 1985, p. 171, trans. FBIS, April 2, 1985, pp. K17–22.

Wang Jiye and Zhu Yuanzhen, eds. *Jingji tizhi gaige shouce* (Handbook on Economic Structural Reform). Beijing: Jingji ribao chuban she, 1987.

Wang Lingshu. "Ji Dengkui on Mao Zedong." In *Liaowang*, Overseas Edition, nos. 6–7 (February 6–13, 1989), trans. FBIS, February 14, 1989, pp. 22–26.

Wang Lixin. "Life After Mao Zedong: A Report on Implementation of and Consequences of Major Chinese Agricultural Policies in Anhui Villages." In *Kunlun*, no. 6 (December 1988):4–53, trans. JPRS-CAR–89–079 (July 28, 1989), pp. 1–65.

Wang Lixin and Joseph Fewsmith. "Bulwark of the Planned Economy: The Structure and Role of the State Planning Commission." Forthcoming in Carol Lee Hamrin and Suisheng Zhao, eds., *Deng's China: Dynamics of the Political Process*.

"Wang Meng Says the Main Purpose of Advocating Freedom in Literary Creation Is to Clear Away 'Leftist' Residue." Zhongguo xinwen she, January 9, 1985, trans. FBIS, January 11, 1985, pp. K7–8.

Wang Mengkui. "Dangqian jingji xingshi he xuyao yanjiu de yixie wenti" (The Present Economic Situation and Some Problems That Need to Be Studied). In *Jingji yanjiu*, no. 12 (December 1989):23–30.

Wang Renzhi. "Guanyu fandui zichan jieji ziyouhua" (On Opposing Bourgeois Liberalization). In *Renmin ribao*, February 22, 1990, pp. 1–3.

———. "Guanyu jianchi shehui zhuyi jihua jingji de jige wenti" (Several Questions on Upholding the Socialist Planned Commodity Economy). In Hongqi, ed., *Jihua jingji yu shichang tiaojie wenji (di yi ji)*, pp. 282–299.

Wang Renzhi and Gui Shiyong. "Jianchi he gaijin zhilingxing jihua zhidu" (Uphold and Improve the System of Mandatory Planning). In Hongqi, ed., *Jihua jingji yu shichang tiaojie wenji (di yi ji)*, pp. 282–299.

Wang Tianduo. "National Economic Work Conference Calls on Enterprises to Stop Losses, Increase Profits." In *Renmin ribao*, February 22, 1984, trans. FBIS, February 28, 1984, pp. K1–2.

Wang Xiaoqiang. "Nongye shehui zhuyi de pipan" (Critique of Agrarian Socialism). In *Nongye jingji wenti*, no. 2 (February 1980):9–20.

Wang Yuzhao. *Da bao gan yu da qushi* (Comprehensive Contracting and the General Trend). Beijing: Guangming ribao chuban she, 1987.

———. "Fengqi yunyong de biange langchao." (The Sweeping Tide of Change). In Wang Yuzhao, *Da bao gan yu da qushi*, pp. 9–18.

———. *Zunzhong nongmin de juece—nongcun gaige de shijian he tansuo* (Respect the Decision of the Peasants—Practice and Explorations in the Rural Reforms). Shanghai: Renmin chuban she, 1989.

"Weihu anding tuanjie zhege daju" (Maintain the Overall Situation of Stability and Unity), *Renmin ribao*, Editorial, October 10, 1989, p. 1.

"Wenzhou zhuanqu jiuzheng 'baochan daohu' de cuowu zuofa" (Wenzhou District's Correction of the "Household Responsibility" Mistake). In *Renmin ribao*, October 9, 1957. Reprinted in Chinese Rural Development Research Group, ed., *Baochan daohu ziliao xuan*, vol. 1, pp. 259–261.

"What Is Shown by the Career Rise and Arrest of 'Du, the God of Fortune'?" In *Renmin ribao*, December 30, 1985, p. 1, trans. FBIS, January 7, 1986, pp. K1–2.

"What Should Be Upheld and What Should Be Opposed?—Fifth Discussion on the Guiding Thought of Doing Everything According to Actual Capabilities." In *Renmin ribao*, Editorial, June 26, 1980, trans. FBIS, July 9, 1980, pp. L8–11.

White, Gordon. *Riding the Tiger: The Politics of Economic Reform in Post-Mao China*. Stanford, CA: Stanford University Press, 1993.

Womack, Brantly, ed., *Contemporary Chinese Politics in Historical Perspective*. Cambridge, UK: Cambridge University Press, 1991.

"Work Regulations for Grass-Roots Organizations of the CCP in State-Owned Industrial Enterprises." Xinhua, January 11, 1987, trans. FBIS, February 5, 1987, pp. 26–30.

"Work Together with One Heart in Building the Four Modernizations—1985 New Year Message." In *Renmin ribao*, Editorial, January 1, 1985, p. 1, trans. FBIS, January 2, 1985, pp. K6–7.

Wu Ji, Zhang Junkuo, Yue Bing, and Li Jiange. "Lun jingji zengzhang de youxiao yueshu" (On the Effective Restraint on Economic Growth). In *Jingji yanjiu*, no. 6 (June 1986):19–24.

Wu Jinglian. "Cong Xiongyali jingyan kan woguo dangqian gaige" (Viewing China's Current Reform from the Perspective of Hungary's Experience). In Wu Jinglian, *Jingji gaige wenti tansuo*, pp. 387–394.

———. Danxiang tuijin, haishi peitao gaige" (Advancing on One Front or Coordinated Reform?). In Wu Jinglian, *Jingji gaige wenti tansuo*, pp. 268–278.

———. "Jingji jizhi he peitao gaige" (Economic Mechanisms and Coordinated Reforms). In *Hongqi*, no. 5 (March 1, 1986), pp. 19–23.

———. "Jingji gaige chuzhan jieduan de fazhan fangzhen he hongguan kongzhi wenti" (The Development Orientation in the Initial Stage of Economic Reform and the Problem of Macroeconomic Control). In *Renmin ribao*, February 11, 1985, p. 5.

———. *Jingji gaige wenti tansuo* (Explorations in Economic Reform). Beijing: Zhanwang chuban she, 1987.

———. "Jingji tizhi gaige yu jingji jiegou tiaozheng de guanxi" (The Relationship Between Economic Reform and Economic Readjustment). In Ma Hong and Sun Shangqing, eds. *Zhongguo jingji jiegou wenti yanjiu*, vol. 2, pp. 790–806.

———. "Women yingdang cong Xiongyali gaige de chengbai deshi zhong qude shenma jiaoshun?" (What Lessons Should We Derive from the Successes and Failures of Hungary's Reform?). In Wu Jinglian, *Jingji gaige wenti tansuo*, pp. 377–386.

———. "Zailun baochi jingji gaige de lianghao jingji huanjing" (Again Discussing Maintaining a Favorable Economic Environment for Economic Reform). In *Jingji yanjiu*, no. 5 (May 1985):3–12.

Wu Jinglian and Hu Ji, eds. *Zhongguo jingji de dongtai fenxi he duice yanjiu* (A Dynamic Analysis of China's Economy and Studies on Countermeasures). Beijing: Renmin daxue chuban she, 1988.

Wu Jinglian, Li Jiange, Ding Ningning, and Zhang Junkuo. "The Key to Bringing About a Benign Cycle in the National Economy." In *Jingji ribao*, January 4, 1986, pp. 1 and 3, trans. FBIS, January 14, 1986, pp. K15–18.

Wu Jinglian, Zhou Xiaochuan, et al., eds., *Zhongguo jingji gaige de zhengti sheji* (The Integrated Design of China's Economic Reform). Beijing: Zhongguo zhanwang chuban she, 1990.

Wu Jinglian et al., "Jingji tizhi zhongqi gaige guihua gangyao" (Outline Plan for Mid-Term Economic Structural Reform). In State Commission for Economic Structural Reform, ed., *Zhongguo gaige da silu*, pp. 197–240.

Wu Kaitai. "Qiushi he yanjin de makesi zhuyi jingji xuejia—Xue Muqiao zhuanlue" (A Truth-Seeking and Serious Marxist Economist—A Brief Biography of Xue Muqiao). In Chinese Economic Daily, ed., *Zhongguo dangdai jingji xuejia zhuanlue*, vol. 1, pp. 231–265.

Wu Shuo. "A Talk on the Second Major Reform of the Rural Economic Structure." In *Liaowang*, no. 4 (1985):16–17, trans. FBIS, February 7, 1985, pp. K19–22.

Wu Xiang. *Cong Xiyang dao Fenyang* (From Xiang to Fengyang). Beijing: Jingji kexue chuban she, 1991.

———. "Deepen Reform and Strengthen the New Structure of the Rural Economy." In *Nongye jingji wenti*, no. 1 (January 1988):9–11.

————. *Woguo nongcun weida xiwang zhi suozai* (The Great Hope of China's Countryside). Beijing: Jingji kexue chuban she, 1984.

————. "Yang guan dao yu du mu qiao" (The Broad Road and the Single-Plank Bridge). In *Renmin ribao*, November 5, 1980. Reprinted in Chinese Academy of Social Sciences, Rural Development Institute, ed., *Nongye shengchan zerenzhi lunwenji*, pp. 27–40.

Wu Xinmin. "For the Workers to Become Masters of the House Is the Key to Creating a New Situation in an Enterprise—Zhou Guanwu, Party Secretary of the Capitol Iron and Steel Company, Talks About the Economic Responsibility System." In *Gongren ribao*, December 24, 1982, pp. 1, 2, trans. FBIS, January 6, 1983, pp. K5–8.

Xiao Jie. "Diversified Views on the Focus of Economic Reform in the Seventh Five-Year Plan Period." In *Shijie jingji daobao*, January 6, 1986, p. 3, trans. FBIS, January 15, 1986, pp. K11–14.

Xing Sheng and Lu Jiafeng. "Zhengque kandai lianxi chanliang de zerenzhi" (Correctly View the Responsibility System That Links Remuneration to Output). In *Renmin ribao*, March 30, 1979, p. 1.

"Xiongyali caizheng tizhi kaocha" (Investigation of the Hungarian Finance Structure). In *Jingji yanjiu*, no. 3 (March 1984):13–22, 8.

"Xiongyali jingji tizhi kaocha baogao" (Investigation Report on the Economic Structure of Hungary). In *Jingji yanjiu*, no. 2 (February 1984):10–12.

Xu Jingan. "Woguo jingji fazhan jinru xin jieduan" (China's Economic Development Has Entered a New Stage). In Chinese Economic Structural Reform Institute, ed., *Zhongguo: fazhan yu gaige (1984–1985, shou zhuan)*, pp. 296–305.

Xu Kong. "Independent Thinker of China's Economic Reform—On Li Yining, Professor of Beijing University." *Zhongguo xinwen she*, trans. FBIS, June 10, 1986, pp. K2–4.

Xu Yi. *Caizheng lilun yu shijian* (The Theory and Practice of Finance). 2 vols. Beijing: Jingji kexue chuban she, 1985.

————. "Dangqian caizheng jingji zhong cunzai de wenti he women de duice" (The Fiscal and Economic Problems Existing at Present and Our Countermeasures). In Chinese Finance Society, ed., *Dangqian caizheng wenti—disice quanguo caizheng lilun taolunhui wenxuan*, pp. 13–34.

————. "Lun shuishou de honggan zuoyong" (The Function of Tax Levers). In Xu Yi, *Caizheng lilun yu shijian*, vol. 1, pp. 175–191.

————. "On the Establishment of a Comprehensive Financial System of Macroeconomic Balance." In *Caizheng yanjiu*, no. 5 (May 1985). Translated in Joseph Fewsmith, ed., "The Debate on China's Macroeconomic Situation (II)." In *Chinese Economic Studies* (Spring 1990):46–68.

————. "Sanshi nian lai caizheng lilun yu shijian de fazhan" (The Development of Finance Theory and Practice Over the Past Thirty Years). In Xu Yi, *Caizheng lilun yu shijian*, vol. 1, pp. 3–31.

————. "Shehui zhuyi jingji guilu yu shehui zhuyi caizheng de zhineng zuoyong" (Socialist Economic Law and the Functions of Socialist Finance). In Xu Yi, *Caizheng lilun yu shijian*, vol. 1, pp. 95–119.

Xue Muqiao. *Dangqian woguo jingji ruogan wenti* (Some Problems in China's Contemporary Economy). Beijing: Renmin chuban she, 1980.

————. "Jianchi baijia zhengming, jianchi lilun lianxi shiji" (Uphold a Hundred Schools of Thought Contending, Uphold Linking Theory to Reality). In Chinese Academy of Social Sciences, Materials Office, ed., *Shehui zhuyi jingji zhong jihua yu shichang de guanxi*, vol. 1, pp. 1–6.

————. "Shehui zhuyi jingji de jihua guanli" (The Planned Management of a Socialist Economy). In Chinese Academy of Social Sciences, Materials Office, ed.,
Shehui zhuyi jingji zhong jihua yu shichang de guanxi, vol. 1, pp. 15–43.

————. *Woguo guomin jingji de tiaozheng he gaige* (Readjustment and Reform of
China's National Economy). Beijing: Renmin chuban she, 1982.

————. *Zhongguo shehui zhuyi jingji wenti yanjiu* (Studies on China's Socialist Economy). Beijing: Renmin chuban she, 1979.

Xue Xiaohe. "Properly Handle the Two Reforms and Overcome the Two Gusts of Ill
Wind—Xue Muqiao on Economic Relations in the Current Year." In *Renmin ribao*,
March 6, 1985, trans. FBIS, March 8, 1985, pp. K13–17.

Yang Fan. *Zhonghua renmin gongheguo de di san dai* (The Third Generation of the
PRC). Chengdu: Renmin chuban she, 1991.

Yang Mu. "Lun yingxiang gongye fazhan sudu de yinsu" (Factors Influencing the Speed
of Industrial Development). In *Zhongqingnian jingji luntan*, no. 10 (October 1985):
17–21.

Yang Peixin. "On Upholding and Perfecting the Enterprise Contract System." In *Jingji yanjiu*,
no. 3 (March 1990):44–50, trans. JPRS-CAR–90–048 (July 5, 1990), pp. 48–54.

Yang Shikuang. "Shehui zhuyi jingji zhong yinggai you jingzheng ma?" (Should Socialist
Societies Have Competition?). In *Jingji kexue*, no. 1 (February 1980):76–78.

Yao Yilin. "Tongxin xieli zuohao jingji gaige de diaocha yanjiu" (Unify to Investigate
Well Economic Reform). In You Lin, Zhao Shaoping, and Wang Mengkui, eds. *Jingji
gaige wencong, di yi ji*, vol. 1, pp. 1–7.

Ye Yonglie. "Wang Li bing zhong da ke wen" (Wang Li, Who Is Ill, Answers His Guest's
Questions). In *Ta kung pao*, January 3, 4, 5, 6, and 7, 1989.

Yeh Chi-jung. "Chen Muhua Received Hong Kong and Macao Reporters This Morning."
In *Hsin wan pao*, March 31, 1985, p. 1, trans. FBIS, April 1, 1985, pp. W8–9.

"Yi fen shengwei wenjian de tansheng" (The Birth of a Provincial Committee Document).
In *Renmin ribao*, February 3, 1978, pp. 1–2.

Yi Ren (pseud.). "Zhuozhou huiyi de qianqian houhou" (Before and After the Zhuozhou
Meeting). In *Renmin ribao*, February 14, 1990, p. 3.

"Yinkou City CCP Committee Correctly Handles a 'Lawsuit' Brought by a Party Secretary Against a Plant Director." In *Renmin ribao*, February 13, 1986, p. 2, trans. FBIS,
February 26, 1986, pp. K1–3.

"You Can Study and Refer to the Experiences of the Capitol Iron and Steel Company."
Hunan Radio, November 28, 1986, trans. FBIS, December 22, 1986, p. K22.

You Lin. "Jihua shengchan shi zhuti, ziyou shengchan shi buchong" (Planned Production
Is Primary, Free Production is Supplementary). In *Jingji yanjiu*, no. 9 (September
1981):3–9.

You Lin, Zhao Shaoping, and Wang Mengkui, eds., *Jingji gaige wencong, di yi ji* (Essays
on Economic Reform), vol. 1. Shenyang: Liaoning renmin chuban she, 1981.

Yu Guangyuan. "Discussion of Ma Ding's Article Should Be Taken as an Opportunity to
Gain Experience in Implementing the 'Double Hundred' Policy." In *Shijie jingji
daobao*, April 21, 1986, trans. FBIS, May 12, 1986, pp. K8–10.

————. "My Views on the Contract System." In *Shijie jingji daobao*, October 5, 1987, p.
10, trans. FBIS, October 28, 1987, p. 31.

————. "On the Question Regarding 'The Theory of the Goal of Socialist Economy'."
Xinhua, October 22, 1979, trans. FBIS, October 24, 1979, L3–8.

————. "Tantan 'shehui zhuyi jingji mubiao lilun' wenti" (On the "Theory of Socialist
Economic Goals"). In *Jingji yanjiu*, no. 11 (November 1979):2–7.

————. "The Thirtieth Anniversary of the Setting Forth of the 'Double Hundred' Policy."
In *Renmin ribao*, May 16, 1986, p. 5, trans. FBIS, June 2, 1986, pp. K1–8.

———. "A Well Received Forum." In *Shijie jingji daobao*, March 25, 1985, p. 5, trans. FBIS, April 4, 1985, pp. K24–25.

"Yuan Baohua Speaks About the Tasks of Enterprise Consolidation in 1984 for the Whole Nation at a Meeting of the National Enterprise Consolidation Leading Group." In *Jingji ribao*, December 22, 1983, p. 2, trans. FBIS, January 12, 1984, pp. K7–14.

Yue Bing. "New Changes in China's Production Structure." In *Liaowang*, Overseas Edition, no. 14 (April 1986), trans. JPRS-CEA–86–057 (May 9, 1986), pp. 53–56.

Zhang Yufeng. "Anecdotes of Mao Zedong and Zhou Enlai in Their Later Years." In *Guangming ribao*, December 26, 27, 28, 29, 30, 1988, and January 1, 2, 3, 4, 5, and 6, 1989, trans. FBIS, January 27, 1989, pp. 16–19 and January 31, 1989, pp. 30–37.

Zhang Zhuoyuan and Bian Lishi. "Price System Reform Must Be Carried Out Step by Step and in Coordination with Other Reforms." In *Jingji ribao*, February 8, 1986, p. 3, trans. FBIS, February 28, 1986, pp. K3–8.

Zhao Fu. "Give Firm Support to Reforms." In *Renmin ribao*, February 13, 1986, p. 2, trans. FBIS, February 26, 1986, pp. K1–3.

Zhao Renwei. "Shehui zhuyi jingji zhong de jihua he shichang" (Plan and Market in the Socialist Economy). In Editorial Department, *Jingji yanjiu*, ed., *Jianguo yilai shehui zhuyi jingji lilun wenti zhengming (1949–1984)*, vol. 1, pp. 470–498.

Zhao Ziyang. "Guanyu tiaozheng guomin jingji de jige wenti" (Some Questions in the Readjustment of the National Economy). In Documents Research Office of the Central Committee of the Chinese Communist Party, ed., *Sanzhong quanhui yi lai zhongyao wenxian xuanbian*, vol. 1, pp. 608–626.

———. "The Question of Strategy for Economic Development of the Coastal Regions." In *Ta kung pao*, March 1, 1988, p. 1, trans. FBIS, March 1, 1988, p. 10.

———. "Report on the Work of the Government." Xinhua, June 23, 1983, trans. FBIS, June 23, 1983, pp. K14–15.

———. "Report to the Second Plenary Session of the Thirteenth Party Congress." In *Renmin ribao*, March 21, 1988, trans. FBIS, March 21, 1988, pp. 20–27.

———. "Report to the Third Plenary Session of the Thirteenth CCP Central Committee." Xinhua, September 26, 1988, trans. FBIS, October 28, 1988, pp. K1–8.

———. "Speech at a Meeting of Propaganda, Theoretical, Press, and Party School Cadres." Xinhua, July 9, 1987, trans. FBIS, July 8, 1987, pp. K1–8.

———. "Yanjiu xin qingkuang, quanmian guanche tiaozheng de fangzhen" (Study the New Situation and Fully Implement the Principle of Readjustment.) In *Hongqi*, no. 1 (1980).

"Zhao Ziyang Talks About Price Reform in Liaoning." In *Wen wei po*, August 3, 1988, p. 1, trans. FBIS, August 3, 1988, p. 9.

"Zhao Ziyang's Speech at New Year Tea Party Held by the CPPCC Central Committee." In *Renmin ribao*, January 2, 1985, p. 1, trans. FBIS, January 9, 1985, pp. K9–11.

Zheng Bijian and Luo Jingbo. "Deepen Scientific Understanding of Socialism." In *Renmin ribao*, November 2, 1984, p. 5, trans. FBIS, November 9, 1984, pp. K2–7.

"Zhengque guji xingshi" (Accurately Appraise the Situation). In *Jingji ribao*, July 19, 1985, p. 1.

"Zhonggong zhongyang guanyu jiakuai nongye fazhan ruogan wenti de jueding" (Decision of the CCP Central Committee on Some Problems in Accelerating Agricultural Development). In Wang Jiye and Zhu Yuanzhen, eds. *Jingji tizhi gaige shouce*, pp. 62–72.

"Zhonggong zhongyang zhengzhiju huiyi tongbao" (Communiqué of the Meeting of the Political Bureau of the CCP Central Committee). In Documents Research Office of the Central Committee of the Chinese Communist Party, ed., *Sanzhong quanhui yilai zhongyao wenxian xuanbian*, vol. 1, pp. 596–600.

Zhongguo baike nianjian, 1980 (Chinese Encyclopedia Yearbook, 1980). Beijing: Zhongguo dabaike quanshu chuban she, 1980.

Zhongguo jingji nianjian (Chinese Economic Almanac). Beijing: Jingji guanli chuban she, 1980–1989.

Zhongguo xiangzhen qiye nianjian, 1978–1987 (Chinese Township and Village Enterprise Yearbook, 1978–1987). Beijing: Nongye chubanshe, 1989.

Zhou Binbin, Liu Yunzhou, and Li Qingzeng. "Nongcun mianlin de tiaozhan yu xuanze" (The Challenges and Alternatives Facing Agriculture). In *Nongye jingji wenti*, no. 12 (December 1986):35–39.

Zhou Guanwu. "On the Contract System." In *Jingji yanjiu*, no. 3 (March 1986):6–10, trans. JPRS-CEA–86–066 (June 4, 1986), pp. 22–30.

Zhou Shulian. "Sanshi nian lai woguo jingji jiegou de huigu" (Looking Back on China's Economic Structure Over the Past Thirty Years). In Ma Hong and Sun Shangqing, eds., *Zhongguo jingji jiegou wenti yanjiu*, vol. 1, pp. 23–55.

Zhou Taihe. "Chen Yun tongzhi sici xia nongcun diaocha de qianhou" (Before and After Comrade Chen Yun's Four Rural Investigations). In *Chen Yun yu xin Zhongguo jingji jianshe* (Chen Yun and New China's Economic Construction), pp. 157–171. Beijing: Zhongyang wenxian chuban she, 1991.

Zhou Zuyou. "Peng Zhen Inspects Zhejiang University." In *Renmin ribao*, January 30, 1986, p. 1.

Zhu Jiaming. "Diaonian wo de pengyou He Weiling" (Mourning My Friend He Weiling). In *Zhongguo zhi chun*, August 1991, p. 29.

———. "Lun woguo zheng jingli de jingji fazhan jieduan" (On the Economic Development Stage Our Country Is Presently Going Through). In *Zhongqingnian jingji luntan*, no. 2 (April 1985):13–23.

Zhu Shuxian. "Ye tan wuchan jieji qude zhengquan hou de shehui fazhan jieduan wenti" (Also Discussing the Question of Developmental Stages Following the Proletariat's Attainment of Political Power). In *Jingji yanjiu*, no. 8 (August 1979):14–18.

"Zhua hengxiang jingji lianxi, cu jingji tizhi gaige" (Grasp Horizontal Economic Cooperation, Promote Reform of the Economic Structure). In *Renmin ribao*, Editorial, March 31, 1986, p. 1.

Zou Gang et al., *Zhongguo weiguan jingji fenxi* (Analysis of China's Microeconomy). Beijing: Renmin daxue chuban she, 1991.

Zuo Chuntai and Xiao Jie. "Balance of Financial Credits Is an Important Question in Macroeconomic Control." In *Renmin ribao*, May 6, 1985, p. 5, trans. FBIS, May 14, 1985, pp. K4–7.

Zuo Mu. "On the Contracted Management Responsibility System." In *Renmin ribao*, June 15, 1987, p. 5, trans. FBIS, June 24, 1987, p. K24.

II. Periodicals

Asian Survey (Berkeley)
Caimao jingji (Beijing)
Caizheng (Beijing)
Ch'ao liu (Hong Kong)
China Daily (Beijing)
The China Quarterly (London)
Ching-pao yueh-k'an (Hong Kong)

Chiu-shi nien-tai (Hong Kong)
Chung-kung yen-jiu (Taipei)
Dong-fang jih-pao (Hong Kong)
Fudan xuebao (Shanghai)
Fujian ribao
Guangming ribao (Beijing)
Gongren ribao (Beijing)
Hongqi (Beijing)
Issues and Studies (Taipei)
Jiefangjun bao (Beijing)
Jingji guanli (Beijing)
Jingji ribao (Beijing)
Jingji yanjiu (Beijing)
Jingjixue zhoubao (Beijing)
Kunlun (Beijing)
Liaowang (Beijing)
Liaowang, Overseas Edition (Beijing)
Ming pao (Hong Kong)
Nongye jingji wenti (Beijing)
Nongye jingji xiaoguo (Beijing)
Nongye jishu jingji (Beijing)
Qiushi (Beijing)
Renmin ribao (Beijing)
Shijie jingji (Beijing)
Shijie jingji daobao (Shanghai)
South China Morning Post (Hong Kong)
Ta kung pao (Hong Kong)
Tung fang jih pao (Hong Kong)
Wen wei po (Hong Kong)
Xinhua (Beijing)
Xuexi yu yanjiu (Beijing)
Zhanwang (Hong Kong)
Zhongguo jingji tizhi gaige (Beijing)
Zhongguo qinggongye jingji (Beijing)
Zhongguo zhi chun (New York)
Zhongqingnian jingji luntan (Tianjin)

INDEX

Joseph Fewsmith is Associate Professor for International Relations at Boston University and Director of the East Asian Interdisciplinary Studies Program. He received his Ph.D. in political science from the University of Chicago in 1980, after which he did post-graduate work at the Center for Chinese Studies at the University of California-Berkeley. He is the editor of *Chinese Economic Studies* and the author of *Party, State, and Local Elites in Republican China* (1985).